AF803057

INDIAN ECONOMY AND SOCIO-ECONOMIC TRANSFORMATION

Emerging Issues and Problems

- **Human Development, Poverty & Empowerment**
- **Impact of Economic Reforms**
- **Strategy of Development and Sustainability**

ESSAYS IN HONOUR OF PROFESSOR BAIDYANATH MISRA

Editor
S.N. MISRA
President Orissa Economics Association

Foreword by
PROFESSOR DEVENDRA CHANDRA MISHRA
Chairman, Nabakrushna Choudhury Centre for
Development Studies, Bhubaneswar.
Former D.P.I. (H.E.), Orissa and
Former Vice-Chancellor, Sambalpur University.

DEEP & DEEP PUBLICATIONS PVT. LTD.
F-159, Rajouri Garden, New Delhi - 110 027

INDIAN ECONOMY AND
SOCIO-ECONOMIC TRANSFORMATION

ISBN 81-7629-525-6

© 2004 ORISSA ECONOMICS ASSOCIATION

All rights reserved with the Publisher, including the right to translate or to reproduce this book or parts thereof except for brief quotations in critical articles or reviews

Printed in India at MAYUR ENTERPRISES,
WZ Plot No. 3, Gujjar Market, Tihar Village, New Delhi - 110 018.

Published by DEEP & DEEP PUBLICATIONS PVT. LTD.,
F-159, Rajouri Garden, New Delhi - 110 027 • Phone : 25435369, 25440916
E-mail : deep98@del3.vsnl.net.in • ddpbooks@yahoo.co.in
Showroom :
2/13, Ansari Road, Daryaganj, New Delhi - 110 002 • Telefax : 23245122

In Honour of
Professor Baidyanath Misra,
the doyen of Indian Economists
as a mark of respect and reverence

Members,
Orissa Economics Association

Foreword

I welcome the move of Orissa Economics Association to bring out a felicitation volume in honour of Professor Baidyanath Misra as a token of its gratitude for him. He has been the main force in founding, nurturing and guiding its destiny for a period of nearly thirty-six years. The small sapling planted by him under the guidance of late Professor Sadasiv Mishra has now grown in to a big tree with spreading branches.

Professor B. Misra has dedicated his whole life to the cause of economic studies, research and teaching and has dominated the economic and cultural scene of the State for the last few decades.

After a brilliant academic career he took to teaching as his first love though he had an occasional foray into politics and journalism. Basically an intellectual of high order, he was not satisfied with soaring high into the rarefied atmosphere of academic life, but wanted to put his foot firmly on solid ground to study the problems of the poor and deprived about whom he had direct experience in his early childhood.

He wrote 14 books initially in fields like Public Finance and Fiscal Policy, Economic Systems and Economic Planning and Development. Later on being moved by the stark poverty of the rural and tribal people in Orissa, he turned his sharp analytical mind to unravel the cause of their distressed condition. He came to a firm conviction that a vigorous thrust to agricultural and rural development would break the vicious circle of poverty and under-development. His later works were devoted to these aspects of the problem in the state and in the country.

His research output has been impressive. He has published sixty research papers and guided twenty-five research scholars to obtain their Ph.D. degrees. He was a brilliant teacher and could keep his students spell bound. His teaching career spanned over thirty two years in various capacities: as lecturer in Economics in Ravenshaw College, Professor of Agricultural Economics and later on Dean of Faculty of Agriculture in Orissa University of Agriculture and Technology, Professor of Economics, Utkal University and Vice-Chancellor OUAT. Later on he was called upon to head the State Planning Board as its Deputy Chairman. While he was Deputy Chairman, it was due to his initiative and efforts, a long-standing proposal for establishing a Research Institute in Social Sciences materialised. It was established in 1987 and he became its first Director. He has been associated with this Institute, now named Nabakrushna Choudhury Centre for Development Studies, since that date in various capacities, as Director, Chairman and Advisor Research Projects with small breaks and has been responsible for its all round development. He has also been member or chairman of a large number of Committees and Commissions at various levels.

In a recent article on "Sustainable Development: Problems and Challenges of 21st Century" he describes how rapid and breath taking advances in technology, has not only brought immense benefits to the mankind on various aspects of life but also produced many adverse effects which unchecked would bring the world to the brink of disaster. He therefore advocated for a "Sustainable Development". It is in fitness of things that the Felicitation Volume has this as a main theme.

For this volume twenty-nine articles have been received. They have very appropriately been divided in to three main sections. Section I deals with the crucial problems of Human Development, Poverty Reduction, Empowerment of Women, Child Protection and Survival, and Food Security. Section II addresses itself to the problem arising of the impact of Economic Reforms on Indian Economy; its impact on various sectors such as agriculture, industry and different groups such as organised and unorganised labour. It also deals with the adverse effects of Economic Reforms on State finances particularly of the poorer states. The third section deals with the Strategy of Development and its Sustainability.

Many of these problems can be more appreciated if viewed from the global perspective. During the last decade of the twentieth century, it became apparent that a new world was emerging, a new world shaped by new technology, new social structure, a new economy and a new culture. Globalisation became the term to describe the new trend. Just as Industrial Revolution gave rise to an "Industrial Society", Information Technology revolution is giving rise to an 'Information Society'. Information Technology has played a decisive role in the rise of "networking" as a form of organisation of human activity in business, politics, the media and non-governmental organisations.

It is not only information technology but also another factor, which spurred globalisation. That was the collapse of Soviet Communism. It led to the spread of capitalism to the whole world. In the words of Castells "it deepened its penetration of countries, cultures and domains of life. In spite of a highly diversified social and cultural land scape, for the first time in history the whole world is organised around a common set of economic rules."

While it is recognised that globalisation is an irreversible process, what is questioned is the present process of globalisation which has its adverse financial, social and ecological impact. According to some critics, the global market is not a market in the strict sense but a network of machines programmed according to a single-value-making money for the sake of making money for its own sake to the exclusion of all other values.

A growing number of economists, sociologists, environmentalists and grass-roots activists from all corners of the world have called attention to the growing discontent about the present process of globalisation. In their view global capitalism in its present form is unsustainable not only economically but also ecologically and socially. It is pointed out that global capitalism does not alleviate poverty and social exclusion but aggravates them. As the new century unfolds, two major developments will have great impact on the life and well-being of mankind. One is the global capitalism, the other is the creation of sustainable communities based on ecological literacy and practice of eco-design. While the former is concerned with the network of financial and information flows, the latter is concerned with the ecological network of energy and material flows. In the words of Fritjof Capra "the goal of global economy is to maximise wealth and power of its elite, the goal of eco-design is to maximise the sustainability of the web of life." (Hidden Connections p. 228)

In India, we have already felt the impact of globalisation in the shape of creation of an elite who form about 20 percent of the total population. The majority of 80 percent of people have borne the adverse effects. The only hope of the tribal and rural communities lies in building up "sustainable societies."

The concept of 'Sustainability' was first developed in early 1980s by Lester Brown. He defined 'Sustainable Society' as one "that is able to satisfy its needs without diminishing the chances of future generations". But this does not tell us how to build a sustainable society. A sustainable human community is one designed in such a way that its ways of life, business, economy, fiscal structure and technologies do not interfere with nature's inherent ability to sustain life. This seems to be a distant echo of Gandhian Economics and values.

I hope the publication of this volume will provide materials to design self sustainable communities in regions like Orissa and similar regions of the country which are ecologically very sensitive and suffer from serious environmental damage on account of reckless exploitation of renewable and non-renewable natural resources in the name of economic development.

Bhubaneswar

DEVENDRA CHANDRA MISHRA
Chairman, Nabakrushna Choudhury Centre for Development Studies,
Former D.P.I. (H.E.), Orissa and
Former Vice-Chancellor, Sambalpur University.

Preface

This felicitous volume comprises of articles written by some of the eminent economists of India in honour of Professor Baidyanath Misra. The book makes a critical appraisal of economic and social changes in India and shows how the strategy of development has created a number of imponderable difficulties in achieving economic and social goals of planning and meeting the challenges of open economy. In examining the strategy, the authors have made a number of constructive suggestions for changing the economic and social structure of the country so as to improve the quality of life of the people. The book is an amalgam of theoretical analysis and compelling reality, a combination of which can really fulfil the needs of the country.

The book has been divided into three sections. The first section deals with Human Development, Poverty and Empowerment. In India the development of the economy over the years has centred and focussed attention on macro-economic variables like GNP, balance of payment, saving rate, fiscal deficit, etc. assigning a secondary role to men and their well-being. There is no doubt that we have attained significant success in many fields of economic activity. Some of the studies show that India will enter into the big league within a few years. Our success in the field of IT, Space Research and Atomic Energy has been recognised world over. Even some of International Organisations predict that India would be the third largest economy in the world by 2050.

However, in the flurry of such activities, great attention has been laid on physical and visible parameters. But there is a difference between human resource and human development. Though these two concepts are inter-related, they are not synonymous. HRD considers man as a resource for all round development—not as a means, but as an end. Therefore, the focus of any change must veer round man. This implies that greater stress must be given to improve the quality of life of our people.

This would be possible if there is substantial improvement in different fields of social sector like education, health, social security, gender empowerment, employment opportunities and so on, so as to enable men and women to lead a decent and dignified life. But unfortunately inspite of all the macro changes in the country, unemployment, poverty, illiteracy, malnutrition, infant and child mortality, gender inequity and such other social disabilities appear to be great challenges at the time. In the first section, eleven authors have thrown some light how to accelerate the process of development without jeopardising social justice. Their analysis shows that we cannot think of economic development where such injustices pervade the economy.

The second section analyses Economic Reforms and its Impact on Indian Economy. The Economic Reforms primarily aims at promoting a market economy through liberalisation, privatisation and globalisation. It is expected that the market economy through perfect competition and without any government intervention will (a) ensure utilisation of resources with maximum growth of output and services at micro level, (b) upgrade methods of production, improve exports and increase foreign investment with up-to-date technology, and (c) reduce the existing rent seeking opportunities within the country through efficient allocation of resources and help in stabilising the domestic price-level. But open economy has created a great deal of controversy in India. Amartya Sen has pointed out that a competitive economy may increase the rate of growth and per capita income by improving the efficiency of economic organisation, but may not increase the quality of life of people. The experiences of last several decades show that globalisation has created a number of distortions in both developed and developing countries. Particularly in case of India, we cannot entirely rely on competition to increase economic growth or attain social justice. Government intervention is necessary in many fields. In the light of experiences of different countries, Panchmukhi makes two important observations: First there is no single universally valid formula for state versus market. Secondly, the state has to govern the market, instead of the state being dictated by the market. Particularly in case of India, state and market should co-exist in any process of development and the governance of the market will have to be the responsibility of the state. All the nine authors in the section have discussed these aspects in great detail with concrete illustrations from India.

The third and final section deals with Strategy of Development and its Sustainability. In most of the countries and so also in India growth has become the goal, a kind of religion or ideology without taking into account our most precious form of capital, our natural resources. Under our present economic system, the earth is a business in liquidation. The new development model (which is generally called fossil-fuel-based automobile-centred throw away economy) has increased income and material consumption to an unprecedented level, but is destroying the Earth's natural system. It is therefore apprehended that such a system of development cannot be sustained for a long time. 'Our Common Future' defines sustainable development as development that meets the needs of the present without compromising the ability of the future generation to meet their own needs. 'Our Common Future' hence emphasises, "In essence, sustainable development is a process of change in which the exploitation of resources, the direction of investments, the orientation of technological development and institutional change are all in harmony and enhance both the current and future potential to meet human needs and aspirations" Environmental movement does not nullify development, but only emphasises to 'care, save and renew' our most precious form of capital, our natural resources. The nine authors who have analysed the strategy of development of different sectors have highlighted the above norms.

I thank all the authors who have ungrudgingly responded to my humble request and contributed articles which can expand the horizon of knowledge. I must say that the response has been beyond my expectation. I again express my gratefulness to them for the kind help rendered to me in achieving a noble endeavour.

S.N. MISRA

Acknowledgements

For the felicitation volume, I have received assistance and encouragement from several quarters. It is difficult to acknowledge the individual contributions of each one of them in this brief write up. However, special mention of a few persons and institutions will not be out of place.

The members of Orissa Economics Association, especially the executive members deserve my special thanks for rightly deciding to bring out a felicitation volume in the honour of Professor Baidyanath Misra, the founder of the association and an eminent economist of the country, in the 35th Annual General Body meeting of the association held at Jagatsinghpur College in the month of February, 2003 and entrusted the responsibility to me, as the President of Orissa Economics Association (2003-2004), to materialise the proposed project at the earliest. I once again offer my sincere thanks to all the members of Orissa Economics Association.

I offer my sincere thanks and gratitude to Professor Baidyanath Misra, founder of the association and former President of Orissa Economics Association for accepting the decision of Annual General Body meeting of the association at Jagatsinghpur College without committing in any form to the decision of the members of the Association.

I express my deepest gratitude to Professor D.C. Mishra, Chairman of Nabakrushna Choudhury Centre for Development Studies and former President of Orissa Economics Association for writing the 'Foreword' for the felicitation volume and for his support and encouragement for the successful completion of the project.

Professor Gyan Chandra Kar, Director Nabakrushna Choudhury Centre for Development Studies and former President of Orissa Economics Association deserves my sincere thanks for his co-operation and encouragement in the publication of the felicitation volume. From day one till the present day, his unstinted co-operation, logistic support and active encouragement in all matters of crucial importance are well appreciated, without which the volume would not have seen the light of the day. I once again thank him.

For the felicitation volume, I have received 18 articles from the All-India level and 11 articles from the state level. This was possible due to my long acquaintance with the members of Indian and Orissa Economics Association. This overwhelming enthusiasm was the result of Professor Misra's academic and professional stature and attainments in the field of economics for which eminent economists at the all-India and regional level responded so enthusiathically. Almost all the authors are celebrated economists in their respective fields. I offer my sincere thanks to all of them for contributing highly qualitative and thought provoking papers which are included in the volume.

Especially I am grateful to Prof. R.K. Sen, President, Indian Economics Association (2003), Prof. A.K. Sinha, Pro-Vicechancellor Bhagalpur University and former President, IEA, Prof. G.S. Monga, Former Professor, Bombay School of Economics and Former President, IEA, Prof. D.K. Srivastava, Professor National Institute of Public Finance and Policy and member 12th Finance Commission, Govt. of India, Prof. P.K. Chaubey, Professor of Economics, Indian Institute of Public Administration, Prof. Smriti Mukherjee, Professor of Economics, Gokhale Institute of Politics and Economics, Prof. P.K. Bhargava, B.H.U, Prof. Prahalad Kumar, Allahabad University, Prof. R. Arunachalam and Prof (Mrs.) N. Rajalakshmi, Madras University, Prof. G.C. Kar, NCDS, Prof. Adwait Mohanty, Utkal University, and Prof. R. P. Sharma, Berhampur University for readily accepting my request for contribution of a paper and timely submitting their esteemed articles.

It is not out of place here to put on record the logistic and moral support I received for the felicitation volume from Prof. Bhavani Prasad Dash, Former President, OEA, Dr. R.N. Patra, Secretary, OEA, and Dr. Jagannath Lenka, Joint Secretary, OEA. I owe my sincere thanks to each one of them.

My thanks are due to all the faculty members of NKC Centre for Development Studies for providing moral and emotional support and co-operation for the publication of the volume.

In NCDS, I am particularly more obliged to Dr. R.K. Meher, secretary and Sri. Srikant Rath, Administrative Officer for providing all assistance, physical and logistic in materialising the project.

I take this opportunity to thank Sri. G.S. Bhatia, Managing Director M/s. Deep and Deep Publications (Pvt) Ltd. for readily accepting to undertake the publication of the book.

Last but not the least, I am thankful to Sri Siba Narayan Pradhan and Smt. S. Pani, for shouldering the responsibility of computerising the entire manuscript with utmost interest.

S.N. MISRA

Contents

Section III
STRATEGY OF DEVELOPMENT AND ITS SUSTAINABILITY

List of Contributors

Adwait Mohanty, Professor of Institutional Finance, R.B.I. Chair, Dept. of Analytical and Applied Economics, Utkal University, Bhubaneswar.

Ajit Kumar Sinha, Pro-Vice-chancellor, T.M. Bhagalpur University & Former President of Indian Economic Association.

A. Ranga Reddy, Professor of Economics, S.V. University, Tirupati, A.P.

Ashutosh Kumar, Visiting Fellow, San Jose State University, California, USA.

B.M. Jani, Professor of Economics, Saurashtra University, Rajkot.

Bhagabat Patro, Reader, P.G. Deptt. of Economics, Berhampur University, Berhampur.

D.K. Srivastava, Professor of Economics, National Institute of Public Finance and Policy and Member, 12th Finance Commission, Govt. of India.

G. Raghava Reddy, Director, Rural Development Academy, Tirupati, A.P.

G.C. Kar, Director, NKC Centre for Development Studies, Bhubaneswar.

G.S. Monga, Former Professor of Economics, Bombay School of Economics and Former President, Indian Economic Association.

I.D. Singh, Reader in Economics, Post-Graduate Degree College, Jaunpur University, Uttar Pradesh.

Jagannath Lenka, Department of Economics, Bhadrak College, Bhadrak.

K. Ravindran, Dept. of Economics, Bombay School of Economics, Mumbai.

Manaranjan Behera, Faculty Member, NKC Centre for Development Studies, Bhubaneswar.

Ms. Smriti Mukherjee, Professor of Economics, Gokhale Institute of Politics and Economics, Pune.

P. Jegadish Gandhi, Hony. Director, Vellore Institute of Development Studies, Vellore.

P.C. Mahapatra, Former Director, T.E. and SCERT and Former President, Board of Secondary Education, Orissa.

P.K. Bhargava, Professor of Economics, Banaras Hindu University, Varanasi.

P.K. Chaubey, Professor of Economics, Indian Institute of Public Administration, New Delhi.

P.S. Raikhy, Professor of Economics, Guru Nanak Dev University, Amritsar, Punjab.

Prahlad Kumar, Professor of Economics, Allahabad University, Allahabad.

R. Arunachalam, Professor of Economics, Madras University, Chennai.

R.N. Patra, P.G. Department of Economics, Ravenshaw College, Cuttack.

R.P. Sarma, Director, Institute of Economic Studies and Former Professor of Economics, Berhampur University, Orissa.

Raj Kumar Sen, Professor of Economics, Rabindra Bharati University and President, Indian Economic Association.

S.K. Misra, Reader in Economics, Post-Graduate Degree College, Jaunpur University, Uttar Pradesh.

S.K. Sahoo, Small Scale Industries Promotion Officer, Cuttack.

S.N. Misra, Professor of Economics, NKC Centre for Development Studies, Bhubaneswar.

Smt. N. Rajalakshmi, Professor of Economics, Madras University, Chennai.

Smt. Rashmi Mishra, Faculty Member, NKC Centre for Development Studies, Bhubaneswar.

Smt. Renu Jain, Reader in Economics, Arya Kanya Degree College, Allahabad.

Somnath Hajra, UGC Research Fellow, Dept. of Economics, Rabindra Bharati University, Calcutta.

Srijit Mishra, Faculty Member, Indira Gandhi Institute of Development and Research, Mumbai.

V.B. Jugale, Professor of Economics, Shivaji University, Kolhapur, Maharashtra.

PROFESSOR BAIDYANATH MISRA

in Wharton School of Finance, Pennsylvania, USA. There he came in contact with Nobel Laureate Professor Simon Kuznets and completed his A.M. degree. After returning home he completed his Ph.D. degree under the guidance of his revered teacher Prof. Sadasiv Misra. The Ph.D. dissertation which was published by World Press Pvt. Ltd., Calcutta under the caption, 'Fiscal Policy in the Context of Planning' has remained a milestone in the economic literature even to-day.

From Ravenshaw College, Prof. Misra moved to Orissa University of Agriculture and Technology as a Professor of Agricultural Economics and served in that capacity for a number of years. During his stay in OUAT he was appointed as Dean of the University.

He was the Professor and Head of the Department of Analytical and Applied Economics Utkal University in 1977 and remained in the said post till the year 1981. From 1981-85 he was the Vice-Chancellor of OUAT and subsequently became the Deputy Chairman of State Planning Board, Orissa. He also became one of the members of the Panel of Economists of the Planning Commission and a member of Orissa Pay Commission during this period.

A Teacher and a Researcher

Professor Misra was well known for his scholastic quality and teaching abilities. As a teacher Professor Misra used to impress upon his students with new ideas. He had the gift of explaining several complex ideas in a simple and lucid style. He is a voracious reader and his coverage of study is not confined only to economics but to a number of fields.

He was instrumental in laying the foundation of modern analytical research based on empirical studies. This earned him the reputation of a successful researcher and on account of this he was able to produce more than 25 Ph.D. scholars both in OUAT and Utkal University.

Institutional Builder

Professor Misra is remembered for instituting academic chairs and new institutions in whatever capacity he served the state. This was duly acknowledged by the former Chief Minister of Orissa Sri J.B. Pattnaik. On the occasion of releasing his autobiography, 'Smruti Tirtha', Sri Pattnaik remarked that 'whenever there is the need for entrusting a new responsibility and an assignment to someone Professor Misra immediately comes to the mind'. When he was the Professor and Head of Dept. of Analytical and Applied Economics, he instituted two academic chairs funded by RBI and SBI. He was in charge of both the chairs till regular incumbents were appointed.

Similarly, while he was the Vice Chancellor of OUAT he established four colleges such as: (a) College of Fisheries, Rangailunda, Ganjam (b) College of Agriculture, Chipilima, Sambalpur (c) College of Engineering and Technology and (d) College of Home Science both in OUAT campus, Bhubaneswar. Besides, he was also able to transfer several agricultural farms from the Government to the University during his tenure as the V.C. of OUAT. He introduced Ph.D. programme in several departments with course programmes with additional professors.

Professor Misra is greatly honoured for his contribution in establishing Nabakrushna Choudhury Centre for Development Studies in Bhubaneswar with the collaboration of Indian Council of Social Science Research and Government of Orissa. He was the founder Director when the institution came into existence in the year 1988-89. Without his active interest and support the institute could not have seen the light of the day. Subsequently he became the Chairman-cum-Director of the institute. In that capacity he gave the institute a solid base by creating regular appointments and spearheading research projects by procuring funds from various external agencies. In the Institute, too, he took the lead in creating academic chairs from sources like TISCO, NALCO, MCL, OMC, OFC and IDC. The present status of NCDS as one of the reputed academic institutions in the country and outside the country derives in a large measure from Prof. Misra's efforts.

The Institutional building capacity of Professor Misra does not end here. In order to create awareness among the students and teachers of economics, he shouldered the responsibility of establishing Orissa Economics Association as early as 1968. By this time the Association has already held 35 Annual Economic Conferences. He was not only the past president of the Association but continues to act as the editor of the Association's mouthpiece 'Orissa Economic Journal'. Through this platform Prof. Misra could help young economists to express their ideas on economic matters confronting the nation and the state.

An Author and a Litterateur

Prof. Misra is an eminent scholar and a prolific writer. He has authored several books; both text and reference which are included in the curriculum of Indian Universities. His books on 'Capitalism, Socialism and Planning' (Oxford & IBH), 'Economics of Public Finance' (MacMillian) have run into several editions showing the popularity of the books among students. Besides, he has to his credit several reference books like 'Economic Profile of India' (Ashish), 'Agriculture Development Problems and Prospects' (Ashish), 'Political Economy of Development' (Ajanta), 'Co-operative Movement of India' (ed), 'Economic liberalisation and Regional Development in India' (ed) (Ashish), 'Poverty, Unemployment and Rural Development' (ed) (Ashish), 'Strategy of Development Planning, Comparative Economic System', and 'Agro-Industries and Economic Development—A Vision for 21st century' (ed) etc.

He has also created a place for himself in the field of literature. He was a Sahitya Academy awardee for his monumental work, 'ADHUNIKA SABHYATARA JANTRANA'. Besides, he also bagged the Nandighosh award and Vishub Milan award for his contribution to Oriya literature. His regular articles in daily newspapers like 'The Samaj', 'The Prajatantra', 'The Pragatibadi' and 'The Samay' are not only simple, lucid but touch on issues which are of interest to all concerned. His critical but thought provoking essays in 'Jhankar', 'Nava Jivan' and 'Pourush' are adjudged to be the best in the field of literary essays and criticisms. Even now he contributes research articles to standard economic and social journals along with research oriented books.

Administrator

In whatever and whichever capacity Professor Misra is placed he used to discharge his responsibilities with utmost sincerity and dignity. Punctuality in office and quick disposal of routine official matters was the hallmark of his personality. As a member of several committees and commissions his contribution in drafting the report, and participation in deliberations was remarkable. As the Chairman of the First State Finance Commission his contribution to revive sick financial health of the state is well acknowledged.

Social and Political Thinker

Right from his college career Professor Misra was deeply involved in social work and tried to solve many social problems. He organised several camps in different parts of the state, during his student and professional career for helping the cause of the poor and the down trodden. As the secretary of the State Welfare Board he organised several camps to eradicate social evils like; untouchability, women atrocities and dowry system etc. He was also Chairman of a number of cultural organisations like Nandighosh, Asha, Jana Sikya Sansthan etc., which tried to promote cultural activities in the state.

He is not averse to politics but is certainly critical of the present day politicians who are corrupt and power seeking.

Man and his Mission

Professor Misra is a large-hearted person. His philosophy of life is 'Karma he Upasana'. Even at the age of 80's one is astonished to see Professor Misra working for more than 12 hours a day; all the time reading, writing and reviewing the project work of the colleagues. He is an indefatigable personality. Simple in behaviour and very accommodative in nature. His mission in life is to do something good for the society and for the people who are helpless. His message to the younger generation is to move ahead with determination, hard work and perseverance. To the colleagues his advice is to be dutiful, honest, sincere, punctual and develop self esteem with integrity and righteousness. To the society at large his message is to promote the state by constricting personal aggrandisement and selfishness.

The Orissa Economics Association considers it most timely and appropriate to honour Professor B. Misra, the economist who has shaped the emerging minds of generation of students in the state and in the country. The felicitation volume consisting of a large collection of thought provoking articles written by his admirers at the national level and students and well-wishers at the state level is dedicated to Professor Misra as a mark of respect and gratitude.

S.N. MISRA

Section I

Human Development, Poverty and Empowerment

CHAPTER

1

Human Development : Where India Stands

P. K. CHAUBEY

IMPORTANCE

A recent newspaper report says that the rank of India has slipped, in terms of human development index, from 124th place in 2000 as reported in Human Development Report published last year to 127th place in 2001 as reported in the Human Development Report this year although in absolute terms Human development index has improved from 0.577 in 2000 to 0.590 in 2001. The news caption often mentions it as a case of deterioration of conditions. When pointed out about inconsistencies in the Report, the UNDP team showed its willingness to revisit the exercise. To be fair, it has also been pointed out in the report that three newly carved out countries/territories, which did not find place in the last year's report are now included and have all better human development index. But then why talk of deterioration? There continues to be a great interest in this exercise though the news item has attracted the front page of only a few dailies, which was the universal case earlier.

Even since the United National Development Program came out with its Human Development Report in 1990 under the guidance of an eminent economist (now, late) Mahbub ul Haq, it is claimed, more than 135 countries have prepared similar reports for their countries. Many sub-national units and some supra-national regional bodies have also published human development reports for their respective areas. Various research organizations have also undertaken extensive exercises. In some cases, it is an annual or a bi-annual feature. More than 500 reports have been prepared and published world over. This shows the importance accorded to the idea of human development. A caveat however, needs to be added here. Very few developed countries have cared to publish such reports though serious scholars always found the idea to be equally relevant for developed countries as well. In fact, some core consultants had wanted human development to be so defined that it has scope for application in developed countries as well.

THE IDEA OF HUMAN DEVELOPMENT

When Mahbub ul Haq joined the UNDP in 1989 as the special advisor to the Administrator of the United Nations Development Program, given the fact that human costs of structural adjustment programmes in the 1980s in several countries under the aegis of the IMF and the WB had been extremely harsh, it naturally occurred to him that a report on conditions of human beings and their well-being be prepared. Favoured by other changes in political climate sweeping the communist countries and disturbances and distress caused in the rich countries in terms of rising crime, growing pollution, spreading AIDS, weakening social fabric, the idea of the annual publication of such a report becomes acceptable to the then Administrator of the UNDP.

By then some developing countries had shown that they could improve human conditions of quality of lives of their fellow citizens in terms of education, health and nutrition despite low per capita income. And it was also found that several other countries despite being rich in terms of per capita income, had failed to secure to a large section of their population the conditions that could be said to be 'humane'. It signified that a country needed not to wait to be rich for securing minimum essentials of life that enhance capabilities of its citizens.

After some deliberations with core consultants, the UNDP team selected the term 'human development' for the report they would finally compile. Now, defining human development was the task. Amartya Sen had been, for quite a few years, toying with the ideas of capabilities and functionings. It came handy to conceive development in terms of intrinsic capabilities as an alternative to that in terms of extrinsic commodities.

Development was always at least implicitly identified with widening of choices. This time the phrase human development was used to denote 'widening of choices through enhancement of capabilities' rather than expansion of commodities. Capabilities were understood to have 'positive' connotation. A capability could be equated with a trait of skill, enhancement whereof improves one's choices without limiting those of others. Living longer, being healthy, being literate and acquiring such traits of persons that help one choose from a wider set of commodities have always been constant endeavour of human race, we should note, as has been expansion of quantities and varieties of goods.

Unfortunately, most of development debate in the West got waylaid and was mired in the din of tonnes, barrels and metres. It was late in the day that the real end of all development was brought back into focus. It took a long route through growth, employment, redistribution and basic needs. Though, inappropriately called human development, the approach has focused our attention on the achievement of a society in terms of longevity of life and health conditions as perceived in terms of morbidity and mortality, literacy and education in terms of enrolment and dropouts, availability of safe drinking water, sanitation and public health, etc. To quote Paul Streeten, in the previous decades those concerned with development have sometimes become lost in technical intricacies of means—growth rates, production, productivity, savings ratios, export ratios, capital output ratios, tax ratios and so on and lost sight of the end. To be candid, if they were true means to some ends then achievement of means should have resulted into achievement of ends. It is therefore difficult to assert that they were really the means to the ends that had to be promoted. Does it not mean that the theories behind propagation of such instruments were faulty?

Moreover, it has now been duly recognized that results of consuming commodities will depend on the characteristics of the consumer and the society of which he/she is a member. You may have enough money to have good food (which is available) and also a good stomach and therefore are capable of enjoying good food yet you may choose to fast. This is a situation of choice. It is different from the one in which either you do not have enough money (entitlement) of there is not enough good food available and you have to starve. All these situations are different from the one in which you are not well to enjoy food (capability). Human development insists on capabilities—capability to enjoy good food. Capability to be well-dressed, capability to be well-read, capability to participate in one's community and so on. A more capable person enjoys greater freedom to choose to lead the life that he or she values.

Finally, though human development has undoubtedly enriched the development dialogue it is not the ultimate insight into development but one of the shifting fashions and new ideas that will replace it, may be ere long.

And India

It has to be noted that human development was always a concern of many societies and their respective states—particularly when they became independent despite the fact that there existed clash of interests between different sections. It goes to the credit of our early leaders and plan makers that they never lost sight of these fundamental aspects of development. Right through the freedom struggle our leaders were conscious of these dimensions of development. Our plan documents are eloquent testimony to the fact that development in India was never narrowly conceived, nor was it defined in pure simple terms of economic growth.

In the reckoning of some of us, we might have compromised on growth front because of our wide concern for various other dimensions, which have today come to be known as human development. Our Constitution, particularly its fourth part, shows its concern for people's voice along with human choices, human rights and human development.

It was not the Eighth Plan's report, which has been reported by the UNDP as having paid attention to the idea of human development; the phrase 'human development' was of course mentioned in the first sentence of the concerned chapter (and nowhere thereafter!). Actually, all of our Plans, particularly the earlier ones, were concerned with human development and devised strategies to promote it. They tried to put human heart, not human face, in the capitalistic framework till late in the day. They were careful to include within its fold both economic development and social development and the latter included institutional development.

THE INDEX OF HUMAN DEVELOPMENT

Human development approach, insists the UNDP, concentrates on the ends, not the means. Whether people are living longer and more healthily. Whether people have become more knowledgeable. Whether people are able to participate in their community affairs and in decision—making processes. Whether people have access to adequate food, safe drinking water, basic health facilities and so on. Whether people enjoy freedom-political and social. Whether people are secure. The Human Development Reports provide details and analyses on various dimensions referred to above and many more.

But comparing countries for a variety of aspects requires some kind of quantification such as percentage of people having access to safe drinking water or percentage of children below a certain age in school or child deaths below 5 per thousand. Improvement in these indicators over time may be taken as development. The Reports also try to present many of these achievements by rural-urban/male-female/ethnic divisions to highlight the disparities that a given country suffers from.

We may note that human development has been conceptualized at the individual level and is concerned with capabilities rather than achievement. Capabilities defined as set of functionings have a limitation of being measured. Moreover, when it comes to assessing human development at an aggregate level it is the achievement level, which becomes important. What is the level of health that people are enjoying rather than that they are capable of having? What is the level of literacy that people as a whole are enjoying rather than the level they can possess?

We may want comparison of achievements by two countries or improvements scored by two countries on an overall basis. Then, combining various indicators becomes necessary. Only such indicators as reflect independent dimensions should be combined to construct an overall index. The dimensions chosen should be fundamental ones. After a lot of deliberations, the UNDP team decided to construct what it called human development index and chose following three key components : longevity, knowledge and income.

Mahbub ul Haq insisted that an overall index should be devised. Amartya Sen and many other friends of his tried but failed to dissuade him from venturing into an exercise, which had but to be very crude. Mahbub ul Haq was willing to have an index so long it was as vulgar as GDP. Then, Amartya Sen helped him devise what came to be known as Human Development Index, which may be little more vulgar than GDP.

It consider three dimensions long and healthy life, knowledge and education, and level of living. Longevity was always measured in terms of life expectancy at birth and it is taken to reflect total health conditions of people though Amartya Sen has called it quantity of life. Knowledge to begin with was measured in terms of adult literacy rate, adults being defined as persons above 25. Later, knowledge was replaced by educational attainment and it was measured by adult literacy rate and mean years of schooling with 2/3rds and 1/3rd weights. Still later, mean years of schooling was replaced by combined enrolment ratio, denominator being the population of age group 6-23. The reasons cited for such changes were non-availability of data, poor discriminatory power of adult literacy rate, etc. in the case of developed countries.

Level of living was represented by a transform of per capita income. As the exercise was international in nature and exchange rate was found to be a poor indicator of comparative purchasing power, the UNDP measured per capita income in purchasing power parity dollars, which was transformed. The transform was changed twice. The attempt through the transform was to make it reflect diminishing returns to income in terms of well-being. Technical experts have found the UNDP formulations suffering from certain theoretical weaknesses.

It may be noted that these aggregates were converted into unit-less achievement levels before they were aggregated. For this, actual achievement levels are first rescaled with reference to corresponding minimum achievement levels, which is then divided by the range/span of achievement over the minimum. Choice of minimum and maximum values has a chequered history. First the minima and maxima were chosen from the current profile of the achievements of the countries and then, on realization that this can create problem for valid comparison, the minima and maxima were chosen from a longer history. As that too did not resolve the problem, plausible figures were chosen as goalpost : 25 years and 85 years for life expectancy, 0 per cent and 100 per cent for literacy, 0 and 100 per cent for combined enrolment ratio and PPP$100 and $40000 for income per capita.

All three dimensions are said to have been given equal weights. But, in fact, one can see that there are four variables and only two of them have the weight of 1/3. Adult literacy rate has the weight of 2/9 while combined enrolment ratio has that of 1/9.

Critics have pointed out many problems with the UNDP formulation(s), an important one being the mixing of stock variables like life expectancy and adult literacy ratio with flow variables of gross enrollment ratio and gross domestic product per capita. They also point out that income per capita is not an end to be pursued for its own sake and human development approach does not permit its inclusion. The UNDP defends its decision by holding that it is a proxy for all those variables which have not been included.

And India

In India, many state governments (or, on their behalf, some research organizations) had already published their human development reports before the Planning Commission came out with National Human Development Report 2001 (NHDR) last year. Practically, all State Reports have devised their methods of calculating human development index for their district units, which was quite an exacting task. We shall however refer to the National Human Development Report 2001, which has calculated the index for 1981 and 1991 for all states/union territories and for 2001 only for major states.

Compared to the UNDP, this report chooses to represent longevity and health through a combination of life expectancy at age one (with weight 0.65) and reciprocal of infant mortality rate (with weight 0.35). It is reminiscent of physical quality of life index where both had equal weight of 1/3rd.

To represent knowledge component the NHDR chooses what it calls adjusted intensity of formal education (with weight 0.65) and literacy rate for the age group 7 years and above (with weight 0.35). Intensity of formal education is defined as weighted average of enrolled students from class I to class XII with weight. Proportional to the level of class—that is the number of years a current enrollee has been in school. Since only a proportion of population (relevant age group for schooling which is 6-18) actually goes to school, this intensity of education is adjusted by multiplying it with this proportion. Because this proportion is less than 60 per cent, the intensity of formal education, which is about 4.64 years, gets adjusted to just 2.70 years for the year 1993.

In case of the level of living, instead of income per capita, monthly consumption expenditure per capita is used. It is adjusted for inflation and inequality both. Adjustment for inequality (calculated for rural and urban areas separately) changes per capita monthly expenditure of Rs. 591 into that of Rs.418 for the year 1999-2000. But adjusting it to inflation through use of state specific deflators (obtained by division of nominal poverty lines of the year by corresponding original poverty lines) brings it down to only Rs. 111 at 1983 price level. Thus, a kind of inter-state comparability is ensured. However, no further transformation is carried out suggesting by implication that no state is considered affluent or superrich warranting application of the principle of diminishing returns.

Scaling norms for different indicators were chosen keeping in view the reasonable period of time starting 1980 and ending in 2020. The worst level of consumption expenditure per capita per month adjusted for inequality was found to be Rs. 70.56 for rural area in Dadra and Nagar Haveli in 1983. So the minimum was chosen to be Rs. 65. The maximum so far attained was for urban Chandigarh in 1999-2000, which was Rs. 256.55. So the maximum was chosen to be Rs. 325—about 25 per cent more than the present maximum. The minimum value of adjusted intensity of formal education was pegged at zero years as the worst case was forund to be of 0.38 years in Rajasthan for rural girls in 1978 and was still 0.83 years in 1993. The maximum was fixed at 7 years as the best attained in 1993 belonged to urban boys of Goa, which was close to 6 years. Rural females in Rajasthan had a literacy rate of 6.78 per cent. In view of the fact some section in some small area for which one could aspire to compute human development index, may have still lower literacy rate, the minimum was chosen to be zero. The maximum was obviously 100 per cent. As the multiplicative inverse of infant mortality rate is used for augmenting the index of life expectancy at one, one needs only the minimum value, which is selected to be 20 per thousand live births—far lower than that achieved by Manipur and Meghalaya.

The worst life expectancy at age one prevailed in rural areas of Uttar Pradesh among females and it was 55.2 years. The minimum value was therefore chosen to be 50 years. We are still far short of 80 years, which has been chosen as the maximum value. This detailed description underscores the meticulous care that was accorded to various choices. Indian exercise could be considered somewhat superior to the international ones but for the fact that most of the database is quite dated. For the year 2001, there exists hardly anything and extrapolations have their limitations.

THE LEVEL OF HUMAN DEVELOPMENT

According to the original Human Development Report (HDR) published in 1990, India's human development index was computed to be 0.439 for 1987. However, subsequently it was computed to be 0.297/0.309 for 1990 in the HDR 1992/1993. Obviously this downward revision owed to methodological changes. However, with one more turn of revision in methodology, we come to know that HDI level for India was 0.510 for 1990. It was compute to be 0.405 even in 1975. Very few people—scholars and researchers, in India questioned the UNDP exercises carried out in haste and used these figures to buttress their own views.

Since the UNDP divided countries into low, medium and high HDI countries depending upon the level of HDI below 0.5, between 0.5 and 0.8 and above 0.8, India was declared as low HDI country by earlier reports and as medium HDI country by later reports for the same levels of achievement. The UNDP ranks of various countries went up or down also because some of the countries were included or not included in the UNDP's HDRs. The

HDI for India was found to be 0.571, 0.577 and 0.590 for 1999, 2000 and 2001 in reports recently brought out by the UNDP. It would be a good idea to compare the HDI figures for India that were first flashed. See Table 1.1.

TABLE 1.1
Human Development Index for India—First Flashed

Year of HDR	*Year of Data*	*Value Reported*	*Year of HDR*	*Year of Data*	*Value Reported*
1990	1987	0.439	1997	1994	0.446
1991	1988	0.308	1998	1995	0.451
1992	1990	0.297	1999	1997	0.458
1993	1990	0.309	2000	1998	0.563
1994	1992	0.382	2001	1999	0.571
1995	1992	0.439	2002	2000	0.577
1996	1993	0.436	2003	2001	0.591

Source : Various Human Development Reports of the United Nations Development Program.

Later their exercises suggested that for 1990, the index was not 0.297 but 0.510—full 70 per cent higher. Similarly, for 1995 the figure was subsequently revised to 0.545. The country was declared one with low human development index. Hundreds of scholars accepted these and wrote thousands of papers undermining India's achievement before liberalization phase. Some damage was thus done. It is difficult to decide whether this was innocently done or deliberately.

Anyway, the Planning Commission did an exercise, which shows adequate consistency and ensures comparability across states and over time. India has improved its HDI from 0.302 in 1981 to 0.472 in 2001, that is, by 60 per cent in 20 years. See Table 2.2.

Based on this Table, the Tenth Plan (Volume III) tries to impress upon that Southern States generally have done better. If we compare the figures for 1981 and 2001, we find Rajasthan has done much better than Andhra Pradesh. while in 1981, Rajasthan had an HDI level of 0.258 and Andhra Pradesh, of 0.298, in 2001, Rajasthan has scored the level of 0.424 but Andhra Pradesh could reach up to 0.416. Thus, while Rajasthan's HDI improved by 0.176 points, Andhra Pradesh's improved by 0.118 points only.

West Bengal (0.305) was way behind Karnataka (0.346) in 1981; in 2001 the gap is merely 0.006—West Bengal has 0.472 as against Karnataka's 0.478. Yes, compared to Gujarat, Haryana and Maharashtra, Tamil Nadu has performed better. Kerala is definitely way ahead of Punjab (by full 0.1 point), growth performance of Madhya Pradesh in HDI is better. It could definitely be argued that grwoth rate is likely to slow at higher level. But Gujarat, Haryana, Punjab and Maharashtra, if we confine to only major states, have all done better than Karnataka. Yet, it should be accepted that

TABLE 1.2
Human Development Index 1981, 1991 and 2001
(According to rank of 1991)

Sl. No.	States/ Union Territories	1981		1991		2001	
		Value	Rank	Value	Rank	Value	Rank
1.	Chandigarh	0.550	1	0.674	1	n.e	
2.	Delhi	0.495	3	0.624	2	n.e	
3.	Kerala	0.500	2	0.591	3	0.638	1
4.	Goa	0.445	5	0.575	4	n.e	
5.	A & N Islands	0.394	11	0.574	5	n.e	
6.	Pondicherry	0.386	12	0.571	6	n.e	
7.	Mizoram	0.411	8	0.548	7	n.e	
8.	Daman & Diu	0.438	6	0.548	8	n.e	
9.	Manipur	0.461	4	0.536	9	n.e	
10.	Lakshadweep	0.434	7	0.532	10	n.e	
11.	Nagaland	0.328	20	0.486	11	n.e	
12.	Punjab	0.411	9	0.475	12	0.537	2
13.	Himachal Pradesh	0.398	10	0.469	13	n.e	
14.	Tamil Nadu	0.343	17	0.466	14	0.531	3
15.	Maharashtra	0.363	13	0.452	15	0.523	4
16.	Haryana	0.36	15	0.443	16	0.509	5
17.	Gujarat	0.36	14	0.431	17	0.479	6
18.	Sikkim	0.342	18	0.425	18	n.e	
19.	Karnataka	0.346	16	0.412	19	0.478	7
20.	West Bengal	0.305	22	0.404	20	0.472	8
21.	Jammu & Kashmir	0.337	19	0.402	21	n.e	
22.	Tripura	0.287	24	0.389	22	n.e	
23.	Andhra Pradesh	0.298	23	0.389	23	0.416	10
24.	Meghalaya	0.317	21	0.365	24	n.e	
25.	Dadra & Nagar Haveli	0.276	25	0.361	25	n.e	
26.	Assam	0.272	26	0.348	26	0.386	14
27.	Rajasthan	0.256	28	0.347	27	0.424	9
28.	Orissa	0.267	27	0.345	28	0.404	11
29.	Arunachal Pradesh	0.242	31	0.328	29	n.e	
30.	Madhya Pradesh	0.245	30	0.328	30	0.394	12
31.	Uttar Pradesh	0.255	29	0.314	31	0.388	13
32.	Bihar	0.237	32	0.308	32	0.367	15
	All India	0.302		0.381		0.472	

Note : n.e: No estimate was made for these States
Source : Tenth Five Year Plan 2002-2007, Vol. III (based on National Human Development Report 2001, Planning Commission).

Tamil Nadu is fast getting close to Punjab in terms of HDI level while Maharashtra is steadily losing.

The figures for smaller states/union territories—some of which are not so small—are not available for 2001. Chandigarh and Delhi were better off in 1991 and likely to maintain the lead. There were quite a few units scoring HDI between Kerala and Punjab and they are likely to maintain their positions. Himachal Pradesh is likely to improve its score faster.

SOME REVEALING FACTS

Achievements of Kerala in terms of human development have been lauded internationally. It is very often compared with Sri Lanka and China, ignoring the fact that China should also be having its own Keralas. Kerala has high human development index-33 per cent higher than the national average. If it is proportionately raised by the factor of international to national index of India, Kerala's score crosses 0.8, which is the lower mark for designating a country with high human development index. This is all good. However, this time the UNDP has praised Madhya Pradesh, Kerala and West Bengal for some achievements—particularly efforts in the direction of decentralization.

However, there are revealing weaknesses. Depending on the data in the NHRD, we try to draw attention to some less known facts and improve our understanding with a view to helping policy makers to be extra careful while devising policies.

Let us take up human poverty index and head count ratio of poverty. Kerala in 1991 had human poverty index of 32.10 and had sixth ranks though the states having lower human poverty index smaller ones, exception being Delhi. (we have not described human poverty index here.) As regards head count ratio of poverty, while Punjab has 6 per cent of its population below poverty line, Kerala has almost 13 per cent such population and the scene in its urban area is much worse. It is worth noting that urban areas in many states in comparison to their rural counterparts are now showing higher proportions of their populations below poverty line.

Kerala has highest literacy rates and adult literacy rates—male and female, rural and urban and also highest enrolment ratios for age groups 6-11 and 11-14 rural and urban, male and female. There is hardly any improvement in adjusted intensity of formal education. It improved from 3.79 years in 1978 to 3.94 years in 1993, which is hardly an improvement in fifteen years. Only Delhi was better than Kerala in 1978 but in 1993, Goa, Himachal Pradesh, Delhi and many other smaller states have done better. Tamil Nadu is pretty close with 3.86 years of adjusted intensity of formal education. Tamil Nadu is doing better than Kerala in many respects. In the case of education in Kerala, much needs to be done.

Unemployment scene, among major states, is the worst in Kerala, particularly in respect of female, youth and educated, and those in urban locale, despite the fact a great many Keralites are absorbed in other parts of the country as well as in other countries, particularly in the Gulf countries. As against average in 1999-2000 for rural female and urban female unemployment rates of 1.5 per cent and 7.1 per cent respectively, these rates are found to be around 19.7 per cent and 26.4 per cent in Kerala. Similar is the scene in Goa (rural female 26.0 per cent, urban female 35.2 per cent and urban male 15.3 per cent), which is otherwise a rich state also in Lakshdweep, a tiny union territory. It suggest that there is something greatly amiss in their development strategy.

Percentage of household having access to safe drinking water is not very high and its rural population is almost worst placed. If we believe in the definition of safe drinking water and the statistics complied by the Planning Commission, then in 1991, in rural Bihar 55 per cent households had access to safe drinking water while in rural Kerala only 12 per cent households did so. This present controversy of soft drinks containing large traces of pesticides says a lot about the quality of water available as it says about these multinationals. In terms of electricity connection Kerala is somewhat worse than Tamil Nadu and Karnataka and much worse than Punjab, Haryana, Himachal Pradesh, Gujarat and Maharashtra but better than Uttar Pradesh, Madhya Pradesh, Bihar, Rajasthan and West Bengal.

The point that is asserted is that human development index howsoever calculated is a partial index and one has to look beyond it. Human development index is an index of achievement, not of capability. Certain kinds of capabilities are meaningful only in conjunction with commensurate availability of commodities. Good literacy rates and good health indicators, indeed very valuable, are not enough. Capabilities have been defined as a set of functioning vectors and functionings have been allowed to include both being and doings but human development index concentrates more on being.

PUBLIC SPENDING FOR HUMAN DEVELOPMENT

Different societies choose to spend resources through public exchequer and private purses in different proportions on activities concerning human development. Again, organizations and institutions providing the services that promote human development may be in public domain or in private hands. Yet, in most societies public spending plays an important role and indicates the level of seriousness with which the state pursues the goal of human development.

One should however not lose sight of the fact whether the money is well spend of not. For a given situation, a well spend low expenditure may yield good outcomes where a less planned high expenditure may fail to achieve it. There are numerous such examples. In fact, if some underdeveloped countries with much less resources could achieve spectacular results in far shorter period than many developed or rich countries failed to achieve, it suggest that the policy design of the former has been far superior.

Human Development Report of 1991 had used the following four ratios : (1) public expenditure ratio, (2) social allocation ratio, (3) social priority ratio and (4) human expenditure ratio. While the first and the last are expressed in terms of proportion to the gross domestic product, social allocation ratio is the proportion of public expenditure spend on social sector and social priority ratio is the proportion of social expenditure on human priority concern. Human expenditure ratio, which is the product of the first three ratios, has been said to be a powerful operational tool that helps policy makers to restructure the budget to reflect their intension.

Analysing some of the figures complied by UNDP, we discovered that at one stage India, Sri Lanka and Thiland were each spending resources equivalent to 2.5 per cent of their gross domestic products but their achievements level differed significantly. Moreover, their public expenditure ratios differed significantly. In late eighties while India had a public expenditure ratio of 37 per cent, Thiland had it barely 16 per cent. It meant that their social allocation ratios and social priority ratios significantly differed. Similar inference can be drawn for Kuwait and Korea, both spending around 4 per cent on human development concerns. But Kuwait's public expenditure ratio was 36 per cent and social allocation ratio, 42 per cent while Korea's public expenditure ratio was just 16 per cent and social allocation ratio, 30 per cent, but what is significant is that while Kuwait spends about one-fourth of its social expenditure on priority concerns Korea spends three-fourths on them.

And India

India is far bigger than Thiland. Various states would spend different proportions on these activities and would achieve different outcomes and may not show a significant pattern.

We do not have the data complied in the manner the UNDP had done it. But we have readymade information on education and health expenditure ratios for 1980-81 and 1998-99. See Table-3.

EDUCATION

Over these two decades, the Table shows that education expenditure ratio has increased in all States barring Kerala , Punjab, Andhra Pradesh and Sikkim. In the case of Kerala, where it has drastically come down from over 25 per cent to less than 19 per cent, it is understandable as decline in enrolment in lower classes in the wake of reduction in absolute number of births will relatively stagnate educational expenditure while total expenditure will rise-given the rise of activities that come under taxation even if the rates are not raised, giving higher tax proceeds. Important to note is that even ratio is one among the higher ones—one per cent point higher than West Bengal's (which spends a little less than U.P in terms of proportion to total) and barely one per cent point lower than Tamil Nadu's. Moreover, it has not to incur much capital expenditure. Punjab's case could still be explained in terms of additional enrolment being taken care of by the private sector, which is making inroads in schooling for children of the rich. In the case of Haryana rise in the ratio is of low order. Andhra Pradesh's case of decline in educational expenditure ratio however remains intriguing as neither they had high accomplishments in literacy and education nor did they ever spend very high. Their ratio in 1980-81 was 14.35 per cent, comparable with of a little better than other states but has come down to 13 per cent, much less than what other states spend. The evidence about significant rise in the private sector activities is also lacking.

The educational expenditure ratio of the Union Government, which is not primarily responsible for the sector although the sector is in the concurrent list, has increased by about 50 per cent over these eighties and nineties from 2.7 per cent to 3.9 per cent of total public expenditure. In Rajasthan, Madhya Pradesh and Bihar, among the major states and Meghalya, Tripura and Manipur among smaller states this has risen by more than 50 per cent and in Assam it has risen more than 100 per cent. Assam spends more than a quarter of its budget (26.34 per cent) and Bihar, more than one-fifth (21.16). While this ratio of Bihar and Assam exceeds that of Tamil Nadu (19.76) and Rajasthan (19.53), Assam's ratio is ever highest in India. For a good number of reasons, the outcomes are not found too be commensurate with the ratio. First, total public spending may not be very large, making absolute level per capita rather low; second, they may be making up for the past; and third, implementation and follow-up may not be very effective. Similar is the case of Uttar Pradesh where this ratio exceeds that of Karnataka and West Bengal and is little behind Tamil Nadu. Even Orissa does much better than Bihar though it spends far less in terms of education expenditure ratio and is not a rich state.

HEALTH

So far as health expenditure ratio is concerned, during the eighties and nineties all southern states barring Kerala have improved it and the outcomes are pretty good in terms of life expectancies and infant morality rates. Once people's health improves and there are not many children needing medical care, health expenditure, which is largely on medical care, needs no increase. Good public health measures are likely to keep it down. However, if Sikkim reduces its health expenditure ratio from 5.65 per cent to 2.84 per cent or Nagaland reduces it from 9.57 per cent to 5.39 per cent, there is need for further probing. Still more intriguing is the case of Jammu and Kashmir where this ratio has significantly gone down from 11.8 per cent to 5.16 per cent. Could it be that expenditure on internal security forms a large proportion of total state budget! Even education expenditure ratio in this state has barely increased from 10.37 per cent to 10.90 per cent. In contrast, Tamil Nadu has raised both the ratios significantly.

In quite a few states health expenditure ratio has actually gone down whether it is the east or the west or the north or the Northeast whereas the

TABLE 1.3
Share of Expenditure on Education and Health in Total Public Expenditure

(*in* %)

States	*Education*		*Health*		*Social Sector*	
	1980-81	*1998-99*	*1980-81*	*1998-99*	*1980-81*	*1998-99*
Andhra Pradesh	14.35	12.98	7.63	8.45	21.98	21.43
Arunachal Pradesh	**	12.04	**	5.43	**	17.47
Assam	12.76	26.34	5.23	4.65	17.99	30.99
Bihar	13.19	21.16	5.49	4.81	18.68	25.97
Goa **	14.47	**	5.11	**	19.58	
Gujarat	12.55	16.38	6.08	5.41	18.63	21.79
Haryana	12.06	14.50	6.51	3.84	18.57	18.34
Himachal Pradesh	13.38	16.83	10.65	6.38	24.21	23.21
Jammu & Kashmir	10.37	10.90	11.82	5.16	22.19	16.06
Karnataka	13.30	17.94	5.48	6.02	18.78	22.16
Kerala	25.30	18.73	9.57	5.47	34.87	24.20
Madhya Pradesh	10.82	16.36	7.59	5.80	18.41	22.16
Maharashtra	14.63	17.67	6.53	4.84	21.26	22.51
Manipur	12.25	18.52	8.66	4.67	20.91	23.19
Meghalaya	9.97	16.95	15.34	7.22	25.31	24.17
Mizoram	**	12.97	**	4.93	**	17.90
Nagaland	8.03	9.55	9.57	5.39	17.6	14.96
Orissa	12.35	17.16	6.70	5.58	19.05	22.74
Punjab	16.99	15.76	6.52	4.73	23.42	20.49
Rajasthan	13.07	19.53	10.21	6.42	24.28	25.96
Sikkim	8.11	7.31	5.65	2.84	13.76	10.15
Tamil Nadu	14.38	19.76	6.56	8.32	20.94	25.08
Tripura	11.60	17.23	4.57	4.69	10.17	21.92
Uttar Predesh	13.15	18.31	5.89	4.10	19.04	22.41
West Bengal	15.92	17.78	9.07	6.49	24.99	24.27
Union Government	2.70	3.90	1.40	5.78	4.10	9.68

**Not Available
Source : Planning Commission Tenth Five Year Plan 2002-2007, Vol. III.

Union Government is spending 5.78 per cent of its total budget on health measures. If it is happening in richer states, may be more people are spending more money from their private purses in private clinics and therefore the state could relatively withdraw from the scene. But decline in the states like Bihar, Orissa, Uttar Pradesh, Madhya Pradesh, and Rajasthan puts one thinking why the demand should decline and if the demand has not declined why the states are falling behind in their duty. Health conditions should have improved as is suggest by significant rise in life expectancies across ages in all states and drastic reduction in infant mortality rates.

IN LIEU OF CONCLUSION

What use more people living a longer life if they have to live an idle life for longer part of a year? What use more people being better educated if they have to loiter on roads because the doors of establishments are shut on their face when they seek wage employment or if they do not get remunerative prices when they choose to be self-employed in the wake of constricted wage labour market? Human Development approach does not favour treatment of human beings as a resources but Human Development Reports did show some worry over the fact that economic growth presently taking place is jobless.

The idea of capability includes both being and doing through human development index could not adequately capture the doing part. Even while one may not like being treated as a resource one does want to be productive and creative and useful to the society and would like to earn one's wherewithal. Western economics has treated work/employment as a means rather an end, which people pursue for its own sake.

That employment elasticity with respect to GDP, on current daily status basis, has been drastically reducing in the eighties and nineties. It declined from 0.52 during 1983-1994 to 0.16 during 1994-2000. As a result, the rate of unemployment increased from 6.0 per cent to 7.3 per cent during this period. Total number of unemployed person years rose from 20 million to 26.6 million. The rate of unemployment has risen across age, sex and area of residence exception being the females in urban area but in their case the rate of unemployment is much higher than their male counterpart. This was the case when growth rate of labour force had drastically decelerated. In the years to come it is likely to accelerate from 1.3 per cent per annum during 1994-2000 to 2.5 per cent per annum during 2002-2007, and then to decelerate to 2.25 per cent per annum during 2007-2012 and 1.9 per cent per annum during 2012-2017.

In order to absorb the growth in labour force, at present level of employment elasticity, the required growth in GDP would be more than 15 per cent per annum—twice the rate we could think of. If the backlog has to be taken care of then growth rate required has to increase further. The Tenth Plan proposes policy changes and special employment programmes which will raise the employment elasticity to 0.34 and thus take care of possible rise in increase in labour force. While growth along with policy changes will induce employment for around 30 million, special programmes will generate employment for about 20 million. As per admission of the Planning Commission, the plan will still leave behind by 2007 more than 5 per cent of labour force (413.5 million) unemployed—frustrated and dejected. Most of the time we have failed in fulfilling promises. Earlier Plan (s) had not planned an employment elasticity of 0.16 but had it. If we again fail this time, a high growth rate will spell disaster in terms of poverty and inequality.

Long life is good but with health. Physical health is good that comes along with mental health. Mental health comes with being employed. If combination of productivity rise and growth rate does not produce enough work for all willing hands, could we think of redistributing work to all?

References

Chaubey, P.K. (2003), Human Development Index : Exercises in Methodology and Reconstruction, Indian Institute of Public Administration. (A Project Report).

Fukuda-Parr, Sakiko and Shicva Kumar, A.K. (ed. 2003), Reading in Human Development : Concept, Measures and Policies for Development Paradigm, Oxford University Press, New Delhi.

Planning Commission (2002), National Human Development Report 2001.

Planning Commission (2002), Tenth Five Year Plan 2002-2007-Vol. III.

United Nations Development Program (1990-2003), Human Development Reports, Oxford University Press, Delhi.

CHAPTER

2

Human Development in India : A Trend Analysis

P. JEGADISH GANDHI

INTRODUCTION

The roots of the concept of human development can be traced to early periods in human history and can be found in many cultures and religions. The central concern of development became the quality of people's lives- what they were capable of doing and what they actually did, the discrimination they faced, the struggles they waged and the expanding choices they enjoyed. The purpose of development is to create an atmosphere to develop people's capabilities, and opportunities, for both present and future generation. The real foundation of human development is universalism in acknowledging the life claims of everyone in society.

The UNDP Human Development Report since 1990 published the Human Development Index which ranks different countries, sexes, regions and ethnic groups on the basis of the human development. HDI takes into account longevity (for capability of leading a long and healthy life), educational attainment (for the capability of acquiring knowledge, exercising choice, communicating and participating in the life of the community) and access to resources (for capability for adequate nutrition and other consumption). The actual indicators selected are life expectancy at birth (for longevity), percentage of literate adults and average number of years of schooling for individuals over 25 years (for educational attainments) and real per capita gross domestic products and Purchasing Power Parity (PPP) dollars.

AGENDA FOR HRD

Dr. Mahbub ul Haq, the "guru of human development" and principal author of the United Nations Development Programmes, Human Development Report, 1993, had called for six-point agenda of action on human development for the Asia region. The six points are as follows : (1) All Asian governments must immediately prepare human development strategies and, in order to do this, collect and process data which can be used to quantify a variety of HD indicators, (2) Freeze military spending at existing levels if not reduce it, and privatize the public sector to generate resources for retiring public debt, (3) Initiate a sweeping decentralization of power and financially strengthen local bodies, (4) Create a forum for South-South co-operation and set-up regional centres for research on an exchange of experience in human development, (5) Form a new partnership with developed world based on a commitment to meeting human development targets and, in turn, demand developed countries to disarm for development, (6) Organise new alliance for change, including non-governmental organizations (NGOs), political parties and so on.

HRD IN INDIA

The Constitution of India, in its various Articles, gives a prominent place to the development of the human factor. The preamble of the Constitution itself is a recognition of this fact. The Articles of the Constitution relating to 'Fundamental Rights' and 'Directive Principles of State Policy', among others, lay down that the State shall make an effective provision for the development of human resources. Articles 38, 39, 42, 44, 45, 46, 47 and 48 of Part IV of the Constitution are directly relevant to the development of human resources. Growth with social justice was adopted as the basis for development planning in India. It did not take long for the policy planners to recognize the bi-directional linkages between education and development. Education was viewed as a crucial input in various sectors of the economy. The development of human resources required adequate provision of health services, water supply, education, housing, nutrition and family welfare facilities which are essential determinants of the quality of life. The provision of one without the other is bound to affect the life adversely, hence the strategy of human resources development is to take an integrated view of these factors.

NEW DIMENSIONS

The development of India's vast human resource potential is the essence of the social sector development strategy being followed in the country. Significant progress has been made over the years in human resource development which is reflected in improved demographic indicators, health care services, progress in the field of education and adult literacy level. The Approach Paper to the Tenth Five Year Plan (2002-07) which outlines a strategy to achieve a GDP growth rate of 8 percent, has a specific focus on human development. The Approach Paper stipulates that economic growth expressed in terms of increases in GDP or per capita income should be accompanied by a broader enhancement of human well-being and quality of life. This includes not only an adequate level of consumption of food and other consumer goods but also access to basic social services, especially education, health, drinking water and basic sanitation. It also includes the expansion of economic and social opportunities for all individuals and groups, reduction in disparities and a greater participation in the decision making process. The attainment of monitorable targets set out in this regard not only necessitates a substantial allocation of resources for the social sectors but also involves an enhanced role for the Government in the provision of social services, rural infrastructure, road development etc. As a ratio to total expenditure, the combined plan and non-plan expenditure of the Centre on these areas rose from 7.8 percent in 1992-93 to 11.1 percent in 2001-02 and also in 2002-03. Expressed as a ratio to GDP at current market prices, the expenditure on social services of the Central government increased from 1.4 percent in 1992-93 to 1.8 percent in 2001-02 and further to 1.9 percent in 2002-2003.

There has been significant progress in human development in the country as reflected in broad indicators such as the improvements registered in educational attainments, health coverage and in the provision of basic social infrastructure. India ranks 115th out of 162 countries in terms of the UNDP's Human Development Index (HDI) and is classified in the group Medium Human Development with an HDI of 0.571 in 2001. India's comparative position on Human and Gender Development is listed in Table 2.1. Though the overall index on gender-related development has improved in 2001 as compared to 1992, it is still low in comparison with the country's human development levels.

LATEST TRENDS IN HUMAN DEVELOPMENT

The 2002 Human Development Report presents a disappointing picture of India's position in the global arena. It shows, in particular, that India ranks 124 in the world. India's Human Development Index—a figure that is complied on the basic of life expectancy, literacy and GDP—is estimated at 0.577. This compares with higher HDI of 0.942, which is held by Norway, 0.939 of USA, 0.933 of Japan, and 0.928 of UK. Hong Kong has a HDI of 0.888 and Singapore 0.885. The low HDI of India is primarily the result of a combination of three factors-low per capita income, low life expectancy and low literacy achievement. Even compared to other developing countries, which have an average HDI of 0.654, India stands lower. India's per capita GDP being only $3,546 in purchasing power parity terms as compared to the developing countries' average of $3,783 (also in purchasing power parity terms) is one of the main reasons for the low index. In

TABLE 2.1
India's Global Position on Human and Gender Development

Country	*Human Development Index*		*Gender Development Index*		*Gender Empowerment Measure*	
	1992	*2001*	*1992*	*2001*	*1992*	*2001*
Norway	0.933	0.939	0.911	0.937	0.752	0.836
Australia	0.927	0.936	0.901	0.935	0.568	0.738
Sri Lanka	0.704	0.735	0.66	0.732	0.288	0.308
China	0.594	0.718	0.578	0.715	0.474	0.321
Indonesia	0.637	0.677	0.591	0.671	0.362	0.362@
India	0.439	0.571	0.401	0.533	0.226	0.240@
Pakistan	0.483	0.498	0.360	0.466	0.153	0.176@
Nepal	0.343	0.480	0.310	0.461	0.315	-
Bangladesh	0.364	0.470	0.334	0.459	0.287	0.309
Mozambique	0.246	0.323	0.229	0.309	0.350	0.428@
Ethiopia	0.227	0.321	0.217	0.308	0.205	-
Niger	0.207	0.274	0.196	0.260	-	0.120@

Note : @ relates to 1999.
Source : Human Development Reports, 1995, 1999 and 2001.

addition, life expectancy at birth in India is 63.3 years as compared to the marginally higher figure of 64.7 years in developing nations as a whole. The fact that India has remained low in the rank of developing nations in respect of human development is clear enough a reflection of the considerable distance that we have to go before we can claim a rank amongst the better-off nations in the world from the point of view of indicators of human development. It shows that there has been some progress- India's HDI has moved up from 0.407 in 1975 to the present 0.577 in 2000.

The HRD Report also produces what it calls a Human Poverty Index (HPI), which sums up an index of the total deprivation of the human conditions. It gives a summary index of the probability of a citizen not surviving up to the age of 40, adult literacy rate, the percentage of population not using improved water sources, the percentage of under-weight children under age 5, and finally the ratio of population below income poverty line. Taking all these into account, India ranks 55 amongst those for whom the HPI has been calculated. China ranks higher with a rank of 24 and Pakistan a rank of 68. The poorer we are, obviously the lower we rank in the HPI. Most importantly, the UN Human Development Report 2002 has pointed out how we in India have been sliding in the ranks of developing nations. This warning should serve as an alarm call to speed up our process of economic development with special emphasis on such indicators as education, public health and gender equality. We have a long way to go even judged by the progress achieved by other developing countries, leave alone China and South East Asia.

INDIA REPORT 2001

The Government of India published in May 2001 its first National Human Development Report, refining the Human Development Index (HDI), developed by the United Nations Development Programme, in the Indian context. The main recommendations continue to be that public expenditure on health and education should be increased. However, a comparison of the States' performance leads us to believe the opposite.

The HDI is a composite of variables capturing attainments in three dimensions of human development viz, economic, education and health. The HDI for country as a whole improved from 0.032 in 1981 to 0.472 in 2001 (Refer Table 2.2). Kerala remains at the top of the NHDR table with an HDI of 0.638 in 2001 while Orissa is almost at the bottom of the list, with an index of 0.267 in 1981, 0.345 in 1991 and 0.404 in 2001. The HDI for Bihar has been the lowest with the HDI for 2001 registering an improvement over the earlier years. Amongst the north-eastern States, Mizoram had the highest HDI and Arunachal Pradesh the lowest, in 1991. States which have done well in terms of HDI in 2001 are Punjab (0.537), Tamil Nadu (0.531) and Maharashtra (0.523). The national index for the rural areas between 1981 and 1991 has gone up from 0.263 to 0.340 and for urban areas from 0.442 to 0.511. The rural-urban gap was the minimum in case of Kerala and maximum for Madhya Pradesh in the early nineties.

Table 2.3 provides select indicators of low-and high-HDI states. The Social Sector Expenditure Ratio is 34.6 for the low-HDI States against 32 for high-HDI States. The low-HDI States spent 4.7 percent of their State Domestic Product on health and education against 3.7 percent by the high-HDI States. Higher public expenditure on the social sector has not resulted in higher HDI, perhaps due to delivery problems. The provision of these services by private parties is preferable because of better delivery. On the other hand, the public provision of these services may create a psychological dependence on the dole. When education is provided 'free' to the people, it may lead to better education status but also create the feeling that it is the government's responsibility to provide the jobs as well. On the other hand, the impact of private expenditure on health and education appears to have a positive impact.

Infrastructure appears to have a much greater impact on HDI. The expenditure on infrastructure as a percentage of plan expenditures by the low-HDI States is 29.2 against 38.1 for the high-HDI States. Road connectivity at the village level is at 50 percent for the low-HDI States against 75.8 percent for those of the high-HDI. Only 28.6 percent households in the low-HDI States have electricity connections against 59.6 percent for the high-HDI States. Better infrastructure appears to have a much greater impact on HDI. Though marginal, the impact of governance appears to be

TABLE 2.2
Human Development Index 1981, 1991 and 2001
(arranged in rank order of 1991)

Sl. No.	States/ Union Territories	1981		1991		2001	
		Value	Rank	Value	Rank	Value	Rank
1.	Chandigarh	0.550	1	0.674	1	n.e	
2.	Delhi	0.495	3	0.624	2	n.e	
3.	Kerala	0.500	2	0.591	3	0.638	1
4.	Goa	0.445	5	0.575	4	n.e	
5.	A & N Islands	0.394	11	0.574	5	n.e	
6.	Pondicherry	0.386	12	0.571	6	n.e	
7.	Mizoram	0.411	8	0.548	7	n.e	
8.	Daman & Diu	0.438	6	0.548	8	n.e	
9.	Manipur	0.461	4	0.536	9	n.e	
10.	Lakshadweep	0.434	7	0.532	10	n.e	
11.	Nagaland	0.328	20	0.486	11	n.e	
12.	Punjab	0.411	9	0.475	12	0.537	2
13.	Himachal Pradesh	0.398	10	0.469	13	n.e	
14.	Tamil Nadu	0.343	17	0.466	14	0.531	3
15.	Maharashtra	0.363	13	0.452	15	0.523	4
16.	Haryana	0.36	15	0.443	16	0.509	5
17.	Gujarat	0.36	14	0.431	17	0.479	6
18.	Sikkim	0.342	18	0.425	18	n.e	
19.	Karnataka	0.346	16	0.412	19	0.478	7
20.	West Bengal	0.305	22	0.404	20	0.472	8
21.	Jammu & Kashmir	0.337	19	0.402	21	n.e	
22.	Tripura	0.287	24	0.389	22	n.e	
23.	Andhra Pradesh	0.298	23	0.389	23	0.416	10
24.	Meghalaya	0.317	21	0.365	24	n.e	
25.	Dadra & Nagar Haveli	0.276	25	0.361	25	n.e	
26.	Assam	0.272	26	0.348	26	0.386	14
27.	Rajasthan	0.256	28	0.347	27	0.424	9
28.	Orissa	0.267	27	0.345	28	0.404	11
29.	Arunachal Pradesh	0.242	31	0.328	29	n.e	
30.	Madhya Pradesh	0.245	30	0.328	30	0.394	12
31.	Uttar Pradesh	0.255	29	0.314	31	0.388	13
32.	Bihar	0.237	32	0.308	32	0.367	15
	All India	0.302		0.381		0.472	

Note : n.e: No estimate was made for these States
Source : Human Development Report 2001, Planning Commission.

TABLE 2.3
Select Indicators of Low-and High-HDI States

	Low-HDI States	*High-HDI States*
	Bihar	West Bengal
	Assam	Karnataka
	Uttar Pradesh	Gujrat
	Madhya Pradesh	Haryana
	Orissa	Maharashtra
	Andhra Pradesh	Tamil Nadu
	Rajasthan	Punjab
		Kerala
Human Development Index	0.4	0.52
Impact of Public Social Sector Expenditures		
Social Sector Expenditure Ratio	34.6	32.0
Public Spending on Health & Education % of SDP	4.7	3.7
Impact of Private Social Sector Expenditures		
Non-Food Consumption Expenditure % of Total	38.0	42.5
Impact of Infrastructure		
Expenditure on Infrastructure as % of Plan Expenditure	29.2	38.1
Road Connectivity at Village Level		
(Less than 1000 persons)%	50.0	75.8
Households with Electricity Connection %	28.6	59.6
Impact of Governance		
Public Expenditure Ratio	20.0	**17.0**

Source : Extracted from National Human Development Report, 2001, Government of India.

positive. The low-HDI States have a public expenditure ratio of 20 percent against 17 percent for high-HDI States. This indicates that a lean government—a proxy for good governance—has a positive impact on HDI.

The implication is clear. Public expenditure on social sectors does not show a positive impact while private expenditures do. However, public expenditure on infrastructure clearly has a positive impact. *The strategy for improving human development has to be that of a lean government spending more on infrastructure and encouraging people to increase their private expenditure on social sectors. This is contrary to what the Government, the United Nations Development Programme and other protagonists of social sector expenditures recommend (Bharat Jhunjhunwala, 2002).*

CHALLENGES IN THE 21st CENTURY

'One of the principal ways of linking economic growth and human lives is to invest liberally in the education and health of the people. Such investment is quite limited in India at present—only $14 a person per annum, compared to $160 in the Republic of Korea. Wherever India has made adequate investment in the education and skill-training of its people and in strengthening its human capital, the strategy has paid rich dividends. For example, India has already emerged as the second larger exporter of computer software as a result of expensive investment in skill formation in Bangalore, which has fast become India's own 'Silicon Valley'. In fact, India enjoys the great advantage of possessing a rich tradition of scientific and technological research, a large reservoir of low-paid hard-working people, the largest middle class in the world, and functioning democratic institutions. Its take-off desperately requires a massive investment in human development' *(Human Development in South Asia Report, 1997).*

As per Economic Surveys, 'Fifty years after achieving independence, poverty, illiteracy, disease and lack of minimum social services continue to affect hundreds of millions of our people' *(1996-97)*. 'The ongoing economic reform process should be reappraised and revitalized to give the entire national development effort a more human face. The eradication of poverty and unemployment must be the abiding goal of our development policies and programmes. The achievement of this goal will require sustained and rapid economic growth combined with well functioning public programmes for social services, rural development and employment generation to provide an effective safety-net for all those millions at the margins of the growth process' *(1997-98)*. 'Policies and programmes undertaken in recent years with a special focus on various components of the social sector have yielded positive results in terms of improvement in basic socio-demographic indicators, quality of life, reduction of overall poverty levels, and increased access to basic necessities of life. However, sustained efforts are still needed to reduce the visible disparities amongst States, between rural and urban areas and between males and females. Sustaining budgetary allocations at higher levels on a long-term basis, also entails concerted resource mobilization efforts on the part of the Centre and the States' *(2001-2002)*. The ongoing economic reforms have a human face and in pursuance of the commitment towards development of human resources and enhancement of human well being, additional resources for the social services sector are being allocated by the Government. Suitable target for the reduction of poverty, hunger, mortality and illiteracy have also been incorporated in the Tenth Five Year Plan *(Economic Survey 2002-2003 p. 211)*.

The main purpose of development is to enlarge people's choices. This covers the objective of creating a favourable environment for people to enjoy long, healthy and creative lives. The basic difference between economic growth and human development is that the former focuses exclusively on the expansion of only one choice-income-while the latter encompasses an enlargement of all human choices-economic, social, cultural or political. Generation of more income for the people and for investment in economic and social infrastructure have a pervasive influence. If higher incomes are available to the people and if basic minimum needs are met, it would provide the pre-conditions for improving the quality of life. The high incidence of poverty in India is an anti-thesis for sustainable human development. In the 21st century, the new paradigm of human development should be systemized around the more than proportionate incremental investment strategy in favour of pro-poor programmes. To quote A.P.J. Abdul Kalam, the President of India: *"While aggregated indicators are important, it does not make sense to achieve a 'developed' status without a major and continuing upliftment of all Indians who exist today and of the many more millions who would be added in the years to come. They should all have a secure and enjoyable 'present' and also be in a position to look forward to a better 'future'. Such a developed India is what we are looking for".*

REFERENCES

Gandhi, P.J. (1996), Indian Economy Issues, Pointer Publishers, Jaipur, Reprinted Edition.

———, (1997), Development : The 21st Century Perspectives, Business Line, May 24.

———, (1998), "Human Development in India: More Grey Areas, Less Bright Spots, Southern Economist, October 15.

———, (1998), Socio-economy of India: The First 50 years and Beyond, Deep and Deep Publications, New Delhi.

———, (2001), "Budget Sidelines Social Sector Dynamics", Southern Economist, March 15.

———, (2001), "Humanising Development: The 21st Century perspectives", Presidential Address, 21st Annual Conference of the Association of Economists of Tamil Nadu and Pondichery, Coimbatore, January 20.

———, (2001), "Social Sector Needs Money", Business Line, February 27.

———, (2002), "Social Sector and Economic Reforms, A Critical Analysis, Southern Economist, May 1.

———, (2003), Globalised Indian Economy—Contemporary Issues & Perspectives, Deep and Deep Publications, New Delhi.

———, (1996), 'The Concept of Development: Its Dialects and Dynamics, Indian Journal of Applied Economics, *October-December*

Governmental of India (1996-97, 1997-98, 2001-2002 and 2002-2003): Economic Surveys,

———, (2001), First Human Development Report.

Human Development Centre (1997), Human Development in South Asia Report.

Indira Gandhi Institute of Development Research: (1997), India Development Report.

Jhunjhunwala, Bharat (2002), 'Human Development: Popular Myths disabused', Business Line, June 3.

Kalam, A.P.J. Abdul and Y.S. Rajan (1998), India 2002, A Vision for the New Millennium, Viking, New Delhi.

Nanjundappa, D.M. (1997), "Formulating a Development Paradigm", Business Line, April 22.

UNDP (1994, 1996, 1997 and 2002), Human Development Report.

Venkitaramanan, S. (2002), "UN HRD 2002, Why India still Languishes?" Business Line, August 5.

CHAPTER

3

Combating Poverty : Regional Concentration and Fiscal Reforms

D.K. Srivastava

INTRODUCTION

This paper examines the phenomenon of growing regional concentration in the changing profile of poverty in India and argues that changes in fiscal policies are needed to further combat poverty particularly its increasing spatial concentration. Most analysts agree that there has been a fall in the poverty ratio over time, although there may be some debate as to the magnitude of fall. However, since the rate of fall has been lower in areas with large incidence of poverty, it is now regionally more concentrated.

Ever since the official estimates of poverty based on the 55th round of the National Sample Survey were presented, there has been a continuing debate as to the rate of decline of the poverty ratio. Several alternative estimates have been prepared aimed at correcting the so-called 'bias' in the official estimates. Some of these alternative estimates are also described in this paper.

This paper is divided into six sections. Section 2 describes the profile of poverty based on official estimates. Section 3 reviews the debate that followed the publication of the official estimates of poverty based on 55th round of the NSS. Section 4 examines the growing regional concentration of poverty. Section 5 considers relevant changes in policy, particularly fiscal policy for devising an appropriate strategy for combating poverty. Section 6 summarises the results and provides concluding observations.

OFFICIAL POVERTY ESTIMATES IN INDIA

Understanding the incidence of poverty in India, and its inter-state pattern has engaged the attention of economists, policy makers, and planners over the last forty years. Poverty estimation exercises took off in 1962 with a Working Group of the Planning Commission defining poverty line with reference to a national minimum level of living as involving a private consumption expenditure of Rs. 20 per month per capita at 1960-61 prices. Various attempts at working out state-specific poverty lines were made from time to time, separately for rural and urban areas. The Planning Commission has been providing estimates of poverty since the Sixth Plan. The present set of official poverty lines are based on the recommendations of the Expert Group, headed by D.T. Lakdawala, whose report was presented in July 1993. the Expert Group had set out an alternative estimation methodology and provided estimates of poverty Head Count Ratios (HCR) based on state-specific poverty lines. Based on this methodology, a set of estimates of incidence of inter-state poverty are available for five reference points, *viz.*, 1973-74, 1977-78, 1983, 1987-88, 1993-94 and 1999-00. These estimates utilise data from NSS quinquinniel surveys of consumer expenditure.

Table 3.1 presents estimates of HCRs of rural and urban poverty in India for these five reference points. While the rural poverty ratio has come down from 56 to 27 per cent during 1973-74 to 1999-2000, i.e. over a period of 26 years, the urban poverty ratio has also significantly declined. Considering the overall poverty ratio, a decline of about 29 percentage points is visible over the period of 26 years, i.e., indicating a fall by a margin of a little over 1 percentage point per year, on average.

TABLE 3.1
Poverty Head Count Ratios in India

Years	*Rural*	*Urban*	*Total*
1973-74	56.44	49.01	54.88
1977-78	53.07	45.24	51.32
1983	55.65	40.79	44.48
1987-88	39.02	38.2	35.35
1993-94	37.27	32.36	35.97
1999-00	27.09	23.62	26.10

Source : (Basic Data) : Government of India, Press Information Bureau, Poverty Estimates, Press Releases, Dated March 11, 1997 and February 22, 2001.

Table 3.2 gives the inter-state profile of the incidence of poverty both for rural and urban areas for 1999-2000. These estimates are based on the state specific poverty lines, which vary between Rs. 270 for Andhra Pradesh

TABLE 3.2
Number and Percentage of Population Below Poverty Line by States : 1999-00

(30-Day Recall Period)

Sl. No.	States/UTs.	*Rural* No. of Persons (Lakhs)	*Rural* % of Persons	*Urban* No. of Persons (Lakhs)	*Urban* % of Persons	*Combined* No. of Persons (Lakhs)	*Combined* % of Persons
1.	Andhra Pradesh	58.13	11.05	60.88	26.63	119.01	15.77
2.	Assam	92.17	40.04	2.38	7.47	94.55	36.09
3.	Bihar	376.51	44.30	49.13	32.91	425.64	42.6
4.	Goa	0.11	1.35	0.59	7.52	0.7	4.40
5.	Gujarat	39.80	13.17	28.09	15.59	67.89	14.07
6.	Haryana	11.94	8.27	5.39	9.99	17.33	8.74
7.	Himachal Pradesh	4.84	7.94	0.29	4.63	5.13	7.63
8.	Jammu & Kashmir	2.97	3.97	0.49	1.98	3.46	3.48
9.	Karnataka	59.91	17.38	44.49	25.25	104.4	20.04
10.	Kerala	20.97	9.38	20.07	20.27	41.04	12.72
11.	Madhya Pradesh	217.32	37.06	81.22	38.44	298.54	37.43
12.	Maharashtra	125.12	23.72	102.87	26.81	227.99	25.02
13.	Orissa	143.69	48.01	25.40	42.83	169.09	47.15
14.	Punjab	10.20	6.35	4.29	5.75	14.49	6.16
15.	Rajasthan	55.06	13.74	26.78	19.85	81.84	15.28
16.	Tamil Nadu	80.51	20.55	4997	22.11	130.48	21.12
17.	Uttar Pradesh	412.01	31.22	117.88	30.89	529.89	31.15
18.	West Bengal	180.11	31.85	33.38	14.86	213.49	27.02
	All India	1932.43	27.09	670.07	23.62	2602.50	26.10

Source : (Basic Data) : As in Table 3.1.

to Rs. 375 for Kerala for rural areas, and between Rs. 344 for Assam and Rs. 540 for Maharashtra for urban areas. These estimates indicate the general pattern that poverty ratios are higher for lower income states. This is particularly evident in the case of rural poverty. Some of the low income States like Assam, Bihar and Orissa have a rural poverty HCR that is higher than 40 per cent i.e. more than 13 percentage points above the national average. State like Uttar Pradesh, Madhya Pradesh and West Bengal have a rural poverty HCR that is of above 30 per cent. In general, the lower the per capita GSDP, and the larger the size of population, the higher is the rural poverty HCR.

In the case of urban poverty, some of the better off states like Maharashtra also show a higher incidence of poverty. In this case some of the highest poverty ratios among the general category states are seen in the case of Orissa, Maharashtra, Bihar, Andhra Pradesh and Uttar Pradesh. On the other hand, the lowest urban poverty ratios among the general category states are seen in the case of Punjab, Goa, and Haryana.

The relativities in the poverty lines across states and between rural and urban areas are also notable. Table 3.3 provides the estimated official poverty lines. Looking at the difference (urban minus rural) as percentage of rural poverty line, it is seen that except for Assam, in all cases, the urban poverty line is higher than the rural poverty line. In the case of Andhra Pradesh, the urban poverty line is nearly 74 per cent higher than the rural poverty line. For Maharashtra, it is 69 per cent higher, and for Tamil Nadu, about 55 per cent higher. Rural and urban poverty lines in the states as percentage of all India corresponding poverty lines are also given in Table 3.3. Inter-state variation relative to the all India rural poverty line is in the

TABLE 3.3

State Specific Poverty Lines in 1999-00

(Rs. Per Capita Per Month)

Sl. No.	*States*	*Rural*	*Urban*	*Difference as % of Rural PL*	*Rural PL as % of All India PL*	*Urban PL as % of All India PL*
1.	Andhra Pradesh	262.94	457.40	73.96	80.27	100.72
2.	Assam	365.43	343.99	-5.87	111.56	75.75
3.	Bihar	333.07	379.78	14.02	101.68	83.63
4.	Gujarat	318.94	474.41	48.75	97.37	104.47
5.	Haryana	362.81	420.20	15.82	110.76	92.53
6.	Himachal Pradesh	367.50	420.20	14.34	112.19	92.53
7.	Jammu & Kashmir	327.56	420.20	28.28	100.00	92.53
8.	Karnataka	309.59	511.44	65.20	94.51	112.62
9.	Kerala	374.79	477.06	27.29	114.42	105.05
10.	Madhya Pradesh	311.34	481.65	54.70	95.05	106.06
11.	Maharashtra	318.63	539.71	69.38	97.27	118.85
12.	Orissa	323.92	473.12	46.06	98.89	104.19
13.	Punjab	362.68	388.15	7.02	110.72	85.47
14.	Rajasthan	344.03	465.92	35.43	105.03	102.60
15.	Tamil Nadu	307.64	475.60	54.60	93.92	10473
16.	Uttar Pradesh	336.88	416.29	23.57	102.85	91.67
17.	West Bengal	350.17	409.22	16.86	106.90	90.11
18.	Delhi	362.68	505.45	39.37	110.72	111.31
	All India	327.56	454.11	38.63	100.00	100.00

Source : (Basic Data) : As in Table 3.1.

range of 80 to 114 per cent. The range in the case of the urban poverty line is 75 to 119 per cent. It may be noted that even in the case of Assam, the urban poverty line may be higher than the rural poverty line as per modified estimates provided by Deaton and Dreze (2002), an issue that is discussed in the next section.

THE RECALL PERIOD CONTROVERSY AND ALTERNATIVE ESTIMATES

In the expenditure survey under NSS, most questions are canvassed on the basis of a 30-day recall period. There are some items, particularly relating to some infrequently purchased items where a 365 days recall period is also used. In some of the earlier surveys, some 7-days recall period questions were also canvassed instead of the 30-days recall period. However, the sample of households were kept different where 7-days questions were canvassed. In the other case, for most questions, the recall period was 30-days and for some of the infrequently used items, it was 365 days. While a clear distinction was made in the earlier rounds, for the 55th round, which produced results for 1999-00, in the 30-365 days version, there was a mix-up in the sense that for the same households for certain items, *viz.*, food, pan, tobacco and intoxicants, information was canvassed for the 7-day and 30-day recall periods and recorded on two columns that were put side by side for the same set of households. It has been contended that the 30-day recall answers were affected by the 7-day recall answers. Since the latter generally show higher consumption, the expenditure estimates in the 30-days schedules were inflated, and showed a sharper decline in poverty than would have been the case if the 55th survey did not have this mix-up of recall periods. In the earlier rounds, the 7-day and 30-day reference periods were canvassed on two independent sets of sample households. Some analysts like Deaton and Dreze (2002 and 2003) have provided alternative estimates after correcting for this bias. Table 3.4 provides estimates provided by Deaton and Dreze.

It will be noted that at the aggregate level rural poverty is not much different from the official estimates, but the estimate of urban poverty has gone down quite significantly.

POVERTY CONCENTRATION : RURAL AND URBAN AREAS

Table 3.5 highlights the concentration of rural poverty among a limited of states using estimates for 1999-00. It is seen that nearly 74 per cent of the rural poor live in just six states viz., Orissa, Bihar, Assam, Madhya Pradesh, West Bengal and Uttar Pradesh. Although the urban poverty is spread out a little more (Table 3.6) but even in this case, it can be seen that just eight states account for a little less than 80 per cent of the urban poor. These eight states are Orissa, Madhya Pradesh, Bihar, Uttar Pradesh, Maharashtra, Andhra Pradesh, Karnataka and Tamil Nadu. It can be seen that four out of

TABLE 3.4

Estimates by Deaton and Dreze : Head Count Ratios

Sl. No.	States	Rural 1987-88	Rural 1993-94	Rural 1999-00	Urban 1987-88	Urban 1993-94	Urban 1999-00
1.	Andhra Pradesh	35.0	29.2	26.2	23.4	17.8	10.8
2.	Assam	36.1	35.4	35.5	13.6	13.0	11.8
3.	Bihar	54.6	48.6	41.1	38.1	26.7	24.7
4.	Gujarat	39.4	32.5	20.0	16.4	14.7	6.4
5.	Haryana	13.6	17.0	5.7	11.8	10.5	4.6
6.	Himachal Pradesh	13.3	17.1	9.8	1.7	3.6	1.2
7.	Jammu & Kashmir	15.3	10.1	6.1	3.8	3.1	1.3
8.	Karnataka	40.8	37.9	30.7	26.0	21.4	10.8
9.	Kerala	23.8	19.5	10.0	21.0	13.9	9.6
10.	Madhya Pradesh	43.7	36.6	31.3	20.7	18.5	13.9
11.	Maharashtra	44.3	42.9	31.9	21.2	18.2	12.0
12.	Orissa	50.4	43.5	43.0	20.8	15.2	15.6
13.	Punjab	6.6	6.2	2.4	6.6	7.8	3.4
14.	Rajasthan	35.3	23.0	17.3	19.8	18.3	10.8
15.	Tamil Nadu	49.0	28.5	24.3	26.2	20.8	11.3
16.	Uttar Pradesh	34.9	28.6	21.5	29.3	21.7	17.3
17.	West Bengal	36.3	25.1	21.9	22.3	15.5	11.3
	All India	39.0	33.0	26.3	22.5	17.8	12.0

Source : Deaton and Dreze (2002), Economic and Political Weekly, September 7.

TABLE 3.5

Number and Percentage of Population Below Poverty Line by States—1999-00 (30-Day Recall Period) : Rural

Sl. No.	General Category States and Assam States/Uts.	No. of Persons (Lakhs)	% of Persons
	States Arranged in Descending Order of Head Count Ratio		
	Fist Six States		
1.	Orissa	143.69	48.01
2.	Bihar	376.51	44.30
3.	Assam	92.17	40.04
4.	Madhya Pradesh	217.32	37.06
5.	West Bengal	180.11	31.85
6.	Uttar Pradesh	412.01	31.22
	Total Number of Rural Poor	**1421.81**	
	Share of First Six States in Total Rural Poor (%)		**73.6**

Source (Basic Data) : Government of India, Press Information Bureau, Poverty Estimates, Press Releases, Dated March 11, 1997 and February 22, 2001.

TABLE 3.6

Number and Percentage of Population Below Poverty Line by States-1999-00 (30-Day Recall Period) : Urban

Sl. No.	States/Uts.	No. of Persons (Lakhs)	% of Persons
First Eight States in Descending Order of HCR			
1.	Orissa	25.40	42.83
2.	Madhya Pradesh	81.22	38.44
3.	Bihar	49.13	32.91
4.	Uttar Pradesh	117.88	30.89
5.	Maharashtra	102.87	26.81
6.	Andhra Pradesh	60.88	26.63
7.	Karnataka	44.49	25.25
8.	Tamil Nadu	49.97	22.11
	Total Number of Urban Poor	**531.84**	
	Share of First Eight in Total Urban Poor (%)		**79.37**

Source (Basic Data) : Government of India, Press Information Bureau, Poverty Estimates, Press Releases, Dated March 11, 1997 and February 22, 2001.

these eight states are relatively better off states. These observations relate to the official poverty estimates prepared by the Planning Commission for 1999-00.

Table 3.6 indicates that five states, *viz.*, Orissa, Madhya Pradesh, Bihar, Uttar Pradesh and Maharashtra account for 56 per cent of the urban poor. Their individual poverty HCR ratios range from little above 26 per cent (for Maharashtra to about 43 per cent for Orissa). The next four states accounting for a significant share in the total urban poor of the country are Andhra Pradesh, Karnataka, Tamil Nadu and Kerala and middle to high income states.

The pattern of growing spatial concentration of poverty provides some useful insights into the changing incidence of poverty. We have worked out changes in poverty concentration over the five sets of available information during the 26 years' period which is under reference. The spatial concentration of poverty is measured by using the Herfindal Index, which was originally used to measure industrial concentration. In the present case, the basic information relates to the share of each sate in the total number of poor in the country. The index is based on measuring the sum of squares of these shares.

The poverty concentration index (PCI) using states as the basic unit may be defined as below :

Let population of all poor be M, and the number of poor in State i by M_i. The share of State i in total poor is given by m_i = (Mi/M). The poverty concentration index (PCI), using states as the basic units, may be defined as below :

$$PCI = \sum \left(\frac{1}{m_i} \right)^2 \quad i = 1, 2, \ldots, n,$$

Where n is the number of states. It may be noted that the index has a maximum value of 1 when the poor are located only in one state and there are no poor in any other state. Thus we can write

$$PCI\ (max) = 1$$

The minimum concentration is seen when each state has an equal share in the number of poor. If the total poor are M and n is the number of states, and each state has an equal share equal to M/n, the summation of the shares of these terms would give the minimum value of PCI as indicated below:

$$PCI\ (min) = \sum [(M/n)/M]^2 = \sum (1/n)^2 = 1/n$$

As n is increased PCI (min) would tend to zero. Thus, the index of concentration varies between 1/n and 1.

The estimated value of the concentration index are given in Table 3.7. It will be seen that as far as the rural areas are concerned, the concentration index was estimated at 9.05 for 1973-74. It steadily increased over the years and reached the level of 12.19 in 1999-00. In the case of urban areas, the concentration index is estimated at 8.51 for 1973-74. In this case also, a

TABLE 3.7

Poverty Concentration Ratio

Years	*Rural*	*Urban*	*Total*
1973-74	9.05	8.51	8.71
1977-78	8.95	8.67	8.66
1983	10.12	8.97	9.47
1987-88	10.06	9.09	9.39
1993-94	11.00	9.38	9.91
1999-00	12.19	10.14	10.96
Concentration Level Relative to 1973-74 Level			
1973-74	100.0	100.0	100.0
1977-78	98.8	101.9	99.5
1983	111.8	105.3	108.7
1987-88	111.0	106.8	107.9
1993-94	121.5	110.2	113.8
1999-00	134.6	119.1	125.9

Source (Basic Data) : Government of India Press Information Bureau, Poverty Estimates, Press Release Dated March, 11, 1997 and Feb 22, 2001.

gradual increase is visible and the index has moved up to the level of 10.14 in 1999-2000 relative to 1973-74. We can see that the rural poverty concentration index has increased by about 35 per cent in 1999-00, relative to 1973-74, whereas the urban poverty concentration has increased by about 19 per cent during this period.

We thus observe that :

(i) Spatial concentration or rural poverty has been higher than that of urban poverty throughout these years ; and
(ii) In both cases, the poverty concentration has increased.

The main trends in the changing profile of poverty incidence in India may be summarized as below :

(i) The incidence of poverty has steadily gone down both for rural and urban areas in all states.
(ii) Rural poverty has become more and more spatially concentrated.
(iii) Urban poverty has also been focused more and more in a limited number of states, but the list includes some of the better off states.
(iv) The concentration of poverty is higher in rural areas, and the spatial concentration has increased markedly over the years.

The Spatial concentration of poverty also leads to some negative externalities. For example, the urban poor, living in densely populated slums, are more easily drawn into the illegal activities. When the poor live closely together in geographical clusters, i.e., when there is a higher concentration of the poor, they are more easily drawn into disruptive activities. Therefore, higher concentration ratios and higher urbanization of poverty provide fertile ground of recruitment of people into activities that have a bearing on the negative externalities associated with poverty. Urban concentration of poverty leads to development of slums and squalor, which generates health-related negative externalities. It can also be seen that the higher concentration of poverty has been associated with lower growth in the concerned states.

Slums areas generate negative externalities feeding into health hazards for the non-poor population within the slum or nearby areas. Many of these hazards emanate from poor availability of drinking water. The recent report of the Committee on problems of Slums in Delhi (2002) observes : "Almost all slum dwellers belong to the very poor strata of society in the country" and further that "The characteristics of a slum is the excessive congestion and unhygienic nature of the housing, lacking in basic amenities".

A Nationwide survey on 'Particulars of Slums', conducted by the (NSSO) in its 19th round had found that nearly 81 per cent rural slums did not have access to a tap for drinking water. In the case of urban slums about 35 per cent did not have a 'tap' as source of drinking water, and in many states about 50 per cent of urban slums did not have access to a tap for drinking water. About 60 per cent of the urban slums remain waterlogged during monsoon. Around 83 per cent of urban slums did not have an underground sewerage system. An open pucca system of drainage did not exist in 65 per cent of the urban slums. About 35 per cent of urban slums did not have any arrangement for garbage disposal, the figure being far larger in many of the bigger states. These conditions of urban slums make them a clear source of health hazards not only for the inhabitants themselves, but nearby non-slum residents as well. One aspect of poverty's negative externalities is its link to health indicators. States with a high incidence of poverty also have low life expectancy and a high IMR.

ROLE OF FISCAL POLICY IN POVERTY ALLEVIATION

Among a list of important 'Fiscal Tasks', Musgrave (1999) includes one as "Relief on Poverty". The rationale for fiscal intervention arises in the context of the existence of the negative externalities associated with poverty. Unless this is done, fiscal costs will have to be incurred by the non-poor individually for coping with the negative externalities of poverty.

An extensive policy regime in India provides for fiscal intervention with the objective, explicit or implicit, of poverty alleviation at the level of central, state and local governments. The Central government provides fiscal intervention by using a large number of central sectors and centrally sponsored schemes. It also runs a large subsidy regime, particularly for food and fertilisers. The state governments also run large subsidy regimes supporting such economic sectors as agriculture, irrigation, power and transport. Most of this fiscal intervention is untargeted and general in nature. The volume of subsidy is large, but the pattern is regressive, and the benefits are appropriated to a large extent by the non-poor population. A discussion paper brought out by the Ministry of Finance, Government of India in 1997 had estimated the total explicit and implicit budgetary subsidies in India as accounting for more than 13.5 per cent of GDP at market prices.

There are other difficulties with the quality and implementation of policy aimed at social welfare and poverty reduction. Some of the main shortcomings arise from the fact that these are too numerous to be effectively implemented. The same design for all states is irrelevant in the context of centrally sponsored schemes. Further, the administration of schemes at the local level is characterised by considerable leakages and states, often due to lack of resources at their end, are unable to take full advantage of the central schemes. Generally, untargeted programmes waste a lot of resources.

It can be seen that a restructuring of fiscal intervention to reduce poverty would involve only a limited amount of additional resources if these are used in well-designed and targeted programmes in the context of spatial concentration of poverty. Given the context of negative externalities, these will provide a double dividend by significantly reducing poverty levels as also providing a platform for higher growth in the concerned regions. In the next section, an estimate is made of the minimum additional resources required to reduce poverty through targeted income-support programmes. It can be shown, as estimated below, that less than 1 per cent of GDP is required as targeted allocation for combating rural poverty and keeping at near-zero levels. The first level of targeting should be towards these states, where concentration of rural poverty is higher.

In this section, an attempt is made to estimate the requirement of additional resources to fully eliminate poverty by a perfectly targeted programme of income support. This amount would simple be the sum of the difference between the gap of the individual incomes of the poor from the poverty line. Alternatively, it can be obtained by multiplying the number of poor by mean poverty gap, for each state for the rural areas.

Thus, Aggregate Resource Gap (ARG) can be written as :

$$ARG = \Sigma\ (z-y_i),\quad i = 1, 2 \ldots m,$$

where z is the poverty line and m is the number of poor. Alternatively

$$ARG = m\ (z-m_p)$$

Where m_p is the mean income of the poor. Since the poverty Gap Index (PGI) is defined as $PGI = 1/n\ \Sigma\ (z-m_p)$

We can obtain ARG = PGI . n/m = (PGI/H) where H is the Head Count Ratio.

The information needed for this estimation requires knowledge of the state specific poverty lines, the poverty gap index and the head count ratio. Using these estimates with reference to the 1999-2000 HCRs, the official poverty lines, and the PGI index with reference to the official poverty lines {Deaton and Dreze (2002)}, estimates have been made separately for the rural and urban areas.

Table 3.8 provides estimates for the total resource gap in rural and urban areas. The total gap is estimated at Rs.14580.4 crore for rural areas, which constitutes 0.75 per cent of GDP at current market prices for 1999-00.

One has to recognize, however, that a case is not being made for using an income support policy that makes up for the exact difference between the poverty line and the average income of the identified poor so as to keep poverty incidence at zero level year after year. In practice, there would be many difficulties in following such a policy.

First, such a policy can have significant adverse incentives. As soon as the poor learn that such a policy is in place, their effort to earn whatever meagre income they are earning would go down, leading to an increase in the gap between poverty line and the mean income. Secondly, a targeting of such high precision would require substantial administrative costs.

Thirdly, the exact design of such a policy would need to be worked out. Fourthly, although income gaps will be filled up, this is with reference to a

TABLE 3.8
Estimation of Minimum Resources Required for Closing the Poverty Gap : Rural

Sl. No.	States/UTs.	No. of Persons (Lakhs)	HCR	Total Population (Crore)	PGI (Official Methodology	Poverty Line (Official)	Estimated Resource Gap (Rs. Crore)
1.	Andhra Pradesh	58.13	11.05	5.26	1.8	262.9	298.8
2.	Assam	92.17	40.04	2.30	8.5	365.4	858.0
3.	Bihar	376.51	44.30	8.50	8.7	333.1	2955.3
4.	Gujarat	39.80	13.17	3.02	2.2	318.9	254.5
5.	Haryana	11.94	8.27	1.44	1.3	362.8	81.7
6.	Himachal Pradesh	4.84	7.94	0.61	1.0	367.5	26.9
7.	Jammu & Kashmir	2.97	3.97	0.75	0.6	327.6	17.6
8.	Karnataka	59.91	17.38	3.45	2.7	309.6	345.8
9.	Kerala	20.97	9.38	2.24	1.5	374.8	150.8
10.	Madhya Pradesh	217.32	37.06	5.86	7.7	311.3	1686.9
11.	Maharashtra	125.12	23.72	5.27	4.4	318.6	887.4
12.	Orissa	143.69	48.01	2.99	11.7	323.9	1361.1
13.	Punjab	10.20	6.35	1.61	0.8	362.7	55.9
14.	Rajasthan	55.06	13.74	4.01	2.1	344.0	347.4
15.	Tamil Nadu	80.51	20.55	3.92	3.8	307.6	549.6
16.	Uttar Pradesh	412.01	31.22	13.20	5.8	336.9	3094.3
17.	West Bengal	180.11	31.85	5.65	6.5	350.2	1544.5
	Sum of 17 States			70.1			14516.7
	All India	1932.43	27.09	71.3	5.2	327.6	14580.4
As percent of GDP at current market prices				Sum of 17 States			0.752
Memo : GDPmp 1999-00		1929641		All India			0.756

Source (Basic Data) : As in Table 5.1.

nutrition-related poverty line. Gaps in respect of other dimensions of poverty particularly, health and education will remain. Fifthly, the existing levels of poverty are dependent to an extent on the present policies however untargeted these may be. If these are restructured, or reorganised, then the impact on the existing poverty levels would need to be identified.

The empirically relevant question is that if such programmes could be designed as could deliver income support to the targeted poor, in a manner which minimise the adverse incentives, it will take a very limited amount of resources to overcome poverty and minimize its negative externalities. The features of the poverty profile that have been highlighted in this paper, *viz.*, its high spatial concentration, and the rising share of urban poor provide critical information in designing the targeting strategy.

Further, allocation of additional resources can be justified on the ground of the negative externalities. As poverty is reduced and kept at a minimum level, considerable savings will be generated through the elimination of these negative externalities, reducing health expenditures as well as resources allocated for countering incidence of illegal activities. On the positive side, growth rate will be stepped in areas of high poverty incidence, as investment and economic activities grow.

Much of the required resources can actually come form reorganising several present welfare oriented policies that derive their justification in the context of supporting the poor, but are either not targeted properly or are wasted in subsidizing inefficiencies. The vast subsidy regimes that are run by central and state governments, for example, constitute untargeted policy intervention, which is known to subsidize largely inefficiencies.

Table 3.9 shows the distribution of per capita grants across states relating to central sector and centrally sponsored schemes for the generally category states and Assam. It will be noted that the per capita grants to states with a high concentration of poverty like Uttar Pradesh and Bihar and

TABLE 3.9

Per Capita Grants for Central and Centrally Sponsored Schemes

States	*Average : 1991-92 to 1992-93*	*Average : 1993-94 to 1995-96*	*Average : 1996-97 to 1998-99*	*Average : 1999-00 to 2000-01*
Andhra Pradesh	68.21	84.58	87.70	105.98
Assam	59.57	92.74	67.87	91.24
Bihar (Old)	54.10	65.72	15.65	57.05
Goa	98.08	129.15	118.22	151.83
Gujarat	35.81	71.75	50.73	57.41
Haryana	61.50	78.87	95.15	91.87
Karnataka	63.39	89.98	83.08	136.17
Kerala	56.20	84.14	73.90	72.73
Madhya Pradesh (old)	71.87	100.05	110.02	87.97
Maharashtra	61.88	67.94	56.37	63.28
Orissa	93.10	95.46	82.62	88.31
Punjab	52.74	67.22	63.05	87.24
Rajasthan	91.77	123.98	117.88	124.96
Tamil Nadu	61.28	68.74	69.23	94.63
Uttar Pradesh (old)	72.64	65.82	44.11	45.90
West Bengal	29.62	29.84	48.96	54.54

Source (Basic Data) : Reserve Bank of India Bulletin on State Finances.

Orissa are lower in relative terms. States with a lesser incidence of poverty have been able to get higher per capita grants that are aimed to combat poverty. It can also be seen that per capita grants on central and centrally sponsored schemes can be used to effectively combat poverty. For example, Rajasthan has been able to keep its poverty head count ratio level low because it has obtained more than twice, in per capita terms, the grants on these schemes, for example, obtained by Uttar Pradesh.

SUMMARY AND CONCLUDING OBSERVATIONS

In the Indian context, a variety of central sector and centrally sponsored schemes have a direct or indirect bearing on poverty alleviation. However, their design is generally common across states, and they are too numerous to be effectively implemented at the field level. A special Subcommittee of the NDC headed by Shri K.C. Pant had indicated that there were as many as 360 Centrally Sponsored Schemes in operation at the inception of the Tenth Plan. An effective option would be to collapse these schemes into just a few, and focus these on high poverty concentration areas. Targeting poverty alleviating policies by areas and groups with suitably designed programmes can deliver far more effective results. Many analysts have argued in favour of targeted programmes in the context of their studies in other contexts also. For example, Grosh (1995) observes that targeted programmes have much greater incidence than general price subsidies. On the other hand, untargeted programmes waste considerable resources as the benefits are appropriated by the non-poor population. Such leakages have been estimated in a number of studies as ranging from 40 to 80 per cent (See, Giovanni and Stewart, 1995). On the other hand, the administrative costs of targeting have been estimated in the range of 6 to 9 per cent of the cost of programmes (See Grosh, 1995). The critical trends in poverty profile of the country indicate spatial concentration. This trend suggests that better results can be obtained by focusing poverty reduction policies on specific regions rather than having generalised subsides or poverty-alleviating schemes having a common design for all states as in the case of many centrally sponsored schemes. It has been indicated that total resources required for near elimination of poverty in the country are not large and could well be justified as a draft on budgetary resources due to their high negative externalities.

REFERENCES

Bourguignon, F. (1991), Optimal Poverty Reduction, Adjustment, and Growth, *World Bank Economic Review*, May 5(2), pp. 315-38.

Callan, Tim and Brian Nolan (1991), Concepts of Poverty and Poverty Line, *Journal of Economic Surveys*, 5 (3), pp. 243-61.

Chelliah, Raja J. and R. Sudarshan (1999), Income Poverty and Beyond Human Development in India, Social Science Press, New Delhi.

Collier and Dollar (2001), Can the World Cut Poverty in Half ? How Policy Reform and Effective Aid Can Meet International Development Goals, World Development, Vol. 29, No. 11, November.

Cornes, Richard (1995), "Measuring the Distributional Impact of Public Goods", in Dominique van de Walle and Kimberly Nead (eds.), Public Spending and the Poor, Johns Hopkins University Press, pp. 69-90, The World Bank.

Cornia, Giovanni Andrea and Frances Stewart (1995), "Two Errors of Targeting", in Dominique van de Walle and Kimberly Nead (eds.), Public Spending and the Poor, Johns Hopkins University Press, pp. 350-386, The World Bank.

Cutler, David M. and F. Lawrence Katz (1992), "Rising Inequality? Changes in the Distribution of Income and Consumption in 1980's", *American Economic Review,* Papers and Proceedings, 82 (2), pp. 546-51, May.

Dandekar, V. M. and N. Rath (1971), "Poverty in India", *Indian School of Political Economy,* Lonavala.

Datt, G. and M. Ravallion (1996), "Why Have Some States of India Performed Better than Others in Reducing Absolute Poverty?", Policy Research Working Paper 1594, World Bank, Washington, D. C.

Datt, Gaurav and Martin Ravallion (1992), "Growth and Redistributive Components of Changes in Poverty Measures : A Decomposition with Applications to Brazil and India in the 1980s", *Journal of Development Economics* 38 : 275-295.

Deaton, Angus and Jean Dreze (2002), "Poverty and Inequality in India : A Re-Examination", *Economic and Political Weekly*, September 7, pp. 3729-3748.

Dreze, Jean and Amartya Sen (1989), Hunger and Public Action, Oxford University Press, Oxford, England.

Foster, James (1984), "On Economic Poverty : A Survey of Aggregate Measures", in R.L. Basmann and G. F. Rhodes (eds), *Advances in Econometrics*, 3, JAI Press, Connecticut.

Grosh, Margaret E. (1992), "The Jamaican Food Stamps Program : A Case Study in Targeting", Food Policy, Vol. 17(1), pp. 23-40.

Grosh, Margaret E. (1994), Administering Targeted Social Programs in Latin America : From Platitudes to Practice, World Bank regional and Sectoral Studies, Washington, D.C. : World Bank, pp. ix, 174.

Hazell, P. and C. Ramaswamy (1991), The Green Revolution Reconsidered, Johns Hopkins University Press, Baltimore.

Ravallion, Martin and Gaurav Datt (1996b), " How Important to India's Poor is the Sectoral Composition of Economic Growth ?", *World Bank Economic Review* 10 (1) : 1-25.

CHAPTER

4

Poverty Alleviation for Development

AJIT KUMAR SINHA

The process of sustainable development must bring the degree of abject poverty to a minimum level as far as possible. The relative poverty is a universal fact and has existed in every society at all times. The matter of serious contemporary concern is, a maintained level of abject poverty of the exposed poor masses, deprived of basic human needs under the Glass Curtain Economy. The process of sustainable development is badly obstructed by the Neo Vicious Circle of poverty which implies a circular constellation of forces tending to act and react upon one another in such a way as to keep a poor country in a state of poverty. It is a humiliating reality before the civil society and world's greatest challenge of the 21st century.

South Asia has been the centre of poverty. Out of 1.2 billion developing world's poor (20% of the total population living on less than $1 a day), 43.5 per cent live in South Asia (India, Pakistan, Bangladesh, Nepal, Bhutan, Maldives, SriLanka and Afganistan), 24.3 per cent in Sub-Saharan Africa, 23.2 per cent in East Asia and Pacific, 6.5 per cent in Latin America and Carribean, 2.0 per cent in Europe and Central Asia and 0.5 per cent in the Middle East and North Africa (Sinha:2002).

The poverty has resulted into low survival rate; low adult literacy rate; population without access to safe water, health services and sanitation and under weight children below the age of five amongst poor in the developing world.

Poverty has been historically identified as the main persistent malady of the Indian Economy. Calculations of poverty indices for the Indian economy including Head-Count Index (HCI), Poverty Gap Index (PGI) and

Squared Poverty Gap Index (SPGI) from August 1951 to December 1997 have clearly revealed that poverty had persisted in our system in a chequered way and the absolute number of poor has risen (Table 4.1).

State wise variation in poverty level is an added dimension of the problem. Undivided Bihar had the highest poverty level from all the three poverty estimates i.e. HCI, PGI and SPGI. The classified estimations for rural and urban poverty indicate that rural poverty was the highest in Bihar, but this place was occupied by Madhya Pradesh in case of urban poverty (Table 4.2). Since 74.29% & 86.86% poor live in rural areas in India and Bihar respectively, the rural setting has a predominant impact on the poverty situation.

Reduction in poverty and unemployment and improvement in the quality of life have been the basic goals of our plans which have remained unchanged since the beginning of the plan era. The earlier Indian plan models had visualised that the 'Trickle Down effect' would result in higher income opportunities for the poor sector and significant dent on the incidence of poverty. But the average annual growth rate was around 3.5 per cent against the desired growth rate of 5.0 per cent during the first three decades of planning and the growth rate of population could not be brought down which jointly resulted extremely low per capita income growth and exposed the trickle down hypothesis.

A distinct change in the strategy of poverty alleviation was visualised since later part of 1970s. Instead of relying on growth to percolate, efforts were initiated to directly attack the problem of poverty by endowing the poor with productive assets/skill to employ themselves to earn larger income. Policy initiatives were also taken to create additional opportunities for wage employment essentially as a supplement to fill the gaps of unemployment in lean seasons. A number of poverty alleviation measures were introduced in the Sixth Five Year Plan and the subsequent plans followed suit. The Tenth Five Year Plan has also introduced a number of poverty alleviation measures.

The poverty alleviation programmes have not made any significant dent on the problem of poverty. Poverty of poverty alleviation programmes jointly with anti development institutional frame work have successfully kept the poverty intact. The abject poverty is prevalent over the system in tune with the global counterparts with the following characteristics :

1. Lack of income and assets to attain basic necessities-food, shelter, clothing and acceptable level of health and education.
2. Sense of voicelessness and powerlessness in the institutions of state and society.
3. Vulnerability to adverse shocks, linked to an inability to cope with them (World Bank; 2000/2001).

TABLE 4.1
Extent of Poverty in different NSS Rounds in India

NSS round	Survey Period	HCI			PGI			SPGI		
		Rural	Urban	Total	Rural	Urban	Total	Rural	Urban	Total
(1)	(2)	(3)	(4)	(5)	(6)	(7)	(8)	(9)	(10)	(11)
3	Aug. 1951 – Nov. 1952	47.37	35.46	45.31	16.05	11.14	15.20	7.53	4.82	7.08
4	Apr. 1952 – Sep. 1952	43.87	36.71	42.63	14.64	10.91	13.99	6.71	4.41	6.31
5	Dec. 1952 – Mar. 1953	48.21	40.14	46.8	16.29	13.25	15.76	7.56	5.96	7.28
6	May. 1953 – Sep. 1953	54.13	42.77	52.15	19.03	13.83	18.12	9.12	6.29	8.12
7	Oct. 1953 – Mar. 1954	61.29	49.92	59.3	21.95	17.24	23.12	10.26	7.74	9.83
8	Jul. 1954 – Mar. 1955	64.24	46.19	61.07	25.04	15.76	23.41	12.50	7.02	11.10
9	May. 1955 – Nov. 1955	51.83	43.92	50.44	18.44	14.65	17.78	8.80	6.40	8.38
10	Dec. 1955 – May. 1956	48.34	43.15	47.43	15.65	13.34	16.24	6.71	5.41	6.48
11	Aug. 1956 – Feb. 1957	58.86	51.45	57.55	19.45	18.16	19.22	8.50	8.51	8.50
12	Mar. 1957 – Aug. 1957	61.11	48.88	59.77	21.69	16.31	20.73	10.01	7.25	9.52
13	Sep. 1957 – May. 1958	55.16	47.75	53.84	19.01	15.95	18.47	8.78	7.00	8.46
14	Jul. 1958 – Jan. 1959	53.26	44.76	51.75	17.74	13.75	17.03	7.88	6.87	7.52
15	Jul. 1959 – Jan. 1960	50.89	49.17	50.58	15.29	15.83	15.39	6.13	6.75	6.24
16	Jul. 1960 – Aug. 1961	45.40	44.65	45.27	13.6	13.84	16.64	6.33	5.83	6.50
17	Sep. 1961 – Jul. 1962	47.20	43.55	46.54	13.6	13.79	16.64	6.31	6.05	6.46
18	Feb. 1963 – Jan. 1964	48.53	44.83	47.85	13.88	13.29	16.77	6.49	5.17	6.13
19	Jul. 1964 – Jun. 1965	53.66	48.78	52.75	16.08	15.24	15.93	6.60	6.38	6.56
20	Jul. 1965 – Jun. 1966	57.60	52.9	56.71	17.97	16.82	17.75	7.60	6.98	7.49

(Contd.)

TABLE 4.1 (Contd.)

(1)	(2)	(3)	(4)	(5)	(6)	(7)	(8)	(9)	(10)	(11)
21	Jul. 1966 – Jun. 1967	64.30	52.24	62	22.01	16.81	21.02	10.01	7.19	9.47
22	Jul. 1967 – Jun. 1968	63.67	52.91	61.6	21.8	16.93	20.86	9.85	7.22	9.35
23	Jul. 1968 – Jun. 1969	59.00	49.29	57.11	18.96	15.54	18.29	8.17	6.54	7.85
24	Jul. 1969 – Jun. 1970	57.61	47.16	55.56	18.24	14.32	17.47	7.73	5.86	7.36
25	Jul. 1970 – Jun. 1971	54.84	44.98	52.88	16.55	13.35	15.91	6.8	5.35	6.51
27	Oct. 1972 – Sep. 1973	55.36	45.67	53.37	17.35	- 13.46	16.55	7.33	5.26	6.90
28	Oct. 1973 – Jun. 1974	55.72	47.96	54.1	17.18	13.6	16.43	7.13	5.22	6.73
32	Jul. 1977 – Jun. 1978	50.60	40.5	48.36	15.03	11.69	14.28	6.06	4.53	5.72
38	Jan. 1983 – Dec. 1983	45.31	35.65	43	12.65	9.52	11.9	4.84	3.56	4.53
42	Jul. 1986 – Jun. 1987	38.81	34.29	37.69	10.01	9.1	9.79	3.7	3.40	3.63
43	Jul. 1987 – Jun. 1988	39.23	36.2	38.47	9.28	9.12	7.24	2.98	3.06	3.00
44	Jul. 1988 – Jun. 1989	39.06	36.6	38.44	9.5	9.54	9.51	3.29	3.29	3.20
45	Jul. 1989 – Jun. 1990	34.30	33.4	34.07	7.8	8.51	7.98	2.56	3.04	2.69
46	Jul. 1990 – Jun. 1991	36.43	32.76	35.49	8.64	8.51	8.61	2.93	3.12	2.98
47	Jul. 1991 – Dec. 1991	37.42	33.23	36.34	8.29	8.24	8.28	2.68	2.90	2.74
48	Jan. 1991 – Dec. 1992	43.47	33.73	40.93	10.88	8.82	10.35	3.81	3.19	3.65
50	Jul. 1993 – Jun. 1994	36.66	30.51	35.04	8.39	7.41	8.13	2.79	2.42	2.69
51	Jul. 1994 – Jun. 1995	39.75	33.5	38.4	8.89	8.38	—	2.9	2.80	—
52	Jul. 1995 – Jun. 1996	37.46	28.04	35	8.31	6.78	—	2.64	2.22	—
53	Jan. 1997 – Dec. 1997	35.69	29.99	34.4	8.39	7.77	—	2.83	2.73	—

Note : (1) HCI = Head Count Index, PGI = Poverty Gap Index, SPGI = Squared Poverty Gap Index
(2) Poverty Line = Rs.49 Per Capita per month for rural areas and Rs. 57 per capita per month for urban areas at 1973-74 prices.

Source : World Bank, India – Reducing Poverty, Accelerating Development, Oxford University Press, New Delhi, 2000.

TABLE 4.2
Extent of Poverty in Different States in India

State	*Total*			*Rural*			*Urban*		
	HCI	*PGI*	*SPGI*	*HCI*	*PGI*	*SPGI*	*HCI*	*PGI*	*SPGI*
Punjab	11.46	1.84	0.46	11.69	1.90	0.48	10.90	1.69	0.40
Andhra Pradesh	21.87	4.54	1.48	15.89	2.88	0.86	38.82	9.27	3.20
Gujarat	24.15	4.77	1.42	22.16	4.07	1.16	28.28	6.22	1.96
Kerala	25.12	5.59	1.86	25.38	5.61	1.84	24.31	5.53	1.88
Haryana	25.22	4.94	1.51	28.26	5.60	1.74	16.47	3.05	0.85
Rajasthan	27.46	5.62	1.72	26.40	5.21	1.55	34.02	7.00	2.24
Himachal Pradesh	28.58	5.19	1.50	30.36	5.55	1.61	9.26	1.25	0.26
Karnataka	32.91	7.73	2.69	30.11	6.27	2.01	39.90	11.36	4.36
Tamil Nadu	35.40	8.33	3.00	32.95	7.30	2.49	39.92	10.23	3.92
Maharashtra	36.82	9.61	3.65	37.91	9.28	3.34	34.99	10.15	4.16
West Bengal	36.94	7.42	2.21	41.18	8.29	2.45	22.95	4.55	1.41
Assam	41.09	7.46	2.00	44.19	8.21	2.20	7.93	0.92	0.22
Uttar Pradesh	41.55	10.23	3.50	42.32	10.37	3.53	35.10	9.03	3.26
Madhya Pradesh	42.40	10.40	3.68	40.75	9.48	3.26	48.08	13.48	4.08
Orissa	48.64	11.89	4.10	49.81	11.96	4.07	40.64	11.41	4.29
Bihar	55.15	13.83	4.77	57.95	14.66	5.06	34.84	7.86	2.63
All India	36.13	8.42	2.86	37.07	8.43	2.80	33.06	8.38	3.07

Note : (1) HCI = Head Count Index, PGI = Poverty Gap Index, SPGI = Squared Poverty Gap Index
Source : World Bank, Reducing Poverty in India, Report No 1788-in, June 29, 1988.

CHALLENGES AHEAD

Development is growth plus change. Change indicates the structural transformation of the system. Developing nations cannot be satisfied on the achievement of positive growth. But structural transformation cannot be possible with abject poverty of common masses. Alleviation of abject poverty is the primary condition for development of the countries like India.

Democracy is the best alternative from development point of view also. This was the reason of economic transformation of the socialist economies to market exonomics. They have transformed their system due to internal scrutiny and without any external pressure. Even the economic development of Punjab and human development index of Kerala is better placed and without any coercion in comparison to China in respective areas. But for overall development of the system it is essentially needed to salvage the system from the traps of Crime Syndicates functioning in perfect nexus with bureaucracy, Police, Politicians and Mafias who siphon off any type of resources with chikenery methods (Sinha: 2000).

For alleviation of poverty, as a precondition of development, the recommendation of the Independent South Asian Commission on Poverty Alleviation should be implemented in the form of 'Sociogram'.

Participatory Monitoring of the Process of Social Mobilisation for Poverty Alleviation Sociogram

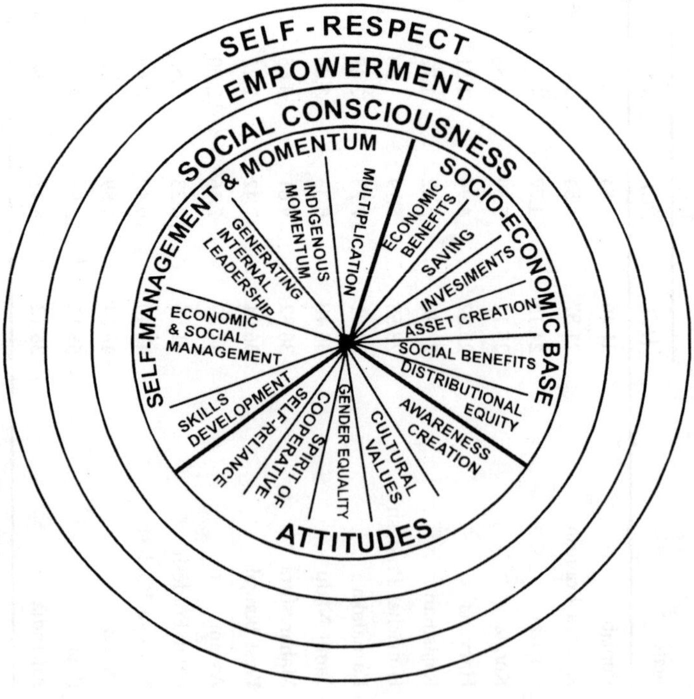

The criteria in the sociogram are all interrelated and mutually reinforcing. However, they deserve to be presented separately not only for their own sake but more importantly, because they contribute to each other's growth and thereby to the total process. If one element in the process is not moving forward it can easily be identified and strengthened. The three major planks that deepen social consciousness and lead to the empowerment of the poor are attitudinal change, the capacity for self-management and the economic and social base of the poor. It is axiomatic that the economic base of the poor has to be improved over a period of time through a dual process of savings, investment and asset creation and the emancipation of the poor from economic and social bondage, to enable them not only to be more productive and keep the surplus in their own hands. The establishment of a self-reliant activity base will mutually reinforce the process of promoting positive attitudinal values. Conscious attempts to diagnose, assess and mutually stimulate such values will bring them to the fore and will contribute to turning them into a driving force for further action, contributing to a deepening expansion of the process itself. Ultimately the process as whole, which starts with the release of the creativity of the poor, has to be judged by the increase in their social consciousness, empowerment and self-respect. It would have the way to be break the Neo-Vicious Circle of Poverty (Vicious Circle of Poverty under institutional framework) and initiate the virtuous circle of development.

References

World Bank (2000), India Reducing Poverty, Accelerating Development. Oxford University Press, New Delhi.

Sinha, Ajit Kumar (2000), Organised Crime And Development, Forum of Free Enterprise, Bombay.

Sinha, Ajit Kumar (2002), Dynamics of Poverty Alleviation Programmes, Deep & Deep Publications, New Delhi, World Bank (2000).

World Bank (1998), Reducing Poverty in India, Report No. 1788.

CHAPTER 5

Poverty Alleviation and Environment

ADWAIT MOHANTY

INTRODUCTION

Environmentalists are unequivocal about poverty and growing deforestation in the low-income economies in the tropics. In their view, the poor are both agents and victims of deforestation. Clearing of forests for agricultural purposes (Yu Xiaogang, 2001) increases output, but not without adverse side effects. Other factors like logging and extensive ranching also cause widespread deforestation, but a growing body of literature adduces nearly 300 million or so small farmers as the prime agents of forest clearing. They practise shifting cultivation in nearly half the land area of the world's tropical and mountain ecosystems (Dove, 1983, Southgate, 1990; 1994; Myers, 1992; 1994; Pearce and Warford, 1993). Tropical forests in Asia are rich in valuable trees, which provide incentive for extensive logging. Logging, however, is not responsible for clearing of forest stretching over a vast landmass. It is a selective work and felling of such trees may not lead to deforestation over an area.

There is no dearth of literature examining the correlation between poverty and deforestation. These studies have underlined inappropriate settlement, migration and pattern of infrastructural development (Jones and O' Neill, 1992, Myers, 1994, Chomitz and Gray, 1996, Southgate, 1990), land tenure regimes (Allen, 1985; Larson and Bromley, 1990), pricing of forest products (Repetto and Gillis 1988, Larson and Bromley, 1990; von Amsberg, 1994), government subsidy and tax policies (Binswanger, 1991; Deacon, 1995), population pressure (Cleaver and Schreiber, 1994), and food prices (Barrett 1999) to be the reasons behind. Correlation between commodity pricing and deforestation which has also remained an area of interest in environmental studies (Cleaver, 1985; Southgate 1990,1994; Larson and Bromley, 1990,1991; Ehui and Hertel, 1989; Elnagheeb and Bromley, 1994; Pearce and Warford 1993). Authors like Perrings (1989) have examined the relationship between poverty, risk and deforestation. But research works tracing the causal relation between poverty and deforestation and assessing the efficacy of different poverty alleviation measures as a solution are few and far between.

A close examination of the relationship between deforestation, poverty and poverty alleviating programmes is of great interest to the environmentalists. Areas under tropical rain forest stand out as major victims of deforestation, thus demanding urgent policy prioritisation. Large scale clearing of these forest areas has been caused by the slash-and-burn agricultural practices, which have the unique feature that land acquisition needs no payment for land itself. The person making the land cultivable or utilisable otherwise does not pay, but pays only the labour time necessary to clear the forest. Faced with adverse shocks the poor are forced to clear forest for land acquisition, but desist from it when their income position improves in favourable environment.

Economic policies have both direct and indirect bearings on the availability as well as utilisation of natural resources (Bromley, 1986). An attempt has been made here to throw light on the linkage between deforestation, poverty and policy variables like poverty alleviating programmes with a view to assessing the efficacy of selected policy measures in arresting deforestation. Choice of appropriate policy measures may reduce poverty as well as forest clearing.

The present study is based on data relating to the extent of deforestation and rural families below the poverty line across the thirty districts of Orissa, a less developed state in the Indian Union. Forest cleared for developmental activities like irrigation works, mineral activities and other such purposes are kept out of purview. The area deforested refers to the forest area in which there is no forest now. The rural poverty ratio measures the extent of poverty in a district. The number of beneficiaries indicates the beneficial impact of a poverty-alleviating programme in a district. The latest year for which data are available is 1997.

ORISSA : A BRIEF OVERVIEW

The state of Orissa is rich in natural and forest resources. The total forest area stretching around 58,000 sq kms comprises nearly 37% of the state's total geographical area. A total of 26, 000sq kms categorised as reserve forests are managed by the State Forest Department under various working plans and schemes, while 32,000 sq kms are under the administrative control of the Revenue Department. Around 12,000 sq kms of forest are under private ownership. Besides, the state has a vast area of mangrove forest stretching across its coastline. As revealed by the satellite survey conducted by the remote sensing authorities, the forest area in the state is shrinking day by day mainly due to over exploitation of the forest land for timber, fuel wood and above all, land acquisition.

Forest land is mostly acquired by the tribals on an extensive scale through the practice of shifting cultivation or 'podu' cultivation as it is locally called. This type of slash and burn agriculture has been a cause of great concern for the state government on account of the consequential deforestation and soil erosion. The State Government has banned this practice and this is strongly opposed by the tribal populace. The tribals, in turn, take recourse to forest clearing not only for timber, but also to acquire land for the cultivation of mustard, turmeric and pulses like arhar.

The Economic Surveys of the state have recorded an increase in the net area sown over the years. Interestingly, records reveal an increase in the area under forests as well. This increase is, of late, mainly due to social forestry programmes undertaken by various government and private undertakings. But social forests created by the plantation of particular types of trees on barren and unproductive land are not a perfect substitute for the typical biodiversity of the natural forests, so opine the environmentalists. Increasing depletion of natural forest base in the state, therefore, remains a cause of concern. Factors like population growth, change in non-wood fuel prices, and forest and land-tenurial policy may cause deforestation. Over and above all these, low and insufficient income of the people has a more direct impact on deforestation, as the poor, in the absence of alternatives, tend to go for easy acquisition of land by clearing forest to earn livelihood.

FINDINGS

The poor in the tropics depend on forest resources to earn livelihood. But, income from this source is uncertain and insufficient to meet their subsistence needs. In such a situation, to supplement their income, the poor go for forest clearing not only to obtain wood but also to acquire land for cultivation. Thus forest clearing may provide the poor with an income support to make up the shortfall in livelihood.

To examine the hypothesis, this study has examined the correlation between the proportion of rural families below the poverty line (% BPL) and the area of the cleared forest as a ratio of the total forest area (CF/TF) in the districts. Two regression models, a linear and a double log, were fitted. Statistically significant negative coefficients with acceptable R^2 reflect a negative correlation between the two variables. High value of the coefficient in the double-log model reveals that a very low level of poverty causes large forest deforestation. Speaking otherwise, areas where poverty is high, deforestation is low or the proportion of land under forest is high. Poverty induces forest clearing. The study has also traced a positive coefficient of net area sown as the dependent variable with CF/TF as the independent variable in linear and double log regressions. It seems, the poor have cleared forest to get productively utilisable land or sold timber to earn some income and so as to cross the poverty line. Allen and Barnes (1985), Johnson (1991) and the World Bank (1991) have underlined a significant role of agricultural settlement and timber use as causes of deforestation. A negative correlation between BPL and CF/TF could also be observed in linear and non-linear regression models computed by taking data for the year 1993. This finding extends support to the earlier observations of the researchers.

TABLE 5.1
Regression Results Dependent Variable CF/TF
Independent variable % BPL

Linear	*D - Log*
–0.98	–3.38
(–2.09)*	(–2.86)*
R^2 = 0.14	R^2 = 0.23

Figures in parenthesis are T values.
* Stand for statistical significance up to 10%.

In the next step, the forest conserving impact of various poverty-alleviating programmes have been examined. The impact of the poverty alleviating programmes can be assessed from two angles: provision of subsidies and generation of income. Programmes like Antyodaya Anna Yojana (AAY), and Public Distribution System (PDS) provide foodgrains at a subsidised rate to the families below the poverty line, Integrated Rural Development Programme (IRDP) aims at supplying income earning asset and loan finance to the rural poor at a low rate of interest. Programmes like Jawahar Rojgar Yojana (JRY) are implemented to extend wage employment to the members of the BPL families by engaging them in the creation of social assets and rural infrastructure. Impact of the number of families benefited by AAY, PDS and IRDP and the amount of expenditure incurred under JRY on the proportion of cleared forests have been examined with linear as well non-linear regression models and the estimates are given in Table 5.2.

It could be read off the table that the subsidy programmes have a negative impact on forest clearing. But the coefficients are statistically insignificant in both the models. They reveal that the impact of these measures are not adequate to lift the rural poor above the poverty line so as to dissuade them from clearing forest. On the other hand, expenditure incurred under JRY has a significant impact. It seems, wage income earned under this programme can provide the poor a livelihood and the labour endowment engaged under the programme could not be diverted towards forest clearing. It is possibly because the workers are kept engaged during the fixed hours in a day, for which they cannot find time to sneak out for other works. In such a situation, missing the work time would imply losing

TABLE 5.2
Regression Results Dependent Variable CF/TF

Indecent Variable	*Value of the Coefficient (Linear)*	*Value of the elasticity (Double-Log Model)*
AAY	-0.0004 (-0.77) R^2 = 0.021	-0.13 (-0.54) R^2 = 0.010
PDS	-0.00 (-0.46) R^2 = 0.008	-0.004 (-0.012) R^2 = 0.00
IRDP	-0.00 (-0.04) R^2 = 0.00	0.22 (0.64) R^2 = 0.01
JRY Expenditure	-1.13 (- 2.15)* R^2 = 0.14	-0.06 (- 2.47)* R^2 = 0.05

Figures in parenthesis are t-values, * indicate statistical significance up to 10%.

wage income for a whole day. But under other schemes, the worker has flexibility in allocating times between work and deforesting, for which the impact of these programmes on is less deforestation significant. However, engagement under any of these programmes leaves less time with the workers to go for deforesting. However, it could well be suggested that wage employment programmes like JRY be revamped in the areas with larger number of families below the poverty line. Income generating effect of these programmes can dissuade the poor from forest clearing.

In which direction should JRY be revamped? Should the programme go for a wage hike so that the poor could be given more income support in exchange for less man-days of employment ? Or, should the wage rate be fixed at a moderate level providing employment for a larger number of days with a more assured income, ? It was observed that wage hike had man-days of employment reduced the number of under JRY, the value of the coefficients under linear and non-linear regressions estimated to be -.59 (-2.36) and -1.16 (-2.20) respectively, with R^2 of 0.17 and 0.15.

Impact of the market wage rate for rural labourers and the number of days of employment generated under JRY on the proportion of forest clearing were also assessed. Wages have a positively significant effect on forest clearing while the impact of the number of man-days of employment was the reverse (Table 5.3).

It seems, with higher wage rate the poor could earn relatively larger income by working less number of days and divert the unutilised labour endowment towards forest clearing to gain access to timber, fuel wood and also productive land. On the other extreme, increased man-days of

TABLE 5.3
Dependent Variable CF/TF

Independent variables	*Linear coefficient*	*Elasticity (D log model)*
Wage rate	2.88 (1.79)* R^2 = 0.10	3.69 (2.62)* R^2 = 0.20
Man-days of employment under JRY	- 2.82 (-3.37)* R^2 = 0.17	-1.03 (-1.98)* R^2 = 0.12

Figures in parenthesis are t values, * indicate statistical significance up to 10%.

employment held out for the workers gave a more assured source of income for a longer time and leaving less time for forest clearing.

JOINT FOREST MANAGEMENT : A POSSIBLE ALTERNATIVE

In an attempt to preserve forest resources, the State Government imposed moratorium on tree felling in the districts of Kalahandi, Bolangir and Phulbani during 1988. From 1991, the jurisdiction of the statute was extended to encompass the districts of Ganjam and Koraput and 1993, onwards the entire state was brought in to the fold of the law. This apart, necessary steps were taken to preserve mature trees in the forest, and protect and ensure growth of forest resources.

Recognising the dependence of the poor on forest resources and to provide them with sustained benefit from the forests, the State has initiated participatory management or Joint Forest Management (J.F.M.). In which both the State and local community participate in the management of forest resources. This gives the local community a right to protect its own interest and access to these resources to earn an income. It is advantageous for the localities to raise, preserve and manage local forest. They know about the usefulness of the forest resources and the loss of income resulting from denudation of forests. Therefore, it is felt that the local people are the best decision-makers as regards the use and preservation of the forest are concerned when their stakes are very high. Keeping this in view, the State Government have adopted a scheme of Joint Forest Management, which underlines a judicious sharing of the forest resources between the local people and the forest authority. The State owns one of the major forest products, timber and chalks out the rules and regulations for its preservation and utilisation. The community, on the other hand, owns other Non-Timber Forest Products (N.T.F.P.) and is permitted to harvest and utilise these for an earning.

Apart from other resolutions, the most recent one in 1996 gives the village community an active role in the protection and management of forests. Formation of Vana Sanrakhyan Samitties (V.S.S.) is a firm step in this direction. Nearly 6686 such Samities have been constituted to preserve and take care of nearly 6,346 sq kms of forestland. Simultaneously, 4,928 Village Protection Committees have been formed to protect 10,07,705 hectares of forestland. The State has implemented afforestation programmes in barren and uncultivable areas under the social forestry projects. Under the scheme, 9,141 Village Forest Committees have been constituted with the responsibility of protecting 1,18,122 hectares of village woodland. These Committees not only make people aware of the ecological benefits of forest, but also motivate them to go for equal sharing of forest product between the Government and the masses.

Such a judicious programme like J.F.M. has not made much headway in protecting the interest of the local people. Studies (Contreras et. al., 2000) reveal that in India, China and Philippines, the provisions under the stipulated laws of J.F.M. when practised largely cater to the needs of the forest department at the cost of the livelihood concern of the local inhabitants. The ultimate result is a conflict between the forest department and the local people. The former does not agree to part with the timber use, and try to circumvent the instructions imposed on the harvesting of the products in which they supposedly have a share. Recently the State Government of Andhra Pradesh have allowed the villagers a share in the sale proceeds of timber to avoid contradictory forms of production and land use. In North-Eastern States of India, particularly in Meghalaya, it has been observed that a Supreme Court ban on logging in the community owned forest land has an adverse effect on forest conservation. Instead of growing trees, the locals have cleared them for conversion into agricultural land. The law has no control over such an act (Nathan and Kelkar, 2001). When the land-use pattern is to be decided by the local community, deforestation is likely to increase. In the absence of access to timber and wood, harvesting of trees will give the locals low and insufficient return and as such, they will divert their efforts from forest preservation to forest clearing so that they can gain access to cultivable land. Therefore, the land-use pattern decided by the State and contested by the locals are neither favourable for the livelihood of the latter, nor for forest conservation. As the local people, depending on forest resources for their subsistence are the poorest, sustainable improvement in their livelihood should be at the core of any forest development and management programme. Payment to the locals for the area reforested and conserved is a practice in China. Upland forest reserves in Guangxi are able to collect handsome amount from nearby countries as 'water source regulation fees' (Harkness, 1998). The Rio Earth Conference also advocated this practice (see Wilson Costa and Stuart, 1999 for such alternative schemes). However, schemes prescribing payments for non-quantifiable environmental services like carbon sequestration are few and far between. A less developed state like Orissa lags far behind in this regard.

In Orissa, the cultivable land raised through forest clearing are fertile with bio-fertilizer from the forest wastes and very productive in the cultivation of turmeric, arhar etc. This has not only induced the poor to clear forest, but also the small and marginal farmers to convert the forestland adjacent to their farms into agricultural land. Apart from ecological imbalance, this practice has adversely affected the production of various natural food products like natural honey, wild tubers etc. High nutritional value of these products fetched a handsome income for the poor who also took these as staple food. Production of a number of green and leafy vegetables, and mushrooms has also fallen alarmingly, thus causing serious income loss as well as malnutrition. Reduced availability of these natural foodstuff rich in protein, carbohydrates and minerals can be made good by converting more vegetative land into farm land and forest clearing is the easiest possible alternative.

The forest management programme introduced in the 1980s, first earmarked the forest areas, in which, the local people were forbidden from using forest. In the subsequent years, the forest department realised that it was difficult to reverse continuing deforestation without the involvement of local ecological knowledge and services. A sound forest policy called for participation of local wisdom in forest management through Joint Forest Management (JFM). While utilising indigenous ecological knowledge, JFM should give due recognition to the rights of the locals over the forest. Payments for forest raising and other ecological services are necessary to motivate the local. The poor households, squeezed between the state policies and market forces may go against conservation of forest resources for their own short-term gains. They need a safety net, which could adequately compensate the gains from forest depletion. A welfare state alone can provide this.

CONCLUSION

Poverty forces the poor to go for forest clearing to obtain wood as well as productive land. Assessing the impact of different poverty alleviating measures on deforestation, it was observed that wage-income programmes like JRY were more effective in reducing deforestation than schemes providing food subsidy or loan subsidy. Moreover, moderate wage rate combined with longer days of employment is more effective in acting as disincentive for forest cleaning than high wage rates with less man-days of employment. Length of engagement, no matter if at lower wage rate, providing greater security of income infuses a sense of complacency for which a poor worker does not get inclined to clear forest which, no doubt, involves risk of being caught and penalised. A programme of Joint Forest Management giving due weightage to the subsistence needs of the local people, and payment for forest harvesting and conservation would be appropriate policy measure.

I acknowledge the assistance rendered by Jyotimayee Kar in preparing this paper

References

Allen, J. and Barnes, D. (1985), "The Causes of Deforestation in Developing Countries", Annals of the Association of American Geographers, 75,2.

Allen, J.C. (1985), "Wood Energy Preservation of Woodlands in Semi-Arid Developing Counties: the Case of Dodoma Region, Tanzania," Journal of Development Economics 19: 59-84.

Barret, C.B. (1999), "Stochastic Food Prices and Slash - and Burn Agriculture", Environment and Development Economics, 4, 2, 161-176.

Barrett, C.B and P.A. Dorosh (1996), "Farmers Welfare and Changing Food Prices: Nonparametric Evidence from Rice in Madagascar," American Journal of Agricultural Economics 78: 656-669.

Bromley, D.W. (1986), "Natural Resources and Agricultural Development in the Tropics: is Conflict Inevitable ?, in A. Maunder and U. Renborg, eds., Agriculture in a Turbulent World Economy, Oxford: Gower.

Chomitz, K.M and D.A. Gray (1996) "Roads, Land use and Deforestation: a Spatial Model Applied to Brazil", World Bank Economic Review 10: 487-512.

Cleaver, K.M. (1985), " The Impact of Price and Exchange Rate Policies on Agriculture in Sub-Saharan Africa," World Bank Staff Working Paper No. 728.

Cleaver, K.M. and G.A Schreiber (1994), Reversing the Spiral: The Population, Agriculture, and Environment Nexus in Sub-Saharan Africa, Washington: World Bank.

Derrings, C. (1989) "An Optimal Path to Extinction? Poverty and Resource Degradation in the Open Agrarian Economy', Journal of Development Economics 30: 1-24.

Dove, M.R. (1983), "Theories of Swidden Agriculture, and the Political Economy of Ignorance", Agro Forestry Systems 1: 85-99.

Earson, B.A. and D.W. Bromley (1991), " Natural Resource Prices Export Policies, and Deforestation: The Case of Sudan', World Development 19: 1289-1297.

Ehui, S.K. and T.W. Hertel (1989), "Deforestation and Agricultural Productivity in the Cote D'lvoire, American Journal of Agricultural Economics 71: 703-711.

Elnagheeb, A.H. and D.W. Bromley (1994), "Extension of Agriculture and Deforestation: Empirical Evidence from Sudan," Agricultural Economics 10: 193-200.

Harkness, James (1998) "Recent Trend in Forestry and Conservation of Bio-diversity in China" in China Quarterly, No 156 December, London, SOAS

Johnson, B. (1991), "Responding to Tropical Deforestation, "An Eruption of Crisis and Array of Solutions, Conservation Foundation, London: World Wildlife Fund, Washington, D.C.

Jones. D and R.V. O'Neill (1992)," Endogenous Environmental Degradation and Land Conservation: Agricultural Land use in a Large Region," Ecological Economics 6: 79-101.

Larson, B.A and D.W. Bromley (1991), "Natural Resource Prices, Export Policies and Deforestation: The case of Sudan", World Development, 19, 1289- 1297.

Meyer, J. (1987), Two-moment Decision Models and Expected Utility Maximization,' American Economic Review 77: 421-430.

Myers, N. (1992), "The Primary Source: Tropical Forest and Our Future, New York: W.W. Norton.

Myers, N. (1994), " Tropical Deforestation: Rates and Patterns', in K. Brown and D.W. Pearce, eds., The Causes of Tropical Deforestation, Vancouver: UBC Press.

Nathan, Dev and Govind Kelkar, (2001), Case for Local Forest Management: Environmental Services, Internalisation of Costs and Markets" VolXXXVI< No 30 Economic and Political weekly, July 28 pp. 2835-2845.

Pearce, D.W. and J.J. Warford (1993), "World without End: Economics, Environment, and Sustainable Development, Oxford: Oxford University Press.

Perrings, C (1989), "An Optimal Path to Extinction ? Poverty and Resource Degradation in the open Agrarian Economy, Journal of Development Economics, 30, 1-24.

Repetto, R. and M. Gillis (1988), Public Policies and the Misuse of Forest Resources, Cambridge: Cambridge University Press.

Southgate, D. (1990), "The Causes of Land Degradation along "Spontaneously" Expanding Agricultural Trontiers in the Third World,' Land Economics 66: 93-101.

Southgate, D. (1994), "Tropical Deforestation and Agricultural Development in Latin America,' in K. Brown and D.W. Pearce, eds. The Causes of Tropical Deforestation, Vancouver: UBC Press.

Von Amsberg, J. (1994),"Economic Parameters of Deforestation, "World Bank Policy Research Working Papers No. 1350, Washington: World Bank Policy Research Department.

Wilson, Charlie; Pedro Moura Costa and Marc Stuart, (1999) "Transfer Payments for Environmental Services in Local Communities :A Local-Regional Approach" Rome IFAD FAO and IUCN.

World Bank (1991), "The Forest Sector: A World Bank Policy Paper" Washington, D.C.

Yu Xiaogang (2001),"Conflict in Resource Management for Ecosystem Services: Water in Lashi Watershade, Lijiang" Economic and Political Weekly Vol XXXVI, No 30 July 28 pp. 2851-2858.

CHAPTER

6

Education and Values : Guide Posts for Educational Reforms

P.C. MAHAPATRA

EDUCATION IS ESSENTIAL FOR ALL

Education has a fundamental role to play in personal and social development. It is one of the principal means available to foster deeper and more harmonious form of human development and thereby to reduce poverty, exclusion, ignorance and oppression. In our national perception education is essential for all. This is fundamental to our all round development, material and spiritual. Education has an acculturating role. It refines sensitivities and perceptions that contribute to national cohesion, a scientific temper and independence of mind and spirit—thus furthering the goals of socialism, secularism and democracy enshrined in our Constitution. In sum, it is a unique investment in the present and for the future.

As per international commission on education, (UNESCO 1996) Education in the coming century will be based on four pillars—learning to know, learning to do, learning to live together and learning to be. They should aim at developing the child's personality. Education like music has two distinguishable notes, which keep on sounding. The first note of rhythm reflects how the power potential in a person grows, powers of the body and mind, of intellect and imagination, of creativity and intuition. The second note in the rhythm of education is somewhat sterner; it requires discipline and control of the self within. It leads to self discipline; self searching and self integrity which underlie man's rational thinking, his judgments and understanding of life.

FRAME WORK OF EDUCATION

The very first thing about the coordinate frame is that modern world is one world. It is a global village. The destiny of mankind hangs together. The great lesson of science today is that mankind is one. In a scientific and technical sense, Mankind—in fact the entire flora and fauna is ecologically one system. We can not within a country and between countries have development of only one part and let the other parts lag behind.

There is the explosion of population. There is the explosion of violence in diverse form—greed, hatred and delusion form a rapidly rising spiral-GHD spiral. To check this, education must inculcate self-control and self-discipline and should not be divorced from values, from character building. "I regarded character building as the proper foundation of their education and if the foundation is firmly laid, I was sure that children could learn all other things themselves or with the assistance of friends". (Gandhiji, My Experiences with Truth). It is basically character building an endeavor to promote morality in our actions individually, collectively and globally. Character translates ideals into deeds.

In Einstein's inspiring words (November 1960) "The most important human endeavour is the striving of morality in our action. Our inner balance even our very existence depend on it. Only morality in our actions can give beauty and dignity of life. To make this a living force and bring it to clear consciousness is perhaps the foremost task of education."

"We are passing through a period of unprecedented crisis in human history, transition from one level of civilizations to an altogether new one. The industrial age led to the atomic age. Now it appears we are moving to a New Age. It may be best characterized as the age of science and Ahimsa. It is also called the solar age as in future the main source of energy will be solar energy which is plentiful every where. . . . The so called crisis and chaos in education it is almost a universal phenomena is in a sense a part of the transitional process. What may be termed the ground law of education in the modern world is that education every where is in a state of Chaos and Crisis" (Dr. D.S. Kothari—Education and Values).

Therefore in a world changing at a fantastic, terrific pace, it is important that there should be continuous and serious thinking by professionally committed people on educational problems and developments, with special emphasis on value education.

In a knowledge based society linkages between education and productivity should be given due weightage. Education is dead education" unless it has a research component and it has little utility, unless it is to some degree related to productivity. There is a real and urgent need of research as regards what is to be taught, how it is taught and how children learn and whole psychology of child development. Due emphasis shall be laid on excellence in education. Divorced from excellence, education develops negative attitudes and has a negative influence on students and teachers. Excellence in an individual implies a corresponding obligation to serve the community, Therefore our youth may be influenced to thinking before taking any action whether it satisfies by the simple 4 ways test "Is it the truth? Is it fair to all concerned? Will it build good will and better friendships? Will it be beneficial to all concerned?

Ethos forms the very essence of a nation. It is to a nation what roots are to the tree. It provides the guiding principles of community life, shapes cultural experiences, creates values, frames community's attitude and sustains society's spirit. It is natural therefore that all the spheres of our national life are influenced by national ethos.

Some of the salient features of the Indian national ethos may be mentioned—as integral approach to life, blending of materialism and spirituality, recognition of divinity in every form of life, attitude of respect and reverence to elders and love of nature, freedom of belief and worship, respect to women. It shall be the goal of the education system and the role of the agencies of education to enable children to imbibe values which are of great significance from the national as well as from the global point of view.

IMPORTANCE OF VALUE EDUCATION

We want a world class education "high peaks of excellence" to compete internationally. The gifted and talented youth is the nation's most precious asset. A world class education can only be driven by values-personal values, community values, aesthetic value and universal values. The deculturisation, dehumanization and alienation must be avoided at all costs. Due emphasis shall be laid on cultivation of a strong and sterling character among the students and the emerging youth. Utmost care shall be taken to have suitable convergence between "Truth preached and practised".

In the words of Prof. V.K. Gokak "the theory of education as it is generally practised today is summed up in five simple words. They are Knowledge, skill, peace, understanding and gentleness or courtesy. These five values of education are connected with faculties of man and his soul. The faculties are his intellect, will and heart. Love is the binding chord. Therefore education means the cultivation of both secular as well as spiritual values with the ultimate aim of becoming a cultured citizen and illumined volunteer in the service of humanity and an active pilgrim in the path of reality. Gentleness is the hallmark of an educated individual.

The growing concern over the erosion of essential values and an increasing cynicism in society have brought to focus the need for the readjustments in the curriculums in order to make education a forceful tool for the cultivation of social and moral values. In our culturally plural society, education should foster universal and eternal values, oriented towards the unity and integration of our people. Such value education should help to eliminate obscurantism, religious fanaticism, violence, superstition and fatalism. Apart from this combative role, value education has a profound positive content, based on our heritage, national and universal goals and perceptions. It should lay primary emphasis on this aspect (National Policy on Education-1986 and modified 1992). However learned and accomplished a person may be, his education is not complete till he has learnt to be balanced and gentle.

The national system of education will be based on a national curricular frame work which contains a common core along with other components that are flexible. The common core will include the history of India's freedom movement, the constitutional obligations and other content essential to nurture national identity. These elements will cut across subject areas and will be designed to promote values (National Curriculum Framework). Education may be viewed as wholeness and wholeness combining truth, beauty and goodness in one majestic symphony.

Thus education is a passport to life, and it is universal, secular and specific.

The relationship between education and development is not unidirectional. Education contributes to development and development of the economy contributes to further development in education. This bi-directional relationship is very important to understand the role of education. Development based on knowledge society will call for education with quality based in values. In the knowledge society's of the present century, education will be increasingly valued as an end in itself and not as a means to an end.

AGENCIES FOR VALUE DEVELOPMENT

The active agencies for inculcation of values among the children are Home/family, school, community and the passive agencies are media and religious institutions. The active agencies act as formal institution and training centres for this purpose.

(i) Home/Family

Home/Family is said to be the first living human institution and learning centre of a child. It is the first unit of an organic society and the in-built moral and social training centre in which values are learnt. Without family a child cannot get the initial education and moral values. Love is the binding chord and harmony is the major key. A child grows in the lap of mother and care of father and relatives. The relationship is more emotional than functional. It should provide the individual the much needed psychological and emotional security which is at present declining.

Family thus provides the link between emotion and intellect and passes value and standards to the children. Every family has a hidden curriculum and code of conducts based on culture, tradition and values. It has been rightly said that charity begins at home. For inculcation of values among their children, the parents and the elders at home shall be the role model because the child learns first from his parents and kith and kin and imitates them. He learns to speak and asserts himself by crying and fighting with others and at the same time learns to share with others and care for others. Love is the binding force. Fellow feelings, obedience, discipline, respect to elders and love for younger, appreciation of dignity of labour, love for nature, affection, kindness, consideration, understanding, good conduct and cordial dealing with others, cleanliness, division of labour and participatory management, the major values are practically taught and experimented here through love/ affection, care and control. The joyful atmosphere and conducive home environment are important software of a good family for greater influence over children.

The parents should be encouraged to spare sometime every day for their children and should behave properly in front of them. They should also open their eyes and ears about the movement and behaviour of their children outside home and should take immediate preventive measures to check any unethical behaviour. Prevention is better than cure.

The foundation of the character building is laid at home and early childhood is the formation period because " while the branch is green and tender, it can easily be made straight". On the other front the values and norms learnt as part of socialization should get a culture expression during the year of schooling.

It is seen that what is taught in school may indeed conflict with the traditional family values. Disadvantaged families often see the schools as an alien world, whose code and practices they do not understand. A real dialogue between parents and teachers is thus essential for harmonious development of children. Education given by school is to be backed up by the education given at home. In that connection Pre-school education should be given greater emphasis. This can bring School system and Home closer to each other. Being joint partners, appropriate strategies can be thought of for social, mental, physical, moral and emotional development of the child. The major package of value development in the child at this stage will be moral and social training. Suitable convergence between home and school should be established.

(ii) Schools

It has been rightly said that "Knowledge received in the childhood is like an engraving made on stone" (John Locke). When the child joins the school, a larger world unfolds before him. He comes in contact with his peer groups, teachers and others at school. Values that he had learnt at home, helps him to adopt with this new environment. At school he is recognised as an individual. The school as an active agency of education plays an important role for his allround development and innate potentialities.

Harmonisation of the traditional and modern is the need of the hour to achieve the desired goal of individual as well as national development. Our educational endeavour must aim at the harmonious blend of the physical, the intellectual and the spiritual for sustainable development, the need for which is intensely felt to-day.

The main purpose of the school as an active agency of education is to fulfil the basic needs of the child-knowledge, skills, values and attitudes for their survival, to live and work in dignity to improve the quality of life and above all to live in peace. An educational institution is considered as a storehouse of culture, transmission centre for knowledge and information promotion centre of research and innovation and a catalytic agent for extension of knowledge and information to the society.

The present century is marked with the growth of two spirals. They are GHD spiral in one hand (Greed, Hatred and Delusion) and the other is the STP(Science, Technology and Productivity). Therefore educational institution has to play an important role for imparting education for values, conducting research in education for development and suitable reunion between education, research and productivity-ERP.

The school in our society, remains a much neglected institution. The school may be performing below our expectation, much what is taught in the school may not be relevant to the needs and aspirations of the learners. But it remains a fact, that it is the foundation of education system in the country. It is a fundamental educational establishment where practical educational activities are carried out systematically. Each school must have a culture of its own. It is only in the school that the building blocks of vibrant value system/values have to be laid to prepare a gentleman- a cultured man. Therefore value education shall become an integral part of school curriculum for creating a human society and balanced individual. Efforts should be made to integrate various components of value education in the curriculum at all stages of school education with ample scope of participation of staff and students. Individual attention should be given for the cultivation of national, social and moral values.

The heart of any educational system is the relationship between teacher and taught. The quality of curriculum, text books, teaching learning process, curricular and co-curricular activities, suitable monitoring and evaluation of scholastic and non-scholastic activities form important components for nurturing values for children, generating understanding and respect to all people as well as to all religions and for creation of a tolerant and cohesive society.

For making education value based, textbooks should be reviewed/ screened carefully and rewritten in such a manner that the values are represented in an explicit manner and not remain as hidden agenda. Supplementary reading materials may also be used for development of the human and universal values and appreciation of cultural heritage in the form of stories, parables, fables and biographies drawn from varieties of cultural and religious traditions.

Co-curricular activities are very potent medium to communicate values and to get practical exposure. Emphasis shall be laid on different youth development activities, programmes- NCC, NSS, Scouts and Guides, community activities, Social service, Rovers, Redcross, group activities, integrated activities, exchange programme, camping activities, games, sports, cultural activities, speaker's meeting, observation and celebration of different religious festivals and events of national importance. Guidance and counselling programme in inculcation of value education could play an important role in schools.

Above all is the central role and role model of teacher. His role is that of a mentor, spiritual guide and the sculpture of new generations. The personality of the teacher, his activities, behaviour and attitudes, his competence, professionalisation and value premises, his vision and perspective and his inclass and outclass behaviour have direct bearings not only on the student but on his fellow members and the community as a whole to develop a value based society drawn from national goals, universal perception, ethical consideration and character building. Even a small number of committed teachers can exercise a great influence. It can be crucially important.

The other aspect of the educational system that has significant influence of formation of values among the children is the total structure of educational system itself—the rules, the procedure and functioning of the institution and various educational authorities. In that circumstances the decisions and the behaviour of all individuals connected with the school system directly or indirectly must be in conformity with the democratic, secular, national and universalistic values which are held up as the cherished goal and guiding principle of the society and the nation. The school has to be reinvented-the abode of learning-vidyalaya has to be strengthened so as to engender an environment of learning that can promote value based world class education. Re-engineering school has become the urgent necessity. It has to be done now to save the country from deterioration.

(iii) Community

Man is a social animal. He lives and moves in the society. Society is within him and around him. He also learns from the social milieu and social environment formed by the community. Knowledge of the child widens in the society and community culture feeds some data during the formation years. He marks and observes what respectable persons in the society do or behave. He inherits values through observation, contact, communication and participation. He keeps on acquiring knowledge and values from elders directly or indirectly, consciously or unconsciously. The mutual relationship and behaviour of the people in the society contribute in developing his personality. The process of education is basically a process of communication and relationship. Community leaders play a significant role while communicating social goal and social content to the children. Here education proceeds from the will to live together and to base the groups cohesion on a number of shared undertakings such as membership of voluntary organisations/youth groups of religious denomination or a political party, which all contribute to form different values in the grown up children. Thus the social environment of the community and the process of socialization to which a person belongs is a powerful educational influence. This socialization helps to develop a democratic, secular and socialistic society.

The most important factor influencing the inculcation of values among the children is the extent of concordance between values preached through education and values practised in a larger society. If education communicates altruistic values and life in society is characterised by self oriented values or if education verbalizes rationalist norms whereas life in society is characterised by a wide prevalence of superstitious credulous actions and corrupt practices, the social content of education will tend to give rise to hypocracy and criticism. The youth will come to believe that what they are taught is not expected to be practiced.

Erosion of value in the community and specially among the community leaders, is felt all over the country. How will they become role models for children if they are drowned with all the vices and corruption, exhibiting self perceived superiority and play the role of exploiters. Intellectual arrogance of the educated people and their alienation from the community is also accelerating degradation of values in the society. A value less society will lead to Jungle rule. Therefore it is high time that social environment should be charged with values. The community as a whole should take the responsibility of value education of its members for gaining active experiences in formation of right kind of values. Therefore the community leaders, opinion makers, religious leaders and the political leaders should become the role models and join hands together to prepare a code of ethics and conduct for inculcation of social, national and universal values among the community members specially among the emerging youth. If elected representatives and the community leaders are motivated, people will automatically be motivated. Thus the community as a whole should take up the responsibility of the value education of its members either by means of constant dialogue or by forming pressure groups or taking the charge in a formal/informal settings.

In the ultimate analysis, the basis of everything in education is self-discipline and self-control. Self discipline is not imposed discipline. It comes through the examples of persons of conviction and character. Such examples are highly infectious and will have a multiplying effect. The parents, teachers, administrators, community leaders, civil society members, politicians, religious leaders, people's representatives and religious preachers have crucial role to play in this regard.

(iv) Media

The media have a profound influence on the minds of the children as well as adults. Media specifically the television is frequently criticised by educationists and social reformers for imposing a kind of lowest cultural common denominator, cutting down the time devoted to reading and thought, forcing scene of violence on people and more generally playing on emotions.

But the media are an integral part of our cultural environment in the broadest sense of the term. Their aims are not necessarily educational but their very real power of attraction has to be taken into account. The radio and TV programmes which clearly militate against the proper educational objectives and the values will be prevented. Steps may be taken to discourage such trends in films and other media. An active people's movement may be started to promote the production of value based children's film of high quality in large number in different languages. Special value education programmes in TV and radio may be broadcasted. Suitable linkages may be established between educationists and media as an effective means of providing education in general and value education in particular.

(v) Education about religion

Another significant factor that merits urgent attention now is religion. Although it is not the only source of essential values, it certainly is a major source of value education. Religion is the foundation for value base survival of human beings in a civilized society depends upon moral values. What is required to-day is not religious education but education about religions, their basics, the values inherent there in and also a comparative study of the philosophy of all religions. This needs to be inculcated at appropriate stages in education right from the primary years. The students have to be given awareness that the essence of every religion is common, only the practices differ. They also be led to believe that differences of opinion in certain areas are also to be respected. Education about different religions of the world will act as an instrument of social cohesion and religious harmony. The knowledge of various religious philosophies is material for bringing communal harmony as ignorance breeds hatred because of wrong notions, assumption, preaching and propaganda by misguided interested persons.

In a world where intra and inter religious conflicts have become the order of the day, there is a need for "spiritual convergence". For this purpose steps may be taken to promote dialogue among the different religious and spiritual leaders, for the introduction of specific teaching of inter-cultural, inter-religious, common spiritual and cultural heritage from early childhood (KG) to Post Graduate(PG). Children should be introduced to the discovery of "otherness" and to the values of tolerance, respect and confidence in others that will bring about a change of behaviour and attitudes towards others. Even if there are differences of opinion in certain areas, people have to learn to co-exist and carry no-hatred against any religion. As a matter of caution, all steps should be taken in advance to ensure that no personal prejudices or narrow minded perceptions are allowed to distort the real purpose of imparting education on religion. No righteous dogmas and superstitions should be promoted to propagate in the name of education about religion.

CONCLUDING OBSERVATIONS

Truth (Satya), Righteous conduct (Dharma), Peace (Santi), Love (Prem) and Non-violence (Ahimsa) are the core universal values which can be identified as the foundation stone on which the value based education programme can be built up. These five values represent the five domains of human personality, intellectual, physical, emotional, psychological and spiritual. They are also correspondingly co-related with five major objectives of education namely knowledge, skill, balance, vision and identity. It requires a sustained efforts by all the agencies of education and joint endeavour of all elders to inculcate basic human values among the children from the early child stage.

The past five decades after independence have witnessed constant erosion of the essential social, moral and spiritual values and an increase in cynicism at all levels. Various committees and commissions namely Radhakrishna commission (1948-49), Kothari commision (1965-66), National Policy on Education (1986-92), Ramamurti committee (1990), Central Advisory Board of Education(CABE) Committee on Policy (1992), Planning Commission core group on value orientation of education (1992) and SB Charan's committee report (1999) have highlighted the urgent need for making the educational system value based. Hence orientation programme and workshops in large numbers may be organized to motivate and energize parents, teachers, community leaders, opinion makers, media persons as change agents for human solidarity, holistic development and integral peace.

Child is the mirror in which the future of a nation is fully reflected. In order to preserve, maintain and advance the status of our country in the world, it is imperative that there should be a comprehensive programme of value education starting from pre-primary level, embracing the entire spectrum of educational process. The minds, hearts and hands of children are to be engaged in forming their own character to know what is 'good', 'love good' and 'do good'. We are guilty of many errors and many faults, but our greatest crime is abandoning our children, neglecting the fountain of life. Many things you and I need can wait. The child can not. To the child we can not say tomorrow, his name is to-day (Gabriel Mistral). We can not perhaps express our concern for value education more forcefully than in these words.

Value based education would help the nation to fight against all kinds of fanaticism, ill will, violence, fatalism, dishonesty, avarice, corruption, exploitation and drug abuse. Therefore the clarion call will be "Live together or disappear, Educate essential values or perish".

References

Fututan. A Mothers, Fathers and Children, Practical Advices to Parents, Bahai Publishing House, New Delhi.

Government of India, Department of Culture, Reforms for Resurgent Republic, Report of the National Seminar on Education Reforms.

Govt. of India, Ministry of Human Resource Development, Department of Education (1992), National Policy on Education-1986 with modifications.

NCERT, National Curriculum Framework for school education-1996, New Delhi.

NCERT, School Education in India, Present Status and Future Needs, New Delhi.

NCERT, Supreme Court of India Judgement (12th September2002) in the matter of National Curriculum Framework for the School Education, 2000, New Delhi.

UNESCO, Learning the Treasure within, Report to the International Commission on Education for Twenty First Century.

CHAPTER

7

Child Survival in Orissa

SRIJIT MISHRA

INTRODUCTION

I had the good fortune of being associated with Professor Baidyanath Misra (BM) who was chairman of Nabakrushna Choudhury Centre for Development Studies (NCDS) when I was with the institute. It was a blessing again to be a consultant to the Orissa Finance Commission under Professor BM's chairmanship. In his 80s, Professor BM is even today actively involved in research. I hope to take a leaf out of his principles and conviction that researchers should address issues of social concern and public policy.

The present note addresses an issue of social concern - child survival, one of the eight 'millennium development goals' (MDGs), identified by the global community [UNDP, 2003]. The focus on Orissa is somewhat deliberate because of Professor BM's association with the state, but more importantly because Orissa is an under-researched state and to address this aspect Professor BM was very much instrumental in establishing NCDS of which he was the founder-Director. It is noteworthy that an earlier paper on infant and child survival in Orissa using National Family Health Survey 1993 (NFHS-1) [PRC, Bhubaneswar and IIPS, 1995] has come out from research done in NCDS [Padhi, 2001].

My present concern is not as exhaustive as of Padhi (2001), but builds on it by making use of some recent estimates of infant and under-five mortality from Census 1991 [Rajan and Mohanachandran, 1998, 2000 and 2001], National Family Health Survey 1998-99 (NFHS-2) [IIPS and ORC

Macro, 2000 and 2001] and Sample Registration System (SRS) for the years 1995-1999 [CBHI, 2002].

SITUATING ORISSA

From 10 million child deaths in the world 22 per cent are in India [Black, Morris, and Bryce, 2003]. Within India, five of the 16 major states have infant mortality rates (IMR) and under-five mortality rates (U5M) above the national average (see Table 7.1). In recent years the most widely used estimates are from NFHS-2 and these show that the five worst states

TABLE 7.1
Infant and Under-five Mortality in 16 Major States of India from Various Estimates for 1990s

States	*Census 1991*				*NFHS-2 1998-99*				*SRS 1995-99*	
	IMR		*U5M*		*IMR*		*U5M*		*IMR*	
Andhra Pradesh (AP)	49	(2)	68	(3)	65.8	(10)	85.5	(10)	65.4	(9)
Assam (AS)	85	(13)	117	(13)	69.5	(11)	89.5	(11)	75.8	(12)
Bihar (BI)	70	(10)	89	(10)	72.9	(12)	105.1	(13)	69.6	(11)
Gujarat (GU)	69	(9)	85	(8)	62.6	(9)	85.1	(9)	62.4	(7)
Haryana (HA)	55	(5)	72	(5)	56.8	(7)	76.8	(8)	68.6	(10)
Himachal Pradesh (HP)	75	(11)	97	(11)	34.4	(2)	42.4	(2)	62.4	(8)
Karnataka (KA)	60	(7)	81	(7)	51.5	(6)	69.8	(6)	56.8	(6)
Kerala (KE)	37	(1)	46	(1)	16.3	(1)	18.8	(1)	14.2	(1)
Madhya Pradesh (MP)	107	(15)	159	(15)	86.1	(15)	137.6	(16)	95.8	(15)
Maharashtra (MA)	58	(6)	72	(6)	43.7	(3)	58.1	(3)	49.4	(2)
Orissa (OR)	108	(16)	160	(16)	81.0	(14)	104.4	(12)	98.0	(16)
Punjab (PU)	54	(4)	66	(2)	57.1	(8)	72.1	(7)	52.6	(3)
Rajasthan (RA)	81	(12)	109	(12)	80.4	(13)	114.9	(14)	84.0	(13)
Tamil Nadu (TN)	53	(3)	69	(4)	48.2	(4)	63.3	(4)	53.0	(4)
Uttar Pradesh (UP)	89	(14)	120	(14)	86.7	(16)	122.5	(15)	85.0	(14)
West Bengal (WB)	67	(8)	88	(9)	48.7	(5)	67.6	(5)	54.6	(5)
All India (AI)	74		96		67.6		94.9		71.8	

Notes : NFHS-2 (National Family Health Survey 1998-99) estimate is for five-year period preceding the survey and does not include the month in which survey took place. SRS (Sample Registration System) figure is simple annual average of estimates for the five years, 1995-99. SRS estimate for all India excludes Jammu and Kashmir during 1995-97 and 1999, Mizoram during 1997, and Nagaland rural during 1998-99 for inadequate data. IMR and U5M denote infant mortality rate and under-five mortality rate respectively. Figure in parentheses denote rank across 16 major states.

Source : CBHI, 2002; IIPS and ORC Macro, 2000; and Rajan and Mohanachandran, 1998.

are the four BIMARU (Bihar, Madhya Pradesh, Rajasthan and Uttar Pradesh) states and Orissa. Note that BIMARU literally means sick and Orissa has been excluded from it because this popular acronym seemed to match with poor performance in demographic indicators and Orissa's position is relatively much better in indicators like sex ratio and fertility decline. This is ironical because morbidity burden (incidence of sickness) seems to be relatively higher in Orissa [Mishra, 2003B; Padhi and Mishra, 2000].

Comparing NFHS-2 with the other two estimates may not be entirely appropriate, but one expects that it would be lower than Census 1991. This is by and large true for all the major states except for four—Andhra Pradesh, Bihar, Haryana and Punjab. In fact, Bihar moves from below national average to above whereas the reverse is true for Assam. However, decline is quite remarkable in Himachal Pradesh and it would be worthwhile to further probe (beyond the scope of the present study) whether this performance goes hand in hand with strides in literacy attainment in recent years [Drèze and Gandhi Kingdom, 2001; and PROBE, 1999]. As NFHS-2 estimates in Table 7.1 are based on five-year period preceding survey, the time period broadly coincides with that of SRS estimates. The latter, like NFHS-2, when compared with Census show that IMR has declined over time for Andhra Pradesh and Haryana, but for Assam it is greater than and for Bihar less than national average whereas Orissa has the worst rank among the 16 major states.

In the country as a whole the Scheduled Castes (SCs) and Scheduled Tribes (STs) generally have greater infant and under-five mortality, but for STs this seems to be a reversal over time from relatively better position because of lower rates of decline [Maharatna, 1998 and 2000]. A question that comes to mind is whether Orissa's high infant and under-five mortality is mostly among the large constituents of SCs (15 per cent) and STs (22 per cent). The relative position of SCs and STs in rural and urban areas in 16 major states for IMR and U5M are given in Tables 7.2 and 7.3 respectively.

As expected, SCs have greater IMR and U5M in all rural and urban regions. However for STs, particularly in rural regions, Assam seems to be doing much better and Madhya Pradesh and Orissa are also marginally better than the overall population. In fact, rural SC IMR in Orissa is also not much higher than IMR for overall rural population. Thus, low child survival in Orissa, as per the Census 1991 estimates of IMR/U5M, does not seem to be unevenly distributed across castes.

Caste wise IMR and U5M estimates for Orissa are also available from NFHS, but before discussing these we analyse socio-economic sub-group wise and districts wise Census 1991 estimates for Orissa.

SOCIO-ECONOMIC SUB-GROUPS WISE AND DISTRICT-WISE CENSUS 1991 ESTIMATES

A search beyond caste takes us to analyse other possible proximate determinants such as levels of mother's education, religion, and occupation.

TABLE 7.2

Infant Mortality Rate (IMR) Estimates for Rural/Urban Regions and for SC/ST in each Region Relative to that Regions overall IMR, 1991

States	*Rural All*		*Rural SC*		*Rural ST*		*Urban All*		*Urban SC*		*Urban ST*	
	IMR	*Rank*	*Relative IMR*	*Rank*	*Relative IMR*	*Rank*	*IMR*	*Rank*	*Relative IMR*	*Rank*	*Relative IMR*	*Rank*
AP	54	(2)	16	(3)	19	(3)	31	(2)	18	(2)	21	(1)
AS	87	(12)	7	(11)	-17	(2)	57	(13)	15	(13)	-1	(2)
BI	73	(9)	10	(9)	9	(7)	48	(8)	15	(10)	12	(5)
GU	79	(11)	15	(12)	1	(6)	49	(9)	8	(8)	15	(8)
HA	58	(3)	17	(4)			39	(4)	13	(3)		
HP	77	(10)	9	(10)	12	(9)	49	(10)	14	(11)	33	(12)
KA	65	(6)	13	(8)	17	(8)	45	(7)	14	(9)	33	(11)
KE	38	(1)	14	(1)	35	(4)	30	(1)	18	(1)	32	(7)
MP	114	(16)	8	(16)	-1	(14)	74	(15)	8	(15)	18	(13)
MA	66	(7)	9	(5)	24	(10)	39	(5)	14	(4)	18	(4)
OR	112	(15)	3	(15)	-2	(13)	76	(16)	18	(16)	23	(14)
PU	61	(5)	16	(7)			37	(3)	16	(5)		
RA	88	(13)	8	(13)	21	(12)	53	(12)	13	(12)	13	(9)
TN	58	(4)	11	(2)	4	(1)	42	(6)	14	(6)	28	(10)
UP	94	(14)	10	(14)	2	(11)	58	(14)	15	(14)	2	(6)
WB	72	(8)	3	(6)	6	(5)	50	(11)	6	(7)	6	(3)
AI	79		10		10		48		14		22	

Note : Two-alphabet notations for states are as in Table 1. Relative IMR for SC/ST refers to net increment in comparison to overall IMR. For instance, IMR for rural SC minus IMR for overall rural gives relative IMR for rural SC. Figures in parentheses denote ranks across 16 major states (14 major states for STs as Haryana and Punjab do not have STs) for that sub-group (All/SC/ST) for that region (rural/urban) for IMR (not relative IMR for SC/ST).

Source : Rajan and Mohanachandran (1998, 2001).

This is given separately for rural and urban and contrasted with the national average (Table 7.4).

It is observed that estimates for Orissa are greater than national average for each subgroup. In line with Caldwell (1979, 1986), increase in mother's educational level seems to be a robust indicator that improves child survival. With regard to religion rural Muslims do better in Orissa, as for the national average. This is perhaps, as Bhat (2002) reasons out on lower maternal mortality, because Muslims mostly reside in large villages with

TABLE 7.3
Under-five Mortality Rate (U5M) Estimates for Rural/Urban Regions and for SC/ST in each Region Relative to that Regions Overall U5M, 1991

States	*Rural All*		*Rural SC*		*Rural ST*		*Urban All*		*Urban SC*		*Urban ST*	
	U5M	*Rank*	*Relative U5M*	*Rank*	*Relative U5M*	*Rank*	*U5M*	*Rank*	*Relative U5M*	*Rank*	*Relative U5M*	*Rank*
AP	78	(4)	21	(3)	20	(3)	41	(2)	23	(2)	28	(1)
AS	115	(12)	15	(11)	-16	(4)	71	(13)	23	(13)	1	(3)
BI	94	(8)	20	(9)	15	(7)	54	(7)	22	(9)	22	(5)
GU	101	(11)	29	(12)	6	(6)	57	(8)	13	(6)	24	(8)
HA	81	(5)	18	(4)			45	(5)	20	(3)		
HP	99	(9)	15	(10)	23	(9)	61	(11)	18	(10)	51	(12)
KA	91	(7)	21	(8)	24	(8)	57	(9)	22	(11)	48	(11)
KE	48	(1)	18	(1)	46	(2)	39	(1)	18	(1)	39	(6)
MP	175	(16)	15	(16)	-3	(14)	97	(15)	19	(15)	32	(13)
MA	82	(6)	28	(7)	44	(10)	44	(4)	21	(4)	35	(7)
OR	168	(15)	11	(15)	0	(13)	101	(16)	27	(16)	41	(14)
PU	73	(2)	29	(5)			43	(3)	22	(5)		
RA	121	(13)	26	(13)	30	(12)	66	(12)	25	(12)	32	(10)
TN	77	(3)	13	(2)	0	(1)	52	(6)	20	(7)	39	(9)
UP	132	(14)	26	(14)	2	(11)	73	(14)	25	(14)	1	(4)
WB	100	(10)	5	(6)	0	(5)	60	(10)	15	(8)	9	(2)
AI	107		20		19		57		22		32	

Notes : Two-alphabet notations for states are as in Table 1. Relative U5M is like relative IMR in Table 2. Figures in parentheses denote ranks for U5M across major states, as in Table 2 for IMR.

Source : Rajan and Mohanachandran (1998, 2001).

greater access to care. However, in contrast to the national average, rural Christians have worse estimates than that for Hindus. This needs further probing that is not attempted in this paper.

Across occupational groups one observes that main workers have lower estimates than marginal workers in the national average, but this is not true for rural Orissa. The most visible distinction is perhaps between manual workers (high estimates) and non-manual workers (low estimates), but this again is not true for urban Orissa where the most vulnerable turn out to be marginal workers.

TABLE 7.4
Socio-economic Sub-group wise Infant and Under-five Mortality Estimates from Census 1991, Orissa and India

Socio-economic Sub-groups	*Orissa*				*India*			
	Rural		*Urban*		*Rural*		*Urban*	
	IMR	*U5M*	*IMR*	*U5M*	*IMR*	*U5M*	*IMR*	*U5M*
Mother's Educational Level								
Illiterate	114	171	88	124	84	117	55	72
Literate but below Middle	108	158	63	87	67	88	45	53
Middle but below Matric	98	142	68	90	56	68	37	42
Matric but below Graduate	73	95	44	50	47	54	33	38
Graduate and above	69	91	36	41	48	59	32	37
Religion								
Hindus	112	168	77	103	80	109	48	59
Muslims	93	130	70	91	78	107	47	60
Christians	127	201	70	96	66	82	40	47
Occupation								
Main Workers	114	170	90	127	80	103	60	76
Cultivators	106	162	71	93	80	109	67	86
Agricultural Labourers	118	174	99	145	81	115	67	96
Other Main Workers	112	167	70	92	80	107	58	70
Manual Workers	122	187	71	139	85	113	62	82
Non-manual Workers	77	87	77	104	60	79	44	51
Marginal Workers	111	148	110	164	88	124	65	88
Non-Workers	111	167	73	97	76	101	48	55

Note : IMR and U5M refer to infant and under-five mortality rates respectively.
Source : Rajan and Mohanachandran (2000).

District wise rural and urban estimates of infant and under-five mortality rates are given in Figure 7.1. As observed earlier, the rural regions have greater mortality rates in all districts. One also seems to have an explanation for absence of distinction between ST and overall rural Orissa estimates—Mayurbhanj (with nearly 60% tribal population) has the lowest estimate and Balesore (with less than 30% as SCs and STs) has the highest estimate. Besides Balesore, the coastal districts of Cuttack, Ganjam and Puri that are economically relatively prosperous and with relatively lower

Fig. 7.1

IMR and U5M in Rural and Urban Regions of Orissa, 1991

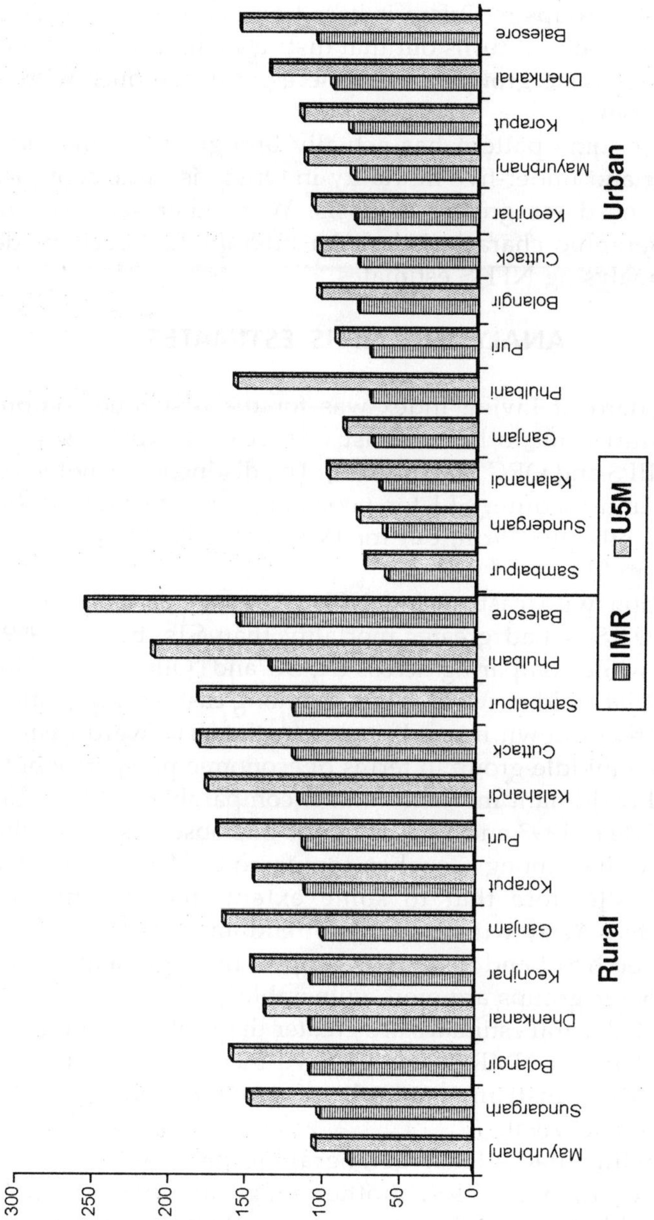

Note : IMR and U5M denote infant and under-five mortality rates respectively. The districts in rural and urban regions are arranged in ascending order based on IMR estimates.

Source : Rajan and Mohanachandran (1998).

proportions of SCs and STs do not seem to have better child survival. Similarly, the predominantly tribal districts of Keonjhar, Koraput, Phulbani and Sundargrh that also have relatively greater proportion of poor are also spread across the spectrum. Our understanding of poverty across districts and across caste groups in Orissa is based on Panda's (2003). Thus, as per Census 1991 estimates, it turns out that districts with greater proportions of poor and poorer caste groups are not necessarily the ones with relatively lower child survival.

Search for some pattern has actually brought forth the fact that the issue of infant and under-five mortality in Orissa is quite complicated and brings in the need for greater analysis. With other socio-economic and medico-demographic characteristics. An attempt has been made in this direction by analysing NFHS estimates.

ANALYSING NFHS ESTIMATES

The Standard of Living Index was for the first time computed with NFHS-2 and turns out to be a robust indicator to explain some outcome differentials [IIPS and ORC Macro, 2000]. The distinction is not very obvious between low and medium SLI for neonatal mortality rate (NMR)—death within one month after birth, but for IMR and U5M the estimates decline with increase in SLI.

Explanation with caste using NFHS-1, as in the case of Census, is elusive. In 1993 SCs had greater mortality than STs, but in 1999 STs fare worse. Thus, while comparing across ST, SC and 'Other' castes in NFHS-2 one observes that child survival is lower among castes with greater poverty. However, it breaks down if one brings in 'other backward caste' (BC), i.e. considered as a middle group in terms of economic prosperity but has very high neonatal and infant mortality that is comparable to STs. Again, if one can consider NFHS 1993 and 1999 as trends one observes relatively low rate of mortality decline among STs when compared to SCs [also see Maharatna, 1998, and 2000]. Note that to some extent in redefinition of caste composition does away with caste wise trend analysis for BC and 'Other'. Nevertheless, both SLI and caste 1999 support the argument of Victora et al (2003) that poorer groups are more vulnerable.

As expected, rural estimates are greater than urban and there is decline over time, but urban NMR seems to have increased over time. One also observes a strong instrumental role of mother's educational level in improving child survival.

In line with international demographic patterns child survival for males is lower than females, mother's age at birth has a U-shaped relationship with the middle age group of 20-29 faring the best (least mortality) and both these are declining over time. One cannot compare birth order over time, but 1993 seems to have a U-shaped relationship with birth order of 2-3 faring best, in 1999 the relationship is not clear. However, it is

TABLE 7.5
Neonatal, Infant and Under-five Mortality Rates by Various Socio-economic and Medico-demographic Characteristics from NFHS Orissa, 1993 and 1999

Background Characteristics		*NMR*		*IMR*		*U5M*	
		1993	*1999*	*1993*	*1999*	*1993*	*1999*
Standard of Living Index	Low	—	59.0	—	101.1	—	137.9
	Medium	—	59.5	—	83.5	—	96.7
	High	—	18.9	—	32.8	—	34.1
Caste	Scheduled Caste	76.3	48.9	160.8	83.9	175.8	122.7
	Scheduled Tribe	53.2	56.1	113.4	98.7	148.8	138.4
	Other Backward	—	71.0	—	95.6	—	113.8
	Others	65.7	43.1	115.3	79.1	128.1	92.9
Residence	Rural	68.4	55.7	125.7	90.9	143.3	117.7
	Urban	40.2	55.6	84.9	77.9	101	99.7
Mother's Education	Illiterate	68.7	62.4	132.2	104.1	153.6	137.3
	Literate, < Middle	60.0	55.4	103.9	78.6	112.4	95.0
	Middle, < High#$	44.9	34.4	71.5	49.2	87.0	58.8
	High and above$	38.7	10.2	59.0	21.7	63.1	21.7
Sex of Child	Male	70.4	64.6	126.9	94.5	141.0	121.3
	Female	57.6	46.4	111.6	84.3	132.5	109.9
Mother's Age at Birth	< 20	76.5	80.1	144.3	119.6	163.1	148.7
	20-29	58.5	46.3	111.8	78.7	126.7	104.0
	30-39	71.1	52.1	114.3	82.5	137.7	107.8
Birth Order	1	87.3	62.3	141.3	93.1	151.7	108.8
	2 (2-3 in 1993)	48.4	46.9	101.1	83.8	117.4	111.5
	3	—	65.1	—	94.2	—	126.6
	4+ (4-6 in 1993)	62.5	50.2	122.4	87.9	143.9	119.8
	7+ (in 1993)#	82.5	—	144.0	—	178.8	—
Previous Birth Interval	< 24 months	90.8	88.3	181.6	130.0	210.7	172.2
	24-47 months	38.4	41.2	83.5	74.7	101.0	105.4
	48+ months	44.9	31.0	73.7	57.5	82.3	65.0
Birth Size*	Large#$	66.9	27.8	79.4	50.8	89.2	—
	Average	31.4	37.2	68.3	68.5	86.4	—
	Small$	99.6	64.5	160.8	99.4	169.0	—
Antenatal or Delivery Care*	Neither of these	69.4	—	125.8	—	159.8	—
	Either one	50.5	—	76.5	—	148.8	—
	Both of these#	35.6	—	56.7	—	128.1	—
Total		64.2	55.7	119.5	89.5	136.9	115.7

Note : NMR, IMR and U5M indicate neonatal, infant and under-five mortality rates respectively. The mortality estimates are based on 10-year period preceding the survey, but when indicated by * they are based on five-year period preceding the survey. # and $ indicate that estimates for 1993 and 1999 respectively are based on 250-499 unweighted children surviving to the beginning of the age interval. Estimates for 'standard of living index', has been done for the first time in 1999; for 'caste' and 'birth order' are based on different composition in 1993 and 1999; for 'antenatal or delivery care' it has not been computed in 1999; and for 'birth size' it is not available for U5M in 1999. Also note that birth size is as reported by mother and not by actual measure.

Source : IIPS and ORC Macro (2001); PRC, Bhubaneswar and IIPS (1995).

important to note that child survival increases with longer birth interval, greater birth size and antenatal or delivery care.

Another dimension of child fatality is that younger the child the more vulnerable she/he is. As per NFHS-2 estimates of Orissa nearly 77 per cent of U5M (death before five years) is IMR (death before one year), 62 per cent of IMR is NMR (death before one month) and 68 per cent of NMR is perinatal mortality (death before one week, 0-6 days) [IIPS and ORC Macro, 2001]. Such a relationship is nothing specific to Orissa, but this along with other information should set the stage for public policy intervention.

CONCLUDING REMARKS

Comparing across states one observes that Orissa ranks poorly in the child survival indicators. At the same time fertility, and hence, live birth rates are relatively lower and coupled with relatively lower population—this means that absolute number of child deaths in Orissa is much lower compared to the BIMARU states [Mishra, 1993A]. This, however, does not mean that the problem is less serious. Given Orissa's topography and problem of difficulty in access to care [Padhi, 2001; Padhi and Mishra, 2000] a successful and cost-effective intervention would be the home-based neonatal care [Bang et al., 1999; Bang, Reddy and Deshmukh, 2002; Bhutta, Darmstadt, and Ransom, 2003].

Public policy should work towards putting knowledge into action [The Bellagio Study Group on Child Survival, 2003] to provide known effective interventions [Jones et al., 2003] and help differentiate biological and behavioural intervention from the systemic interventions [Bryce et al. 2003]. Again, successful intervention requires it to be holistic that goes beyond disease-, programme- and sector-specific approaches [Claeson, Bos and Padmanathan, 2000] and also integrates access to knowledge with physical and financial access [Mishra, 2003A]. Equally important is the need to put in place a system that collects timely and reliable data, uses it to analyse local variations, and acts on it [Lee, 2003].

(The author thanks Surendra Nath Misra for giving him this opportunity. Discussions with Shovan Ray were helpful in explicitly mentioning the intriguing aspect of Census 1991 estimates. Sarika Rathi (Kansal) provided research assistance. Nandini's constant reminder saw it through).

REFERENCES

Bang AT, Bang RA, Baitule SB, Reddy MH, Deshmukh MD (1999), Effect of Home-based Neonatal Care and Management of Sepsis on Neonatal Mortality: Field Trial in Rural India, *Lancet*, 354 (9194): 1955-61.

Bang AT, Reddy MH, Deshmukh MD (2002), Child Mortality in Maharashtra, *Economic and Political Weekly*, 37 (49): 4947-65.

Bellagio Study Group on Child Survival, The (2003) Knowledge into Action for Child Survival *Lancet*, 362 (9380): 323-27.

Bhat, PNM (2002), Maternal Mortality in India: An Update, *Studies in Family Planning*, 33 (3): 227–236.

Bhutta ZA, Darmstadt GL, Ransom EI (2003), *Using Evidence to Save Newborn Lives*. Washington DC: Save the Children, Population Reference Bureau.

Black RE, Morris SS, Bryce J (2003), Where and Why are 10 Million Children Dying Every Year? *Lancet*, 361 (9376): 2226-34.

Bryce J, Arifeen S el, Pariyo G, Lanata CF, Gwatkin D, Habicht J-P, and the Multi-Country Evaluation of IMCI Study Group (2003), Reducing Child Mortality: Can Public Health Deliver? *Lancet*, 362 (9378): 159-64.

Caldwell, JC (1979), Education as a Factor in Mortality Decline: An Examination of Nigerian Data, *Population Studies*, 33 (3): 395-413.

Caldwell, JC (1986), Roots to Low Mortality in Poor Countries, *Population and Development Review*, 12 (2): 171-220.

CBHI (Central Bureau of Health Intelligence) (2002), *Health Information of India 1999*, New Delhi: Government of India.

Claeson M, Bos ER, Pathmanathan I (2000), Reducing Child Mortality in India in the New Millennium, *Bulletin of the World Health Organization*, 78 (10): 1192-99.

Drèze, J and Gandhi Kingdom, G (2001) School Participation in Rural India, *Review of Development Economics*, 5 (1): 1-24.

IIPS (International Institute for Population Sciences) and ORC Macro (2000), *National Family Health Survey (NFHS-2), 1998-1999, India*, Mumbai: IIPS.

IIPS and ORC Macro (2001), *National Family Health Survey (NFHS-2), India, 1998-99: Orissa*. Mumbai: IIPS.

Jones G, Steketee RW, Black RE, Bhutta ZA, Morris SS, and the Bellagio Child Survival Study Group (2003), How Many Child Deaths Can we Prevent this Year? *Lancet*, 362 (9377): 65-71.

Lee JW (2003), Child Survival: A Global Health Challenge, *Lancet*, 362 (9380): 262-2.

Maharatna A (1998), On Tribal Fertility in Late Nineteenth and Early Twentieth Century India, Working Paper Series No. 98.01, Cambridge, MA: Harvard Center for Population and Development Studies, Harvard University.

Maharatna A (2000), Fertility, Mortality and Gender Bias among Tribal Population: An Indian Perspective, *Social Science & Medicine*, 50 (10): 1333-51.

Mishra S (2003A), Access to Knowledge with Physical and Financial Access will Improve Child Survival, *Lancet*, 362 (9381), http://www.thelancet.com/journal/vol362/iss9381/full/llan.362.9381.child_survival.26716.1 (accessed August 2, 2003).

Mishra S (2003B), Public Health Scenario in India, mimeo, Mumbai: Indira Gandhi Institute of Development Research (Prepared for R Radhakrishna edited *India Development Report 2004*, New Delhi: Oxford University Press, forthcoming).

Padhi S (2001), Infant and Child Survival in Orissa: An Analysis with NFHS Data, *Economic and Political Weekly*, 36 (34): 3316-26.

Padhi S, Mishra S (2000), *Premature Mortality, Health Status and Public Health Care Facilities in Orissa: A Study in Accessibility and Utilisation*. Bhubaneswar: Nabakrushna Choudhury Centre for Development Studies.

Panda, M (2003) Poverty in Orissa: A Disaggregated Analysis, mimeo, Mumbai: Indira Gandhi Institute of Development Research (Draft, February 2003).

PRC (Population Research Centre), Bhubaneswar and IIPS (1995), *National Family Health Survey (MCH and Family Planning), Orissa 1993*. Bombay: PRC, Bhubaneswar and IIPS.

PROBE Team, The (1999), *Public Report on Basic Education in India*, Oxford University Press, Delhi.

Rajan SI, Mohanachandran, P (1998), Infant and Child Mortality Estimates - Part I, *Economic and Political Weekly*, 33 (19): 1120-40.

Rajan SI, Mohanachandran, P (2000), Infant and Child Mortality Estimates, 1991 Census by Religion, Occupation and Level of Education, Part II, *Economic and Political Weekly*, 35 (51): 4541-88.

Rajan SI, Mohanachandran, P (2001), Infant and Child Mortality Estimates for Scheduled Castes and Scheduled Tribes: Based on the 1991 Census, Part III, *Economic and Political Weekly*, 36 (48): 4506-08.

UNDP (United Nations Development Programme) (2003), *Human Development Report 2003 - Millennium Development Goals: A Compact among Nations to End Human Poverty*. New York: Oxford University Press.

Victora CG, Wagstaff A, Schellenberg JA, Gwatkin D, Claeson M, Habicht J-P (2003) Applying an Equity Lens to Child Health and Mortality: More of the Same is Not Enough. *Lancet*, 362 (9379): 233-41.

CHAPTER

8

Incidence of Ultra-Poverty in the Tribal Community of Orissa

R.P. SARMA

Ever since Thomas Robert Malthus (1766-1834) familiarised the problems of population, growth of food grains and poverty of the masses in the early nineteenth century, economists have become conscious about poverty. He considered that the poor are entirely responsible for their poverty and expressed the opinion that it was not the responsibility of the state to support the poor. He even objected to the Poor Law enacted by the British Parliament to help the poor. One cannot accept now his analysis of causes and remedies for poverty, but the fact is that now poverty is an important economic problem concerning every economy in one form or other. Perhaps from Malthus onwards economics became a subject to "enquire into the nature and causes of poverty" and governmental interference has been accepted as a policy to remove poverty.

Per capita income has so far been the main criterion for measuring poverty of a community, even though it is not a perfect measuring rod from many considerations. Even though the analysis of poverty started in India in the early sixties of the last century, an additional criterion to measure the backwardness of the people is widely used now in addition to per capita income. Perhaps now the percent of people/families below a poverty line is given more preference in evaluating the level of economic development of a region than the traditional criteria of per-capita income.

THEORETICAL FRAMEWORK

Share of population with income below certain predetermined amount is taken generally as the measure of poverty or 'Poverty Line', a dividing line below and above certain number of families. Beginning from D.P. Ojha's estimation of poverty in 1660-61 all economists and statisticians have been estimating the poverty line at the expenditure level at which a minimum calorie intake daily by an individual in the family as the basis. All of them computed the poverty line almost on the basis of about 2100 to 2400 calorie in-take daily for the urban and rural people separately converted into current prices.

Line of poverty expressed as per cent of total population or total families is called by "Head-count Ratio". Prof. Amartya Sen in his study *On Economic Inequality,* 1973, provided a new dimension to measurement of poverty. Instead of the traditional below-poverty-line concept he has devised a new formula based on income inequality of the people below the poverty line. Analyzing the Bengal Famine of 1943 in his book on *Poverty and Famines: An Essay on Entitlement and deprivation, (1981)* he propounded the thesis that starvation and starvation deaths are more than sufficient to be diagnosed as the prevalent of poverty but drought and famine are not the causes of poverty, poverty is due to insufficient purchasing power with the people to buy their minimum needs.

In 1981 in another monumental work, *Choice, Welfare and Measurement,* he has devised a new formula based on income inequality of the people below the poverty line. In the USA another measure is used to analyze poverty, called "Poverty Gap". It is the average short fall of income of all the poor taken together from the poverty line. On the basis of poverty gap Sen elaborately explained "Poverty Index" which is considered as a better measure of poverty of the people.

Sen's inequality measure explains the Indian phenomenon, that is, why in spite of different measures of the government to alleviate poverty the poverty line is not being lowered. This paradox can be explained with the help of a simple diagram.

In Fig. 8.1 the line ABC is the income line and P is the line of poverty. The area between poverty line and income line indicates the Poverty Gap. It is the aggregate short fall of income of all the poor taken together from the poverty line. Point B at which the income line intersects the poverty line indicates the percentage of people below poverty line, as shown in the figure it is about 50 per cent. As a result of planner's efforts to alleviate the poverty adopting different income earning schemes among the poor people, the income line increased to DB (the red line) below the poverty line and accordingly the poverty gap reduced, but the people below the poverty line remained constant hence there is no change in the poverty line.

Sen's poverty measure is explained in this formula :

$$P = H\,[I + (1-I)\,G]$$

In the formula, H is the Head count ratio, I is the aggregate shortfall of income from the poverty line and G is the Gini coefficient of the inequality

FIG. 8.1
The Poverty Gap

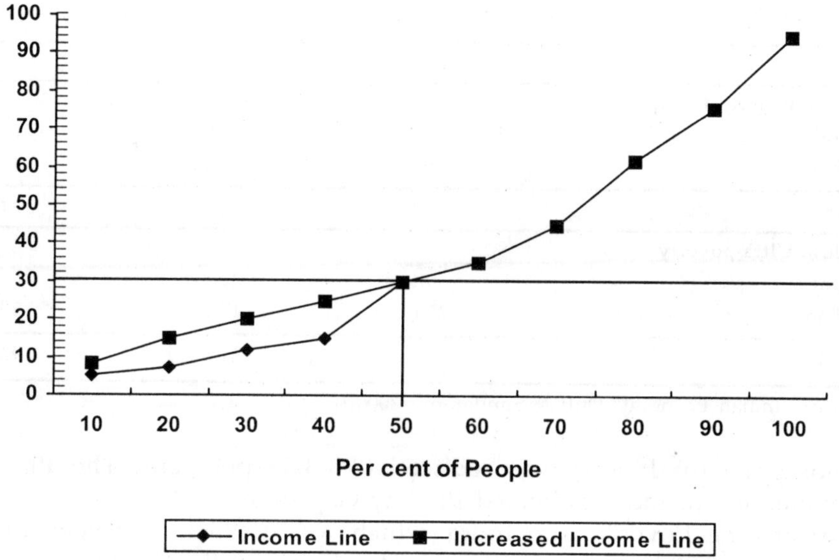

measure. Co-efficient measure P lies between 0 and 1; lower the co-efficient of P lower is the degree of poverty. When it reaches 0 means every one has income above the poverty line. What Sen wanted to analyse is that below the poverty line all are not equally poor; the degree of poverty changes substantially below the poverty line which has to be taken into consideration in formulating schemes to alleviate the poverty.

ULTRA POOR

In the poverty gap where the gap is very wide, at the beginning of the income line, those few people are termed as Ultra Poor. A dead line can also be fixed arbitrarily, below the minimum expenditure fixed for the poverty line, as ultra poverty line. Planning Commission (1996-97) estimated the criterion of poverty line on the basis of per capita consumption expenditure of Rs. 115.43 for rural and Rs. 165.58 urban area. Those who are not able to spend even 50 per cent of it can be taken as ultra poor.

The country studies of World Bank Report, *India: Poverty, Employment and Social Services* (1989) used the procedure adopted by Planning Commission of India in estimating poverty line. The World Bank computed the Ultra Poverty line along with the general poverty line. Table 8.1 shows the World Bank estimations of poverty line and ultra poverty line.

In 1970 people below poverty line was estimated at 52.4 per cent of which 29.8 per cent were below ultra poverty, that is out of the total poor 56.73 per cent are ultra poor. By the year 1988 the percentage of ultra poor

TABLE 8.1
Poverty and Ultra Poverty Estimates

(Figures in per cent)

Sector	*1970*	*1983*	*1988*
Below Poverty Line			
Rural	53.0	44.9	41.7
Urban	45.5	36.4	33.6
Total	52.4	42.5	39.6
Below Ultra-poverty			
Rural	30.1	22.8	20.4
Urban	25.6	17.7	15.8
Total	29.8	21.8	19.2

Source : Indian Economy, Dutt & Sundaram, (2000).

among the total poor was reduced to 48.55 per cent. The Planning Commission of India estimated Poverty Gap Index and according to their estimate the Poverty Gap Index which was 15.95 in the year 1973-74 declined to 8.30 by the year 1993-94. The decline of the Poverty Gap Index from 1973-74 to 1993-94 is presented in Table 8.2. The average annual decline of poverty gap was 3.31 in the rural sector, but in the urban sector the gap was lowered by 2.71 points.

TABLE 8.2
Poverty Gap Index of India : 1973-94

Year	*Rural*	*Urban*	*Total*
1973-74	16.56	13.64	15.95
1977-78	15.73	13.13	15.15
1983-84	12.32	10.61	11.96
1987-88	9.11	9.94	9.32
1993-94	8.45	7.88	8.30
Annual Average Decline	3.31	2.71	3.21

Source : Planning Commission, 1998.
Ninth Five Year Plan 1997-2002 Vol.I.

ORISSA SCENARIO

Tribal Economy

After independence of India planned efforts have been made continuously for the socio-economic development of the tribal communities, but during the last half century of planned development even though they have been provided with special privileges to develop them they are still remaining in the lowest income group in the society.

The tribals constitute about 8.08 (1991) per cent of the total population of India. About 283 lakhs of tribals that is about 3.35 per cent reside in three states of Madhya Pradesh, Maharashtra and Orissa. The tribal economy greatly influences the state economy of Madhya Pradesh and Orissa, in which the tribals constitute 39 and 25 per cents of respective states. Out of the total tribal population of 283 lakhs in these three states about 50 per cent reside in Madhya Pradesh and around 25 per cent each in the state of Maharashtra and Orissa. The figures presented in Table 8.3 indicate the facts. In Orissa even though tribal population is found in all the districts they are mostly concentrated in eight districts, where the tribal population of the districts exceeds 50 per cent. In another eight districts the tribal population constitutes less than 5 per cent, which can be termed as non-tribal districts.

TABLE 8.3
States Dominated by Tribal Population-1991

State	*Population (In Lakhs)*	*State Per cent*
Madhya Pradesh	140(49.49)	39.0
Maharashtra	73(25.76)	9.5
Orissa	70(24.75)	25.0
Total	283(100.00)	3.35*

•Per cent of tribal population from India's total population

Note : The figures I the parentheses indicate per cent of tribal population in the state out of total tribal population of the three states.

As it can be verified from Table 8.4 that in eight tribal districts about 63.15 per cent of the total tribals of Orissa are concentrated and in the non tribal districts their percentage is about 4.25 per cent. The eight tribal districts are five of the southern Orissa district of Malkangiri, Koraput, Nabdarangpur, Rayagada, Kandhmal and three northern districts of Sundargarh, Keonjhar and Mayurbhanj. The non-tribal districts in the coastal Orissa are Bhadrak, Kendrapara, Jagatsinghpur, Puri, Cuttack, Khurda and Ganjam.

Tribals have maximum poverty in both rural and urban areas. About 63.6 per cent of the rural families and 58.6 per cent of urban families were under the poverty line in 1993-94, according to the latest official figures available for analysis. District wise poverty figures are not available for the tribals concerning their percentage of poverty. District wise 1997 figures are available for the general poverty; accordingly differences in poverty score between the general population and the tribal population can be derived.

These four tribal dominated districts and four general districts have been taken as sample for comparison. The four general districts taken are

TABLE 8.4

Tribal Population in the Districts of Orissa, 1991

Per cent of Tribes	*No. of Districts*	*Population (In Lakhs)*	*Per cent*
<5	8	3.06	4.35
5-20	7	7.96	11.32
21-50	7	14.89	21.17
>50	8	44.41	63.16
Total	30	7.32	100.00

Source : Statistical Outline of Orissa,1991.

Bhadrak, Jagatsinghpur, Kendrapara and Puri, because in these four districts about 0.69 per cent of tribals are found. On the other hand four districts with a dominant tribal population, on an average about 55.75 per cent in the district's population have been taken for comparison. These districts are Malkangiri, Mayurbhanj, Nabrangpur and Kandhmal.

In 1993-94 the Planning Commission accepted as Rs.11,000 as the minimum need of the family in the rural sector and any family getting less than that was included in below poverty line. The lower two grades of people, described as destitutes and very very; poor with the family income up to Rs. 6000, are taken together as Ultra Poor. Beyond Rs. 6000 up to Rs. 11,000 income of the families are included under poor category.

Figures of percentages of ultra-poor and poor are presented for comparison between the four sets of districts of general and tribal dominated districts in Table 8.5. In the tribal districts the percentage of poverty of the rural families calculated as 91.54 per cent in comparison to general districts of 71.18 per cent, a gap of more than 20 per cent. Among the poverty stricken families in the rural sector the ultra poor in tribal districts constitutes 72.51 per cent, which is about 79.21 per cent of the total poor families. In the general districts the average percentage of poverty was

TABLE 8.5

Poor and Ultra-Poor Families in Tribal and Non-Tribal Districts,1997

General Districts	*Ultra Poor*	*Poor*	*Total Poverty*	*Tribal Districts*	*Ultra Poor*	*Poor*	*Total Poverty*
Bhadrak	48.88	22.88	71.16	Malkangiri	67.33	24.53	91.86
Jagatsinghpur	42.56	27.01	69.57	Mayurbhanj	70.41	20.36	90.77
Kendrapara	42.14	27.17	69.31	Nabrangpur	66.94	23.56	90.50
Puri	49.43	25.26	74.69	Kandhmal	76.36	16.67	93.03
Total	45.75	25.43	71.18	Total	72.51	19.00	91.51

Source : Orissa Development Report, (2000) Planning Commission, New Delhi.

71.80 per cent, down of about 20 per cent from the tribal districts, of which the ultra poor constitutes 45.75 per cent, which comes to about 64.27 per cent of total poor families.

CONCLUSION

Officially it is stated that the tribals were 79.1 per cent of poverty line in 1983, which was reduced to 63.6 per cent in 1993-94. As against this the general community's poverty which was 43.8 per cent in the rural sector was reduced to 32.9 per cent by 1993-94. But these figures were not analysed by district wise. The analysis of general districts versus tribal districts shows that the tribals have far more percentage of families under the poverty line. Among the poverty stricken families the ultra-poor families are at the higher percentage in the tribal districts analyzed in general terms. The conclusion is summarized in Table 8.6.

TABLE 8.6
Poverty and Ultra-Poverty among Tribals and Others

(Figures in Per cent)

Category	*Tribal Districts*	*Non-tribal Districts*
Ultra-Poverty	79.21	64.27
Poverty	20.79	35.73
Combined*	91.54	71.81
	(100.00)	(100.00)

* Per cent of rural families below poverty line in the district.

In non-tribal districts the percentage of poverty for the schedule castes is included, both in general poverty and ultra poverty which cannot be calculated separately. A special demographic characteristic of Orissa is that the districts where the tribals are dominate the population of scheduled castes is very much limited. Hence even though the poverty of scheduled castes is included in general poverty of the tribal districts it is not significant.

REFERENCES

Dutt, Rudra & K.P. S. Sundaram. (2002), *Indian Economy,* S. Chand, New Delhi Government of India, 2000, Orissa Development Report, Planning Commission, New Delhi.

———, Economic Survey. (2003), Ministry of Finance and Company Affairs, New Delhi.

Government of Orissa, Economic Suirvey-2000-2001, 2001, Bureau of Economics & Statistics, Bhubaneswar.

Hajela, T.N. (1995), *History of Economic Thought,* Konark Polishers, New Delhi.

Sen, Amartya, (1982), *Choice, Welfare & Management,* London.

Sinha, Ajit Kumar & Sen, Rajkumar, (Eds.) (2000), *Economics of Amartya Sen,* Deep & Deep, New Delhi.

CHAPTER

9

Measurement of Poverty among the Beneficiary Households Under Different Anti-Poverty Programmes in a Backward District of Orissa

MANARANJAN BEHERA

Poverty is a relative concept. Definition of poor and poverty varies from person to person. It is not only a state of existence but also a process with many dimensions and complexities. To understand poverty, it is essential to examine the economic and social context, including institutions of the state, markets, communities, and households. Poverty differences cut across gender, ethnicity, age, location (rural versus urban), and income source. In households, children and women often suffer more than men. In the community, minority ethnic or religious groups suffer more than majority groups and the rural poor more than the urban poor: among the rural poor, landless wage workers suffer more than small landowners or tenants (Khan, 2001). While recognising that poverty is multi-dimensional in character and that it manifests itself in a variety of socio-economic characteristics, individual scholars and official agencies have nevertheless, considering the immensity of its incidence, thought it necessary to evolve a single yardstick that would help estimate the number of people in poverty in the country (EPW Research Foundation, 1993).

Various discussions on the measurement of poverty show that there are two methods of measuring poverty on the basis of a minimum calorie intake. One is to check the set of people who do not satisfy the minimum calorie intake. This may be called the direct method and "does not involve the use of any income notion, in particular not that of a poverty-line income" (Sen, 1981). The second method may be called the 'income method' and involves the calculation of the minimum income at which the specified minimum nutritional needs are satisfied, given the consumption patterns of the population. While the Planning Commission (and much of the literature on poverty estimation) has used the income method to measure poverty in India, an estimate of poverty by the direct method allows for an independent check on how well the income method is doing in capturing the calorie at the poverty line (Jones and Sen, 2001).

For measuring poverty and income inequality, most of the recent studies (Parthasarathy, 1995; Rath, 1996; Desai and Namboodri, 1998; and Feast, 2000) are based on NSS data and/or some other published data. These studies have tried to quantify the trend of rural poverty over the years. But, in the present context, attempt has been made to estimate the incidence, depth and severity of rural poverty among the beneficiary households under different anti-poverty programmes in a backward region. In order to develop the backward areas and improve the living conditions of the poor people living in rural areas, many developmental activities have been started by the Government of India in the post-independent period. The government have implemented as many as 40 rural development and poverty alleviation programmes. Some of the important programmes are Integrated Rural Development Programme (IRDP), Development of Women and Children in Rural Areas (DWCRA), Training of Rural Youth for Self-employment (TRYSEM), Supply of Improved Tool Kit to Rural Artisans (SITRA), Ganga Kalyan Yojana (GKY), Jawahar Rojgar Yojana (JRY), Employment Assurance Scheme (EAS), Indira Awass Yojana (IAY) and Million Wells Scheme (MWS). From 1.04.1999, instead of IRDP, DWCRA, TRYSEM, SITRA, GKY and MWS, Swarnjayanti Gram Swarozgar Yojana (SGSY), which is jointly funded by Government of India and the state government in the ratio of 75:25, is in operation. Similarly, Sampoorna Gramin Rojgar Yojana (SGRY), funded by Government of India and the state government in the same ratio, has been introduced with effect from 25.09.01 by merging two wage employment schemes, i.e., Jawahar Gram Samridhi Yojana (JGSY) (Its old version name was Jawahar Rojgar Yojana) and Employment Assurance Scheme (Misra and Behera, 2002). Unfortunately, only the acronyms rose in number, schemes and programmes multiplied, but poverty showed no sign, whatsoever, of declining. With this background, as SGSY and SGRY are the newly introduced schemes, the present study takes into account five selected but important anti-poverty programmes, namely, IRDP, TRYSEM, JRY, EAS and MWS, for the measurement rural poverty in a backward district of Orissa, i.e., Mayurbhanj.

OBJECTIVES

The present paper seeks to study the following two objectives:

(i) To examine the backwardness of the district through various socio-economic indicators; and

(ii) To measure the incidence, depth and severity of poverty among the beneficiary households under the five selected anti-poverty programmes, namely, IRDP, TRYSEM, JRY, EAS and MWS, in the district of Mayurbhanj.

METHODOLOGY

The study is based on both primary and secondary sources of data. Secondary data have been collected form District Statistical Handbook, Mayurbhanj (1999); District at a Glance, Orissa (2003); Orissa Agricultural Statistics (2000-2001); and Directorate of Economics and Statistics, Government of Orissa.

For collection of primary data* on income and other related information, multi-stage purposive sampling method has been used. In the first stage, 10 per cent of the total number of blocks of Mayurbhanj district subject to a minimum of two have been selected. Since the total number of blocks in the district is 26, therefore, three blocks, namely, Betanati, Kaptipada and Kusumi, have been selected purposively from north-western, eastern and southern region of the district.

In the second stage, 10 per cent of the total Gram Panchayats subject to a minimum of two Gram Panchayats from each sample block have been selected. Since the number of Gram Panchayats in Betanati, Kaptipada and Kusumi blocks are 16, 16 and 11 respectively ; so two Gram Panchayats from each sample block have been selected purposively. One Gram Panchayat is very near to the block headquarters, and the other one is far away from the block headquarters. The Panchayats selected from the sample blocks are: Betanati and Santara from Betanati block, Badakhiladi and Sarat from Kaptipada block, and Talak Pokhari and Jorada from Kusumi block.

In the third stage, three villages, one is in close proximity, the second one is of medium distance, and the third one is farthest to the Gram Panchayat headquarters, have been selected purposively from each of the sample Gram Panchayats. While selecting the villages, due consideration has been given to the size of population, geographical spread and accessibility of the villages.

In the last stage, all the beneficiaries under IRDP, TRYSEM, JRY, EAS and MWS from the sample villages for the years 1993-94, 1994-95 and 1995-96 (These three years have been taken as per the instruction of Panchayati

---

*The primary data collected for the Project "Evaluation of Anti-poverty Programmes in Mayurbhanj District, Orissa; Sponsored by Panchayati Raj Department, Government of Orissa; and Conducted by S.N. Misra and M. Behera, Nabakrushna Choudhury Centre for Development Studies, Bhubaneswar-13, have been used in the study.

Raj Department, Government of Orissa) have been surveyed. The total numbers of beneficiaries surveyed under the above five different schemes in the three sample blocks are shown as below.

Number of Beneficiaries Surveyed under different Anti-poverty Programmes in the Sample Blocks

Sl. No.	*Name of the Block*	*IRDP*	*TRYSEM*	*JRY*	*EAS*	*MWS*	*Total*
1.	Betanati	58	21	57	44	11	191
2.	Kaptipada	53	14	65	59	23	214
3.	Kusumi	65	27	54	55	20	221
	Total	176	62	176	158	54	626

For measuring incidence, depth and severity of poverty among the beneficiary households under different anti-poverty programmes, the model developed by Foster, Green and Thorbecke (1984) has been used. The model is explained as follows :

$$P = \frac{1}{N}\left\{\sum_{i=1}^{m}\left[\frac{Z - Y_i}{Z}\right]^a\right\}$$

Where,

Y_i = Income per beneficiary household
Z = The Poverty line
N = Number of households in the sample
M = Number of beneficiary households having income below the poverty line
a = Measure of inequality aversion
P = Poverty

(i) When a = 0, the above equation reduces to M/N, i. e., the number of poor households in the sample divided by the total number of households in the sample population. This is commonly used as a measure of incidence of poverty, and is called the headcount ratio. If it is expressed in percentage, it is known as headcount index.

(ii) When a = 1, the poverty gap ratio (depth of poverty) is produced, which shows the shortfall of the poor households' income from the poverty line expressed as an average of all households in the sample.

(iii) When a = 2, the squared poverty gap ratio is obtained, which measures the severity of poverty.

In the present study, all the three measures have been used to estimate the incidence, depth and severity of poverty among the beneficiary households of five selected anti-poverty programmes.

As per the new methodology communicated by the Planning Commission, Panchayati Raj Department, Government of Orissa has fixed Rs. 15, 000 per households per annum at 1996-97 prices as the poverty line for rural Orissa. So, in the study Rs. 15,000 per household per annum has been taken as the poverty line for measuring the incidence, depth and severity of poverty. As the study was conducted in 1999-2000, the incomes of the beneficiary households have been deflated by the wholesale consumer price index to 1996-97 prices.

Another point to be mentioned here is that all the beneficiaries under different poverty programmes were below the poverty line before they became beneficiaries, as this is the pre-condition in order to become a beneficiary under any anti-poverty programme.

THE STUDY AREA

Mayurbhanj is the largest district in the State of Orissa in terms of geographical area. As per 2001 Census, the total population of the district was 22.22 lakhs constituting 6.05 per cent of the total population of the state. The percentages of male and female populations were 50.50 and 49.50 respectively. More than 93 per cent of the total population were living in the rural areas. The shares of ST and SC population in the district as per 1991 Census were 57.88 per cent and 7.00 per cent respectively. The density of population per square kilometre of area was 213 as against the state average of 236. Higher decennial growth rate of population was found in the district in 2001 over 1991 (17.89 per cent) as compared to that of the state average (15.94 per cent). In terms of literacy rate, the district lags far behind the state. It was 52.43 per cent in the district in 2001 as against 63.61 per cent in Orissa. When sex-wise literacy rate is taken into consideration, it was very less (38.28 per cent) in case of females compared to that of males (66.38 per cent). Further, the rural literacy rate in the district was only 49.96 per cent, whereas, in urban area, it was 83.35 per cent.

The work participation rate of the people in the district is not so good. In 2001 Census, it was 46.37 per cent as against the state average of 38.88 per cent. Main workers constituted 27.81 per cent of the total population. Out of total workers of the district, the percentages of cultivators and agricultural labourers were 27.91 and 66.42 respectively.

The land utilisation pattern of the district shows that 42.14 per cent of the total geographical area belonged to forest area, and the share of forest area to that of state total was 7.55 per cent in 2000-01. The cropping intensity of the district was as low as 119 as against 135 in Orissa. This shows that the area sown more than once was very less. This was due to the poor irrigation facility available in the district. The percentage of net irrigated area to net area sown was 19.70 in 2000-01 in the district, whereas, it was 27.28 in

Orissa. The fertiliser consumption per hectare of gross cropped area was 28 kilogram compared to 41 kilogram in case of Orissa. Paddy is the principal crop in the district with a yield rate of 19.03 quintals per hectare in 2000-01. Out of the total land holders of the district 84.00 per cent marginal and small farmers in 1995-96, and the corresponding state level figures was 81.98 per cent.

The number of post offices per lakh of population was 31.95 in 2001-02 in the district. With regard to electricity facility, 69.55 per cent villages were found to be electrified in the district, whereas, at state level, it was 78.94 per cent. The road communication facility of the district was also not good. In 1999-2000, the total road length per 100 square kilometres of area in the district was 121.17 kilometres, which was less than that of the state average (145.53 kilometres). The per capita net value added by manufacture in 1997-98 in the district was as low as Rs. 27.33 as against Rs. 591.46 in Orissa. Similarly, the per capita foodgrain production in Mayurbhanj district in 1998-99 (147.19 kilogram) was less than that of Orissa (173.76 kilogram).

In terms of per capita income, the district figure was Rs. 7084 in 1998-99 at current prices, whereas, the corresponding state figure was Rs. 8435. The percentage of below poverty line of (BPL) families living in rural areas in the district was 77.74 in 1997 as against the state average of 66.37 per cent.

The analysis of the above socio-economic indicators shows that the district Mayurbhanj is one of the backward districts of the State of Orissa. Hence, measuring extent of poverty among the beneficiary households under different anti-poverty programmes in the district is very much important for further action by the government for its development.

EXTENT OF POVERTY

The extent of different types of poverty (i.e., incidence, depth and severity of poverty) among the beneficiary households under the selected anti-poverty programmes in the three sample blocks of Mayurbhanj district are explained in detail below.

INTEGRATED RURAL DEVELOPMENT PROGRAMME (IRDP)

The various measures of poverty among the IRDP beneficiary households in the sample blocks of Mayurbhanj district are shown in Table 9.1. The table shows that, in Kusumi block, 47.69 per cent of the IRDP beneficiary households were below the poverty line. The incidence of poverty was lowest, i. e., 26.42 per cent, in Kaptipada block and, in Betanati block, the incidence of poverty was 29.31 per cent. On an average, in the three sample blocks, 35.23 per cent beneficiary households were still living below the poverty line. This implies that 64.77 per cent IRDP beneficiary households crossed the poverty line after they became the beneficiary under IRDP. When depth (poverty gap ratio) and severity of poverty (squared poverty gap ratio) are taken into consideration, these were found to be highest in Kusumi block followed by Betanati and Kaptipada blocks. The overall poverty gap ratio and squared poverty gap ratio were 0.0728 and 0.0209 respectively. This shows that the depth and severity of poverty were not very high among the IRDP beneficiary households. Improper selection of trade and improper utilisation of funds received for the trade were found to be the major reasons for not achieving the hundred per cent target of reducing poverty among the beneficiary households.

TABLE 9.1
Estimates of Poverty among the IRDP Beneficiary Households in the Sample Blocks

Sl. No.	Name of the Block	Head Count Index	Poverty Gap Ratio	Squared Poverty Gap Ratio
1.	Betanati	29.31	0.0506	0.0134
2.	Kaptipada	26.42	0.0474	0.0119
3.	Kusumi	47.69	0.1132	0.0350
	Total	35.23	0.0728	0.0209

Source : Estimated from the data collected from the field study.

TRAINING OF RURAL YOUTH FOR SELF-EMPLOYMENT (TRYSEM)

Under TRYSEM, 35.48 per cent of the beneficiary households of three the sample blocks were living below the poverty line. It was as high as 48.15 per cent in Kusumi block followed by 28.57 per cent in Kaptipada block and 23.81 per cent in Betanati block. Thus, compared to Betanati and Kaptipada blocks, TRYSEM has not become very much successful in reducing poverty in Kusumi block. Similar to IRDP, under TRYSEM, depth and severity of poverty were found to be lower level, i.e., 0.0611 and 0.0153 respectively. The depth and severity of poverty followed the same trend as that of incidence of poverty among the TRYSEM beneficiary households in the three sample blocks, which can be seen from Table 9.2. Many TRYSEM

TABLE 9.2
Estimates of Poverty among the TRYSEM Beneficiary Households in the Sample Blocks

Sl. No.	Name of the Block	Head Count Index	Poverty Gap Ratio	Squared Poverty Gap Ratio
1.	Betanati	23.81	0.0442	0.0103
2.	Kaptipada	28.57	0.0229	0.0023
3.	Kusumi	48.15	0.0941	0.0257
	Total	35.48	0.0611	0.0153

Source : Estimated from the data collected from the field study.

beneficiaries complained that the funds for purchasing raw-materials were not given to them immediately after they received the training under the programme, otherwise, they could have started their businesses successfully. This was one of the reasons for the poor performance of TRYSEM in reducing poverty (Misra and Behera, 2000).

JAWAHAR ROJGAR YOJANA (JRY)

Compared to IRDP and TRYSEM, the performance of JRY in reducing poverty among the beneficiary households was very miserable. In Kusumi block, all the JRY beneficiary households were living below the poverty line. The percentages of beneficiary households living below the poverty line in Betanati and Kaptipada blocks were 98.25 per cent and 92.31 per cent respectively. The depth and severity of poverty were also highest in Kusumi block followed by Betanati and Kaptipada blocks. Table 3 shows that the poverty gap ratio and the squared poverty gap ratio were 0.8185 and 0.6733 respectively in Kusumi block. The overall respective head count index, poverty gap ratio and squared poverty gap ratio in the sample blocks were 96.59 per cent, 0.7039 and 0.5395. The main reasons for the incidence of poverty among the JRY beneficiaries were: (1) payment of wage less than the minimum wage, (2) use of contractors/middle men (Though there is complete ban in the use of contractors/middle men under JRY) resulting low payment of wage, and (3) considerably less man-days of employment (about 18 man-days per beneficiary per annum instead of providing 100 mandays of employment to at least one member of each rural landless household.

TABLE 9.3

Estimates of Poverty among the JRY Beneficiary Households in the Sample Blocks

Sl. No.	*Name of the Block*	*Head Count Index*	*Poverty Gap Ratio*	*Squared Poverty Gap Ratio*
1.	Betanati	98.25	0.6827	0.5065
2.	Kaptipada	92.31	0.6274	0.4573
3.	Kusumi	100.00	0.8185	0.6733
	Total	96.59	0.7039	0.5395

Source : Estimated from the data collected from the field study.

EMPLOYMENT ASSURANCE SCHEME (EAS)

The performance of EAS in reducing poverty was a little bit better compared to JRY. It can be seen from Table 9.4 that 67.72 per cent EAS beneficiary households were below the poverty line in the study area. The head count index was again found to be highest, i.e., 81.82 per cent, in Kusumi block followed by Kaptipada (61.02) per cent and Betanati (59.09

per cent) blocks. But the poverty gap ratio and squared poverty gap ratio were comparatively better under EAS than that under JRY. Like JRY, EAS also failed to create the target number of mandays employment in all the three sample blocks of Mayurbhanj district.

TABLE 9.4

Estimates of Poverty among the EAS Beneficiary Households in the Sample Blocks

Sl. No.	*Name of the Block*	*Head Count Index*	*Poverty Gap Ratio*	*Squared Poverty Gap Ratio*
1.	Betanati	59.09	0.1056	0.0310
2.	Kaptipada	61.02	0.1346	0.0462
3.	Kusumi	81.82	0.2454	0.0839
	Total	67.72	0.1651	0.0551

Source : Estimated from the data collected from the field study.

TABLE 9.5

Estimates of Poverty among the MWS Beneficiary Households in the Sample Blocks

Sl. No.	*Name of the Block*	*Head Count Index*	*Poverty Gap Ratio*	*Squared Poverty Gap Ratio*
1.	Betanati	100.00	0.4898	0.2557
2.	Kaptipada	69.57	0.2318	0.0940
3.	Kusumi	80.00	0.2540	0.0998
	Total	79.63	0.2926	0.1291

Source : Estimated from the data collected from the field study.

MILLION WELLS SCHEME (MWS)

In case of MWS, the incidence, depth and severity of poverty were found to be highest among the beneficiary households in Betanati block. Table 9.5 shows that all the EAS beneficiary households were below the poverty line in Betanati block. The depth and severity of poverty in the block were 0.4898 and 0.2557 respectively. The head count index was 80.00 per cent in Kusumi block and 69.57 per cent in Kaptipada block. On an average, 79.63 per cent of the MWS beneficiary households were below the poverty line in the study area. The main reason for the poor performance of MWS was that, out of 54 Million Wells, 74.07 per cent wells were in working condition, and only 51.85 per cent wells were providing water both in *Kharif* and Summer seasons. As a result, MWS had little impact on agriculture, and most of the wells were used for drinking water purpose only (Misra and Behera, 2000).

CONCLUSION

The measurement of incidence, depth and severity of poverty among the beneficiary households under IRDP, TRYSEM, JRY, EAS and MWS in the three sample blocks, namely, Betanati, Kaptipada and Kusumi, of Mayurbhanj district show that all the above five important anti-poverty programmes have not been very much successful in reducing poverty among the beneficiary households. Compared to the self-employment programmes, i.e., IRDP and TRYSEM, the performances of wage-employment programmes, i.e., JRY, EAS and MWS, were worse. JRY was found to be the worst performed programme in reducing poverty among the beneficiary households in all the sample blocks. Except MWS, all the other four programmes had performed very miserably in Kusumi block. The performances of IRDP, JRY, and EAS in reducing poverty were found to be better in Betanati block, whereas, in Kaptipada block, the performances of JRY and EAS were, to some extent better, compared to that in Betanati and Kusumi blocks. The reasons for the poor performance of anti-poverty programmes in reducing incidence, depth and severity of poverty among the beneficiary households in the three sample blocks were : (1) improper selection of beneficiary households, (2) poor supervision and motivation of the government and bank officials involved in the implementation of the anti-poverty programmes, and (3) more attention towards the fulfilment of the target rather than to make the schemes successful by the concerned officials.

References

Desai, B.M. and N.V. Namboodri (1998), 'Policy Strategy and Instruments for Alleviating Rural Poverty', *EPW*, Vol XXXIII, pp. 2669 – 2674.

EPW Research Foundation (1993), 'Poverty Levels in India: Norms, Estimates and Trends', *EPW*, August 21.

Feast, B. (2000): 'Poverty Statistics', *EPW*, Vol. XXXV, pp. 2372-2379.

Foster, J.J. Green and E. Thorbecke (1984), 'A Class of Decomposable Poverty Measures', *Econometrica*, Vol. 52, pp. 571-576.

Jones, R.P. and K. Sen (2001), 'On India's Poverty Puzzles and Statistics of Poverty', *EPW*, Vol. XXXVI, No 3, January 20-26.

Khan, M.H. (2001), 'Rural Poverty in Developing Countries—Implications for Public Policy', International Monetary Fund, Washington, D.C.

Misra, S.N. and M. Behera (2000), 'Evaluation of Anti-poverty Programmes in Mayurbhanj District, Orissa' (mimeo), Nabakrushna Choudhury Centre for Development Studies, Bhubaneswar.

Misra, S.N. and M. Behera (2002), 'Poverty and Living Condition', *Orissa Development Report*, Planning Commission, Government of India.

Parthasarathy, G. (1995), 'Public Intervention and Rural Poverty: Case of Non-sustainable Reduction in Andhra Pradesh', *EPW*, Vol XXX, No 41 and 42.

Rath, N. (1996), 'Poverty in India Revisited', *Indian Journal of Agricultural Economics*, Vol. LI, No. 1 and 2.

Sen, A. (1981), 'Poverty and Famines: An Essay on Entitlement and Deprivation', Oxford University Press, Oxford.

CHAPTER

10

Structural Adjustment, Overflowing Godowns, Starvation Deaths and Food Security in India

RABI N. PATRA

INTRODUCTION

The situation in rural India in the years 1942 and 2001 is similar in kind but different only in degree, at least in one respect. In 1942, more than 3 million people died in Bengal and Orissa while 20 deaths were reported from Kashipur block in Koraput district of Orissa in 2001; the cause of death in both the years being the same i.e., starvation. Scale of children for paltry sums, eating toxic mango kernels due to lack of entitlement to food and yet the government denying such reports in their bid to highlight the liberalization – privatization – globalization policies are the stark realities, particularly in the KBK districts of remote Orissa. The condition in parts of rural areas in Andhra Pradesh, Bihar, Chhatisgarh, Gujarat, Madhya Pradesh, Maharashtra and Rajasthan is no less serious. The vast majority of our population suffers from widespread hunger and malnutrition, and starvation deaths occur every year. In independent India, Government intervention in the food grains economy might have succeeded in averting famines of any large magnitude but it has certainly failed in eliminating chronic hunger, malnutrition and deaths by starvation. There is thus an urgent need of an accountable and effective food grains management and food delivery mechanism to ensure food and nutrition security especially in the rural areas.

As is clear from the title, the paper is an attempt to focus on the food security system in India and changes therein following shifts in the economic policy paradigm since 1991. The paper is organized in four sections. Section I being introductory defines the problem, section II presents a general outline of the food management system in India with special reference to the pre-reform period, the food security system under the LPG-SAP regime is analysed in section III and section IV contains a summary of the key points and some workable suggestions to improve the system.

FOOD SECURITY SYSTEM IN THE PRE-1990s

Every civilized society has a social responsibility of ensuring food and nutrition security in the system i.e, making available adequate food rains of standard quality at affordable prices to the people, especially to those at the lower echelons of the economy. Thus viewed an appropriate food management system is a precondition to achieve the objective.

Any effective food grains strategy has two broad aspects: managing the supplies and stocks, and overcoming demand bottlenecks. Certain amount of government intervention is, therefore, necessary to manage the food economy in tune with the overall objectives of economic policy.

In India government intervention in the food grains management system has concerned on the supply side forces through a scheme of public procurement and support prices, storage and buffer-stock operations, public distribution, and regulation of internal and international trade in food grains. By and large, the consumption and nourishment aspects are either omitted or dealt with only obliquely.

Analytically the food security system in India may be studied under two broad periods with 1991, the year since when there have been significant shifts in economic policies under the economic reforms paradigm, as the year of divide. For purposes of better comparison we have limited our analysis to the 1980s and the 1990s.

Broadly speaking, the performance of the food economy during the 1980s was noteworthy. It witnessed large public expenditures on rural development, employment generation and infrastructure (which accounted for 13.2% of GDP in the Seventh Plan period) leading to (a) a substantial growth in food grains production, (b) an increase in rural employment, especially non-farm rural employment, (c) high agricultural wages and (d) a sharp fall in the incidence of rural poverty. The production of food grains registered a growth rate of 3.54% per annum during the 1990s (Table 10.1), rural employment exhibited a growth rate of 1.36% during 1983-1987-8 and 2.03% during 1987-8-1993-94 (Table 10.2), the non-farm sector accounted for 29% of the rural employment by 1990, agricultural wages in real terms rose by about half and the rural headcount poverty fell sharply from about 45% in 1983 to about 36% in 1990 (Table 10.3). This proves that the public sector works and it matters too.

TABLE 10.1
Index Based Annual Growth Rates of Food-grains Production

(Base: Triennium ending 1981-2=100)

Period	*Growth Rate*
1979-80 – 1989-90	3.54
1989-90 – 1998-99	1.80

Source : Patnaik (2003).

TABLE 10.2
Annual Percentage Growth Rate of Rural Employment

Period	*Growth Rate*
1983-1987 – 8	1.36
1987-8-1993-4	2.03
1993-4-1999-0	0.58

Source : Patnaik (2003).

TABLE 10.3
Rural Poverty Estimates

(Headcount Ratio)

NSS Rounds	*Rural Poverty*
38(1983)	45.31
45(1989-0)	34.30
46(1990-1)	36.43
54(1998)	44.90

Source : Patnaik (2003).

FOOD SECURITY SYSTEM IN THE 1990s

Compared to the 1980s, the food security system in the 1990s reflects a contrasting picture. In 1991 the Government of India, in its bid to rescue the economy from the temporary abnormal condition caused by the Gulf war, availed of an IMF loan amounting to US $4.8 billion under the extended financing facility with the commitment to adopt the LPG model and implement the SAP. Though the commitment has several aspects we will be concerned here with those which have a bearing on our food and nutrition security. Three such aspects of the LPG-SAP regime are important : Trade Liberalisation, Fiscal Compression and PDS targeting.

TRADE LIBERALISATION

Liberalisation of trade including international trade in agricultural commodities is a key component of the new regime. Trade Liberalisation induced shifts in the structure of land utilization and cropping pattern favouring export crops, such as, cotton, floriculture and horticulture, prawn fisheries. Soyabeans, and sugarcane leading to a lower, growth rate in food grains production in the 1990s. The index based annual growth rate of production of food grains nearly halved from 3.54% during the 1980s to 1.80% in the 1990s (Table 10.1). Surprisingly, for the first time since the spread of Green Revolution technology, the growth rate of food grains production fell below the declining population growth rate. This has led to a reduction in the per capita net output and availability of food grains (Table 10.4). Thus the very norm of adequacy is at stake. It is, therefore, safe to say that the market does not always deliver.

TABLE 10.4
Per Capital Annual Net Output and Availability of Food-grains

(in Kgs)

Period	*Output*	*Availability*
1989-0-1991-2	174.3	173.5
1992-3-1994-5	176.2	169.7
1995-6-1997-8	170.3	170.4
1998-9-2000-1	169.7	157.2

Source : Patnaik (2003).

A more serious outcome of the cropping pattern shifts has been large scale suicides of farmers. The shift in the cropping pattern and land use favouring export crops yielded good dividends initially but it petered out subsequently on account of the world market glut and international price crash. The hike in power tariff rates and the squeeze on lower cost institutional credit following the economic reform policies, and the use of poor quality seeds and pesticides due to ignorance put the cotton farmers in Andhra Pradesh and Maharashtra in great distress. Unable to meet competitive and efficiency requirements, they plunged into a debt trap and many of them took suicide as the escape route. In Andhra Pradesh alone as many as 634 farmers were reported dead due to suicide during 1998-2002 (Patnaik, 2003), hats off the 'efficient market mechanism' and the incarnation of 'Cyberabad'. Thus market per se is not efficient and instead of ensuring food security can be a man-eater.

FISCAL COMPRESSION

Fiscal compression is another important constituent of the LPG-SAP model. In the name of containing fiscal deficit and on the basis of the seven decades old fallacious crowding out principle, public expenditure, especially those on rural development and infrastructure, was drastically cut. The latter was lowered to 7.8% of GDP by 1992 and has remained more or less at that level as yet. This has resulted in a sharp rise in the extent of rural poverty and a still sharper fall in the growth rate of rural employment. The rural poverty headcount ratio rose from 34.30% in 1989-90 to 44.90% in 1998 and the annual growth rate of rural employment dropped to the abysmally low 0.58% in the 1990s (Tables 10.1 & 10.2) causing reduced access to available food grains as reflected in the falling offtakes of food grains under the PDS (Table 10.5). Free market, therefore, limits people's access to food grains and can be a deterrent to food security.

TABLE 10.5
Procurement, Allocation & Offtake of Food-grains (Rice and Wheat Under the PDS)

(in Million Tones)

Year	*Procurement*	*Allocation*	*Offrake*
1991	19.60	21.92	19.00
1994-5	25.47	24.12	12.86
2000-1	35.45	28.65	11.72*

* Including Provision of Antyodaya.
Source : Economic Survey, 2001-2.

TARGETING PDS

A third aspect of the new regime relates to targeted PDS i.e, official emphasis on the poor with the ulterior motive of completely dismantling the PDS after some time in future. But such targeting can be an instrument of food and nutrition insecurity.

One important component of targeting has been reduction in food subsidy. Surprisingly, a policy measure aimed at reducing food subsidy has led to its increase from Rs. 7500 crores in 1997-8 to Rs. 12010 crores in 2000-1 (Table 10.6) and has been under attack from the Fund-Bank pundits and the ex-Fund-Bank personnel manned Finance Ministry in India. The increase in nominal food subsidy is not a matter of concern as it hardly accounts for 0.5% of our national income but benefits many million people (Patnaik, 2003). Further the increase in the nominal food subsidy is a misleading indicators in that the real consumer-end subsidy has lowered over time. This is because a large part of the subsidy is due to the intermediate costs of procurement, storage, buffer-stock operations, transport etc. Consequent

TABLE 10.6
Food Subsidy

(Rs. Crore)

Year	Food Subsidy	Buffer Stock Component
1997-8	7500	937
1998-9	8700	1552
1999-0	9200	1754
2000-1	12010	4233

Source : Economic Survey, 2001-2.

upon the rise in such costs the central issue prices of food grains have gone up sharply and even faster than the free market price and the minimum support prices/procurement prices (Table 10.7) exercising a negative effect on the buying capacity of the poor. Increase in the central issue Prices and the resultant narrowing/disappearance of the PDS-open market price differentials have only added to the problem. The consumers are being doubly affected by rising PDS prices, and a low food grain quality; and a poor delivery mechanism, so much so that even some poorer households do not like to utilize the PDS. The most important outcome of this system has been declining offtakes compared to allocation under the PDS (Table 10.5). Thus the nation is spending more to starve the poor.

TABLE 10.7
Minimum Support Price and Central Issue Price of Food-grains

(Rs./Quintal)

Year	Support Price		Issue Price	
	Wheat	Rice	Wheat	Rice
1991-2	275	230	280	377
1994-5	360	340	402	537
2000-1	610	510	BPL 415	565
			APL 830	1130

Source : Economic Survey, 2001-2.

Another component of the targeting exercise is the use of an absurd calculation mechanism to determine the food grains requirements for the PDS. The basis is an average of the actual offtakes from the Fair Price Shops in the preceding 10 years. Looking at the vast increases in population over time and the price hike-led falling offtakes one can well imagine the blatant irrationality of this principle of calculation. Obviously the inherent objective is to understate the requirement for the PDS. It is then no wonder that the public procurement and allocation of food grains from the central pool to the PDS has stagnated over the years during the 1990s (Table 10.5) affecting the entitlement of the poor. Thus targeting has misfired.

The reform linked targeting has affected the food security in a more serious way. Targeting in India is based on the fallacious exclusion principle i.e, excluding the non-poor form the PDS. But this principle has led to (i) large social costs and welfare losses on account of both Type-I or E – mistakes (inclusion of non-income-poor in the scheme) and Type-II or F – mistakes (omission of the income-poor from the scheme) and (ii) high administration and efficiency costs. Thus targeting has caused more people to consume less and led to a system of robbing 'Peter to pay Paul'.

A still more disturbing effect of targeting has been the immoral enormous growth in the central pool stocks of food grains in the 1990s. The volume of stocks is much in excess of the desired buffer norms (Table 10.8) and because of storage problems a good part of it is lying in the open and/or under the tarpaulins. Result is: first, rise in storage and management costs; second, irrationally low farm-gate prices, and third, poor quality of food grains. The government is spending heavily around Rs. 3000 million per day to stock the food grains of which around 25% is rotting. The FCI is refusing to buy from farmers citing lack of storage capacity, meeting its targets through purchase from the millers thereby helping recycling and putting the farmers at the mercy of the exploiting millers and the volatile market forces. Given the high cost of modern farm practices and the unprecedentedly low farm prices the farmers are unable to cover even the explicit costs and repay the debts. And since food grains are not properly stored, the first casualty is their quality. Thus targeting has led to overflowing godowns on the one hand and rising unemployment and widespread hunger, undernourishment and starvation deaths on the other.

CONCLUSION

The aforesaid analysis indicates that our food security is in jeopardy. We have both starvation and (pseudo) food surpluses simultaneously and worse still, such a paradoxical situation is the by-product of a set public policies which we call reforms. Unfortunately we have no subsidies for the common farmers some of whom are forced to suicide deaths but subsidies for a few big industrial tycoons who have been immorally allowed to rob the state exchequer under one pretext or the other without any commitment to nation building and we can afford tax concessions under different clauses to the microscopic minority well-to-do but cannot afford to feed the hungry millions. Thus, we are targeting the poor for starvation.

But we cannot let the people starve. To improve the food security system a people-centric three-tier food grains production and management system may be suggested.

The promotion of an organic method and high internal input-low external input based agricultural production system, and gearing the agricultural innovation-extension network to that end are key components of this strategy. These will raise productivity, lower costs and overcome frustration led suicides in the farm sector.

In view of the inadequacy of supply side policies, effective demand management mechanisms need to be pursued. Since cheaper and wider network based alternative institutional arrangements are not available, a dwindling PDS affects the poor. Hence the PDS needs to be genuinely reformed so as to improve the people's entitlement to food. Increasing public expenditure on rural development and infrastructure to at least 15% of GDP and measures to create gainful employment opportunities in the countryside through the implementation of a vigorous Food for Works Programme are sound policies to fight chronic hunger, deprivation and insecurity.

Our third suggestion is a three-tier food management system with establishment of (i) Community Grain Banks at the village level to protect producers' interests, economies on intermediate costs, provide culturally appropriate food grains to the consumers and locally produced food grains to run all public food related programmes like ICDS, ensure food security for the village and sell the surplus to Regional Grain Banks at fair prices; (ii) Regional Grain Banks at the state level to procure surplus food grains from the Community Grain Banks to provide for the use in state run public institutions like hospitals, canteens in government and semi-government establishments etc., ensure food security at the state level and sell the surplus to the National Grain Bank at approved prices; and (iii) National Grain Bank at the centre/apex to maintain the PDS, hold desired minimum stocks and export the genuine surpluses at fair prices.

The system is in peril and unless appropriate corrective public action is taken at the right earnest our avowed objective of establishing a socialistic pattern of society and ensuring food and nutrition security will remain "a mid summer night's dream".

References

Government of India. *Economic Survey*, 1999-2000, 2000-01, 2001-02, 2002-03.

Patnaik, Utsa (2003), "Global Captitalism, Deflation & Agrarian Crises in Developing Countries". *Journal of Agrarian Change*, Vol. 3, No. 1 & 2.

Swain, Mamata (2003), "Food Security System in Orissa—A Critical Review", *Asian Economic Review*, Vol.45 No.1.

Swaminathan, Madhura (1996), "Structural Adjustment, Food Security & System of Public Distribution of Food", *Economic & Political Weekly*, June 29.

CHAPTER

11

Gender Equity and Empowerment of Women in Orissa : Current Trends and Direction for Future Growth

RASHMI MISHRA

The Country's concern in safeguarding the rights and privileges of women found its best expression in the Constitution of India. The principle of gender equality is enshrined in the Indian Constitution in its Preamble, Fundamental Rights, Fundamental duties and Directive Principles. Giving special attention to the status of women, Article 14 confers equal rights and opportunities on men and women in the political, economic and social spheres. Article 15 (3) empowers the state to make affirmative discrimination in favour of women. There is a growing social awareness across the globe to attain gender equality and empowerment of women. Discrimination against women in the form of male-female differentiation constitutes the core of the gender-based system. Gender bias is generated by the process of extending the biological sex differences to the criteria of social placement. The rise in the levels of education which nourishes progressive outlook and the advent of industrialization and modernization have effected a sea change in the attitude and thinking patterns of the people. Consequently the idea that, women have to be treated at par with men in every aspect has gained momentum.

Empowerment is envisaged as an aid to help women to achieve equality with men or, at least, to reduce gender gap considerably. A deeper understanding of the word throws light on many of its dimensions and implications. The very concept of empowerment of women which is based on equality between sexes, is a long drawn, conscious and continuous process comprising enhancement of skills, capacity building, gaining self-confidence and meaningful participation in decision making. Nevertheless, it comprehensively seeks to ensure an equitable division of resources and carve a clear role for them in the decision-making. It helps them in articulating theirs as well as other rights and participates actively in the democratic processes. Empowerment also wards off retrogressive practices like female infanticide and gender based violence.

Discussion on empowerment warrants a glance at the state of Indian women in different spheres of life. According to Human Development Report (2001), India ranks 105 in gender related development index (GDI) and 95 in gender empowerment measures. Women literates constitute 44.5 per cent of the total literates. The percentage of women in government at ministerial level is 10.1 while the female economic activity is 42 per cent of the total economic activity. Despite considerable progress in the fields of health and nutrition, the maternity mortality rate is 410 per 1lakh births. The above statistics reveal a discouraging picture of women in the field of literacy and employment in the organised sector and also reflect on the inadequate awareness on health and hygiene.

The UN conference in Copenhagen, in the year 1980, stated that although women represent half of the world's population and one third income, they own less than 1 per cent of world's property. Women have only a very limited access to resources and control over income, credit, land, education, decision-making, training and information. The Government of India had ushered in the new millennium by declaring the year 2001 as women's empowerment year, to focus on "our vision in the new century of a nation where women are equal partners with men".

There has been a marked shift in the approach to women issues from welfare to development starting from the fifth five year plan (1974-78) onwards. In recent years, the empowerment of women has been recognized as the central issue in determining the status of women. Accordingly, the National Commission for Women was set up by an Act of Parliament in 1990 to safeguard the rights and legal entitlements of women. Similarly, the Orissa State Commission for Women is functioning in this direction since 1993. Still, there exists a wide gap between the goals stated in the constitution, legislation, policies, plans, programmes and related mechanisms on the one hand and the situational reality of the status of women in Orissa vis-a-vis India on the other.

However, a national policy for the empowerment of women has been framed by the Government of India in 2001 with the objective of bringing about the advancement, development and empowerment of women.

Against this backdrop, the present paper makes an attempt to analyse demographic, socio-economic and political situation of women in Orissa in terms of gender equity and empowerment of women. The paper further suggests some policy measures to ensure gender equity and empowerment of women.

STATUS OF WOMEN IN ORISSA

In the State of Orissa, out of the total population (367 lakh), women constitute nearly half of the population (49.29 per cent) as per 2001 census. The Development of women in Orissa is very slow owing to their poor socio-economic status, illiteracy, lack of awareness and self confidence.

WOMEN AND INFANT MORTALITY

Sex ratio (females per thousand males) is an important index of the long term status of women's welfare. India is one of the few countries where males significantly outnumber females and this imbalance has increased over time. According to 2001 census sex ratio of the country is 933. In Orissa the sex ratio has been declining sharply over the years (Table 11.1). Not only the female of Orissa are fewer to-day as compared to men but their number may even get lesser in coming years (Table 11.2) because the child sex ratio (0-6 years of age) is even more adverse to females (Bhat, 2002). It has declined from 995 in 1981 to 950 in 2001.

TABLE 11.1
Sex Ratio of Orissa and India (1901-2001)

Year	*Orissa*	*India*
1901	1037	972
1951	1022	946
1961	1001	941
1971	988	930
1981	981	934
1991	971	927
2001	972	933

Source : Census of India, 2001.

TABLE 11.2
Trends in Female Male Ratio at 0-6 Year Age during 1981-2001 for Selected States

	Female male ratio of age 0-6 years		
	1981	*2001*	*Change*
Orissa	995	950	-45
WB	981	963	-18
AP	992	964	-28
MP	977	940	-37
India	962	927	-35

Source : Census of India 1981 to 2001.

The falling of child sex ratio may be due to neglect of the girl child resulting in their higher mortality rate, female infanticide and sex selective female abortions. (Bose, 2001) A study (Yadav, 2001) points out that female foeticide is the main cause of this decline. The study indicates that not only the less developed states like Rajasthan, Bihar and Orissa experience female foeticide, the developed states like Punjab and Haryana also lead in female foeticide.

WOMEN AND EDUCATION

For the overall development of the country, educated, healthy, enlightened and empowered women are very much essential. An educated mother always provides light to her children. But gender disparity in the sphere of literacy is still there in rural and urban areas of the country. Nevertheless a movement to women's literacy has taken a concrete shape in Orissa.

The number of female illiterate has come down. The rate of growth of female literacy has outpaced that of male and the gaps between female and male illiterates and dropouts is narrowing down. In Orissa female literacy rates increased at a faster rate than male literacy rates for the decade (1991-2001) reaching a level of 75.95 for males and 50.97 for females (Table 11.3). The gap in male and female literacy stands at 24.98 per cent for total population. Government of India and State Government have ambitions, plans to reduce the gender gap in secondary and higher education during Tenth Plan Period (2002-2007). NGOs, experts and large number of volunteers were mobilized during the Total Literacy Campaign. The National Literacy Mission (NLM) Authority played a pivotal role in the campaign. The estimates of NLM reveal that over 60 per cent women participated in the programme. There are currently 29 Total Literacy Campaigns (TLC) and 12 Post Literacy Campaigns in the State compared to 450 Total Literacy Campaigns and 250 Post Literacy Campaigns in the Country.

TABLE 11.3
Literacy Rate

	1981			*1991*			*2001(p)*		
	Persons	*Male*	*Female*	*Persons*	*Male*	*Female*	*Persons*	*Male*	*Female*
India	43.56	56.37	29.75	52.11	63.86	39.42	65.38	75.85	54.16
Orissa	40.96	56.45	25.14	48.55	62.37	34.40	63.61	75.95	50.97

Source : Census of India, 2001.

In the state of Orissa, out of the target of 65.61 lakh people to be covered under TLC, 57.43 lakh have been enrolled, but the achievement level is as low as 26.63 lakh adults. This type of situation occurs because education is considered to be a waste, particularly in case of females due to the age old practices relating to household chores, customs and tradition.

WOMEN AND EMPLOYMENT

Water together with land is one of the major natural resources for livelihood and food security. Access to and control over land and water are sources of power and influence for women. Women contribute significantly to the economy, as they are pioneers in various professions. Women are working in different sectors of the economy as agriculture labourers, road construction workers, domestic helps, petty crafts women, self employed women besides doctors, engineers, lecturers and white collared executives. Employment of women is an index to their status in the society. Table 11.4 shows the rate of female work participation in public and private sectors. Proportion of women as percentage to total employment is 9.8 per cent in the year 1996. It has increased to 12.6 per cent in the year 2001. In the same year public sector provides employment to 91.84 thousand women compared to 9.91 thousand women employment provided by the private sector.

Participation of women in rural economy has increased in agricultural and allied activities. The development strategy aims at increasing the production, reducing poverty, inequality and unemployment and improving the quality of life, but in reality women have been the critical manifestation of adverse impact and growing imbalance (Beteille, 2001).

According to 2001 census, most female workers are involved in agriculture. They are agricultural labourers rather than cultivators. Apart from agriculture, women in rural areas are engaged in animal husbandry, weaning handicraft, tailoring, forestry, sericulture etc. Table 11.5 shows classification of female workers engaged in different sectors of the economy in the state of Orissa vis-à-vis other selected states as on June 2002. It shows that after a decade of economic reforms, three fifths of total workers of Orissa are employed in agriculture. There is more or less absence of new employment opportunities in industrial and other sectors in Orissa as well as in the country. Percentage share of female agricultural labourers to total female workers is 54.33 per cent in comparison to 17.99 in Punjab. Thus majority of the female workers derive their livelihood from agriculture and agriculture sector is over burdened. States like West Bengal and Punjab seem to have succeeded largely in diverting its workforce to non-agricultural activities.

In Orissa a substantial quantum of development funding is spent on employment generation in rural areas. It is envisaged that this fund shall be utilized by women's groups in developing productive infrastructure for them. Preference has been given to food for work that will help in improving the environment and resource base. Similarly labour laws that provide basic welfare support like crèche, drinking water facilities etc. are available at work sites. Though development policies and programmes have created a

TABLE 11.4

Employment of Women in Organized Sector in Orissa

Year	Total Population (in '000)	Total Women Population (in '000)	Employment of Women in Organized Sector														
			Central Govt		State Govt		Quasi Govt		Local Bodies		Total Public Sector		Private Sector		Total Employment		Proportion of women as (%) of total Employment
			Total Emp	Women Emp	Total Emp	Women Emp	Total Emp	Women Emp	Total Emp	Women Emp	Total Emp	Women Emp	Total Emp	Women Emp	Total Emp	Women Emp	
1996	34,568	17,030	81873	3311	3311	462198	212695	12189	18862	4611	775628	73149	96097	12379	871725	85528	9.81
1997	34,946	17,222	81728	3413	394480	58988	218528	12411	18235	4145	712971	78954	96607	10934	809578	89888	11.10
1998	35,304	17,400	81853	3535	399648	62154	212336	12548	18448	4000	712285	82237	99221	11039	811506	93276	11.49
1999	35,641	17,565	82804	4084	397909	56202	209526	18622	18593	4137	708832	83045	92717	10322	801549	93367	11.65
2000	35,956	17,717	79770	3753	403896	66511	207659	14546	19346	4025	710671	89015	86916	10002	797587	99017	12.41
2001	36,248	17,858	79390	3712	408505	71071	209977	12828	19289	4234	717161	91845	88778	9917	805939	101762	12.63

Source : Economic Survey 1996 to 2001, Government of Orissa.

TABLE 11.5
Classification of Female Workers Engaged in different Sectors in Selected States (Classification of Workers, Females in 000)

State	Total workers	Culti-vators	Agril laboures	H. hold Industry	Other Industry	% share in total workers			
						Culti-vators	Agril. labour	H. of Industries	Other industry
Orissa	4454	867	2420	379	788	19.47	54.33	8.51	17.69
W.B	7003	941	2269	1258	2535	13.44	32.40	17.96	36.20
A.P	13139	2616	7387	903	2233	19.91	56.22	6.87	17.00
Punjab	2118	276	379	149	1314	13.03	17.99	7.03	62.04

Source : The Economic Times, June 17, 2002.

positive impact on position of women in society, some major issues and problems are: (a) women are powerless and have less choice regarding their job (b) their contribution to the family economy and national economy remains largely invisible and undervalued and they have a low level of participation in decision making.

Further, high degree of illiteracy among rural women in the state like Orissa increases their involvement in household activities. It is a well known fact that household work consumes around half of their time and energy, which is unrecognized and unpaid. Rural women are mostly engaged in agricultural and allied activities including small farm agriculture, livestock, food processing, gathering, small trading and vending. Women have successfully diversified their off farm activities such as poultry farming, animal husbandry, bee keeping, tailoring, construction site, bidies rolling in factories and worksheds; providing services such as cleaning, washing etc. Agriculture sector is the largest women employer. More than 50 per cent of women are employed as wage labourers. Their earning capacity is further depressed as they are mostly involved in activities like sowing, weeding, hoeing, cutting of fodder as well as harvesting and processing etc, which are treated as normal functions involving a small profit. Recognizing the vital economic and social contribution of women, it is envisaged that women are to be integrated fully into development and for building a better life women should be active leaders than passive recipients.

WOMEN AND HEALTH

The question of women's health is intricately woven into the process of development of any nation. Greater health for women impacts positively on the health of other family members. Changes in the status of livelihood both in quality and quantity are visible significantly in Orissa viz., (a) birth rate which was 39 per thousand in 1968 has declined to 25.7 in 1998. Death rate which was 15.3 in 1968 has come down to 11.1 in 1998, (b) life expectancy at birth for female which was 49.5 during the period 1980 has gone up to 61 during 2001, (c) child marriage is no more in vogue, (d) infant mortality rate which stood at 149 in 1979 has declined to 98 in 1998, (e) programmes for increasing awareness through women's education, total literacy campaign, Mahila Samitis and ICDS have been undertaken, (f) the proportion of literates among females which was 4.5 in 1951 has increased to 50.97 as per 2001 census (provisional), (g) the male literacy percentage is 75.95 per cent, (h) Universal immunization programme is being implemented successfully and (i) incidence of severe malnutrition among 0-3 year children has reduced from 3.78 per cent in January 1998 to 2.65 per cent in September 1999.

Inspite of all these measures gender differentials in the matter of nutrition and healthcare especially in case of pregnant women and nursing mothers are still prominent. Antenatal care, safe deliveries with medical paramedical personnel and post-partum monitoring are the main factors behind safe motherhood. The proportion of pregnant women receiving antenatal care (at least twice) and those who have had deliveries under medical attention are highly correlated. Accordingly, Safe Mother hood Index (SMI) is constructed for each state by taking simple average of these two proportions, separately for rural and urban areas. For computing Health Care Supply Index (HCSI) the variables considered include : (a) per capita expenditure on health, supply of doctors, hospitals and beds, each as a ratio of population. These data are expressed as percentage of value of Kerala (taken as 100) in order to get the indices (Table 11.6). It presents two health

TABLE 11.6

Health Indicators

State	*SMIU 92*	*SMIR 92*	*SMIT 92*	*SMIU 98*	*SMIR 98*	*SMIT 98*	*HCSI 92*	*HCSI 98*
Madhya Pradesh	59	22	30	59	26	33	30	32
Bihar	50	17	21	50	18	20	30	22
Haryana	59	37	42	61	32	38	34	33
Uttar Pradesh	50	20	25	43	15	20	35	23
Orissa	55	28	32	67	44	46	37	35
Andhra Pradesh	80	50	58	87	63	69	43	52
Rajastan	40	15	19	55	23	30	43	40
Assam	61	22	26	61	22	26	48	44
Karnataka	76	52	59	85	58	66	53	57
West Bengal	72	43	50	87	56	62	57	47
Maharastra	79	48	60	86	55	.67	66	57
Tamil Nadu	93	69	78	95	84	88	66	63
Gujarat	72	45	53	78	54	63	73	76
Punjab	64	53	55	73	49	55	78	72
Kerala	96	91	92	99	95	96	100	100

Note : SMIU 92, SMIR92 and SMIT92 stand respectively for safe motherhood index for urban, rural and total for 1992; the next three columns referring to the same indices for 1998. The last two columns refer to health care supply index respectively for 1992 and 1998.

indicators so constructed for safe mother hood and health care supply. The first of these is relevant to maternal deaths and the second to health care in general. As per the ranking on HCSI in 1992, the leaders in this respect are Kerala, Punjab, Gujarat, Tamil Nadu. Kerala is an out standing one. M.P., Bihar, Haryana, UP and Orissa are laggards. Thus, regions/states with well developed health care facilities have also managed to bring down the levels of fertility and promote safe motherhood simultaneously Krishnaji and James, 2002. The results indicate that rural urban differentials in mortality are large and persistent and require health infrastructure development to bridge the gap in Orissa.

Nevertheless, human care plays a fundamental role in the development of human capabilities. Not only the physical and financial care are important for the well being of the entire society, but emotional care is also extremely a significant factor in social well being and development and sustenance of human capabilities. Women share a major responsibility of providing this service to the society and that too without any remuneration or recognition. As has been observed over the years, due to increase in expectation of life, the population of India is aging fast. It leads to the fact that there are more and more elderly people to be taken care of, inevitably by women. Women, whom our society has made primarily responsible for taking care of elderly, sick and children, are finding it more and more difficult to perform this conventional role because of their increasing participation in the work force.

WOMEN AND VIOLENCE

Gender related development indices like sex ratio, infant mortality rate, age at marriage, educational level, wage discrimination, unequal rights to property and socio-political life widen the inequality between man and woman. As a result of which women are subjected to harassment and exploitation.

The magnitude of violence against women in Orissa has risen significantly (44.5 per cent) during the period 1987-91 (National Commission for Women, 1994-95). Orissa has also recorded highest rate of rise in number of dowry deaths in the country. There has been an over all rise in magnitude of all types of crimes against women in Orissa in this period.

The crime head-wise incidence of reported cases from 1996-2000 along with percentage increase is presented in Table 11.7. It is observed that crimes against women in 2000 reported an increase of 21.75 per cent over the year 1996. The available data indicate an increasing trend in respect to all types of crimes against women excepting eve-teasing. Molestation has recorded the highest increase (29.66 per cent) followed by dowry homicide (26.55 per cent). On the other hand, dowry torture has an increase of 23.47 per cent in 2000 over the year 1996.

The major factors responsible for criminal violence against women both inside and outside the home are gender discrimination, patriarchal norms,

TABLE 11.7
Showing Reported Crimes against Women in Orissa

Sl. No.	*Type of Crime*	*Year* 1996	1997	1998	1999	2000	*% Increase*
1.	Rape	617 (15.79)	683 (16.51)	796 (17.04)	816 (17.16)	753 (15.83)	22.04
2.	Molestation	1281 (32.78)	1363 (32.94)	1418 (30.36)	1555 (32.98)	1661 (34.92)	29.66
3.	Kidnapping/ Abduction	325 (8.32)	398 (9.62)	421 (9.01)	429 (9.1)	358 (7.53)	10.15
4.	Eve-teasing	169 (0.43)	176 (4.25)	194 (4.15)	183 (3.88)	154 (3.24)	-(8.87)
5.	Dowry Homicide	354 (9.06)	324 (7.83)	387 (8.29)	382 (18.10)	448 (9.42)	26.55
6.	Dowry Suicide	37 (0.95)	54 (1.30)	55 (1.18)	30 (0.64)	41 (0.86)	10.81
7.	Dowry Torture	720 (18.42)	727 (17.57)	901 (19.29)	875 (18.58)	889 (18.69)	23.47
8.	Non-dowry Torture	405 (10.35)	413 (9.98)	499 (10.68)	445 (0.64)	452 (9.50)	11.60
	Total	3908 (100.00)	4138 (100.00)	4671 (100.00)	4715 (100.00)	4756 (100.00)	21.75

Note : Figure in parenthesis indicates percentage.
Source : Home Department, Government of Orissa, 2000.

erosion of human values, materialistic attitude, frustration and learned helplessness. Due to societal and family pressures, women are often forced to keep the violence private and hidden. Furthermore, women are not inclined to report these crimes due to public apathy and distrust in the enforcement machinery. Uncomfortable cross-questioning by the police, the judiciary and constant pressure from the heartless surrounding force convince the victim to succumb to these pressures and allow the culprit to get away (Mishra, 2001).

Government of Orissa has initiated several steps to combat violence against women. Sensitization of law enforcement personnel and policy makers is being carried through initiatives by the government and voluntary sectors. Special police cells and police stations managed by women have been set up for encouraging women to report cases of violence against them. Correctional administration system in police and jails extended by the State Government ensures that women under trials and convicted women are provided with opportunities for training/income generation so as to enable them to integrate into society on their release. The steps have been taken by the Government to set up supportive structures for women victims of violence e.g. short stay home at district level with medical provision, psychological and economic rehabilitation opportunities.

There are National Commission and State commission for women to safeguard constitutional and legal provisions for women. These are also looking into specific complaints of atrocities, denial of rights and harassment and exploitation of women with a view to taking remedial action and assisting and restoring their legitimate rights.

Domestic violence has traditionally been viewed as a private matter. Measures have been taken through media campaign for raising awareness of domestic violence as a public health issue and a violation of women's rights.

Government has been making concerted efforts to tackle this problem by strengthening the existing legislation and developing new institutional machinery to encourage women to report crimes against them. In spite of all these provisions crimes against women recur and there is struggle for gender justice. Women's organizations play a more constructive role in generating awareness and providing assistance to the victims. They are permitted to meet the victim in the rescue homes so that they can offer her the necessary help, guidance and reassurance.

WOMEN AND LAW

The Constitution of India not only granted equal rights and opportunities to men and women in the political, economic and social spheres, but also empowered the States to adopt measures to prevent discrimination. The Government has enacted several laws for providing equal status to women. The special social enactments to safeguard women are :

(a) The Family Courts Act, 1954, (b) The Special Marriage Act, 1954, (c) The Hindu Marriage Act, 1955, (d) The Hindu Succession Act, 1956,(e) Immoral Traffic (Prevention) Act, 1956, (f) The Maternity Benefit Act, 1961, (g) Dowry Prohibition Act, 1961, (h) The equal Remuneration Act, 1976, (i) The Child Marriage Restraint (Amendment) Act, 1979 (j) The Criminal law (Amendment) Act, 1983, (k) Commission of Sati (Prevention) Act, 1987, (l) Prevention of Atrocities Act, 1989.

The Hindu Marriage Act of 1955 codifies the law governing marriage and divorce. Under this Act, bigamy is made illegal. Under Hindu Succession Act women can claim property rights. Section 176 Cr. PC and Section 113-A and 113-B help in the investigation of dowry death and dowry related crimes. The Hindu Adoption and Maintenance Act provides for maintenance not only of wife but also for a widowed daughter-in-law, children and aged parents. The dowry prohibition Act, 1961 has banned the practice of dowry, means any property given or agreed to be given by the parents of a party to the marriage at marriage or before marriage or at any time after marriage in connection with marriage.

The legislature seems to have recognized the need for intervention in the private domain of families and introduced significant changes in the law relating to offences against wife, notable among them is section 498-A IPC, which provides opportunities to women of publicly stating that they are treated with cruelty within the four walls of their homes and section 376-A IPC dealing with forced sex with a wife who is divorced or separated. Government has requested judiciary to establish family courts at district level where adhoc judges will be appointed. There is complaint committee on sexual harassment of women at work place, which is operating at district level. Efforts have been made to include legal literacy as part of the high school and college curriculum. Legal advice cell has been set up at the state level to scrutinise legislations and the concomitants government rules with a view to identifying the gender bias in these and to suggest suitable modifications and prepare new legislation to enable women to attain genuine equality in the society.

WOMEN AND PANCHAYATI RAJ

Panchayat is empowered for monitoring of formal education like enrolment and drop-out rates especially for girl children, Scheduled Caste and Scheduled Tribe students. The main responsibility of the PRIs is to accelerate the pace of development and involve all people in this process so that the felt needs of the people and their development aspirations are fulfilled. Women participation in PRIs is essential for efficient, equitable and sustainable people-centred development. Before 73rd Constitution amendment came into force, Government of Orissa had incorporated some of its important provisions such as reservation for Women, Scheduled Caste and Scheduled Tribes in its existing Panchayat Raj Acts. Subsequently, the Orissa Panchayat Raj Acts were further amended in conformity with 1992 Constitutional Amendment. Elections to the Gram Panchayats and Panchayat Samitis in Orissa had been held before the Seventy Third Amendment came into force. Possibly, Orissa became the first state to introduce one-third reservation for women in Panchayati Raj Institutions.

In the Panchayat election held in 2002 in Orissa, it has been reported that out of total 1,01,206 PRI representatives women constitute 36214 in number (35.8%). Though in the State of Orissa there are women representatives of different categories in the Panchayat Raj Institutions as stated in Table 11.8, yet they are not treated on par with male members either by the members of the institutions or by the officials and felt that as they are women their views are not given weightage on many occasions.

Subordination of women in society acts as a structural constraint to their participation in political activities. This constraint operates more or less for all classes and communities of women. Prevalent culture which is very complicated and often decisions are taken behind the scene may be regarded as another constraint in this regard. (Bohra, 1997)

TABLE 11.8
Representation of Women in Panchayati Raj Institutions in Orissa

Sl. No.	Position	Total	General UR	SC	ST	BCC	Women				
							SCW	STW	BCCW	RW	Total
1.	Ward Member	87547	20353	7874	13885	14021	7056	9164	8665	6529	31414
2.	Sarapanch	6234	1287	480	1510	769	336	894	462	496	2188
3.	Panchayat Samiti Member	6227	1387	576	1030	1046	449	674	577	488	2188
4.	Panchayat Samiti Chairman	314	61	15	85	36	23	54	18	22	117
5.	Zilla Parishad Member	854	189	85	133	150	54	86	82	75	297
6.	Zilla Parishad President	30	08	02	06	04	02	04	02	02	10
	Total	101206	23285	9032	16649	16026	7920	10876	9806	7612	36214

UR = Unreserved; SC= Scheduled Castes; ST = Scheduled Tribes; BCC= Backward Class.
RW = Reserved Women
Source : State Election Commission, Orissa, BBSR, 2003.

One of the greatest hurdle in contesting elections for higher posts both at Gram Panchayat and Panchayat Samiti level is the over increasing expenditure of election. Thus, in our State women with lower socio economic capabilities can not bear such a burden and it is difficult for them to come forward for the election. It appears that election completely eliminates those women who are below the poverty line.

Since the reservation under Panchayati Raj for women is at present in the transitional phase, their participation in decision-making is poor and very often they depend upon other members for taking decisions. The male relatives of women representatives are sometimes taking active part in their official activities.

EMPOWERMENT OF WOMEN AND CHALLENGES

The economic empowerment includes employment generation poverty elimination, efforts to develop organizational and managerial skills, development of entrepreneurship and access to various socio-economic institutions which act as self sustaining and self protective weapons for women. Since women comprise majority of the population below the poverty line and are very often in situations of extreme poverty, poverty eradication programmes should be reoriented to address the needs and problems of such women. Although many women entered into workforce, the work they entered in most cases offered no possibility for economic advancement and upward mobility. Any woman who has a career and a family, automatically develops two personalities. She can achieve happiness only as long as she keeps the two in balance. Divorce, separation, desertation further compounded the economic plight suffered by many women. With the burgeoning women workforce there is a necessity to formulate certain constitutional guarantees for them so that they are not exploited. Thus economic empowerment is that conscious state of womanhood where she would find herself equipped to stand against all odds impinged upon her by the outer world (Soundari and Sudhi, 2003). Nevertheless employment of women proves crucial to the economy and society as they supplement to the family income.

Despite constitutional guarantees and penal enactments women are subjected to exploitation, alienation in the society. They suffer from gender discrimination at home and at the work place. Preference to boys for food and health care has been prevalent in most of the communities. Orissa has highest infant mortality rate (IMR) in the country, as well as an unacceptably high maternal mortality rate (MMR). Though strategies have been built up to improve the health status of women, yet there is a high prevalence of malnutrition among women.

Other inequalities include household inequality, economic and political inequality, social and educational inequality. While the literacy rate among the women in Orissa has increased from 34.40 per cent in 1991 to 50.57 per cent in 2001, the fact that nearly half of the female population are still illiterate is a matter of deep concern. The drop out rate among girls is far greater than boys.

Discrimination and denial of education to girls stand in the way of improving career and life chances for women. According to the Child Marriage Restraint Act, the minimum age for a girl to marry is 18 years. But in practice in many tribal regions it has been violated. Society is also subjected to various types of domestic violence. Recently as on 8 March 2002, a bill was introduced in Lok Sabha on the Protection of Domestic Violence Bill 2002 which seeks to provide that if any relative of the victim subjects her to habitual assault or makes her life miserable or causes injuries or harms her or forces her to lead an immoral life would constitute Domestic violence. The offence is punishable with imprisonment up to 1 year.

The Anti Dowry Act has not acted as a severe deterrent to prevent dowry deaths across the state vis-à-vis country. Giving and taking huge amounts of dowry is still widely accepted in many castes or families. In case of negative response brides are harassed, beaten, tortured and burnt in many instances. Government should come forward to push vigorously the measure to confer co-parcenary rights to property on women, which might also act as an effective deterrent to this social malice-dowry.

Representation of women in Panchayat Raj system a unique experiment which translates the idea of empowerment of women into reality. Women's entry into grassroots level democratic institution is a positive indicator of change in the socio-political dynamics of the rural society in Orissa There is low rate of participation of women in the decision making process compared to the male members in the state. Caste and political background are the important factors in influencing the entry of women into political field (PR update, Jan. 97).

POLICY AND DEVELOPMENT APPROACHES TO WOMEN IN ORISSA

- There has been a growing awareness among planners and policy makers to integrate women in the development process. The main hindrances in socio-economic development of women are illiteracy, poverty, lack of employment opportunity, resistance to change, prevalent caste system, political backwardness and lack of infrastructural facilities etc.
- To overcome these problems, an integrated and balanced development oriented policy may be adopted. Economic growth can be achieved by creation of employment opportunities by utilizing the available resources in that region.
- Provision of micro-credit assistance proved to enhance the social empowerment of women. It increases the outreach of credit and enhances the women's access to credit for consumption and production. The SHGs (Self Help Groups) are to be formed with Bank linkage programmes. SHGs need to directly address gender specific causes of poverty. Social empowerment of women assumes special significance which includes equal status, participation and power of decision making at the household level and also at the community and village level.
- In view of the critical role of women in agriculture and allied sectors as producers, concerted efforts are to be made to ensure that the benefits of training, extension and various programmes reach them in proportion to their number. The training programmes for women in soil conservation, social forestry, dairy development and other occupations allied to agriculture like horticultures, livestock including small animal husbandry, poultry fisheries etc shall have to be expanded to benefit women workers in agriculture.
- The important role played by women in electronics, information technologies and food processing and agro industry and textiles has been crucial to the development of these sectors. They should be given comprehensive support in terms of labour legislation, social security and other support services to participate in various

industrial sectors. Provision of support services for women like child care facilities including crèches at work place and educational institutions, homes for the aged and disabled have to be expanded and improved to create an environment to ensure their full co-operation in social, political and economic life.

- Equal access to education for women and girls may be ensured by eradicating illiteracy, creating a gender sensitive educational system, to increase the enrolment and retention rates of girls. There is a need for occupation, technical and vocational skill development of women. In areas where girls are not allowed to receive even primary education, stipends may be provided in order to encourage them to attend school.
- Women should have access to comprehensive, affordable and quality healthcare. In order to meet the problems of infant and maternal mortality, there should be strict implementation of Child Marriage Restrict Act and implementation of registration of birth and death. Registration of marriages may be made compulsory.
- In view of the high risk of malnutrition and disease that women fall at the different stages viz infancy and childhood, adolescent and reproductive phase, efforts may be made to meet the nutritional needs of women in all stages of life. Widespread use of nutrition education is required to address the intra-house imbalance in nutrition.
- Special attention may be given to the needs of the women in the provision of safe drinking water, sewage disposal, toilet facilities and sanitation within accessible reach of households especially in rural areas and urban slums. Special attention is to be given for providing adequate and safe housing and accommodation for women including single women, working women, students apprentice and trainees.
- More and more women are to be involved in spreading the use of solar energy, biogas, smokeless chulahs and other rural applications so as to have a visible impact of these measures in influencing ecosystem and changing the lifestyle of rural women. Efforts are to be made to motivate girls to take up science and technology for higher education. Thus, special skill development will be made suited to women's needs. Special assistance maybe provided to the disadvantageous groups like women in extreme poverty, destitute women, women in conflict situations, women affected by natural calamites, women in less developed regions, the disabled women, single women in difficult circumstances those displaced from employment, migrants and women who are victims of marital violence, deserted women and prostitutes etc.
- A change in sex-role is necessary and a confidence may be built up into the minds of the women to recognize their identity. Change in

social attitude towards women is required for equitable distribution of resources and for empowering them. It can instill a healthy sense of dignity in women and enable them to lead an honorable life.

REFERENCES

Beteille, A. (2001), "Equity and Universality", *Economic and Political Weekly*, Vol. 36 (38), pp. 3619-25.

Bhat, P.N.M. (2002), " On the Trail of Missing Indian Females, *Economic and Political Weekly*, Dec. 21-27, pp. 50 05-18.

Bohra, O.P. (1997), "Women in Decentralised Democracy", *Journal of Rural Development*, Vol. 16 (4), pp. 673-83.

Bose, Ashish (2001), "India's Billion Plus People, 2001 Census Highlights, Methodology and Media coverage", B.R publishing Corporation, Delhi.

Govt. of Orissa, (2001), *Draft Report*, Women and Child Welfare Department.

Institute of Social Sciences (1997), Panchayati Raj Update, January.

Krishnaji, N. and K.S. James (2002), "Gender Differentials in Adult Mortality", *Economic and Political Weekly*, Vol. 37 (46), pp. 4633-37.

Mishra, R (2001), "Violation of Human Rights : A Study on Violence against Women in Orissa", Proceedings of the Seminar on Marginalized Women : A Human Right Perspectives, School of Women Studies, Utkal University, Bhubaneswar.

National Commission for Women (1995), "A Situational Analysis of violence against women in Orissa", New Delhi.

Soundari, S.M.H and M.A. Sudhi (2003), " Gender Disparity in Tamil Nadu", *Social Welfare*, Vol. 49 (12), pp. 24-27.

The Economic Times, (2002), June 17, 2002.

Yadav, B (2001), "Haryana's Setting Daughters", *Economic and Political Weekly*, Vol. 36 (45), pp. 4257-59.

SECTION II

Economic Reforms and its Impact on Indian Economy

CHAPTER

12

Regional Inequality and Growth During the Time of Reforms

SMRITI MUKHERJEE

Uneven development as between the different regions of a country has always been a subject matter of investigation by the economists. Ever since the theory of unbalanced growth was offered a strong theoretical basis was given in support of regional inequality. Given the limited nature of resources at its command a country could not develop different sectors of the economy at the same pace. There was a question of choice and this choice was mostly exercised in terms of national priorities. Social overheads were left at the care of public sector so that future growth might not suffer due to lack of infrastructure. Regions that benefited from such large projects experienced a boost in income and employment generation. Regions where industrial expansion was left at the hands of private sector also developed depending upon the scope for earning profits.

Quite apart from the public and private sector participation in development there were other factors that helped explain the variation in regional growth pattern. One is said to be the initial level of per capita income. When a region starts with a higher level of per capita income it has some comparative advantage and it becomes easier to attract investors on the basis of better infrastructure facilities. If this logic is correct the regions with higher per capita income will continue to grow at a higher rate and the relative position in income distribution will remain the same. There is, however, an alternative view which says that growth tends to be faster in regions with lower initial base. According to this view a tendency towards convergence over time is the most likely thing to happen across the regions.

More well of regions will find it increasingly difficult to maintain the same pace over time as a result of which other regions will come into prominence and ranking order of regions will change. The gap between the rich and the poor states will be narrowed down in an automatic manner and given sufficient time convergence to a steady state income level is quite possible.

Another factor that is mentioned frequently in more recent studies happens to be political in nature. Thus the type of government in a country, whether it is federal or unitary has something to do with the pattern of development. In the case of a unitary government decisions at the regional level lose validity and the entire country is treated as a unit. Chances of regional divergence in growth due to inappropriate policies pursued by the sub-national governments are minimum in a unitary type of government. Policy frictions on account of different ruling parties at the centre and the states can be avoided in a unitary set up and hence growth can be expected to be faster.

The paper is organised as follows. Section one discusses some of the measures generally used to highlight regional inequality. Section two presents the results as applied to different Indian states. Sections three and four examine the two hypotheses relating to convergence and different political parties ruling at the centre and the states. Lastly we present the conclusion.

I

MEASURES OF REGIONAL INEQUALITY

Maximum to Minimum Ratio

The simplest measure one can think of in relation to regional inequality is a variant of range in measures of dispersion. Here one calculates the ratio of lowest and highest per capita state domestic product during the initial and final period. A fall in the ratio over the two time periods would indicate a movement towards greater inequality. Although a very crude measure, it is handy and gives a rough idea about region wise income distribution.

Coefficient of Variation

Let y_I denote the per capita income of states and $\overline{y}$ be the average per capita income of the states. $\overline{Y}$ may not be equal to the national per capita income in case all the states are not included. In that case average of the per capita incomes of states selected in the study is to be calculated. $\sqrt{\Sigma (y_i - \overline{y})^2/N}$ gives the required measure where N represents the number of states. To standardise the result it is divided by $\overline{y}$ and that serves as a useful measure of the gap that exists between units. If there is no inter state variation in per capita income the value will be equivalent to zero. The further one moves away from zero the greater is the regional inequality. There is some criticism against the measure because it does not take into account the difference in population figures which is quite important. A state with a very high per capita income may have very small population and hence the deviation from the states' average income may give a misleading picture. To correct for the deficiency relative share of each state in national population is included. The revised measure is given by $\sqrt{\Sigma (y_i - \bar{y})^2/P_i/P}$. The result is again divided by $\bar{y}$ to ensure the presence of a scaling factor.

Relative mean Deviation

Both the versions of coefficient of variation that have been reproduced suffer from one limitation. Because they deal with sum of the squared deviations actual differences may be magnified. To eliminate this weakness instead of squaring the deviations one can take the modulus of the difference between state income and average income of the group and then obtain the total. It is given by $\Sigma|y_i - \bar{y}|P_i/P.1/\bar{Y}$.

Theil Index

Another measure of inequality tried in this paper is better known as Theil Index. It is given by

$T = \Sigma x_i \log(x_i/p_I)$ where x_i is GDP share of region I and p_I is population share of region i. If regional income and population shares are identical the second term on the right hand side will be equal to zero reducing the entire measure to be zero.

II

The result of our calculations are given below.

TABLE 12.1
Regional Disparities in India

Measures	*1990-91*	*1999-2000*
Maximum minimum ratio	3.8344	7.3241
Simple coefficient of variation	0.3473	0.5231
Weighted coefficient of variation	0.2924	0.3430
Relative mean deviation	0.2618	0.2746
Theil Index	0.0053	0.0118

All the measures of disparity within a union that have been tried point towards the same conclusion namely increase in the degree of inequality during the reform period. Inequality measures for the year 1999-2000 included four states less than in the year 1990-91 because data were not available. While it is true that state level reforms have not been uniform and hence relative share of different states in national income has not maintained the same trend the question is whether the observed increase in inequality is solely due to reforms. If it can be shown that states with lower level of per capita SDP at the base year continued to have lower growth rates as well then India represents a case of anti convergence. Poor states continue to remain poor or grow to be poorer while rich states vie for higher rankings. Some attempts to measure that association are discussed below.

III

TRENDS IN REGIONAL DISPARITY

With a view to ascertaining the trend in regional inequality all the five measures that have been mentioned above were calculated for each of the years between 1990-91 and 2000-01. The results are reported in the following table.

TABLE 12.2
Trends in Regional Inequality

	1990-91	*1991-92*	*1992-93*	*1993-94*	*1994-95*	*1995-96*	*1996-97*	*1997-98*	*1998-99*	*1999-2000*	*2000-01*
L/H	.2608	.2119	.1943	.1950	.1873	.1618	.1514	.1229	.1112	.1078	.1132
Cvu	.3348	.3881	.3919	.4132	.4134	.4211	.4701	.4731	.5093	.4808	.5003
CVw	.2648	.3075	.3280	.3497	.3498	.3641	.4818	.3953	.3643	.3549	.4664
THEIL	.0053	.1518	.1187	.1846	.1466	.1034	.7170	.7246	24.3043	.7909	.7991
RW	.2048	.2205	.2448	.2638	.2638	.2679	.3694	.3067	.2617	.2509	.2048

The first measure which is simply the ratio of states with the highest and lowest per capita incomes in a given year proves in a conclusive manner the growth in regional inequality. Without any break the L/H ratio goes on declining over the years. The state with the lowest per capita income has remained the same in the process, it being Bihar. Up to 1995-96 Delhi happened to be the state with the highest per capita income but since 1996-97 the place has been taken over by Goa. Growth rate of per capita SDP being higher than in the case of Delhi, the gap in regional income distribution has continued to widen. The unweighted coefficients of variation also tell the same story. Disparity in regional income has continued to grow during the reform period. While interpreting these results too much credence should not be given to the measures because size of the state as given by population is not taken into account. The fact that Delhi or Goa commanded the highest per capita SDP does not mean much because population base was rather small. Population weighted coefficient of variation CV_w throws some interesting light on the question of regional inequality. Between 1990-91 and 1996-97 it goes on increasing but then it starts coming down in a consistent manner. Relative mean deviation also supports the same conclusion. Inequality value reaches the peak in the year 1996-97 and thereafter a slump takes over. It declines persistently up to 2000-01. These two population weighted measures make it clear that reform period does not reveal a uniform tendency as far as regional inequality is concerned. The first half of reform is characterised by increasing divergence whereas the later period reveals a tendency towards greater equality. The Theil index however comes out with the opposite result. It shows that after declining somewhat between 1993-94 and 1995-96 it is increasing sharply in the more recent period. The states that enjoyed higher per capita incomes are doing still better and middle level ones are losing in their ranking. Therefore, if Theil index results are taken to be the most reliable ones the conclusion is greater divergence during the reform period as between the different states. Of the five measures discussed here only two support the hypothesis of convergence involving Indian states. The other three hold that bridging the internal gap is a serious policy challenge.

IV

REGIONAL IMBALANCE—A VIEW ACROSS THE STATES

In an analysis of regional inequality it is quite interesting to find out whether degree of industrialization plays any part in the observed inequality across the states. In a given country some states may be more advanced industrially compared to others and the share they are enjoying in the country's industrial map is quite important. A state showing regional inequality higher than the national average can have higher ranking in connection with industrialization. Industries are not necessarily evenly distributed across the state and concentration in a few areas leads to greater amount of specialization. Concentration and consequent specialization guarantee higher growth rate in industrial sector and regional balance probably takes a backseat. The opposite case is not difficult to come by where more or less all the regions are equally developed leading to higher rate of development and lesser inequality also. This is more likely the case with planned development and state sponsored industrialization. A balanced view of industrial development can lead to this kind of result.

The case of industrially lagging states is no less interesting. A state can occupy a middle rank in industrialization with pronounced regional inequality. One or two areas may contain all the industries which ensure the middle level rank and produce higher level of inequality at the same time. Areas where old industries have lost in prominence and new ones are not coming up typically present such a picture. Old established industries although decaying still ensure a fair share of factory employment and that accounts for a satisfactory rank in industrialization. Industrialization started with private initiative is more prone to market forces where diminished rate of return leads to fall in employment and output. Competition from other states may also be a factor to reckon with. Excessive dependence on certain industries and that also in a few selected regions are more likely to produce sharp regional gaps.

In order to see whether industrially advanced states in India are showing greater degree of inequality we selected three states namely Maharashtra, Gujarat and Tamil Nadu and calculated the three measures of inequality as given by unweighted coefficient of variation, coefficient of variation weighted by share in population and relative mean deviation. No trend analysis in regional inequality could be undertaken and these measures were calculated for a two year period between 1993-94 and 1994-95. The results showed that unweighted coefficient of variation (CV_U) was lower than the national average in the case of Maharashtra. The other two measures employed by us namely CV_w and R_w gave values much higher than that obtained for India as a whole. For Gujarat and Tamil Nadu however all the measures came out with values lower than the national average.

The hypothesis that we were trying to test ie whether higher industrial prominence is associated with greater degree of regional imbalance came out to be inconclusive. The results obtained for Gujarat and Tamil Nadu clearly went against the hypothesis while two of the three measures supported the presence of higher regional imbalance in the case of Maharashtra. Maharashtra being the most important state in India industrially the result could not be ignored and that is why the test was treated as being one of inconclusive proof. To establish a decisive relation between the two variables one ought to have a bigger sample size.

Next in order to see what happens in the case of an industrially backward state we picked Orissa and calculated the same three measures of regional imbalance for the same set of years. Again the result was inconclusive. The first measure CV_U showed that regional imbalance was less than in the case of the rest of India but the other two measures pointed to the contrary evidence; regional imbalance proved to be much higher than the national average. Collecting all the evidence regarding association between industrial development and regional inequality we come to the view that it is difficult to say anything conclusive in this regard in the case of India. Inequality in regional development occurs in a random manner irrespective of the fact that the state is industrially more or less developed. The determining factors of industrialization like investment, infrastructure facilities, easy availability of credit, proper investment climate etc. probably affect states in India in an equitable manner. Presence of any policy favouring particular regions in a persistent manner seems difficult to prove.

V

CONVERGENCE ACROSS THE STATES

In studies of regional growth β convergence seems to be a popular hypothesis to test. According to neo classical growth theory there is an inverse relationship between growth rate of per capita output or income and the starting level of these variables. If two economies are same in regard to consumer taste and technology the poorer economy tends to grow faster compared to the rich one. The underlying idea behind this result is that per capita output is supposed to be a function of capital per unit of effective labour ie $y_I = f(k_I)$. There is also supposed to be a steady state value of per capita availability of capital. Let that be given by $\overline{k}$. It is common knowledge that if an economy starts with a per capita capital availability that is below the steady state level it will tend towards that value given sufficient time. The other economy where capital per unit of effective labour is near to the steady state level or above it capital availability as well as output per head will decline in a monotonic fashion. This gives rise to the hypothesis of convergence of per capita output across the states. This hypothesis is in conformity with endogenous theory of growth where rate of technological progress is faster in economies with lower level of income per head. The hypothesis has been tested in inter country models also which try to find out the impact of globalization on convergence.

With a view to ascertaining if any long run tendency towards convergence in state per capita income is present in the case of India we started with a basic regression equation where log of current and initial income is sought to be explained with reference to log of initial income. Thus $\log (y_{it}/y_{I0}) = \alpha + \beta \log (y_{I0})$ where the quantity on the LHS stands for growth rate of per capita income and log y_{I0} signifies log of initial per capita income. In the case any convergence is taking place b will come out with a negative sign. Per capita state domestic product were collected for two years 1990-91 and 2000-01 and then the log of this ration was obtained. The ratio thus obtained was regressed on the log of per capita state income as it occurred in the year 1990-91. Altogether twenty eight states were covered in this convergence test. The result of the regression was as follows :

$$\text{Log } (y_{it}/y_{i0}) = -1.0520 + .4115 \log(y_{i0})$$

The result shows that there is no tendency towards convergence across the states in India as far as per capita income growth is concerned. The lack of a clear and substantial negative regression coefficient may imply two things: agricultural states have lower per capita incomes and at the same time capital base is also weak. Technological innovations taking place in one state do not reach easily to other states as a result of which the question of bridging the gap among the states remains a difficult issue. The linkage between the states is not very high which is a precondition for technological transmission. The second factor one can mention in this connection is rather abstract. Suppose the basic assumption that neo-classical theory makes about a constant steady state value of per capita income or capital is not valid. There is no such constant value toward which per capita income is tending and therefore the question of faster adjustment to reach that value does not arise. The pace of technological progress is not the same across the states so that the poor states need more time to come up to a given level.

Whatever be the real reason behind lack of convergence the fact stands out that states in India are not veering round a steady state value.

CONCLUSION

The study undertaken by us was mainly to highlight the trend in regional inequality during the reform period the results of which have already been reported in the text. The time period chosen was 1990-91–2000-01 and altogether twenty eight states were covered. Regional inequality was measured with the help of selected statistical tools without depending much on economic indicators. The results make it clear that in the two years namely 1996-97 and 1999-2000 there were some drop in inequality measures although the overall trend suggested was that of persistent increase. Notwithstanding the statistical results we carried out another test as well just in order to confirm whether any hidden tendency towards convergence was at work. Accordingly β coefficient was found out which indicated the lack of any convergence across the states.

These two findings were important enough to demand comments on our part. As regards growing inequality among the states one can point out the lack of interregional or zonal investment policies and free factor movements across the states. In a federal set up a particular state government may not be encouraging the idea of free movement of labour from other states. Unfriendly attitude towards outside labour implies fall in capital movement also. Ideological stance of sub-national governments may sometimes unnerve investors forcing them to seek greener pastures.

As to the issue of lack of convergence among the states we can point out that our study is no exception. Other studies in the field Raja Shankar (2001), Aiyer (2001) come out with the same conclusion. Some explanation for the lack of convergence has been offered in an earlier section. Here we can mention that India does not fulfil the neo classical assumption of 'other things being equal' as between the states. Population density, literacy rate, appropriate infrastructure etc., differ widely among the states as a result of which β coefficient test so popular in the western countries loses its applicability. May be there is no absolute steady state value in per capita income when parameters differ so widely as between the constituents. If India is to give serious thought to regional inequality then more micro level planning might be necessary. A higher growth rate for the country in aggregate may not mean that it will automatically percolate in an even manner among all the states.

REFERENCES

Aiyer, S. (2001), Growth Theory and Convergence Across Indian States: A Panel Study in Callen, Reynolds and Towe (ed) India at the Crossroads, IMF, 2001.

Barro, R.J. and Sala-i-Martin (1992), Convergence, *JPE*, Vol.100, No. 21.

Cashin, P. and N. Loayza (1995), Paradise Lost? *IMF Staff Papers*. Vol. 42, No. 3.

Das, S. and A. Barua. (1990), Regional Inequalities, Economic Growth and Liberalisation: A Study of the Indian Economy. *The Journal of Development Studies*, London.

Debroy and Bhandari (2003), Ranking of the States, *India Today*, May 19.

Dev, S. Mahendra (2000), Economic Reforms, Poverty, Income Distribution and Employment. *EPW*, March 4.

Ghuman, B.S. and Dhian Kaur, (1993), Regional Variations in Growth and Inequality in the Living Standard: The Indian Experience. *Margin*, Vol.25, No.3, (April-June).

Jha, R. (2000), Growth, Inequality and Poverty in India—Spatial and Temporal Characteristics, *EPW*, March 11.

Rao, M. Govinda, Shand, R. T. and Kalirajan, K.P. (1999), Convergence of Income across Indian States, *EPW*, March 27.

Shankar Raja and A. Shah. (2001), Bridging the Economic Divide Within Nations, *Policy Research Working Paper 2717*, World Bank, November.

Williamson, J.G.(1965), Regional Inequality and Process of National Development: A Description of the Patterns, *Economic Development and Cultural Change*, Vol.xiii, No. 4, (July).

APPENDIX 12.1
Per Capita Net State Domestic Product (at current prices) (in Rs.)

	1990-91	*1991-92*	*1992-93*	*1993-94*	*1994-95*	*1995-96*	*1996-97*	*1997-98*	*1998-99*	*1999-2000*	*2000-01*
Andhra	4816	5556	5748	7006	8145	9274	11224	11683	13993	14878	16373
Arunachal	5231	6524	7514	8853	9417	11303	10871	11723	13129	13352	14587
Assam	4432	4683	4973	5520	6017	6624	7394	7966	8826	9720	10198
Bihar	2966	2903	2998	3417	3737	3533	4001	4014	4474	4813	5108
Delhi	11373	13697	15429	17522	19954	21830	25719	30537	33870	36515	38864
Goa	8952	10693	12800	15332	16703	20141	26418	32647	40248	44613	45106
Gujarat	6343	6256	8235	9054	11810	12914	16153	16536	18815	18685	19228
Haryana	7721	8775	9037	10526	12283	13573	16707	17749	19716	21551	23742
H.P.	5243	5691	6390	6896	7846	8747	11960	13488	16144	17786	18920
J&K	4624	3755	4457	5400	5860	6231	8667	9491	11591	12373	12399
Karnataka	4975	5888	6321	7242	8504	9359	11670	12566	15420	16654	18041
Kerala	5110	5140	5768	6524	7578	9004	13050	14231	16029	17709	19463
M.P.	4798	4257	4544	5516	6034	6775	8819	9455	10682	11626	10803
Maharashtra	7612	8170	10080	12010	13368	15770	17619	18954	20356	22604	23726
Manipur	3912	4653	5623	5929	6542	6914	7961	9039	10504	12721	12823
Meghalaya	4944	4891	5272	5934	6402	7862	8785	9668	11090	12083	13114
Mizoram	4856	4474	6599	7517	7743	9570	142210	12393	13479	14909	N.A.
Nagaland	5893	6166	6273	7730	8550	9758	11805	13052	12408	12594	N.A.
Orissa	3166	3907	4114	4662	5369	.6236	6401	7831	8324	8733	8547
Punjab	8177	9872	11140	12934	14534	16053	17353	18762	21184	23254	25048
Rajasthan	4883	4497	5197	5315	6951	7523	10102	10997	12348	13046	11986
Sikkim	5213	5728	5722	7679	8869	9472	9901	11324	13158	14751	15550
Tamil Nadu	5541	5796	6880	8051	9353	10223	13327	15404	17613	18623	19889
Tripura	4240	3688	3773	4252	4366	5083	8109	9658	11012	13195	14348
U.P.	3937	4069	4335	4794	5339	5872	7501	7779	8633	9323	9721
W.B.	5072	5298	5541	6247	7436	8491	9857	11682	13641	14894	16072
A&N Islands	9729	5927	6277	8729	10476	10911	21017	22855	20450	19777	N.A.
Pondicherry	7657	7932	7584	8537	10489	11512	18677	25806	28761	29348	31358

APPENDIX 12.2
Net State Domestic Product (at current prices)

	1990-91	*1991-92*	*1992-93*	*1993-94*	*1994-95*	*1995-96*	*1996-97*	*1997-98*	*1998-99*	*1999-2000*	*2000-01*
Andhra	30624	37344	39337	48785	57687	66786	81517	85791	103915	11753	12443
Arunachal	446	572	676	815	889	1093	1078	1192	1369	1427	1591
Assam	9775	10632	11543	13095	14580	16385	18465	20211	22710	25333	26891
Bihar	24940	25399	36820	31250	34912	33705	29449	30307	34680	38326	41825
Delhi	10660	13170	15364	18071	21312	24147	30148	37169	42785	47846	52793
Goa	1086	1265	1544	1887	2096	2577	3323	4166	5212	5862	6022
Gujarat	26133	26124	35018	39190	52013	57861	74183	77037	88932	89606	93601
Haryana	12644	14639	15416	18347	21863	24652	31345	33910	38288	42488	47474
H.P.	2795	2975	3411	3744	4340	4931	6803	7807	9507	10657	11536
J&K	3622	3935	3565	4416	4901	5329	7851	8858	11128	12182	12423
Karnataka	22394	26736	29162	33924	40427	45133	58071	63414	78874	86296	94635
Kerala	14747	15102	17175	19688	23176	27909	40699	44883	51061	56926	63094
M.P.	31602	27849	31070	38500	42901	49118	48593	53136	61099	67778	64063
Maharashtra	59325	65230	82076	99729	113197	136119	156687	171969	188331	213151	227893
Manipur	714	866	957	1156	1306	1412	1671	1941	2308	2858	2945
Meghalaya	884	884	979	1133	1258	1590	1900	2170	2580	2904	3230
Mizoram	336	417	478	562	597	761	983	1022	1139	1288	N.A.
Nagaland	693	762	811	1045	1209	1442	1849	2137	2184	2330	N.A.
Orissa	9901	12505	184416	15481	18156	21463	22189	27437	29458	31195	30795
Punjab	16452	20245	23280	27547	31543	35504	39112	43096	49588	55470	60890
Rajasthan	21459	20044	2671	24727	33011	36442	50986	56912	65535	71020	66949
Sikkim	214	237	243	335	404	446	491	583	702	758	827
Tamil Nadu	30966	32563	37922	46152	54131	59718	79460	92788	107123	114309	123140
Tripura	1193	1030	107	1244	1307	1557	2500	3015	3473	4193	4580
U.P.	55122	57206	62056	69846	79135	88511	112861	119346	135262	149352	159408
W.B.	34290	36433	38768	44460	53819	62462	74422	89595	106170	117507	128387
A&N Islands	268	176	193	279	346	374	720	813	754	753	N.A.
Pondicherry	608	648	649	727	911	1020	1675	2358	2677	2783	3030

Appendix 12.3
Convergence Variables

	$log (y_{ti}/y_{to})$	$log (y_{io})$
Andhra Pradesh	0.5314	3.6827
Arunachal Pradesh	0.4454	3.7186
Assam	0.3619	3.6466
Bihar	0.2361	3.4722
Delhi	0.5337	4.0558
Goa	0.7023	3.9519
Gujarat	0.4816	3.8023
Haryana	0.4878	3.8877
H.P.	0.5573	3.7196
J&K	0.4283	3.6650
Karnataka	0.5595	3.6968
Kerala	0.5808	3.7084
M.P.	0.3525	3.6810
Maharashtra	0.4937	3.8815
Manipur	0.5156	3.5924
Meghalaya	0.4236	3.6941
Mizoram	N.A.	N.A.
Nagaland	N.A.	N.A.
Orissa	0.4313	3.5005
Punjab	0.4862	3.9126
Sikkim	0.3900	3.6887
Tamil Nadu	0.4746	3.7171
Tripura	0.5500	3.7436
U.P.	0.5294	3.6273
W.B.	0.3925	3.5951
A&N Islands	0.5009	3.7052
Pondicherry	N.A.	N.A.
All-India	0.6123	3.8840

CHAPTER

13

Why State Level Fiscal Reforms are Necessary?

P.K. BHARGAVA

SUMMARY

The object of this paper is to clearly highlight as to why fiscal reforms at the state level are necessary. In this context, the inadequacy of the existing sources of revenue of the state Governments and at the same increasing dependence of the states on loan finance is clearly revealed. In consequence, the increasing expenditure of the state Governments towards interest payments and the growth in their debt repayments and liabilities becomes self-evident. Attention has also been drawn towards the associated problem of growing revenue and fiscal deficits of the State Governments.

The paper also refers to the initiatives taken by the Central Government to improve the fiscal health of the States. However, the more important aspect of the entire story is that the State Governments themselves have to take steps to ameliorate their condition and strengthen their fiscal situation in the broader national interest.

WHY STATE LEVEL FISCAL REFORMS ARE NECESSARY?

During the last decade, the Indian economy has witnessed a number of changes in the field of economic policy. The various economic reform measures have been undertaken by the Central Government. However, in a federal system, the states are expected to play an increasingly important role. As the States enjoy independence and autonomy in their functions and resources assigned to them under the Constitution, it is desirable that their role and performance should be complementary and supplementary to the efforts of the Centre. Hence, to accelerate the process/programme of second-generation economic reforms, co-operation from the States is not only desirable but extremely essential. The state-level fiscal reforms, therefore, are of extreme relevance in our federal fiscal system and the future of public sector finances, to a large extent, in this country will depend upon as to whether the states are willing to co-operate and undertake the various fiscal reform measures, as expected of them.

The division of functions between the Centre and the states under the Indian Constitution is such that the States are required to perform a number of functions that are expanding and expensive in nature. Table 13.1 shows that total expenditure of the State Governments during the period 1991-92 to 2000-01 (Budget) became three times. While the expenditure on revenue account increased a little faster. Further, the Table also shows that the proportion of non-development expenditure in the revenue account expenditure continue to increase: non-development expenditure constituted 30.9 per cent of the expenditure on revenue account in the year 1991-92 and this percentage increased to 42.5 in 2000-01 (Budget). Another significant feature of the expenditure pattern of the State Governments has been a sharp increase in interest payments during a span of ten years (1991-92 to 2000-01 Budget), interest payments have witnessed almost five fold increase, from Rs. 10,944 crores to Rs. 54,271 crores. Interest payments by the State Governments that constituted 12.7 per cent of the expenditure on revenue account in 1991-92 have gone up to 18.7 per cent in 2000-01 (Budget). Similar is the situation with regards to expenditure on administrative services and pensions. During the period 1991-92 to 2000-01 (Budget), such expenditure became more than 4 times from Rs.11,526 crores to Rs.53,139 crores. Expenditure on administrative services and pensions constituted 13.4 per cent of the expenditure on revenue account in 1991-92 that increased to 18.3 per cent in 2000-01 (Budget). Such a situation in state finances is indicative of the fact that the State Governments have increasingly depended on 'loan finance' and at the same time it also shows the increasing inadequacy that exists in the receipts on revenue account. Rapidly increasingly expenditure on administrative services including pensions, specially from the year 1995-96, is clearly explained by the rapid increase in the salary and allowances of the employees on account of the implementation of the recommendations of the Fifth Central Pay Commission. The Economic Survey 1998-99 in this context rightly observed, "The implementation of the Fifth Central Pay Commission recommendations at the Centre also provided a benchmark for pay revisions at the State Level. This has led to a substantial increase in their salary and pensions outgo thereby adversely affecting the fiscal health" (page 23).

The situation regarding growth in revenue receipts of the State Governments for the decade 1991-92 to 2000-01 is shown in Table 13.2. Revenue from state taxes as a percentage of the GDP continued to be

Table 13.1
Selected Financial Indicators of State Governments

(Rs. Crore)

	1991-92	1992-93	1993-94	1994-95	1995-96	1996-97	1997-98	1998-99	1999-00 (Revised)	2000-01 (Budget)
1. Total Expenditure	107929	119334	134648	161554	177584	202769	228135	266361	325634	350766
2. Expenditure on Revenue Account	86187	96205	109376	128440	145004	168950	186634	220090	271611	290622
3. Non-Development Expenditure	26666	31506	37367	48499	54197	60864	69891	84701	107309	123533
4. Interest Payments	10944	13210	15801	19413	21932	25576	30113	35874	45526	54271
5. Administtrative Services & Pensions	11526	13723	15578	17810	21204	24777	28674	35923	46719	53139
6.3 as % of 2	30.9	32.7	34.2	37.8	37.4	36	37.4	38.5	39.5	42.5
7.4 as % of 2	12.7	13.7	14.4	15.1	15.1	15.1	16.1	16.3	16.8	18.7
8.5 as % of 2	13.4	14.3	14.2	13.9	14.6	14.7	15.4	16.3	17.2	18.3

Source : Economic and Political Weekly, May 19, 2001, pp. 1754 and 1756.

Table 13.2
Revenue Receipts of State Governments

(Rs. Crore)

	1991-92	1992-93	1993-94	1994-95	1995-96	1996-97	1997-98	1998-99	1999-00 (Revised)	2000-01 (Budget)
1. Revenue from State Taxes	35756 (5.5)	39868 (5.3)	46424 (5.4)	55735 (5.5)	63865 (5.4)	71102 (5.2)	81229 (5.3)	88995 (5.1)	105637 (5.4)	125563 (5.8)
Of which: Taxes on commodities & Services	31798 (4.9)	35640 (4.8)	41451 (4.8)	48729 (4.8)	55755 (4.7)	62672 (4.6)	71830 (4.7)	79045 (4.5)	93255 (4.8)	111100 (5.1)
2. States' Own Non-tax Revenue	12706 (1.9)	12884 (1.7)	15569 (1.8)	21660 (2.1)	22895 (1.9)	23543 (1.7)	24438 (1.6)	24168 (1.4)	29634 (1.5)	31588 (1.5)
3. Share in Central Taxes	16848 (2.6)	20580 (2.7)	22395 (2.6)	24885 (2.5)	29048 (2.4)	35038 (2.6)	40411 (2.7)	39421 (2.2)	44458 (2.3)	50805 (2.3)
4. Grants from the Centre	15226 (2.3)	17759 (2.4)	21176 (2.5)	20004 (2.0)	20996 (1.8)	23155 (1.7)	24223 (1.6)	23863 (1.4)	35081 (1.8)	36964 (1.7)

Note : Figures within brackets are percentage of GOP at Current market prices.
Source : Economic and Political Weekly, May 19, 2001, p. 1755.

stagnant; rather there was a marginal fall up to the year 1999-00 (Revised) and it was only in the year 2000-01 (Budget) when there was some improvement in the situation as it was only in that year when state taxes stood at 5.8 per cent of the GDP. The Table also shows the predominance of indirect taxes in the states' tax structure—taxes on commodities and services constituted 4.9 per cent and 5.1 per cent of the GDP during the years 1991-92 and 2000-01 (Budget), respectively. As for the growth in receipts from states' own non-tax revenues, the situation is none too happy and satisfactory. During this period, states' own non-tax revenues that constituted 1.9 per cent of the GDP, increased to 2.1 per cent in 1994-95 but thereafter there was a gradual decline and in the year 2000-01 states' own non-tax revenues constituted 1.5 per cent of the GDP. The Table also shows that the states' share in Central taxes constituted 2.6 per cent of the GDP in 1991-92, marginally increased to 2.7 per cent in 1992-93 but there after it had a declining trend and in the year 2000-01 (Budget) states' share in Central taxes stood at 2.3 per cent of the GDP. Grants from the Centre to the states constituted 2.3 per cent of the GDP in 1991-92, increased to 2.4 per cent in 1992-93 and to 2.5 per cent in 1993-94 but from the following year 1994-95 grants from the Centre to the states as a percentage of the GDP have witnessed a declining trend and in the year 2000-01 (Budget), grants from the Centre to the states constituted 1.7 per cent of the GDP.

It is thus clear that the growth in states' own revenues—both tax and non-tax-as a percentage of the GDP does not present a satisfactory picture at all. Similarly, the transfers from the Centre to the States effected in the from of 'shared taxes' and 'grants' as a percentage of the GDP do not present a healthy situation for state finances. It should thus, be sufficiently clear that the states need to take steps to strengthen their situation by taking suitable measures to mobilize additional resources from their own tax and non-tax revenue resources. Further, the state Government should not expect much from the Centre as the fiscal situation at the Central level too has not been satisfactory.

The unsatisfactory fiscal situation of the State has resulted into increasing gross fiscal and revenue deficits during the decade 1991-92 to 2000-01 (Budget), as is clear from Table 13.3. The Table shows that during this period, the gross fiscal deficit of the State became almost five-fold from Rs. 18,900 crores to Rs. 94,028 crores. Gross fiscal deficit of the states that constituted 2.9 per cent of the GDP in 1991-92, stood at 3.8 per cent of the GDP in 2000-01 (Budget). The situation with regard to the revenue deficits of the State Governments is more alarming. The gap between the revenue receipts and revenue expenditure of the state Governments has continued to enlarge as the revenue expenditure of the State Governments has continued to increase, as referred to earlier. Such a situation has resulted into growing revenue deficits of the State Governments. The quantum of revenue deficits jumped more than eight times from Rs. 5,651 crores in 1991-92 to Rs. 48,424 crores in 2000-01 (Budget). Consequently, revenue deficits as a percentage of the gross fiscal deficit of the states has also witnessed a substantial increase

TABLE 13.3
Measures of Deficit of the State Governments

(Rs. Crore)

Year	Gross Fiscal Deficit	Revenue Deficit	(3) as % of (2)
(1)	(2)	(3)	(4)
1991-92	18900(2.9)	5651(0.9)	29.9
1992-93	20892(2.8)	5114(0.7)	24.5
1993-94	20596(2.4)	3812(0.4)	18.5
1994-95	27697(2.7)	6156(0.6)	22.2
1995-96	31426(2.6)	8201(0.7)	26.1
1996-97	37251(2.7)	16114(1.2)	43.3
1997-98	44200(2.9)	16333(1.1)	37.0
1998-99	74254(4.2)	43642(2.5)	58.8
1999-2000(Provisional)	90765(4.6)	53709(2.7)	59.2
2000-2001(Revised)	94824(4.3)	51445(2.4)	54.3
2001-2002(Budget)	94028(3.8)	48424(2.0)	51.5

Note : Figure within brackets are *percentages of GOP at current market prices.*
Source : Reserve Bank of India, Annual Report 2000-01, page 286.

as is clear from Table 13.3. Revenue deficit that constituted 29.9 per cent of the fiscal deficit in 1991-92, witnessed a further increase and stood at 59.2 per cent in 1999-2000 (provisional) and is estimated at 51.5 per cent in the year 2000-01 (Budget). These data also clearly suggest that the finances of the State Governments have been in disarray and emphasise the necessity of fiscal reforms at the state level to ameliorate the fiscal situation of the states. This is a difficult task but the State Governments have hardly any choice in the matter.

The constant deterioration in state finances has compelled the State Governments to borrow even increasing amounts from the market, Central Government and other sources such as the financial institutions, provident funds and reserve funds, etc. Revenue deficits that constitute a significant part of the gross fiscal deficits have been financed out of such borrowed funds. In the process, therefore, the axe has fallen on capital expenditure that has adversely affected the process of capital formation and development of various socio-economic infrastructure facilities in the economy. On the other hand, the interest bill and liabilities of the State Governments have continued to increase throughout. Table 13.4 shows the pattern of financing of the gross fiscal deficit of the state's and the states' outstanding liabilities during the period 1991-92 to 2000-01 (Budget). During this period, the quantum of the net loans from the Centre increased from Rs.

TABLE 13.4

Financing of State Government's Gross Fiscal Deficit

(Rs. Crore)

Year	Loans from the Central Govt. (net)	Market borrowings	Others*	Gross Fiscal Deficit (2+3+4)	States' Outstanding Liabilities (end March)			States' Outstanding liabilities as percent to GDP at current market prices
					Tatal**	Loans & advances form the Centre	Market Loans	
(1)	(2)	(3)	(4)	(5)	(6)	(7)	(8)	(9)
1991-92	9373 (49.6)	3305 (17.5)	6222 (32.9)	18900 (100.0)	126338	83491	18923	19.3
1992-93	8921 (42.7)	3500 (16.8)	8471 (40.5)	20892 (100.0)	142178	92412	22426	19.0
1993-94	9533 (46.3)	3620 (17.6)	7443 (36.1)	20596 (100.0)	160077	101945	20658	18.6
1994-95	14760 (53.3)	4075 (14.7)	8862 (32.0)	27697 (100.0)	184527	116705	30133	18.2
1995-96	14801 (47.1)	5888 (18.7)	10737 (34.2)	31426 (100.0)	212225	131505	36021	17.9
1996-97	17547 (47.1)	6515 (17.5)	13189 (35.4)	37251 (100.0)	243525	149053	42536	17.8
1997-98	23676 (53.6)	7280 (16.5)	13244 (30.0)	44200 (100.0)	281207	172729	49816	18.5
1998-99	31057 (41.8)	10467 (14.1)	32730 (44.1)	74254 (100.0)	341978	203786	60283	19.4
1999-2000 (Provisional)	32656 (36.0)	12636 (13.9)	45474 (50.1)	90765 (100.0)	419821	236442	72919	21.5
2000-2001 (Revised)	32033 (33.8)	12567 (13.2)	50221 (53.0)	94821 (100.0)	503613	268475	85486	23.1
2001-2002 (Budget)	33633 (35.8)	10666 (11.3)	49730 (52.9)	94028 (100.0)	591509	302108	96151	23.9

* Include loans from financial institutions, provident funds, reserve funds, deposits and advances etc.

** Include internal debt, loans and advances from the Central Government and Provident funds, etc.

Note : Figure within brackets are percentages of Gross Fiscal Deficit.

Source : Reserve Bank of India, Annual Report 2000-01, page 289.

9373 crores (1991-92) to Rs. 33633 crores (2001-02) and the market borrowings went up from Rs.3305 crores to Rs. 10666 crores. Similarly, the dependence on financial institutions, provident funds, reserve funds, deposits and advances, increased from Rs. 6222 crores to Rs. 49730 crores during this period. The outstanding liabilities of the State Governments thus increased from Rs. 126338 crores in 1991-92 to Rs. 591509 crores in 2001-02 (Budget)—around four-fold increase during the decade. This is an alarming situation and emphasise the urgency of fiscal reforms at the state level. It may also be pointed here that states' outstanding liabilities as a percentage of the GDP increased from 19.3 per cent in 1991-92 to 23.9 per cent in 2001-02 (Budget), as is clear from Table 13.4.

While the revenue receipts of the State Governments have substantially lagged behind the growth in expenditure on revenue account, a significant part of such receipts has been diverted by the State Governments towards the servicing of their debt. Table 13.5 shows gross and net interest payments as a percentage of revenue receipts for each of the individuals State Governments as also for all the states taken together. The Table shows that gross interest payments for all the States increased nearly five times in a span of 10 years from Rs. 10944.4 crores in 1991-92 to Rs.54271.0 crores in 2000-01 (Budget). These gross interest payments constituted 13.6 per cent and 22.2 per cent of revenue receipts of the States during the respective years. However, a number of State Governments (as is clear from the Table) were spending a much higher percentage of revenue receipts towards gross interest payments as against 13.6 per cent for all the States taken together in 1991-92: Jammu and Kashmir (23.7%), Bihar (20.7%), Orissa (19.7%), Goa (17.8%), Uttar Pradesh and West Bengal (17.7%), Kerala (16.9%), Gujrat (15.4%), Himachal Pradesh and Rajsthan (14.9%) and Haryana (14.4%). Similarly, in 2000-01 (Budget), a number of State Governments were incurring a higher percentage of their revenue receipts towards gross interest payments as against 22.2 per cent for all the States, as is clear from Table 13.5: West Bengal (40.2%), Orissa (30.1%), Himachal Pradesh (29.9%), Rajasthan (29.8%), Uttar Pradesh (28.7%), Punjab (27.4%), Haryana (22.8%) and Bihar (22.6%).

Similarly, the net interest payments as a percentage of revenue receipts in the case of a number of States exceeded the all States' figure of 10.2 per cent in the year 1992-93 as shown in Table 13.5: Bihar (20.7%), West Bengal (17.6%), Orissa (16.6%), Himachal Pradesh (16.4%), Kerala (15.7%), Assam (15.6%), Uttar Pradesh (14.8%), Goa (14.2%) and Punjab (12.2%), Similarly in the year 2000-01 (Budget) a number of States such as West Bengal (39.3%), Orissa (29.7%), Himachal Pradesh (29.6%), Uttar Pradesh (27.1%), Rajasthan (22.7%), Punjab (21.6%) and Bihar (20.3%), were incurring a higher percentage of their revenue receipts towards net interest payments as against the corresponding percentage of 18.5 for all the States taken together. These data clearly indicate that both the developed and relatively less developed States are parting with a noticeable share of their revenue receipt towards servicing of their debt obligations in the form of gross and net

TABLE 13.5
State-wise Gross and Net Interest Payments

(Rs. Crore)

States	Gross Interest Payments									
	2000-01 (Budget)	1999-00 (Revised)	1998-99	1997-98	1996-97	1995-96	1994-95	1993-94	1992-93	1991-92
(1)	(2)	(3)	(4)	(5)	(6)	(7)	(8)	(9)	(10)	(11)
1. Andhra Pradesh	3968.7 (18.9)	3249.7 (18.6)	2643.8 (18.5)	2153.3 (15.1)	1838.8 (16.4)	1529.1 (15.5)	1256.4 (14.3)	1025.0 (12.4)	829.9 (11.7)	695.0 (11.1)
2. Arunachal Pradesh	99.1 (9.8)	81.8 (8.0)	71.2 (7.7)	59.9 (6.5)	53.3 (6.6)	42.3 (5.6)	34.5 (5.7)	27.5 (5.0)	21.8 (4.3)	21.4 (4.8)
3. Assam	996.1 (15.2)	1084.0 (18.6)	520.7 (11.6)	638.9 (14.2)	559.9 (14.5)	487.6 (14.4)	589.3 (19.9)	490.0 (14.8)	410.7 (15.7)	92.7 (3.8)
4. Bihar	3197.2 (22.6)	2861.4 (22.7)	1872.3 (20.2)	1536.0 (16.6)	1417.1 (17.6)	1667.6 (22.6)	1561.1 (23.0)	1350.9 (20.4)	1240.6 (20.8)	1004.3 (20.7)
5. Goa	221.2 (12.5)	185.4 (14.0)	143.9 (12.5)	118.1 (10.3)	100.5 (12.4)	89.9 (11.0)	69.2 (13.0)	68.2 (14.7)	58.5 (15.0)	57.3 (17.8)
6. Gujarat	3503.1 (21.1)	2827.3 (19.5)	2261.9 (17.8)	1884.2 (14.8)	1610.0 (16.7)	1328.1 (15.5)	1190.9 (15.3)	1046.0 (14.9)	928.8 (15.7)	716.8 (15.4)
7. Haryana	1541.9 (22.8)	1316.2 (22.0)	997.0 (18.2)	820.3 (15.0)	715.9 (11.8)	555.7 (11.1)	486.9 (8.3)	421.7 (12.1)	343.3 (14.4)	321.9 (14.4)
8. Himachal Pradesh	824.3 (29.9)	650.1 (17.9)	498.0 (21.5)	372.1 (16.1)	313.0 (15.7)	285.2 (16.3)	222.6 (17.0)	209.6 (14.3)	177.1 (16.8)	147.8 (14.9)

(Contd.)

Table 13.5 (*Contd.*)

(1)	(2)	(3)	(4)	(5)	(6)	(7)	(8)	(9)	(10)	(11)
9. Jammu & Kashmir	944.1	786.0	664.7	592.7	489.3	440.4	576.7	275.6	359.4	385.7
	(18.3)	(15.0)	(14.7)	(13.1)	(13.3)	(13.5)	(19.1)	(12.4)	(17.5)	(23.7)
10. Karnataka	2392.6	2039.6	1616.6	1393.8	1208.1	1047.5	871.4	718.0	593.7	514.5
	(15.4)	(15.6)	(14.4)	(12.4)	(12.6)	(12.3)	(12.5)	(11.4)	(11.0)	(10.8)
11. Kerala	1926.4	1709.3	1446.3	1286.1	1103.4	924.2	819.7	687.2	542.5	483.4
	(18.9)	(19.6)	(20.1)	(17.9)	(18.0)	(17.0)	(17.6)	(17.5)	(16.3)	(16.9)
12. Madhya Pradesh	2634.0	2254.6	1834.8	1659.9	1376.2	1158.2	1094.3	867.9	741.5	607.7
	(18.1)	(16.3)	(16.2)	(14.6)	(13.7)	(13.4)	(14.4)	(12.3)	(11.5)	(11.3)
13. Maharashtra	6047.3	4651.1	3673.1	2903.6	2447.2	2055.4	1760.0	1510.1	1336.8	1159.6
	(21.4)	(19.1)	(16.9)	(13.4)	(12.7)	(12.4)	(11.7)	(11.6)	(12.4)	(11.9)
14. Manipur	142.7	130.2	91.3	78.9	65.6	57.5	51.8	48.9	44.6	31.1
	(14.5)	(11.1)	(10.2)	(8.8)	(8.1)	(8.3)	(8.7)	(8.5)	(9.3)	(6.9)
15. Meghalaya	130.9	128.9	69.4	60.9	55.6	50.4	45.0	33.3	25.3	21.5
	(11.9)	(12.1)	(8.3)	(7.3)	(7.6)	(7.4)	(8.5)	(6.6)	(5.9)	(5.3)
16. Mizoram	107.0	91.4	73.7	65.8	47.7	34.9	29.8	22.5	28.0	13.2
	(14.5)	(10.4)	(10.0)	(9.0)	(7.1)	(5.6)	(5.5)	(4.5)	(6.6)	(3.3)
17. Nagaland	186.4	163.1	136.5	113.4	97.9	79.4	80.0	61.5	58.1	53.6
	(14.7)	(14.3)	(13.2)	(10.9)	(11.2)	(10.2)	(12.7)	(9.7)	(11.3)	(10.8)
18. Orissa	2317.6	1779.7	1484.8	1291.7	1079.4	929.3	786.7	682.7	542.2	481.0
	(30.1)	(27.3)	(32.6)	(28.4)	(25.2)	(23.9)	(22.0)	(21.3)	(18.6)	(19.7)

19. Punjab	2931.2 (27.4)	2474.7 (29.5)	2316.8 (40.3)	1848.8 (32.1)	1634.4 (29.4)	1489.6 (28.7)	1243.7 (23.5)	1042.2 (31.8)	410.6 (14.7)	360.6 (9.7)
20. Rajasthan	3372.8 (29.8)	2869.8 (28.7)	2242.9 (26.1)	1896.7 (22.1)	1553.1 (20.5)	1233.8 (16.2)	1035.9 (16.4)	885.4 (15.8)	742.8 (15.2)	615.7 (14.9)
21. Sikkim	82.8 (8.3)	70.7 (4.6)	52.5 (3.6)	40.9 (2.8)	33.0 (2.9)	29.0 (3.1)	26.1 (4.8)	21.7 (9.6)	18.9 (9.0)	14.9 (8.2)
22. Tamil Nadu	2749.0 (14.9)	2582.3 (15.7)	2121.9 (14.9)	1763.4 (12.4)	1475.6 (12.3)	1293.2 (12.2)	1089.6 (11.8)	956.5 (11.9)	688.5 (9.8)	557.3 (8.2)
23. Tripura	205.0 (12.6)	170.8 (12.3)	140.6 (11.1)	120.0 (9.5)	110.2 (10.7)	88.7 (9.5)	75.8 (10.2)	68.1 (10.6)	58.7 (9.7)	50.1 (8.9)
24. Uttar Pradesh	7763.0 (28.7)	6749.5 (29.8)	5516.6 (31.7)	4689.3 (27.0)	4061.0 (25.3)	3324.9 (21.9)	3088.6 (23.1)	2111.1 (17.4)	2041.6 (17.5)	1710.3 (17.7)
25. West Bengal	5282.1 (40.2)	4087.6 (35.9)	2949.9 (31.4)	2410.0 (25.7)	1940.3 (23.6)	1616.2 (21.9)	1327.4 (19.3)	1168.9 (19.7)	966.2 (18.5)	827.0 (17.7)
26. NCT Delhi	704.5 (12.6)	530.7 (11.5)	432.3 (11.8)	314.1 (8.6)	189.9 (6.8)	94.0 (4.1)	— —	— —	— —	— —
All States	54271.0 (22.2)	45525.9 (21.2)	35873.5 (20.3)	30112.8 (17.1)	25576.4 (17.7)	21932.1 (16.0)	19413.4 (15.9)	15800.5 (15.0)	13210.1 (14.5)	10944.4 (13.6)

(*Contd.*)

TABLE 13.5 (Contd.)

States	Net Interest Payments								
	2000-01 (Be)	1999-00 (Re)	1999-98 Accounts	1997-98 Accounts	1996-97 Accounts	1995-96 Accounts	1994-95 Accounts	1993-94 Accounts	1992-93 Accounts
(1)	(12)	(13)	(14)	(15)	(16)	(17)	(18)	(19)	(20)
1. Andhra Pradesh	2404.70 (11.4)	1915.70 (11.0)	1498.30 (10.5)	1249.80 (9.0)	1014.80 (9.1)	811.40 (8.2)	488.04 (5.6)	319.50 (3.9)	252.00 (3.6)
2. Arunachal Pradesh	92.4 (9.2)	75.6 (7.4)	65.1 (7.0)	54.6 (6.5)	46.7 (5.8)	36.4 (4.8)	31.3 (5.2)	23.4 (4.3)	18.9 (3.8)
3. Assam	992.9 (15.1)	1080.8 (18.5)	518.5 (11.5)	636.8 (14.7)	557.8 (14.5)	485.2 (14.4)	587.2 (19.8)	487.6 (14.7)	408.2 (15.6)
4. Bihar	2868.7 (20.3)	2532.8 (20.1)	1736.3 (18.7)	1448.2 (16.7)	1360.6 (16.9)	1647.5 (22.3)	1532.2 (22.5)	1318.2 (19.9)	1233.4 (20.7)
5. Goa	217.2 (12.2)	181.0 (13.7)	139.4 (12.2)	115.4 (10.4)	98.0 (12.1)	86.5 (10.6)	66.7 (12.5)	65.5 (14.1)	55.2 (14.2)
6. Gujarat	1828.6 (11.0)	1294.3 (8.9)	669.2 (5.3)	677.0 (6.1)	793.8 (8.2)	472.5 (5.5)	369.2 (4.7)	268.5 (3.8)	490.4 (8.3)
7. Haryana	1285.5 (19.0)	1087.2 (18.2)	813.3 (14.8)	583.3 (9.9)	478.3 (7.9)	298.8 (6.0)	10.8 (0.2)	305.2 (8.8)	248.2 (10.4)
8. Himachal Pradesh	816.9 (29.6)	487.8 (13.4)	488.6 (21.1)	359.1 (16.5)	288.6 (14.5)	259.8 (14.8)	213.4 (16.3)	206.4 (14.1)	172.6 (16.4)

9.	Jammu & Kashmir	824.5 (15.9)	671.1 (12.8)	576.6 (12.8)	492.6 (11.5)	389.3 (10.5)	347.5 (10.7)	480.9 (15.9)	193.8 (8.7)	309.7 (15.1)
10.	Karnataka	1712.4 (11.0)	1379.1 (10.5)	946.9 (8.4)	831.3 (7.8)	533.5 (5.5)	351.7 (4.1)	468.8 (6.7)	380.2 (6.0)	236.8 (4.4)
11.	Kerala	1846.0 (18.1)	1639.2 (18.6)	1375.3 (19.1)	1232.6 (17.3)	1047.7 (17.0)	823.9 (15.2)	781.9 (16.8)	659.6 (16.8)	519.4 (15.7)
12.	Madhya Pradesh	2340.6 (16.1)	1890.2 (13.7)	1687.3 (14.9)	1436.7 (12.8)	1106.4 (11.0)	1017.2 (11.8)	881.2 (11.6)	651.9 (9.2)	399.6 (6.2)
13.	Maharashtra	4821.1 (17.1)	3459.5 (14.2)	2019.2 (9.3)	1209.5 (6.0)	412.7 (2.1)	784.2 (4.7)	582.9 (3.9)	581.5 (4.5)	508.8 (4.7)
14.	Manipur	141.9 (14.4)	129.7 (11.0)	90.5 (10.1)	78.0 (9.0)	64.6 (8.0)	56.3 (8.1)	50.9 (8.6)	47.0 (8.1)	43.7 (9.1)
15.	Meghalaya	125.3 (11.4)	123.3 (11.5)	63.5 (7.6)	56.8 (8.2)	50.8 (7.0)	47.9 (7.0)	43.3 (8.2)	31.5 (6.3)	22.0 (5.1)
16.	Mizoram	106.5 (14.4)	90.9 (10.3)	73.1 (9.9)	65.4 (9.1)	47.3 (7.1)	31.8 (5.1)	29.4 (5.5)	22.2 (4.4)	27.6 (6.5)
17.	Nagaland	183.4 (14.5)	160.1 (14.0)	134.0 (12.9)	111.4 (11.2)	95.8 (11.0)	77.4 (9.9)	78.5 (12.4)	60.1 (9.5)	57.5 (11.2)
18.	Orissa	2292.6 (29.7)	1759.7 (27.0)	1465.2 (32.2)	1273.1 (27.5)	1065.9 (24.9)	790.6 (20.3)	733.0 (20.5)	595.0 (18.5)	483.9 (16.6)
19.	Punjab	2310.9 (21.6)	1857.7 (22.2)	2211.9 (38.4)	865.9 (13.6)	170.3 (3.1)	1402.5 (27.1)	1162.2 (21.9)	968.2 (29.5)	339.3 (12.2)

(Contd.)

TABLE 13.5 (Contd.)

(1)	(12)	(13)	(14)	(15)	(16)	(17)	(18)	(19)	(20)
20. Rajasthan	2572.8 (22.7)	2152.0 (21.5)	1514.1 (18.8)	1298.5 (15.5)	928.2 (12.3)	732.2 (9.6)	613.0 (9.7)	272.5 (4.9)	245.9 (5.0)
21. Sikkim	82.5 (8.3)	70.4 (4.6)	52.2 (3.6)	40.9 (3.1)	31.2 (2.7)	27.9 (3.0)	25.7 (4.7)	20.8 (9.2)	17.6 (8.4)
22. Tamil Nadu	2417.2 (13.1)	2248.6 (13.7)	1736.9 (12.2)	1277.1 (9.4)	1126.6 (9.4)	950.4 (9.0)	810.8 (8.8)	681.3 (8.4)	477.3 (6.8)
23. Tripura	196.5 (12.1)	163.3 (11.8)	137.0 (10.8)	117.8 (10.9)	102.6 (10.0)	86.7 (9.2)	74.1 (10.0)	66.5 (10.3)	58.3 (9.7)
24. Uttar Pradesh	7325.0 (27.1)	6312.7 (27.9)	5088.6 (29.3)	4205.0 (23.9)	3582.1 (22.3)	2861.1 (18.8)	2715.2 (20.3)	1756.3 (14.5)	1723.9 (14.8)
25. West Bengal	5158.8 (39.3)	3977.1 (34.9)	2901.2 (30.9)	2305.1 (25.5)	1827.6 (22.2)	1565.3 (21.2)	1238.4 (18.0)	1097.7 (18.5)	921.8 (17.6)
26. NCT Delhi	338.3 (6.0)	144.7 (3.1)	293.3 (8.0)	181.2 (5.2)	184.5 (6.6)	86.9 (3.8)	(20.1) (-1.0)	(5.4) (-1.0)	— —
All States	45303.1 (18.5)	36884.5 (17.2)	28395.6 (16.1)	22203.1 (13.0)	17405.6 (12.0)	16139.6 (11.8)	14048.8 (11.5)	11075.1 (10.5)	9272.0 (10.2)

(-).... Not available.
Note : Figure within brackets are percentages of revenue receipts of state.
Source : Economic and Political Weekly, May 26, 2001, p. 1928.

interest payments. It may also be noted that West Bengal was parting with as much as 40 per cent of the revenue receipts in the year 2000-01 (Budget) towards meeting its interest obligations in the form of Gross/net interest payments. One can, therefore, easily infer that it is not the less developed States alone that suffer from lack of fiscal discipline.

In order to improve and strengthen the fiscal situation of the states, a number of steps need to be undertaken to enlarge the resource base of the States and at the same time contain and ensure economy in public expenditure. It requires a detailed scrutiny and examination of the finances of the State Governments. However, to begin with the revenue from State taxes, which as a percentage of the GDP continues to be stagnant, need to be enlarged by widening the net of direct and indirect taxes. While indirect taxes, especially the States tax and State excise duties, continue to be predominant in the State' tax structure, it is necessary that the contribution of direct taxes ought to be augmented. One of the proposals in this direction has been that through a constitutional amendment, the limit of profession tax be raised three times from the present ceiling of Rs. 2,500 per assessee per year. There is need for a uniform policy for the purpose and that the tax be implemented on a uniform pattern in all the States. At the same time the various merits and demerits of the tax need to be seriously looked into before a constitutional amendment is made in this area. Similarly the pros and cons about the much talked about ' Entry Tax' and the experience of the States that attempted its introduction should be considered, prior to any decision in this regards. In this context, it needs no mention that VAT that was to be implemented nation wide from April 2002, has been postponed for implementation to April 2003 in the face of various hurdles faced by the states.

There is, however, one area where reform in the States' tax system is long overdue and a number of commissions/committees have favoured time and again to raise resources from this sector, namely the agricultural sector. Keeping in view the various constraints, including the political considerations, time has come when the State Government will have to initiate measures to raise resources, at least, from the better-off sections of the farming community.

It may be pointed out here that agricultural incomes, even of the relatively rich farmers, continue to be untaxed for long in this country. The exclusion of agricultural incomes from the purview of income tax has not only distorted the equity in the tax system but at the same time encouraged the conversion of black money into white money. It is high time that either the constitution be amended so as to bring the agricultural incomes within the ambit of Central income-tax, or alternatively all the State Governments may pass on their right of taxing agricultural incomes to the Central Government that already has an efficient tax administration machinery for the purpose. The revenues so collected, minus the cost of collection, be distributed among each of the States in proportion to the quantum of agricultural incomes brought within the net of Central income-tax. Such an arrangement will not only ensure equity in the tax system but at the same time also provide additional revenues to the States to improve their fiscal health.

Beside, the tax administration needs to be improved to generate additional tax revenues. In fact, there is need for a broad uniformity amongst all the States regarding the scrutiny and examination of the over-all tax structure of each of the individual States so as to access the potential for raising additional resources.

If one looks at the States' own non-tax revenues as a percentage of the GDP, the situation has deteriorated. There has been much debate about the 'user charges' and there is by and large a unanimity that such charges in the sphere of electricity, irrigation and transport should be increased. However, when it comes to practice by the State Governments, they have to face a number of difficulties and hurdles. A number of reform measures, especially in power sector, have already been initiated so as to bail out the State Electricity Boards whose losses continue to be colossal and alarming. However, the response of quite a good number of State Governments has not been encouraging in this direction and the situation has been bad to worse. Uttar Pradesh's example is a case in point where the visiting team of the World Bank during its visit in April 2002 expressed annoyance with the State Governments failure to regulate the functioning of the UP Power Corporation Limited in order to improve the power situation in Uttar Pradesh. Accordingly, the second installment of Rs. 15,000 crore loan meant to carry out structural and fiscal reforms in the State was stalled . it is perhaps for the first time that the World Bank has taken such a step after paying the first instalment.

There is a strong need for a progressive increase in user charges for various social and economic services that are provided by the State Governments. It is high time that, to begin with, all the State Governments arrived at a broad consensus regarding the policy measures to modify and restructure the user charges at least in the areas of electricity, irrigation and transport. Unless it is done immediately on a priority basis, the State Governments should otherwise be ready to face a great deterioration and strain on the fiscal front. It may be noted that the Government of Rajasthan in May 2002 decided to abolish completely the subsidy on irrigation water and that such a move will raise user charges by almost 400 per cent. This makes Rajasthan the only state to usher in reforms at the grass-root level as part of a financial package being provided by the World Bank. Happily, the Punjab Government in its budget for 2002-03 has intended to progressively move in the direction of levying substantial user charges for its social and economic services. While such steps on the part of the State Governments are in the right direction but what is more important and relevant is that all the State Governments agree to follow the rules of the game and implement the policy decisions to improve their fiscal situation.

A number of State Governments, such as Andhra Pradesh, Assam, Gujarat, Karnataka, Madhya Pradesh, Maharashtra, Orissa, Punjab, Tamil

Nadu and Uttar Pradesh are coming forward to join the race for disinvestment and each of these State Governments has put a few public sector enterprise on the block to sell off 51 per cent or more of their equity. Broad guidelines and the norms for the process of disinvestment be clearly decided and each of the State Governments should come forward with detailed information regarding the public sector enterprise where the disinvestment is to be carried out so as to ensure transparency in the system. Further, the proceeds form disinvestment should be used for creation of infrastructural facilities or for the purpose of retirement of the public debt of concerned State Government.

The increasing dependence of the State Governments on loan finance and consequently the increasing interest bill of the States has adversely affected their fiscal strength. In this context, the proposed 'debt swap policy' of the Centre will enable the State Governments to raise fresh low-cost debt for the express purpose of prematurely retiring high-cost debt. The scheme is for States to prepay Rs. 85,000 crores of high-cost debt to the Centre over three years—Rs. 25,000 crores in the current year (2002-03) itself. State Governments would be allowed access to 100 per cent of the small savings collected in their territory instead of 80 per cent accessible until last year provided the additional receipts are used for retiring expensive debt. The proportions of small savings collections that States have to earmark towards prepayment of expensive debt would be raised to 30 per cent. This will yield Rs. 15,000 crores in the current year (2002-03). At the same time, States would be given permission, under Article 293 enabling them to borrow conditionally on the Centre's sanction to borrow an additional Rs. 10,000 crores from the market. The combined sum of Rs. 25,000 crores, as referred to above, would be transferred to the Centre for retiring debt that carry interest rates higher than 13 per cent. The twin benefits of the proposed schemes would be that the interest burden of the States would come down considerably and such capital receipts by the Centre will mean a concomitant reduction in its borrowing as also in its fiscal deficit.

In addition, the Centre is finalizing an ambitious State Fiscal Responsibility Programme that would dramatically change the State finances by 2004-05. As per the programme by 2004-05 the gross fiscal deficit of the States would be brought down to 2.5 per cent of the State GDP, the revenue deficit would be brought down to zero and the interest payments of the States as a percentage of their revenue receipts would be brought down to 18-20 per cent. At the core of the proposed State Fiscal Responsibility Programme is the recommendation of the Eleventh Finance Commission, whose terms of reference were expressly expended to recommend an implementable State level fiscal reforms programme. The programme revolves around creating a Rs. 10,607 cores incentive fund. The corpus for this fund would come from 15 revenue deficit States identified by the Eleventh Finance Commission. These States would contribute 15 per cent of their revenue deficit grants to the fund, with a matching grant from the Centre. The States that implement reforms would be eligible to draw funds from this incentive fund. Each of these States would have to improve their revenue deficit as a proportion of their receipts by at least 5 per cent annually between 2000-05. The States which do not follow the set timetable for reform would forgo their share of withdrawals from the incentive fund in that financial year. In case, they make-up in the following year, they would have to meet the previous as well as current year's target to draw from incentive fund. Further during the first four years, no amount of this fund would be transferred to another State. However, if any State is not able to draw the amount indicated on the basis of performance of the first four years, the amount undisbursed would form part of a common pool. This pool would be distributed to performing States in the fifth year on a pro-rate basis in addition to amounts they are initially entitled to. It may also be pointed out here that the Centre has set up a committee to monitor the fiscal programme of the States.

The Centre's efforts to improve and to strengthen the finances of the State Governments is a healthy development in our federal fiscal system but the most important aspect of the entire story is that the State Governments themselves have to come forward and participate in the process of fiscal consolidation. During the period of reforms, the gains may be recounted on many fronts but the cause of worry and anxiety is that backward and poorer States like Bihar, Orissa or Assam have suffered because of their poor infrastructure. Take the case of Bihar. In the early nineties, it had the eighth highest state domestic product in the country. In 1999-2000 after a decade of economic reforms it has gone down two ranks and was placed at the tenth position after losing considerably in terms of share in aggregate State Domestic Product (SDP) of the major states. Bihar's share in aggregate SDP declined from 5.87 per cent in 1990-91 to 4.42 per cent in 1999-2000. Of the 26 states and union territories whose comparable data are available for the period, 13 states have succeeded in raising their shares in aggregate SDP, 11 states have witnessed a decline while the share has remained unchanged for two states. It means that gains of 13 States came from the loss of 11 states. This is an alarming situation as they were comparatively developed states. This goes against the broad national interest because any programme oriented towards economic reforms, especially in a federal country like India, should ensure regional balance as one of the prime objectives so as to maintain integrity and harmony of the federation as a whole.

CHAPTER

14

Issues and Policy Options for Trade Related Intellectual Property Rights and Indian Economy

B.M. Jani

I

World Trade Organisatization (WTO) has provided guidelines for Agreement on Trade Related Investment measures (TRIMs) and the Trade Related Intellectual Property Rights (TRIPs). There are several economic, social, Political and Legal ramifications. The present paper tries to sort out major issues on the basis of review of latest literature on the subject and offers policy options related with the subject. It is necessary to examine TRIPs on different sectors of Indian economy like Agriculture, Industry and Service sector. For this, Doha Ministerial Declaration needs to be evaluated with reference to the developing countries in general and India in particular. Similarly, visions and provisions of WTO for the developing countries also need rethinking. The main Ministerial declaration at Doha elaborated on the objectives and timetable for the current negotiations in agriculture and services, negotiations of industrial tariffs, trade and investment and competition policy. Periodical changes are necessary in favour of the developing countries.

This paper is divided into three parts: the first one reviews literature so as to sort out issues of discussion, the second one analyses visions and provisions of WTO for TRIMs and TRIPs for the developing countries, whereas, the third one offers policy options for multilateral trade development for Indian economy under new quasi-judiciary system, WTO.

RETROSPECT

There are several studies carried out by the scholar in area of WTO and India. These include, Chadha (2000)1, Panchamukhi (2000)2, Alagh (2001)3 Mishra (2001)4, FICCI(2000)5, Deodhar (1999)6, Gulati (2000)7, Mukhopadhyaya (2000)8 and others. These scholars examined impact of Urugway Rounds Agreements (URA) on global Trade and the impact of URA on Indian trade with respect to agriculture, industrial and service sector trade growth in 21st century.

Moreover, serious attempt is made by institutions and individuals to view the role of WTO with reference to its sectoral impact. All these studies have explored potentiality for further growth of Indian trade under the WTO regimes considering various sectors of the economy.

However, very scant attention is paid by the scholars to offer policy options for the Government of India to negotiate in the next round of the WTO. This paper bridges the gap to show ways and means with different policy options so as to increase the share of India in aggregate World trade.

MAJOR ISSUES DRAWN ATTENTION

On the basis of above-noted literature, one can safely draw following issues which need due discussion :

1. For India's adjustment, strategy to World Trade in Agriculture can be through diversification and sustainable agriculture. In this regard what kind of strategy to be followed by policy-makers to increase India's share in world exports?
2. What should be the nature of anti-dumping tariffs in era of dumping by China and other countries to damage agricultural and small industry products in Global competition?
3. The bringing of intellectual property rights (TRIPs) in the purview of WTO would also have serious effect of Indian agriculture through patenting of seeds, sui-generis system. Will WTO-regime not affect adversely to Indian agriculture?
4. Market access of agricultural products and commodities manufactured by small scale industries in World trade needs, legal protection. Do we have legal reforms in India with respect to WTO and globalization of Indian trade?
5. Who will fund for technological advancement in agriculture, industrial and service sector products in global Indian trade so as to increase its share?
6. Multinationals are selling technology as a commodity in global market and charging discriminately from country to country. In

such a situation, what is the way out for a developing country like India?

7. As WTO being a quasi-judicial body, is there any scope to have a code of conduct for the developed countries to stop exploitation?
8. Technology and knowledge industry, and information technology as the most competitive sectors are core ones in India economy. What kind of strategic policy initiatives should India take to strengthen domestic R & D activities so as to make the indigenous technology and knowledge-industries emerge as the most competitive sector in the next five years.
9. What should be India's approach towards new issues such as Multilateral Agreement on investment, labour standards, child labour trade-environment linkages?
10. What are the consequences of liberalization and globalization in the fields of the banking and insurance sectors on the domestic banking and insurance industries? How should government monitor and control the instabilities that may be generated by the external shocks in this field?
11. Looking to mounting internal and external debt burden both governmental and private on average India, it is most necessary to monitor control such debts. Would it not affect adversely to competitive strength of Indian economy?
12. What kind of global financial architecture should be evolved that volatility and instability of capital markets and exchange rates can be controlled so as to manage Indian capital and forex markets under rule-based disciplines framework?

II

VISIONS AND PROVISIONS

The Uruguay Round Agreement is launched from January 2000 and the WTO members will have to negotiate for trade liberalization in Agriculture and service trade. A new Millennium will force member of the WTO in round of multilateral trade negotiations.

Section 25 of Dunkel proposal reveal: (1) Trade in Goods, (2) Trade in services, (3) Trade related aspects of Intellectual property rights including trade in counterfeit goods (4) Agreement establishing the Multilateral Trade organization to be executed by the WTO. TRIPs and TRIMs have drawn attention of WTO on what is essentially non-trade agenda. The clearest of this approach is the attention given to the inclusion of labour and environment standards into the WTO agenda. It appears that non-trade issues are more important than that of pure trade issues. Free trade rise under the most favoured nations rule of game under General Agreement on Tariffs and Trade (GATT) now a key component of the WTO, a tariff reduction to trading partner must be granted to all GATT members. But on the other hand, this non-participation encouraged the developed countries to leave the sectors of great interest to the developing countries out of the liberalization exercise.

The second interest shows that Post Uruguay round average tariff reduction would be around 3 to 4% by member countries which may virtually lead to free trade with respect to border measures. Apart from textiles, Asian developing countries can have interest in leather, rubber and foot wear be January 2005. Much liberalization process in developing countries continues to have high tariff on industrial products to engage developed countries in the bargaining process. However, it should be noted here that the developed countries have much larger markets, so 1% reduction in tariff by the former will lead to reduction by the latter. In gain sharing exercise the developing countries may not be rich.

The formation of Technology Agreement, telecommunication and financial service needs to be successfully concluded for comprehensive negotiation round to cope with balance of payment situation. Thus, sectoral negotiations can help India to gain from trade and raise its contribution in global trade. WTO Ministerial conference at Singapore accepted that negotiation can proceed along sectoral line on piecemeal basis.

WTO has mandated change in the Patents Acts which are to affect India in the so called Patentable subject matter, so Trade related intellectual rights (Trips) need to be reviewed by mobilizing public opinion. Micro-organism in patentable subject includes patenting of life forms, patents on animal of all hues and patents of biotechnology as strategic field for a country like India considering forest products.

Actually, there are three areas on which India should remain firm: (a) Labour standards; (b) trade and environment and (c) Multilateral agreement on investment. 135 member countries of the WTO debated these issues at Seattle for negotiating agenda for the Millennium Round. It is expected that there would be $15 billion FDI inflow by 2005 with $5 billion worth of outward investment. To achieve them we need access markets. Multilateral investment of OECD club could not frame such arrangements. No country should be discriminated against foreign direct investment once it has been established. Such pre-establishment right cannot be taken away in a multilateral framework. Thus, India needs to be a pro active member in the WTO.

Being the World's second largest emerging market, India is an important destination to business organizations from other countries and Indian companies will have to understand our import regulations and the rules for foreign investments and companies should set up office here and/or hire the best Indian consultants/NGOs. WTO system allow this facility to all members. We should come out with better arguments than the opposite side of modifying the regulations. However, economists have argued that intra-bloc exports have notably increased due to regional trade arrangements (RTA). Within the RTA, the ratio of World exports increased from 74% in 1990 to 86% in 1999. The following table provides the position.

Intra-bloc Exports : Pre-WTO and Post-WTO period

(In billion Dollar)

Bloc	*1970*	*1980*	*1990*	*1999*
APEC	58.6	357.7	901.6	1904.9
EU	76.5	456.9	981.3	1376.3
NAFTA	22.1	102.2	26.3	581.2
ASEAN	1.5	13.4	28.6	81.9
EAEC	9.2	98.5	282.4	621.6
Bangkok Agreement	0.1	1.5	4.5	15.4
SAARC	0.1	0.6	0.9	2.7

Source : World Development Indicators, World Bank, 2001.

It can be observed from the table that the share of the blocs representing the developed countries rose very fast during 1990 to 1999, whereas, in the case of SAARC, it is not satisfactory. As against this, the share of ASEAN trade bloc can be considered better than SAARC and Bangkok agreement blocs. This means that SAARC countries will have to increase their bargaining capacity to raise their share in global trade and during the next round of the WTO, the countries of the bloc will have to go in for policy options as indicated in the next part of this paper. As a corollary, WTO will have to tackle the spread of regionalism considering the factors given in the table.

The WTO agreement on anti-dumping measures stipulates a rigorous framework for dealing with the problem of dumping. China has already started dumping of critical inputs and raw material items. The anti-dumping measures as per the agreement, can be initiated only when (a) an existence of dumping is identified, (b) injury to industry is measured and (c) casual link between dumping and injury to industry is established. All these steps need technical analytical support. Dumping of goods in a general sense means sending goods that are unsaleable because of high prices, they are sent from the home market to a foreign market for sale at low prices.

The formula for anti-dumping duties to offset or prevent dumping are :

1. The anti-dumping duty shall not be greater than the margin of dumping.
2. No anti-dumping duty shall be levied by reason of exemption from or refund of duties for taxes borne by a product when destined domestic consumption in the exporting country.
3. No anti-dumping duty shall be levied unless it is determined that the effect of dumping such as to cause material injury to an established industry.

The lessons from India's experiment with quantitative restrictions in the WTO are clear enough. There are risks in hiding behind exemptions and Indian approach of delaying the inevitable can have its costs. There must be greater awareness of the decisions taken in the WTO if the Indian economy is to be able to respond to changing trade conditions.

TRIP's exercise includes technological protectionism. These include information technology and technology related with manufacturing items. Due to low labour cost, Indian labour needs protection. This is so as cyber law has demanded new labour laws. Multinationals are charging for technology as a commodity and also charging the cost of the technology. One of the key values of globalization is competitive new technology which threatens developing countries particularly when industrilized countries like USA create restriction of the access of new technology and even scientific developments. Biotechnology has opened great opportunities for the commercial exploitation of genetic resources in various fields. The TRIPs agreement provides a basis for the appropriation through Patent Rights of micro organisms and cells while preventing the non-patentability of plants and animals in developing countries Implications of appropriability through patent rights of the parts of nature are far reaching not only in economic but also in ethical and socio-political terms.

III

POLICY OPTIONS TO BE FOLLOWED

1. The Government of India will have to make provision in legal framework to stop exploitation of women and child labours, whereas, relaxation is required for people engaged in Information Technology areas from labour laws point of view, as internet business goes in for 24 hours a day.
2. Liberalization and globalization are inevitable stages in the process of enhancing the economic opportunities with active participation of all countries with capacity building in areas of humanizing the process of economic development. It is most necessary to improve social opportunities and human capability to boost our global trade.
3. WTO has mandated change in the Patents Act. After 20 years protection, it is most necessary for the government of India to revise Indian Patents Act of 1970, under which Pharmaceuticals and agro-chemical patents are given shorter period like five to seven years. Our Pharmaceuticals industry, chemicals and Petro-chemical industry need strong ethical brands to cope with globalization process.
4. The government of India will have to plan for Information Technology Agreement and agreement on basic infrastructure like telecommunication and financial services to boost the markets. This

is so as India is dominating in Internet business and in software exports in order to protect our people in global market.

5. The WTO working Group on trade and labour standard must ensure non-tariff barrier, international NGOs and trade unions on our side in an era of competition. The government must change focus on centralized bargaining in the interest of unorganized markets and unorganized labours flexibility in labour markets.
6. The government of India will have to lower tariffs to benefit from WTO negotiations and it is equally necessary to ban domestically prohibitive goods and products. A recent study by WHO identified 270 medicines capable of meeting 90% of country's entire medical needs and other 10,000 are unnecessary, ineffective, expensive and hazardous. Political economy of transfer of pollution and polluting technologies result from weak bargaining. The government will have to give necessary period for adjustment to the concern industries.
7. An increase in production and income may result an increase in demand of environmental goods like clean air, fresh water and food security to rising population of India. There is a need for Multilateral Environment Agreement and WTO framework in favour of the third world countries like India.
8. The WTO is not clear about the development of non-tariff barrier to imports from the Third World such a anti-dumping duties, particularly for India. It is feared that the major economic power may enforce their will to small players. It must be recognised that India cannot change at its own except global code of conduct about this skeptical benefits.
9. WTO rules on dumping and subsidies have crucial implications on IMF supported and sponsored programmes. From IMF side anti-dumping programme must be discouraged largely for two reasons: the first economic cost of large unproductive nature should be avoided and the second there are several countries whose tariff structures are only partially obligatory to the dictates of WTO, which should be corrected by anti-dumping duties.
10. The Government of India will have to go in for Economic Reforms in Agriculture sector to raise strength of the sector by policy initiatives like market: (a) reform including support price, procurement and public distribution system (b) technology and protection of intellectual property, (c) Pricing of input and (d) institutional infrastructure.
11. The task force before Commerce Ministry is wider transparent consultation with state governments in India to develop new mechanism so as to have national position on trade issues for more legal and economic expertise for such big decision making.
12. The WTO should not interfere with the domestic policy of its member nations so long as policy does not relate to World Trade.

If one country pursues policies that distort the flow of world trade or threatens to reduce trade of member countries others should have the right to appeal to the WTO. In such cases the WTO can have right to intervene.

CONCLUSION

It appears that the Government of India will have to protect interest of states having predominance of unorganized sector, unorganized industries and existence of unorganized labour markets. In any case, globalisation of trade process under the umbrella of WTO should not adversely affect from long term point of view to agri-business, small scale exports and pharmaceuticals by the multinationals. It is necessary a share of Indian trade in total global trade. It is high time for corporates of India to encourage R & D to increase competitiveness in global markets to face global competition in 21st century.

For a country like India, which has no trade preferences has some lessons as under :

1. WTO is a powerful tool to reduce trade barriers globally, reducing the preferential access of Third World competitors.
2. Trade preferences to SAARC countries will provide benefit not to a large extent.
3. It is not possible to get wholehearted support from other developing countries in areas of agriculture and textiles in reducing trade barriers.
4. Preferential agreements have always created undesirable dependency. It is found that the economy of some small countries may collapse. Preferences create serious economic distortions considering long term growth of the economy. Resources are drawn away from fundamentally competitive sector to less competitive sectors prone to subsidy enjoying sectors. Allocation of resources needs to be given due weightage.

More equitable global trade will enhance development process and migrants can contribute to increasing trade with their home countries which may ultimately lead to higher employment, output and rising GNP levels.

References

Alagh, Yoginder (2001),"Globalization Debate". The Indian Economic Association Conference Volume.

Bhalla, G.S. Singh and Gurumali (1996), "Impact of GATT on Punjab Agriculture, Institute for Development and Communication", Monograph Series II Ajanta Books International, New Delhi.

Chadha, G.K. (2000), "Economic Reforms and Emerging demand Hiatus Supply in India Rural Labour Market". Indian Economic Association Conference Volume.

Deodhar, S.Y. (1999), 'WTO and India Agriculture', IUF Conference, Ahmedabad. Nov.20-22.
FICCI (1999), 'WTO and Small Scale Industries Sector'. Seminar Organized by FICCI, New Delhi.
Garritse Ronald (1999), 'Producers' subsidies', Printer Publishers, London.
Gulati, Ashok et. al. (1999), "From Marrkesh to Seattle Indian Agriculture Globalizing World", Economic & Political, Political Weekly 34 (412) pp. 2931-42.
Mishra, R.S. (2001), "The WTO Agreement on Agriculture and Agricultural Crisis in India" The Indian Economic Association.
Mukhopadhaya, Somasri (2000), 'Uruguay Round And India's Export Response', Indian Economic Association, Conference Volume 2001.
Panchmukhi, V.R. (2000), 'World Trade Organization And India: Challenges and Perspectives'. The Indian Economic Association Conference Volume.
Palit, Amitendu (1997), 'IMF—WTO Agreement', The Economic Times, 11 January.
National Working Group on Patent Laws (1993) : Patent Regimes in TRIPS, New Delhi.
Panagariya, Arivind (1998), 'WTO and Developing Countries', The Economic Times, 14 December.
Sahota Gian S. (1999), Subsidies in Punjab Report to the Government of Punjab, Chandigarh.
Srivastava, D. K. and Sen, Tapas (1997), Government Subsidies in India, National Institute of Public Finance and Policy, New Delhi.
UNDP(1999, Human Development Report, Oxford University Press, Ins, New York.
World Bank (1999),World Development Report, 1999-2000.

CHAPTER

15

Economic Reforms and Rural Credit : Impact, Issues and Responses

G. RAGHAVA REDDY

INTRODUCTION

Development of institutional credit for agriculture has been one of the important planks of agricultural development strategy. Initially, this was prompted by the concern mainly for the cultivator who was being exploited by the money lender in terms of high rates of interest, obligation to sell his produce at disadvantageous prices and, in some cases, eventual foreclosure of mortgages on his holding. With the commencement of national economic planning, however, there has been a distinct shift in emphasis with the accent on the role of credit as a positive aid to intensified agricultural production. The new agricultural strategy has lent added urgency to the need for a supporting framework of rural banking and credit. Growing high-yielding varieties of foodgrains on a large scale will entail the greatly increased consumption of fertilizer, pesticide and improved seed which unlike traditional inputs, have to be acquired outside the farm. The resulting demand for production credit is thus not only quantitatively larger than ever before but also qualitatively different. Along side this will also grow the requirements of credit to finance the marketing of increasing quantities of inputs and farm machinery and the processing, storage, transportation and sale of a rapidly expanding volume of agricultural produce. With agriculture becoming increasingly modernized, commercialized and profitable and with a spurt in rural economic activity generally and the acceleration of monetization, the need will continue to grow for extensive institutional machinery capable of providing the necessary credit and banking facilities and also of mobilizing savings out of rising rural incomes (Darmy, 1970).

SUPPLY OF RURAL CREDIT AND ITS AGENCIES

Rural credit in India, like most other less developed countries is supplied by a plurality of agencies generally classified into, organized/formal/institutional and unorganized/informal/non-institutional sector/markets. The size of the informal sector is generally larger than the formal sector. The cost and availability of credit in the unorganized market is being influenced by the State by different types of intervention which tend to improve the link between the two credit markets.

In the context of development planning state intervention in the credit market is justified on grounds of market failure, external economies and considerations of equity both social and regional. In India there are three types of state interventions into the rural credit market-one promotional, two regulatory and three both promotional and regulatory. The establishment of NABARD and National Co-operative Development Corporation (NCDC) is an instance of promoting new organizations of development banking. The regulatory role consists of the set of controls, subsidies, allocations, directions on the banking system framed and directed by the Reserve Bank and Government. The nationalization of commercial banks and the different schemes of reorganization of co-operative credit delivery system are instances of both the promotional and regulatory role of the State.

Formal rural credit institutions in India date back to the early 20th century when credit co-operatives were first set up in certain 'provinces' as the Indian States were then known. Since then the co-operative movement, especially in the sphere of credit, had spread to all parts of India and had taken deep roots. From time to time, high level commissions/committees were set up either by the RBI or the Government of India to examine the problems of rural finance and recommend measures for strengthening co-operative rural credit system, keeping in view the nature and dimension of credit requirements. The present 'multi-agency' system in India is the result of these efforts spread over several decades. It consists of the two wings of the co-operative structure (the short-term and the long-term credit): the commercial banks with their branch network and the RRBs with their branch network. At the national level, there is the National Bank for Agriculture and Rural Development (NABARD).

ROLE OF INFORMAL AGENCIES

About 60 per cent of the credit requirements of farmers are now met by the institutional sources and the remaining 40 per cent by informal sources. However, small and marginal farmers including tenants who account for 80 per cent of holdings and one-third of area operated depend for more heavily on informal sources (Rao: 2003). The rates of interest charged by the constituents of the informal sector are generally higher than the formal sector. A number of institutional factors are responsible, besides the market factors, for high rates of interest in unorganized credit markets. The size of the loan is usually small and thus the fixed handling charges are relatively high. Defaults also tend to be larger in unorganized credit markets. These higher defaults are due not so much to a lower standard of morality and unwillingness to repay debts as to the fluctuations in prices and incomes derived from agricultural products, which reduce the ability of the agriculturists to repay debts at inopportune times. Inflation is another contributory factor especially in many Latin American Countries. A general statement, however, is that interest rates in the unorganized money markets of underdeveloped countries are high because the economy is underdeveloped and the money market unorganized. The high rates of interest prevailing in unorganized money market have been a heavy burden on agriculturist. Annual interest payments have been fairly large in relation to the net income of the farmers, thus reducing his ability to make improvement on the land (Meller : 1968). Hence the need for intervention in and regulation of credit transactions in the unorganized money market in the context of development planning.

In India at the base of credit structure, moneylenders and indigenous bankers are the overwhelming source of finance for cultivators.

The traders and commission agents generally advanced short-term clean loans to the producer-sellers. They advance small amount normally for one season and recover them when the sales are effected. Majority of the farmers who borrow from them make voluntary arrangements to sell their produce through them. In Lieu of the interest, some trades and commission agents charge a marginally higher commission from producer-sellers who had obtained credit from them; and those producer-sellers who do not dispose off their produce through them are charged higher interest rates (Kahlon & Singh : 1984).

COMMERCIAL BANKS

Till 1967 financing agriculture was considered to be the sole responsibility of the co-operative credit for agriculture and allied activities, on account of increasing emphasis laid on higher agricultural production as also the technological break through achieved by Indian farmers, the resources of the co-operative sector were found to be inadequate. Against this background, commercial banks were, as a matter of national policy, called upon for the first time in 1967 to provide finance to this sector. Their role in this direction expanded significantly after the nationalization of the 14 major scheduled commercial banks in 1969. Since then commercial banks have been financing agricultural activities and development on an increasing scale year by year and their financial involvement in this sector is growing. The entry of commercial banks into rural finance has initiated new trends by encouraging the planning process at the grass roots level and imparted a significant development orientation to deployment of funds in the rural areas. The Reserve Bank has been an active catalyst in directing the flow of bank credit to this priority sector (RBI 1984). However, the advent of economic reforms has altered the trend drastically.

DECLINING RURAL BRANCH NETWORK AND C-D RATIO

Gunnar Myrdal (1958) remarked that "studies in many countries have shown how the banking system, if not regulated to act differently, tends to become an instrument for siphoning off the savings from the poorer regions to the richer and more progressive ones where returns on capital are high and secure". This is the phenomenon of demand—following finance which operates nationally as well as globally. The purpose of public intervention in the operations of the banking system is to safeguard the interests of not only poorer regions but also the economically weaker segments of society whose access to banking facilities is constrained by a multiplicity of factors both economic and non-economic. In India despite large-scale nationalization of banking since 1969, the urban-bias in commercial banking is hardly reduced. Table 15.1 offers some details in this regard.

TABLE 15.1
Share of Rural Branches in Deposits and Credit of SCBs

(Rs. in Crore)

End of Year	*No. of Offices*	*As % of Total*	*Deposits*	*As % of Total*	*Credit*	*As % of Total*	*C-D Ratio*	
							RBs	*MBs*
1969*	1443	17.6	306	6.3	115	3.3	37.6	98.2
1978*	12534	45.2	2664	10.1	1530	8.4	57.4	87.9
1984*	25541	52.9	9603	13.4	6589	13.5	68.6	84.6
1987*	30585	56.2	17527	14.7	11127	15.3	63.5	71.3
1991	35216	58.1	33163	15.1	19688	14.7	59.4	71.4
1997	33008	52	72511	14.7	32372	11.5	44.6	75.7
1988	32890	51.2	86484	14.6	36697	11.2	42.4	74.9
1999	32856	50.5	102602	14.6	41193	10.6	40.1	76.9
2000	32719	49.9	120447	14.7	47396	10.1	39.4	82.2
2001	32533	49.4	139427	14.7	56017	10.1	40.2	84.3

*December and for other years March.
SCBs : Scheduled Commercial Banks.
RBS : Rural Branches.
MBs : Metropolitan Branches.
Source : Economic and Political Weekly Vol. XXXVII No. 5, February 2-8, 2002 pp. 489-490.

A major component of the banking policy before economic reforms had been the spread of branch network into rural areas. One of the avowed objectives of bank nationalisation in 1969 was to transform the urban bias in commercial banking and make it a supply – leading phenomenon. As a consequence of this rural oriented banking development policy, we find that the number of rural branches as well as their proportion had gone up significantly in the first two decades of bank nationalization. In 1969 the proportion of rural branches was hardly 18 per cent and the figure went up to 58 per cent by 1991. The year 1991 is a significant landmark in the recent economic policy framework as it witnessed the beginning of new economic policy with greater accent on liberalization in all spheres of economic activity including banking. As a result we find that rural-oriented banking development has been given up in the post-reform period, as is evident from Table 15.1. We notice that the proportion of rural branches had declined to 49 per cent by March-2001. Even in absolute terms there has been a significant reduction in the number of rural branches by 2683 between 1991 and 2001. Such institutional vacuum is sure to hurt the process providing institutional credit to the rural sector in particular and in underdeveloped regions in general. Even the new policy of expanding micro-credit facilities through bank-linked Self-Help-Groups (SHGs) will face a serious hurdle, if the rural branch network is not expanded (EPW : 2002).

It is also noticed from Table 15.1 that rural deposits as a proportion of total deposits have been rising from a meagre figure of 6.3% in 1969 to 15.1%in 1991. However, in the post-reform era, they have stagnated around 15 per cent, the proportion of credit disbursed by the rural branches though rising slowly over time since 1969 has tended to decline in the post-reform period. C-D ratio is a rough measure of the flow of rural savings and credit to and from the banking system. The C-D ratio was 37.6 per cent in 1969 and has gradually risen to 68.6 per cent in 1984. This is the highest level attained during the entire period from 1969 to 2001. In the post-reform period there has been a steady decline in the C-D ratio and touched 39.4 per cent in 2000 and slightly moved to 40.2 per cent in 2001. The dwindling of C-D ratio of rural branches from over 64 per cent to around 40 per cent has been the most disquieting aspect of banking development of the past decade. This is all the more disquieting when viewed against the RBI prescription of a minimum of 60 per cent C-D ratio that rural branches are required to achieve (EPW : 2002). However, the C-D ratio of metropolitan branches was 98.2 per cent in 1969. Although it has fluctuated around that figure during the first decade of nationalization, there has been a gradual decline in the C-D ratio of metropolitan branches which touched 71.4 per cent in 1991. Hovering around that level with marginal variations it has tended to rise and reached 84.3 per cent in March 2001. These Trends in C-D ratio of metropolitan branches provide enough evidence of demand following nature of banking development due to the pulls and pressures of the metropolitan credit market.

FLOW OF BANK CREDIT TO AGRICULTURE

On account of agriculture credit friendly banking policies pursued by the Reserve Bank and subsequently NABARD and Government of India, there has been a significant increase in the flow of bank credit to agriculture in quantitative terms in the post-nationalisation era. Table 15.2 provides some particulars in this regard.

TABLE 15.2
Flow of Bank Credit from SCBs to Agriculture and Industry

(Rs. in Crore)

Year	*Amount Outstanding to Agriculture*	*Amount Outstanding to Industry*	*Amount Outstanding to TTM*
1975*	1071(10.7)	5777(57.7)	3167(31.6)
1980*	37722(15.7)	11555(48.8)	8397(35.5)
1990	16626(15.9)	50486(48.7)	36840(35.3)
1995	24948(11.80)	96211(45.6)	89780(42.5)
1999	40889(10.7)	18797(49.1)	153589(40.2)
2000	45638(9.9)	213779(46.5)	200664(43.6)

* End of December and others relate to March.
SCBs : Scheduled Commercial Banks.
Figures in parentheses indicate respective percentages to total.
TTM : Transport, Trade and Miscellaneous.
Source : EPW, Vol. XXXVI No. 5, Feb-8-2002, p. 493.

It may be noticed from Table 15.2 that the share of agriculture in total bank credit, both direct and indirect, which stood at 10.7 per cent in 1975 reached a peak of 15.9 per cent in March 1990. Subsequently, it has been steadily declining and touched a low of 9.9 per cent by March-2000. This has been inspite of the Reserve Bank's prescription of the share of agriculture at 18 per cent which remains unfulfilled. The reduction in sectoral credit allocation to agriculture and allied activities including small scale industry explains the decline in the proportion of priority sector advances in total non-food credit from 40 per cent in March 1990 to 34.7 per cent in March 1995 and to 35.9 per cent in March 2001 (EPW : 2002).

We noticed that the share of bank credit to industry has been getting reduced in the 1980s and stood at 47 per cent by the turn of the century. The tertiary sector has been getting a share of credit ranging from 32 per cent in 1975 and 44 per cent in 2000. Agriculture provides livelihood to nearly 2/3rds of the work-force but receives hardly 10 per cent of bank credit. The non-agricultural sector therefore gets 90 per cent of bank credit though it provides employment to hardly 1/3rd of the work-force in India. No wonder the low-productivity associated with agriculture which is over burdened with population gets neglected in the credit market. The situation is likely to worsen in the years to come due to the policy of deregulation and liberalisation of banking industry. In other words, in the post-reform era, the process of supply-leading banking is getting replaced by demand-following banking which has serious implications for achieving equity and social justice in the new millennium.

RRBS AND RUAL CREDIT

RRBs came into existence in 1975 in 12 districts with 17 branches. Since then there has been a rapid expansion of the number of RRBs, their branches and the districts covered until the end of the Sixth Five Year plan. Roughly the first decade of the establishment of RRBs is a period of rapid growth. The second decade starting with 1986 to 1996 is a period of consolidation. We present the progress of banking activities of RRBs in Table 15.3.

TABLE 15.3
Progress of Regional Rural Banks

(Rs. in Crore)

S.N.	*As at the end of*	*No. of RRBs*	*District covered*	*No. of branches*	*Deposits*	*Outstanding Advances*	*C.D Ratio %*
1.	Dec 1975	6	12	17	0.2	0.1	50
2.	Dec 1976	40	84	489	8	7	91
3.	Dec 1980	85	144	3279	200	243	122
4.	Dec 1985	188	333	12606	1286	1408	109
5.	Dec 1986	194	351	12838	1715	1785	104
6.	Sep 1990	196	380	14511	4268	3555	83
7.	Mar 1995	196	425	14509	11150	6291	56
8.	Mar 1996	196	427	14497	14188	7505	53
9.	Mar 1997	196	427	14461	18032	8718	48
10.	Mar 1998	196	448	14450	22189	9861	44

Source : NABARD, Statistics on Regional Rural Banks, Various Years.

As is well known deposit mobilisation and making advances are the primary functions of modern banking. RRBs are no exception to this rule. This is popularly known as financial intermediation between the saving units and spending units. Financial mobilisation by offering a set of incentives and services and allocation on the basis of social priorities underline this activity. CD ratio is a summary measure of banking activity of any institution or the set of institutions for any region or nation. We notice from Table 15.3 that except in the first two years of the establishment of

RRBs the CD ratio was more than 100% upto 1986. Subsequently, it has tended to decline gradually. It means that in the first phase not only the deposits mobilised by RRBs but also a part of the deposits of the sponsoring banks were drawn into the stream of advances. Since the advent of economic reforms a reverse situation is emerging. It implies that there has been an adverse effect on the clientele of RRBs who are generally poor. The post-reform era therefore has a deleterious effect on the rural banking scene and thereby on the rural poor.

ARGUMENTS AGAINST SUPPLY—LEADING FINANCE

A variety of arguments are advanced against directed bank lending to priority sector in particular and regulation of interest rates and other allocations of bank credit. A few arguments are listed here under.

(A) Directed Lending Undermines the Health of Lending Institutions

The earlier banking and financial sector policy was predicated on the strong assumption of the need for supply-based, subsidy-linked and target-oriented approach to banking development. It was further supplemented by the mandated involvement of banks and some financial institutions in government sponsored programmes like IRDP and other poverty-alleviation schemes. The mainstream literature is generally skeptical about the sustainability of that supply-led strategy of financial sector development; it is generally believed that the infirmities created in the operations of banks were more severe than the achievements made (EPW, 2002).

(B) Adverse Selection and Moral Hazard

A major problem of credit markets and more important that of directed credit programmes is the *'information asymmetry'* and the large agency costs associated with monitoring directed credit programmes. One of the solutions suggested in the literature to reduce *'information asymmetry'* and large agency costs associated with directed credit programme is to utilize the role of peer Groups, Non-Governmental Organisations, Self-Help Groups in credit market. A notable success story in this regard is the case of Bangladesh Grameen Bank (BGB), which has been lending largely to small groups of women to finance small-scale self-employment activities. BGB has been very successful in effectively tackling the problems of adverse selection, moral hazard, and lack of collateral. As of January, 1996 in the case of BGB, the repayment rate was 98 per cent despite the interest rate on loans being 20 per cent. The bank's organisation of borrowers into groups means that the group acts effectively as a form of social collateral substituting for the traditional physical collateral. Thus the inherent problem of *'asymmetry information'* characterizing the directed credit programmes especially in the case of small borrowers, is effectively tackled by the peer monitoring mechanism so crucial for the success of BGB, however, in some cases, peer pressure mechanism may not work effectively, especially if the group is not homogeneous and the risk-profile of the group members is not similar (RBI 1996-97).

(C) Erosion of Repayment Ethics

There is a general consensus that the strategies followed have helped to build a broad based institutional infrastructure for the delivery and deployment of credit. However, the emphasis throughout has been on achieving certain quantitative targets. As a consequence, inadequate attention was paid to the qualitative aspects of lending resulting in loan defaults and erosion of repayment ethics, to a grater of lesser extent, by all categories of borrowers. The end result was a disturbing growth in overdues, which not only hampered the recycling of scarce resources of banks, but also affected profitability and viability of financial institutions (Thorat : 2000).

KISAN CREDIT CARD SCHEME

The complexity and composite operations undertaken by the farmers have led to evolving Kisan Credit Card Scheme for the farmers to meet the total credit requirements in a comprehensive way. As this is a revolving credit facility without much documentation hassles, the scheme is becoming popular among the farmers and branches also find it very easy to operate.

The Kisan Credit Card Scheme requires lot of publicity to bring required awareness among the farmers so that all farmers in the service area villages are covered under the scheme. Besides reducing the transaction cost, the scheme emphasizes on timely and adequate credit which will directly help in improving the production levels and productivity (Kamath : 2000).

The Kisan Credit Card Scheme, introduced in 1998-99, is an innovative mechanism for facilitating access to short term credit to farmers. The scheme has gained popularity and its implementation has been taken up by 27 Commercial banks, 373 District Central Co-operative Banks/State Co-operative Banks (Two tier structure) and 196 Regional Rural Banks throughout the country. As on November 30, 2001, 20.4 million Kisan Credit Cards involving credit sanctions of Rs. 43,392 crore had been issued. Co-operative Banks accounted for 66 per cent of Kisan Credit Cards followed by Commercial Banks (27 per cent) and RRBs (7 per cent) (Economic Survey 2001-2002).

MICRO-FINANCE INNOVATION

With a view to improving the recovery of loans from the poor as well as to reduce the transaction costs and to improve the capability of the poor through the social intermediation, a system of micro finance delivery mechanism has been tried in different parts of the world. Under the system, borrowers get united in a group to deal with their activities including savings and borrowings. These groups are commonly known as Self – Help Groups (SHGs). The importance of SHGs is well recognized long back. However, in India the first formal attempt in this direction was initiated in 1992 with the launching of SHG Bank Linkage Programme under the aegis of the NABARD. The programme is yet to gain significant momentum at least in terms of quantum of amount issued. The cumulative number of SHGs involved in SHG Bank Linked Programme aggregating 114775 as at end of March 2000 covering an estimated number of 1.9 million very poor families in 24 states and union territories. More than 85 per cent of SHGs formed were exclusively of women members. As many as 718 NGOs were involved in SHGs bank linked programme. In all, 266 banks representing Commercial banks, Co-operative banks and Regional Rural Banks participated in the programme. Bank loans amounted to Rs. 1.9 billion (Ddadhich : 2000).

CONCLUSION

Historically, commercial banks have remained cut off from the domain of rural credit. Their location and outlook were such that they were urban-oriented almost everywhere. With the advent of development planning and the emergence of green revolution the demand for agricultural and rural credit accelerated and the non-commercial banking institutions could not meet it. The credit from informal sector was not only inadequate but costly and even exploitative. Hence, a strong case was made for the entry of commercial banks in the field of rural credit. The nationalization of 14 banks 1969 gave a major thrust in this direction. Consequently there was a rapid expansion of rural branches of commercial banks. Banking operations in terms of deposit mobilisation and deployment of credit also picked up. However the C-D ratio of rural branches has always lagged behind the national average, let alone that of the metropolitan branches. As a result, the rural savings were pumped out of the rural sector into the urban commercial sector. The share of agricultural credit in the post-reform era has dwindled. In the name of banking reform the priority sector share is reduced and this is likely to have adverse consequences for meeting the credit needs in agriculture but also for fostering microfinance innovations through the mechanism of SHG-bank linkages.

References

Dadhachi, C.L. 2000, New Savings Linked Loan Products in Rural Finance in the New Millennium, Oriental Bank of Commerce, New Delhi, p. 179.

Darmy, P.N. 1970, Institutionalisation of Agricultural Credit—Indian Experience, Banking and Development, RBI Bombay, p. 123.

Economic and Political Weekly Research Foundation 2002, Special Statistics-31, Money Banking and Finance, February 2, p. 483.

Government of India 2001-2002, Economic Survey, New Delhi, p. 2000.

Gunnar Myrdal 1958, Economic Theory and Under-Developed Regions, Vora & Company, Bombay, p. 40.

Hanumantha, C.H. Rao, Reform Agenda for Agriculture, EPW Feb. 15-21, 2003, p. 619.

Ibid., p. 483.

Ibid., p. 484.

Kahlan, A.S. & Singh Karam 1984, Managing Agricultural Finance : Theory and Practice, Allied, New Delhi, p. 54.

Kamath, R.J. 2000, Strengthening Self-Help Groups in the New Millennium, Oriental Bank of Commerce, New Delhi, p. 168.

Meller John W. et al. 1968. Developing Rural India, Plan and Practice, Corn Well University Press, Ithaca, p. 60.

Reserve Bank of India, 1996-97, Report on Trend and Progress of Banking in India (July-June) Mumbai, p. 51.

Thorat, Y.S.P. 2000 Towards a Stronger and Sustainable Rural Finance in Banking in the New Millennium. Oriental Bank of Commerce, New Delhi, p. 170.

CHAPTER

16

Globalisation and Decentralised Development : A Feminist Perspective

S.K. MISHRA AND I.D. SINGH

In the 1960s the state played a major role in promoting the wellbeing of the majority of people in developing countries. Poverty reduction was at the center of development planning and there was an emphasis on an approach to development which was broad-based and integrated. All of this changed from the decade of 1980s onwards in the context of the debt crisis and the steep rise in the cost of living in industrialized countries, which made inflation and deficit reduction major preoccupation of the governments of those countries. Within a policy framework set by Washington, 'the Washington Concensus', the role of status to promote broad-based socio-economic development was severely eroded. In many countries macro economic policies and structural adjustment programmes took precedence over socio-economic development planning; and economic growth privileged over social development. In the decade of 1980s, the World Bank and the I.M.F. set the policy framework through a strategy of policy dialogue. From the beginning of 1990s, trade replaced development as the central policy issue. WTO now sets the policy framework based on epistemology that liberalization of markets for goods and finance, small government and fiscal discipline is best for capturing the benefits of globalisation.

However, international environment is far from enabling and those of us are committed to the goals of sustainable human development have to fight disillusionment, despair and worst of all, cynicism in form of deteriorating quality of life of poor in general and of women in particular.

Thus, the dramatic changes in power relations brought about by the globalisation of financial and labour markets and by critical reinterpretations of modernity provide fertile ground for rethinking changing gender relations and development practice in the third world (Feldman, 1998).

The present paper aims at examining the impact of globalisation on women in form of its influences on women's awareness (literacy), physical capability (health) and autonomy (employment status). The paper also discusses the role played by feminists in countering the ill-effects of globalisation on women.

A BRIEF ACCOUNT OF DEBATE ON GLOBALISATION AND WOMEN'S STATUS

Globalisation is touted as the panacea for the economic ills of the world. The free flow of capital, labour, goods and information without state and other forms of intervention is claimed to be the only path towards world prosperity promoted by various regional organizations like EU, NAFTA, APEC and world organizations, such as GATT, WTO and financially aided by IMF and IBRD, economic liberalism is sweeping the globe as it leaves millions of skeletons behind. Capital has become free to pursue the greatest profit wherever it may lead. Out flows often cause closures of plants and ouster of workers from job. Capital inflows lead either to greater exploitation of workers and plunder of natural resources, or to destroy nascent local industries and traditional enterprises due to severe competition. Both situations, while creating opportunities for some, drive more to destitution (Lucie Cheng, 1999).

UK governments' white paper on globalisation of December, 2000—Making Globalisation Work for the Poor - recognize that "Globalisation creates new opportunities for sustainable development and poverty reduction" and therefore opines that "there is no alternative to globalisation and we should learn to live with it". But, the paper also admits that globalisation poses great threats to employment and livelihoods, to the environment and to human security in general - and so it argues finally that "making globalisation work for the world's poor is the greatest moral challenge facing our generation. The paper, however, does advocate intervention of the governments in the interests of equity and justice, for the benefits of globalisation will not automatically reach poor people (2001). Therefore, remedy to this challenge was perceived in decentralization, local development, and grass root initiatives that focused attention on the plight of the excluded—the rural landless, the urban poor and women - and shift in development discourse to 'meeting basic needs'.

Boserup (1970), described the institutional barriers that limit women's productive capacity and competitive position in the market. To her, traditional value victimizing women, were associated with subsistence-based production. Rogers shared Boserup's commitment to market competition as the means for increasing gender equity. Though, Boserup and Rogers sought to improve women's status through participation in market-based exchange relations. They underestimated women's reproductive responsibility in status production.

Studies of women's resistance and intra household bargaining have more recently been elaborated (Sen, 1990). However, patriarchal familiar relations between women and household limited women's voice and opportunity. Therefore, the policy goal was to free women from backward oppressive households and patriarchal relations which prohibited their participation in labour market. Hence, becoming wage labourers and self reliant individuals then became the criteria for measuring women's status, mobility and achievement. It was further thought that the availability of credit, in combination of new skills and training would transform subsistence and non-wage relations into marketable skills, enabling women to similar to those of men.

In the last decade, the recent tide of globalisation compelled countries to renegotiate their approach to development, a process that shifted national economic planning from import substitution and agricultural self-sufficiency to strategies of comparative advantage and export led growth. In the mean time, it was felt that the negative effects could be mediated by special programmes for women and children until economic equilibrium could once again be realized (Cornia et. al., 1987). Despite the problems entailed in this analysis, the discussions nonetheless linked the costs of economic reorganization directly to poverty, motherhood, and the privatisation of welfare institutions (Cornia et. al., 1987; Bakkar, 1994).

This all led to a significant departure in 1990s from earlier researches with regards to women's development—Earlier, women's unequal status was attributed to their lack of access to resources, their limited skills, traditional cultural practices and their relationship to patriarchal household structures. In the 1990s, scholars recognized that women bear the unequal burden of reduction in social expenditure caused by introducing economic restructuring and social dislocation and concluded that these costs are not temporary (Elson, 1990, 1992; Feldman, 1992; Bakkar, 1994).

GLOBALISATION AND WOMEN'S STATUS IN OTHER ASIAN COUNTRIES

It is a general perception that women tend to bear the brunt of globalisation. On the one hand, the general deterioration of living conditions and traditional patriarchal attitudes meant that they have had to take care of their families while generating an income. On the other hand, women are often the victims of plant closures.

In both Taiwan (China) and the Republic of Korea as the 'economic miracle' abated, a large number of textile, shoe, and garment plants, the labour-intensive manufacturing industries, closed leaving millions of women workers jobless overnight, for these industries lost their competitiveness. These women struggled for compensation and the right to work.

In Masan, announcement of Japanese Sumida Company's withdrawal of capital caused loss of job by 300 women workers in 1990. In response to a long protest and struggle of the workers, the company promised a significant amount of economic compensation (Lim, 1998).

In Taiwan (China), textile, garment, shoe and electronic plants, women comprising more than 50 per cent of their labour force, began to shut down one by one in the 1980s. To the report of Ministry of Economics more than 174000 companies and plants ceased to operate between 1993 and 1995, many leaving their workers without jobs, severance pay, or even back wages (Huang, 1998). Prevalence of low wages in Taiwan, compelled women in their 30s and 40s to seek employment-to supplement their family income. Most of them could not find comparable work for age-sex discrimination and had to take on food service or janitorial jobs, part time temporary contract, and other flexible work or suffer unemployment.

Likewise, may women workers in Philippines have also been victims of globalisation. Development of a more sophisticated resistance movement, the organization like Gabriela in Philippines has gained an international reputation and is spearheading a transterritorial anti-globalisation movement in the Asia-Pacific. In view of women in Philippines, the problems they face are related to their long colonial past as well as to the globalisation of international capital (Hsia, 1998).

Committee for Asian Women Workers started in 1981 (CAW) with its headquarter at Hong Kong is an example of transnational labour activist group which arose to meet with the problem of brutal exploitation of women due to globalisation. The CAW convenes conferences and workshops of Asian women labour organisers and also brings out a newsletter, carrying stories on women's labour conditions and their struggles in almost all Asian countries. Globalisation and its impact on women workers in Asia have been a frequent topic since 1991.

GLOBALISATION AND WOMEN IN SOUTH AFRICA

To South African Women, most government budgets are gender-biased, overlooking the ways in which programmes and policies either fail to address women's oppression, or exacerbate it (Joanna Kerr, 1999). They therefore take initiative to ensure that every government department annually draws up its own 'women's budget', analysing every line item for its impact on women. The success of the South African model is inspiring women elsewhere to create women's budgets as transformative tools for equality.

Women need a greater voice with this vision in mind, Gender and Economic Reforms in Africa (GERA) have been created to develop alternative and transformative economic policies and programmes that ensure gender equity and economic justice with the help of feminist economists, critical feminist researchers and activists who are able to analyse and influence economic policies and institutions—who can speak the language of economics.

ANALYSIS OF INDIAN EMPIRICAL EVIDENCES

Public expenditure on health and education; and state of women's health, education and work during pre and post reform period in India and in developing countries on the whole have been demonstrated to evaluate the effect of globalisation.

TABLE 16.1

Public Expenditure on Social Sector as Percentage of GDP in Pre and Post Reform Period

Countries	*Expenditure on Health*			*Expenditure on Education*		
	1990	*1998*	*Change*	*1990*	*1998*	*Change*
India	0.9	0.6	-0.3	3.9	3.2	-0.7
Developing Countries	1.9	3.8	+1.9	3.5	3.8	+0.3
Difference	-1.0	-3.2	—	+0.4	-0.6	—

Source : UNDP HDR—1992, HDR—2000 & HDR—2001.

Public expenditure on health and education in India is not only less in comparison to other countries but also shrinking due to influences of economic restructuring. The table shows that public expenditure on health and education as percentage of GDP reduced by 0.3 and 0.7 per cent respectively in India whereas it increased in developing countries in the post reform period.

The difference in expenditures on health and education between India and developing countries increased sharply during this period. It clearly shows that the neglect of social sector in India is far more than that in developing countries.

SOCIAL DEVELOPMENT INDICATORS

Literacy

It is supposed to be a significant indicator of social development, Indian position in literacy is shown in the following Table 16.2.

The Table 16.2 throws light on situation of literacy in population above 15 years of age. The female literacy has improved in post reform period faster than that of males. However, India has much less than half literate adult females in comparison to nearly two-thirds of that in developing countries. Moreover, the gap in female literacy between India and other developing countries was 20 percentage point in pre reform period which

TABLE 16.2
Adult Literacy in Pre and Post Reform Period in India

Countries	*Adult Literacy (In Per cent)*							
	1990			*1998*			*T D L*	
	M	*F*	*GDL*	*M*	*F*	*GDL*	*M*	*F*
India	62	34	28	67.1	43.5	23.6	5.1	+9.5
Developing Countries	74	54	20	80.3	64.5	15.8	6.3	+10.5
S D L	12	20	8	13.2	21.0	7.8	1.2	1.0

Source : UNDP, HDR-1992 and HDR—2000.
Notes : GDL = Gender Difference in Literacy.
TDL = Temporal Difference in Literacy.
SDL = Spatial Difference in Literacy.

rose to 21 percentage point after economic reforms. Thus, India has not taken appropriate care of a very significant indicator of social development like female literacy.

Health

Availability of health facilities to the women may be measured by Maternal Mortality Ratio, Expectation of Life at birth and also by sex ratio.

Maternal Mortality Ratio for India in 1998 was almost same as it was for overall average all developing countries a decade ago.

Life expectancy at birth for women in India has made substantial increase and now it is greater than that for men by 0.8 years (1998). However, the same figure of difference for overall developing countries is noted to be 3.2 years.

Sex ratio, i.e., number of females per thousand males is a significant indicator of attitude of society towards females and the facility of health and nutrition given to them.

TABLE 16.3
Sex Ratio in Pre and Post Reform Period in India

Sex Ratio	*Census*		*Change over 1991*
	1991	*2001*	
General	927	933	+6
Child Population age 0 – 6 years	945	927	-18
Population aged 7+	923	935	+12

Source : M.K. Premi, The Missing Girl Child, *EPW*, May 2001, p.1875.

Increase in sex ratio in general population seems to be a matter of satisfaction. But, it conceals more significant facts than what it reveals.

Increase in sex ratio is a result of tremendous rise in survivorship of elderly women. A sharp decline in sex ratio among the children of upto age six from 945 to 927 shows mass growth of foeticide and infanticide of girl child. This may be attributed to the realization of social attitude against the girl child into practice through foetus sex test. This action may not be considered that much immoral under the influence of globalisation of thought at the social and individual level.

STATUS OF EMPLOYMENT

Earning and workforce participation of women have been considered by UNDP as important factors to workout Gender Development Index. Globalisation has significantly influenced women's WFPR.

TABLE 16.4

Women's (15+) Workforce Participation Rate in Pre and Post Reform Period in India

Country	*WFPR of Women (In Percentage)*		
	Year		*T D E*
	1988-90	*1998*	
India	25.6	41.8	16.2
Developing Countries	32.5	55.6	23.1
SDE	6.9	13.8	6.9

Sources: UNDP, HDR-1992 & HDR-2000.
Notes : TDE = Temporal Difference in Employment.
SDE = Spatial Difference in Employment.

The table shows that Women's Work Force Participation rate increased by 16.2 percentage point during the last decade which is far less than 23.1 percentage point, the rate of increase for overall developing countries. Likewise, Work Force Participation rate for developing countries was higher than that for India by 6.9 percentage in 1990 which rose by double, i.e., to 13.8 percentage point in 1998.

One of the very disturbing features of growth pattern in the post liberalisation period is very low employment generating potential of growth in the secondary and the tertiary sectors. The result is concentration of work force in agriculture and a persistent deterioration of relative productivity and income of both male and female workers engaged in the primary sector (Bhalla : 2001).

In the wake of globalisation, there has also been casualisation and informalisation of labour market both for males and females (Jeemol Unni, 2001). However, this was comparatively more for females than that for males. Increase in percentage of casual employee has been by 2.4 and 3.3 percentage points for males and females respectively whereas there was reduction in percentage of regular employee by 1.7 and 1.1 percentage point for males and females respectively.

REMEDIAL MEASURES

The decade of ninetees has been of paramount significance as regards to feminist research, strategy and advocacy. Attempts made by feminists to promote equality and women's empowerment have begun to bring fruition. Act of devoting an entire issue of the prestigious journal 'World Development' to gender and macro economics in 1995 clearly indicates interest and seriousness of main stream economists in feminist economic theory. Other remedial measures and their impacts are as follows:

Influencing Corporate Behaviour

Corporations are the biggest players in the global economy and also the biggest winners. Foreign private investment in developing countries alone has grown five-fold and translates into investments of almost US $ 1 trillion (Sutherland an Sewell, 1998:2). In comparison, the investment in development cooperation is a drop in the bucket.

Campaigns to make corporations more responsible have been waged for decades for environmental protection, better working conditions for labour, ban on child labour etc. Now, Southern Women's groups have become active on behalf of women factory workers. As a result of external pressure, some corporations are introducing voluntary codes of conduct covering ethical, environmental, and labour practices in all their operations, both domestic and abroad (Hibler and Beamish, 1998). However, enforcement of voluntary codes of conduct needs independent monitoring. Moreover, most importantly, codes of conduct can not ultimately influence a global production system dependent on cheap and flexible female labour.

UN Endeavours

Institutions like the World Bank are increasingly seeing women as active agents of social, political and economic change instead of passive recipients of development. The 1995 UN World Conference on Women was probably the most visible and international focus on governments and their responsibilities. More than thirty five thousand women from all over the world went to Beizing, many of them to share their experiences of working conditions, inadequate health care, or lack of access to technology in the context of globalisation. Non-governmental organisations had unprecedented access to government delegates attending the numerous preparatory meetings and Beizing summit, and they lobbied intensely for substantive changes in the final document—The Platform for Action. However, the Beizing summit does not seem to have gained ground. Firstly, sectoral approach adopted by UN denies any strategizing about the structural causes of gender discrimination. Secondly, the participants attending the summit mostly represented the 'minor' government ministries. Lastly, most of the Beizing recommendations addressing problem of globalisation are vague.

Pressure on Governments

The observations reveal that the globalisation, well supported and strengthened by the government policies, has deteriorated the quality of life and work of women and disappointed to all those who are committed to the goals of sustainable human development. Nelson (1994) rightly says that it is women who have had to be the shock absorbers of the Structural Adjustment Programme (SAP). Therefore, government policies must have to pay due attention to the plight of those who are expected to be worsened by the globalisation by extending some sort of safety net to them. For this, government need to be pressured and held accountable to these international commitments by the women's organisations, researchers and activists. Governments can be influenced to address the structural causes of poverty, or restructure the allocation of public expenditures—but unless feminist leaders show them how, it is unlikely to happen.

CONCLUSION

So, if development is to expand people's choices and guarantee their human rights, two things are necessary. First, global economic system must change and secondly, processes of change have to recognize gender imbalances to ensure that all people benefit from development. For this, feminist research and activism has to deepen its impact, expand its approach, and strengthen its alliances.

Deepening of impact means exposing and challenging vested interests and power structures—the historically rooted culture, principles, rules and procedures that underline an organisation. Simply adding women into existing structures is not going to serve the purpose.

Expanding of approach denotes our need to be more multidisciplinary and holistic. Development objectives need to be informed by human rights, ecology, cultural studies, political science and so on. Economic growth will always supersede human welfare as long there is dominance of economics over other disciplines in defining development.

Finally, alliances need to be strengthened between women—North and South, East and West, rich and poor. We must be respectful to one another, taking care not to misrepresent the diverse positions of different women. The tensions that exist within international feminism need to be acknowledged and tackled. Global sisterhood can be replaced by a form of sisterhood which is both strategic and effective.

References

Bakkar, I. (ed.) (1994), 'The Strategic Silence: Gender an Economic Policy', London: Zed.

Bhalla, G.S. (2001), 'Political Economy of Indian Development in the 20th Century', Presidential Address at 83rd Annual Conference of IEA, University of Jammu, Dec. 30, 2000 to Jan. 1, 2001.

Boserup, E (1970), 'Women's Role in Economic Development', New York, St. Martin's.

Cornia, G.A. et. al. (eds.) (1987), *Adjustment with a Human Face*, Vol. I, New York, UNICEF/ Clarendon.

Elson, D. (1990), "Male Bias in Macro Economics: The Case of Structural Adjustment". In Diana Elson (ed.), Male Bias in Development Process, Manchester, Manchester University Press, pp. 164-190.

Elson, D. (1992), "From Survival Strategies to Transformation Strategies: Women's Needs and Structural Adjustment", In Lourdes Beneria and Shelley Feldman (eds) Unequal Burden: Economic Crises, Persistent Poverty and Women's work, Boulder: West View, pp. 26-48.

Feldman, S. (1992), "Crises, Poverty and Gender Inequality: Current Themes and Issues". In Lourdes Beneria and Shelley Feldman (eds), *op. cit.*, pp. 1-25.

Feldman, S. (1998), "Conceptualising Change and Equality in the Third World Context". In Nelly P. Stromquist (ed.), Women in the Third World, New York : Garland.

Harriss, John (2001), "Globalisation and World's Poor", *EPW*, Bombay, India, June 9, pp. 2035.

Hsia, H.C. (1998), "Awaking the Women who nourished the earth'. Taiwan: Lihpao, April 1, p.11.

Huang, C.H. (1998), "Economic Liberalism and Fate of Women Workers', Article presented at the Globalisation and Asia Workshop, Taichung, July.

Kerr, Joanna (1999), "Responding to Globalisation', In Marilyn Porter and Ellen Judd (eds) Feminists Doing Development, London: Zed Books.

Lim, Y.I. (1998), "Han Young Cases Viewed from Korean Experiences', Article presented at the Labour Rights and Labour Organising in the *Pacific Rim Conference*, May 22, 1998, University of California, Los Angeles.

Lucie, C. (1999), Globalisation and Women's Paid Labour in Asia, *International Social Science Journal*, UNESCO: Blackwell, June, p. 225.

Rogers, B. (1980), The Domestication of Women: Discrimination in Developing Societies, New York: St. Martin's.

Sen, A.K. (1990), "Gender and Cooperative Conflicts'. In Irine Tinker (ed.), Persistent Inequalities: Women and World Development, New York: Oxford, pp. 123-149.

Sutherland and Sewell (1998), Quoted in Kerr Joanna, 1999, *op. cit.*

Unni, Jeemol (2001), Gender and Informality in Labour Market in South Asia, *EPW*, June 30.

CHAPTER

17

Trends in Income Distribution in India During Liberalization Period

ASHUTOSH KUMAR AND P.S. RAIKHY

Relationship between economic development and income distribution has been attracting attention of economists mainly since mid-fifties. It was opined that relative inequality increases during the early stages of development, reaches a peak and then declines in the later stages (Kuznets, 1963). When 'trickle down' hypothesis failed to alleviate poverty and reduce income inequalities it was realized that goals of economic development must be redefined in terms of progressive reduction in unemployment, poverty and inequalities (Seers, 1969). As such the study of income distribution, especially in developing countries, assumed more importance (Chenery : 1974). Two different approaches have been applied in the study of income distribution, one related to degree of relative inequality, while the second to degree of absolute poverty. 'Growth with equity and social justice' has been a cherished goal of India's policy and planning, and many programmes, ranging from political slogans like *'garibi hatao'* to effective measures involving public distribution system and employment generation programmes were launched. These programmes did succeed in reducing poverty and inequalities. However, a complete 'U' turn in economic polices was made in July, 1991, when the country adopted policies of structural adjustment involving decontrol, delicensing, deregulation, privatization etc. These policies of liberalization and privatization further got strengthened under the WHO policy regime and integrating the Indian economy with those of other countries. Thus globalization policies have now virtually replaced the initial relatively small reform measures. It is feared that this rapid trend towards free trade and free enterprise economy with state increasingly withdrawing from economic and social welfare activities would worsen poverty and income inequalities in the country. With this objective in view, the present paper examines income distribution in India during the liberalization period. The paper has been divided into three sections. Section-I examines the trends and determinants of income inequalities, Section–II concentrates on the trends and determinants of poverty and Section-III sums up the discussion and brings out the implications.

I

Inequalities in India, have been measured in terms of variations in consumption expenditure of different population groups. The share of total consumption expenditure of different quintile groups of households arranged by per capita consumption expenditure and the Gini coefficients since 1977-78 are given in Table 17.1. It may be seen from the table that the share of the poorest 20 percent population in 1977-78 was 8.5 percent, which increased to 8.9 percent in 1987-88 and further to 9.84 percent in 1999-2000. Share of the top 20 percent during the same period decreased, with some fluctuations in-between, from 40.9 percent in 1977-78 to 36.15 percent in 1999-2000. Relative inequality, measured through the ratio of the share of top quintile with that of the bottom quintile (Q5/Q1) indicated a declining trend, with values of 4.812 in 1977-78, 4.607 in 1987-88 and 3.670 in 1999-2000. The Gini ratio declined from 0.321 in 1977-78 to 0.318 in 1987-88 and 0.260 in 1999-2000. Thus, the 55th round of NSS indicated a rapid decline in inequalities in 1999-2000.

TABLE 17.1
Quintile-wise Percentage Share in Total Consumption Expenditure

Year	Q_1	Q_2	Q_3	Q_4	Q_5	Q_5/Q_1	*Gini Ratio*
1977-78	8.5	12.5	16.4	21.7	40.9	4.812	0.321
1983-84	8.6	12.7	16.5	21.7	40.5	4.709	0.314
1986-87	8.5	12.5	16.4	21.5	41.1	4.835	0.322
1987-88	8.9	12.5	16.3	21.3	41.0	4.607	0.318
1988-89	9.0	12.7	16.4	21.4	40.5	4.500	0.311
1989-90	9.1	12.9	16.6	21.7	39.7	4.363	0.304
1990-91	9.1	13.1	16.9	21.8	39.1	4.297	0.296
1991-92	9.0	12.5	15.9	20.7	41.9	4.656	0.325
1992-93	8.8	12.5	16.2	21.4	41.1	4.670	0.320
1996-97	8.86	12.36	15.84	20.87	42.07	4.740	0.328
1999-2000	9.84	14.16	17.55	22.3	36.15	3.670	0.260

Source : http://www.worldbank.org/html/grwthweb/grth_t.htm
Note : Q_1 share of bottom Quintile in Consumption Expenditure and Q_5 of top Quintile.

DETERMINANTS OF INCOME DISTRIBUTION

On a list of 16 determinants of income distribution, relating to human resource development, infrastructure, structure of the economies in terms of labour force and value added by different sectors and per capita income for 16 major states of the country was prepared. These included :

1. Percentage of Urban Population (PURBAN)
2. Literacy Rate (LITERACY)
3. Life Expectancy (LIFE)
4. Infant Mortality Rate (INFANT)
5. Growth Rate of Population (GRPOP)
6. Percentage of Working Population (PWORKING)
7. Sex Ratio (SEX RATIO)
8. Density of Population (DENSITY)
9. Relative Infrastructure Index (INFRA)
10. Per capita State Domestic Product (PCSDP and in log form LOGPCSDP)
11. Percentage of Labour in Primary Sector (PLABPRIM)
12. Percentage of Labour in Secondary Sector (PLABSEC)
13. Percentage of Labour in Tertiary Sector (PLABTERT)
14. Percentage Value Added in Primary Sector (PVAPRIM)
15. Percentage Value Added in Secondary Sector (PVASEC)
16. Percentage Value Added in Tertriay Sector (PVATERT)

Multiple (step-wise) Regression Analysis was applied with Gini ratio as dependent variable, at two points of time, 1987-88 and 1999-2000 and Factor Analysis was also applied so as to bring out the major changes, if any, in the determinants during the liberalization period.

In 1987-88, percentage of urban population (PURBAN), percentage value added in secondary sector (PVASEC), per capita state domestic product in log form (LOGPSCDP) and literacy rate (LITERACY) were identified as significant determinants. Urbanisation (PURBAN) and literacy rate contributed to enhancing of inequalities, while PVASEC and LOGPCSDP had damping effect on inequalities (Table 17.2). These four variables turned out to be significant at five percent level and were able to explain 78.2 percent of the variations in the inequalities.

During 1999-2000, PVAPRIM, INFANT, LIFE and PLABPRIM turned out to be significant determinants of inequalities. While PVAPRIM affected inequalities negatively, other variables affected these positively. The coefficients of all the four variables turned out to be significant at 5 percent level and could explain 84.3 percent of the variations in the inequalities (Table 17.3).

Thus during the liberalization period, in addition to structural variables like PVAPRIM and PLABPRIM, demographic variables like INFANT and LIFE also tuned out to be important determinants. However,

TABLE 17.2

Determinants of Income Distribution in India : Results of Multiple Regression (Step-wise) Analysis with Gini Ratio as Dependent Variable (1987-88)

Regression Coefficient of						
CONSTANT	*PURBAN*	*PVASEC*	*LOGPCSDP*	*LITERACY*	R^2 *(F)*	R^2 *(D.F.)*
0.2388 (12.20)	0.00222* (2.83)	—	—	—	0.363* (7.99)	—
0.2645 (13.97)	0.00464* (4.15)	-0.0035* (-2.67)	—	—	0.589* (9.32)	0.525* (2,13)
0.5590 (3.19)	0.00608* (4.51)	-0.0040* (-3.16)	-0.091 (-1.69)	—	0.688* (8.05)	0.585* (3,12)
0.6481 (4.25)	0.00635* (5.55)	-0.0047* (-4.22)	-0.126* (-2.63)	0.00086* (2.41)	0.782* (9.91)	0.703* (4,11)

Note : Figures in parentheses are t-values.
* indicates significant at 5 percent level.

TABLE 17.3

Determinants of Income Distribution in India : Results of Multiple Regression (Step-wise) Analysis with Gini Ratio as Dependent Variable (1999-2000)

Regression Coefficient of						
CONSTANT	*PURBAN*	*PVASEC*	*LOGPCSDP*	*LITERACY*	R^2 *(F)*	R^2 *(D.F.)*
0.3106 (13.96)	-0.00198* (-3.66)	—	—	—	0.488* (13.37)	—
0.29793 (14.71)	-0.00256* (-4.76)	0.00056* (2.29)	—	—	0.635* (11.35)	0.579* (2,13)
-0.02198 (-0.17)	-0.00260* (-5.70)	0.00141* (3.50)	0.0043* (2.47)	—	0.758* (12.57)	0.698* (3,12)
-0.23487 (-1.67)	-0.00276* (-7.09)	0.0012* (3.63)	0.0066* (3.78)	0.0016* (2.43)	0.843* (14.77)	0.786 (4,11)

Note : Figures in parentheses are t-values.
* indicates significant at 5 percent level.

from policy point of view, reduction in share of agriculture increased inequalities, which indicated that diversification of the structure of the economies towards secondary and tertiary sectors had inequality-enhancing effect. In a country where about 65 percent population engaged in agriculture produces about 25 percent share of national income, further decline in the share of agriculture in the absence of shift of labour, will increase inequalities.

FACTOR ANALYSIS

In view of the problem of multi-collinearity, more variables could not be included in Multiple Regression Analysis. Therefore, Rotated Factor Analysis (Keiser-Varimax) technique was applied to 1987-88 and 1999-2000 data. Table 17.4 shows that for the year 1987-88, the three identified factors accounted for 81.3 percent of the total variations is the variable set. The First Factor, accounting for 34.6 percent of the variations, included LIFE, LITERACY, PLABTERT and INFRA variables. The Second Factor which included PURBAN, PVASEC, PLABSEC, PVATERT and PWORKING as constituent variables was able to explain 29.9 percent of the variations. The Third Factor included SEXRATIO and PCSDP variables and could explain 16.8 percent of the variations in the variable set.

TABLE 18.4

Determinants of Income Distribution in India : Results of Factor Analysis, Rotated Factor Matrix (1987-88)

Variable	*Factor Loading*			*Communalities*
	F1	*F2*	*F3*	
Life Expectancy [LIFE]	0.919	0.218	0.020	0.892
Literacy Rate [LITERACY]	0.877	0.179	-0.340	0.916
Percentage Labour in Tertiary Sector [PLABTERT]	0.811	0.408	-0.147	0.846
Relative Infrastructure Index [INFRA]	0.806	0.122	0.442	0.859
Percentage of Urban Population [PURBAN]	0.323	0.907	0.147	0.948
Percentage Value Added in Secondary Sector [PVASEC]	0.224	0.801	-0.035	0.692
Percentage Labour in Secondary Sector [PLABSEC]	0.251	0.699	0.335	0.664
Percentage Value Added in Tertiary Sector [PVATERT]	0.367	0.675	-0.241	0.649
Percentage of Working Population [PWORKING]	-0.400	0.669	-.385	0.756
Sex Ratio [SEXRATIO]	0.234	0.093	-0.906	0.885
Per Capita State Domestic Product [PCSDP]	0.566	0.408	0.594	0.840
Variance	3.8070	3.2916	1.8478	Total = 8.9464
Percentage of Variance Explained	34.6	29.9	16.8	81.3
Percentage of Cumulative Variance Explained	34.6	64.5	81.3	—

For 1999-2000, again three factors were identified, which explained 78 percent variations in the variable set (Table 17.5). The First Factor including

TABLE 17.5

Determinants of Income Distribution in India : Results of Factor Analysis, Rotated Factor Matrix (1999-2000)

Variable	Factor Loading			Communalities
	F1	F2	F3	
Life Expectancy [LIFE]	0.898	0.291	-0.161	0.917
Relative Infrastructure Index (INFRA)	0.845	0.126	0.061	0.733
Infant Mortality Rate [INFANT]	-0.802	-0.237	0.310	0.795
Percentage Labour in Secondary Sector [PLABSEC]	0.791	0.325	-0.036	0.733
Literacy Rate [LITRACY]	0.737	0.229	-0.298	0.684
Density of Population [DENSITY]	0.672	-0.380	-0.099	0.605
Percentage of Urban Population [PURBAN]	0.326	0.907	-0.034	0.930
Per Capita State Domestic Product [PCSDP]	0.560	0.772	0.645	0.930
Percentage of Working Population [PWORKING]	-0.521	0.680	-0.462	0.947
Percentage Value Added in Secondary Sector [PVASEC]	0.069	0.639	-0.047	0.415
Percentage Value Added in Tertiary Sector [PVATERT]	0.369	0.580	-0.542	0.767
Sex Ratio [SEXRATIO]	0.179	-0.041	-0.934	0.906
Variance	4.6482	3.0849	1.6296	Total =9.3627
Percentage of Variance Explained [In%]	38.7	25.7	13.6	78
Percentage of Cumulative Variance Explained	38.7	64.4	78	—

LIFE, INFRA, INFANT, PLABSEC, LITERACY and DENSITY, accounted for 38.7 percent of the variations. The Second Factor including PURBAN, PCSDP, PWORKING, PVASEC and PVATERT, explained 25.7 percent of the variations. The Third Factor included SEXRATIO and accounted for 13.6 percent of the variations.

Thus before liberalization, structural variables had the edge over demographic variables in explaining income distribution, but after liberalization, demographic variables have an edge over structural variables in explaining the income distribution. However, still the mix of demographic and structural variables is important in determining income distribution in India.

II

In this section, trends in poverty in 16 major states of the country have been examined and determinants of poverty have been identified.

Estimates of poverty in the country have been mainly made by NSS through its different consumption rounds. However, Planning Commission accepted the methodology of 'Expert Group on Estimation of Proportion and Number of the Poor' (Lakdawala Committee) in 1993 and estimates of poverty have been based on this methodology. Such estimates of poverty for 1977-78, 1987-88 and 1999-2000 have been given in Table 17.6.

TABLE 17.6
Percentage of Population below Poverty Line in Selected States of India, 1977-78, 1987-88 and 1999-2000

State	*1977-78*	*1987-88*	*1999-2000*
Andhra Pradesh	39.31	25.66	15.77
Assam	57.15	36.21	36.09
Bihar	61.55	52.13	42.60
Gujarat	41.23	31.54	14.07
Haryana	29.55	16.64	8.74
Jammu and Kashmir	38.97	23.82	3.48
Karnataka	48.78	37.53	20.04
Kerala	52.22	31.79	12.72
Madhya Pradesh	61.78	43.07	37.43
Maharashtra	55.88	40.41	25.02
Orissa	70.07	55.58	47.15
Punjab	19.27	13.20	6.16
Rajasthan	37.42	35.15	15.28
Tamil Nadu	54.79	43.39	21.12
Uttar Pradesh	49.05	41.46	31.15
West Bengal	60.52	44.72	27.02
All India	51.32	38.86	26.10
C V for Head Count Ratio (Percent)	27.62	32.78	58.00

Sources: 1. Govt of India, Press Information Bureau, 11th March, 1997.
2. http: www.planningcommission.nic.in/prfebt.htm.

The table shows that poverty at the national level in 1977-78, as measured by head count ratio, was 51.32 percent. However, the poverty level in Orissa was as high as 70.07 percent. Bihar, West Bengal, Madhya Pradesh, Maharashtra, Assam and Tamil Nadu had higher poverty than the national average. The minimum level of poverty was in Punjab (19.27 percent).

In 1987-88, the poverty at the national average level was reduced to 38.86 percent. All states showed improvement in respect of poverty level. However still, poverty level in Orissa and Bihar was much above the national average. Poverty level continued to be high in West Bengal, Madhya Pradesh, Tamil Nadu, Uttar Pradesh and Maharashtra. The minimum level of poverty continued to be in Punjab (13.20 percent), followed by Haryana (16.64 percent).

The recent poverty estimate for 1999-2000 indicated national average of poverty as 26.1 percent, which indicates a sizeable improvement. However, the poverty level in Orissa was still as high as 47.15 percent and in Bihar 42.60 percent. Poverty level in Madhya Pradesh, Assam and Uttar Pradesh continued to be higher than the national average. Poverty level in Jammu & Kashmir was the lowest (3.48 percent). Punjab (6.16 percent) and Haryana (8.74 percent) were also having low poverty levels. Very significant improvements in reduction of poverty were experienced in Jammu & Kashmir, Maharashtra, Kerala, Karnatka, West Bengal, Gujarat and Andhra Pradesh.

However, a very significant aspect of the improvement in poverty situation is that while some states experienced remarkable improvement, others indicated only marginal improvement. As a result, coefficient of variation of Head Count Ratio (HCR) increased from 27.62 percent in 1977-78 to 32.78 percent in 1987-88 and further jumped to 58 percent in 1999-2000. This widening gap between states can at least to some extent be attributed to the policies of liberalization, privatization and globalisation and needs to be bridged at the earliest.

DETERMINANTS OF POVERTY

To examine the determinants of poverty, in addition to 16 variables identified on 'a-priori' basis in case of income inequalities, Gini ratio, which was dependent variable in case of the study of inequalities was also included. The analysis has been made at two points of time i.e. 1987-88 and 1999-2000, to study the impact of liberalization policies on the determinants of poverty.

MULTIPLE (STEP-WISE) REGRESSION ANALYSIS

The results of Multiple (step-wise) Regression Analysis for 1987-88 (Table 17.7) showed that PLABPRIM, LITERACY, PLABSEC and LIFE were identified as significant variables, which along with LOGPCSDP and PVASEC could explain 83.7 percent of the total variations in poverty (HCR). Thus structural and demographic variables were important in affecting poverty.

In 1999-2000, variables like PLABPRIM, PVASEC, PURBAN, GINI, DENSITY and GRPOP were found to be significant determinants of poverty (Table 17.8), which could explain 92.2 percent of the total variations in poverty. While GINI, PVASEC, PLABPRIM and DENSITY were found to be poverty enhancing, PURBAN and GRPOP were poverty reducing factors. From policy viewpoint GINI, PVASEC and PLABPRM turned out to be important. Without shift of labour force from agriculture, increase in share

TABLE 17.7

Determinants of Poverty for India: Results of Multiple [Step-wise] Regression Analysis with Poverty Headcount Ratio as Dependent Variable [1987-88]

	Regression Coefficient of							
CONSTANT	LOGPCSDP	PVASEC	PLABPRIM	LITERACY	PLABSEC	LIFE	R^2 (F)	R^{-2} (D.E.)
236.92 (3.61)	-.58* (-306)	—	—	—	—	—	0.401* (9.38)	—
285.85 (4.42)	-.77* (-3.91)	0.78** (1.98)	—	—	—	—	0.539* (7.63)	0.469* (2,13)
187.56 (2.23)	-.60* (-2.82)	1.06* (2.62)	0.54* (1.68)	—	—	—	0.627* (6.75)	0.534* (3,12)
176.38 2.17)	-.63* (-3.08)	1.01* (2.58)	0.72** (2.16)	0.27 (1.42)			0.685* (6.0)	0.571* (4,11)
53.30 (0.48)	-.60* (-3.10)	0.93* (2.51)	1.91* (2.27)	0.66** (2.12)	1.7 (1.53)	—	0.744* (5.84)	0.617* (5,10)
30.05 (0.32)	-.35 (-1.74)	0.52 (1.44)	2.34* (3.19)	1.31* (3.37)	2.7* (2.60)	2.15* (2.27)	0.837* (7.74)	0.837* (6,9)

* indicates significant at 5 percent level.
** indicates significant at 10 percent level.

Table 17.8
Determinants of Poverty for India: Results of Multiple [Step-wise] Regression Analysis with Poverty Headcount Ratio as Dependent Variable [1999-2000]

				Regression Coefficient of				
CONSTANT	*PLABRPIM*	*DENSITY*	*GRPOP*	*PVASEC*	*PURBAN*	*GINI*	R^2 *(F)*	R^{-2} *(D.E.)*
-27.94	0.90*	—	—	—	—	—	0.482*	—
(-1.96)	(3.61)						(13.04)	
-53.08	1.15*	0.0261*	—	—	—	—	0.685*	0.637
(-3.68)	(5.25)	(2.90)					(14.16)	(2,13)
-45.52	1.28*	0.0239*	-6.6**	—	—	—	0.766*	0.708*
(-3.39)	(6.20)	(2.94)	(-2.05)				(13.16)	(3,12)
-58.85	1.31*	0.0230*	-6.1**	0.47	—	—	0.811*	0.742*
(-3.89)	(6.71)	(3.00)	(-2.01)	(1.61)			(11.82)	(4,11)
-22.34	0.90*	0.0118**	-6.4*	1.06*	-0.89*	—	0.915*	0.873*
(-1.50)	(4.98)	(1.89)	(-2.97)	(4.00)	(-3.51)		(21.62)	(5,10)
-38.89	0.64*	0.0086**	-3.7**	0.76*	-1.25*	187*	0.962	0.937*
(-3.36)	(4.29)	(1.90)	(-2.20)	(3.67)	(-5.99)	(3.34)	(38.16)	(6,9)

* significant at 5 percent level of significance.
** significant at 10 percent level of significance.

of secondary sector would enhance poverty. To some extent urbanisation represents shift from agriculture and in this sense it is poverty reducing.

Factor Analysis

To identify important determinants of poverty, Rotated Factor Analysis was applied to the data for 1987-88 and 1999-2000. To have positive association with poverty, PURBAN, LITERACY and PCSDP were changed into PRURAL, ILLIT and INVPCSCP. For 1987-88, four derived Factors could explain 90.9 percent of the total variations (Table 17.9). The First Factor included four variables, namely INFANT, PLABPRIM, INVPCSDP and ILLIT, which could explain 28.1 percent of the total variations. The Second Factor, accounting for 27.9 percent of the variations included

TABLE 17.9
Determinants of Poverty in India: Results of Factor Analysis, Rotated Factor Matrix (1987-88)

Variable	*Factor Loading*				*Communalities*
	F1	*F2*	*F3*	*F4*	
Infant Mortality Rate (INFANT)	0.803	-0.160	0.352	-0.292	0.880
Percentage Labour in Primary Sector (PLABPRIM)	0.797	-0.460	-0.041	0.010	0.848
Inverse of Per Capita State Domestic Product (INVPCSDP)	0.745	-0.418	-0.0480	0.364	0.864
Illiteracy (ILLIT)	0.679	-0.259	0.345	-0.487	0.885
Percentage Value Added in Secondary Sector (PVASEC)	-0.200	0.958	0.056	0.076	0.966
Percentage Value Added in Primary Sector (PVAPRIM)	0.406	-0.848	-0.141	-0.166	0.931
Percentage of Rural Population (PRURAL)	0.541	-0.752	-0.249	0.060	0.923
Density of Population (DENSITY)	-0.101	-0.028	-0.941	0.159	0.921
Percentage of Working Population (PWORKING)	0.063	0.330	0.837	0.297	0.903
Sex Ratio (SEXRATIO)	-0.043	0.067	0.064	0.981	0.973
Variance	2.809	2.794	1.922	1.568	Total=9.093
Percentage of Variance Explained	28.1	27.9	19.2	15.7	90.9
Percentage of Cumulative Variance Explained	28.1	56	75.2	90.9	

PVASEC, PVAPRIM and PRURAL. The Third Factor included DENSITY and PWORKING and explained 19.2 percent of the variations. The Fourth Factor, comprising of SEXRATIO explained 15.7 percent of the variations. As the First Factor included a mix of economic, structural and demographic variables, therefore it can be said that poverty is affected by mix of all such aspects.

For 1999-2000, four Factors were derived, which accounted for 89.9 percent of the total variations in the variable set (Table 17.10). The First Factor included PLABPRIM, INFANT, INVPCSDP, ILLIT and PRURAL variables which explained 32.8 percent of the variations. The Second Factor included PVASEC, GINI and PVAPRIM variables which explained 28.5 percent of the variations. In the Third Factor, DENSITY and PWORKING were included, which explained 16.8 percent of the variations. The Fourth Factor included SEXRATIO and explained 11.7 percent of the variations. Again, poverty was influenced by a mix of economic structural and demographic variables.

TABLE 17.10

Determinants of Poverty in India: Results of Factor Analysis, Rotated Factor Matrix (1999-2000)

Variable	*Factor Loading*				*Communalities*
	F1	*F2*	*F3*	*F4*	
Percentage Labour In Primary Sector (PLABRIM)	0.957	-0.031	-0.228	-0.002	0.969
Infant Mortality Rate (INFANT)	0.854	-0.022	-0.233	-0.242	0.841
Inverse of Per Capita State Domestic Product (INVPCSDP)	0.803	-0.343	0.362	0.121	0.909
Illiteracy (ILLIT)	0.780	-0.204	-0.323	-0.241	0.812
Percentage of Rural Population (PRURAL)	0.649	-0.586	0.359	0.107	0.904
Percentage Value Added in Secondary Sector (PVASEC)	-0.122	0.921	0.124	-0.078	0.885
Gini Ratio (GINI)	-0.011	0.881	-0.136	0.159	0.821
Percentage Value added in Primary Sector (PVAPRIM)	0.445	-0.834	0.018	-0.160	0.919
Density of Population (DENSITY)	-0.197	0.103	0.903	0.134	0.884
Percentage of Working Population (PWORKING)	0.121	0.540	-0.722	0.354	0.954
Sex Ratio (SEXRATIO)	-0.152	0.092	0.024	0.972	0.977
Variance	3.608	3.135	1.843	1.288	Total=9.875
Percentage of Variance Explained	32.8	28.5	16.8	11.7	89.8
Percentage of Cumulative Variance Explained	32.8	61.3	78.1	89.8	

Thus the analysis in Sections-I & II suggested that India has been able to reduce poverty by a sizable extent, but this reduction is not uniform across the board. Still Orissa and Bihar continue suffering from worse form of poverty. In case of relative inequalities also, the country has succeeded in reducing these by a sizable extent and the trend continued during liberalization period also. However, this declining trend needs to be strengthened further, which calls for special policy measures.

III

On the basis of the findings of the present study and other studies pertaining to the field (Kumar, 2003) it may be argued that for attaining the objective of growth with equity and social justice, government intervention could be through different channels like factor markets, changing of ownership and control of assets, taxation of personal income and wealth, public expenditure and provision of public consumption goods and subsidies, changing commodity composition of final demand and state of technology etc. The choice of policy action for equity depends upon socio-economic and structural conditions. The work force has to be shifted from primary sector to secondary and tertiary sectors. Trend towards urbanization, minus its accompanying problems, could also contribute further in reducing inequalities and poverty. In the era of globalisation rapid and diversified growth of manufactured exports is also expected to have equity-enhancing effect. The most effective weapon to fight iniquitous income distribution is human capital formation by providing better educational and health facilities to the poor. Empowerment of the poor through their more participation in social, economic and political decision making could also help in further strengthening the trend of falling inequalities.

A package of appropriate policies may be able to help in overcoming the problems of poverty and inequalities, in this era of liberalisation, privatization and globalisation.

References

Chenery, H.B. (1974), "Restructuring the World Economy" World Development, No. 2, pp. 1-9 (October-November).

Kumar Ashutosh (2003), Economic Development and Income Distribution, Deep & Deep, New Delhi.

Kuznets, S. (1963), "Quantitative Aspects of Economic Growth of Nations", Economic Development and Cultural Change.

Seers, Dudley (1969), "The Meaning of Development" Eleventh World Conference of the Society for International Development, New Delhi.

CHAPTER 18

Capital Inflows and Fiscal Profligacy

G.S. MONGA AND K. RAVINDRAN

In the globalised set up of economies of the world, capital has become a dominant socio-economic factor which is demolishing the international borders while moving in search of greener pastures of higher profitability. In fact, capital now commands greater respect than nations or their cultures, both of which along with their labour forces and other factors at their command have become subservient to work for capital.

Despite being under the influence of anti-capitalist rhetoric over four decades, India has come to a stage where the role and importance of capital and capitalism cannot be written off. The earlier restrictions on capital flows are now ineffective in view of the changed institutional framework of banking and capital markets. Five decades after independence, distinct signs of structural changes can be noticed.

There are perceptible changes in monetary and fiscal policies as well as in regulations affecting exchange rates and capital inflows. The effects can be seen as a mixed blessing whose long term consequences are somewhat difficult to visualise.

FACTORS AT WORK

The interest rate differential was one of the earlier factors which induced faster capital inflow initially. Now that interest rates have dropped, problems of capital outflow can arise. The Reserve Bank has had to intervene in this connection as well as in connection with money supply and inflation. It must also take appropriate measures to utilise the generation of high total domestic savings.

In view of the propensity of capital to make or mar economies India, along with other developing countries has been seeking it from all over. Globalisation of production, creation of jobs, economic growth, higher returns and increased export earnings are some of the obvious expectations from this capital inflow which is a accompanied by technology and time saving exercises. It is also true that capital has been moving around the world in search of lucrative returns. Developing countries want such capital as could come along with management expertise and would enable them to leapfrog several stages of industrial and infrastructural development. Both the providers and takers of capital are in a hurry and often adequate attention is not paid to policy problems and sustainability of transactions. Need has been felt about trekking cautiously in the matter of further liberalising capital flow in view of the problems of exchange rate stability, interest and inflation rates and because of the need to utilise savings rate and control fiscal deficit. Also, financial institutions, capital markets and foreign trade sector need to be strengthened. In recent years the international capital market has been very active and there have been huge movements of capital from some parts of the globe to others. These capital flows have induced speculative activity in different hues and colours. Reluctance in long term loans is associated with favour shown for short term loans keeping the borrower alert in view of the possibility of renegotiations of terms and constant inspection into the progress of the projects undertaken. The leaders keep an eye on the appropriate use of the loans given. International capital flows thus determine the efficiency of global allocations. They also affect the equilibrium between savings, investments and interest rates.

The pace of economic changes in India has been swift. Intensive competition is clearly visible along with new information and production technologies. The developing world has started measuring progress by the extent of availability of capital which is considered to be the key to economics success. Capital, desirably or otherwise, is promoting further globalisation even of those economies which are still undecided; it is also transforming the managerial decision making process.

India has been reasonably favoured by foreign investors despite political constraints. The favourable factors are an inflation rate of below four per cent, softening of interest rates, easy flow of resources, agricultural recovery with high growth rate and an associated rise in rural incomes. The negative factors are a suspect, industrial recovery during the transition period, slow export growth and infrastructure bottlenecks. At current market prices, between 1991-97, the GDP more than doubled from Rs. 6168 b to Rs. 12600b.

OPPORTUNITIES, RISKS

In today's global economy, no country, especially a developing one, can do everything alone. Economic policies in India were adjusted suitably in the nineties between 1991 and 1996. The larger recipients of foreign direct investments were telecommunications (27%) followed by oil and refinery (10%) and power (9%). A greater part of the contribution came from the U.S. and the rest from UK, Japan, Germany and other countries. Capital and technology naturally go for opportunities commensurate with risk, competition, alternatives, and the nature of economic policy reforms. At the same time the pace and momentum of economic reforms in the recipient country must match the requirements of the economy and allow the capital flow into desirable directions from the country's point of view.

The inflow of foreign capital into India has gone through several phases of steady growth in the early years of reforms and rather unsteady growth since 1994. In between there have been wild fluctuations. The flow should have been maintained at a sustainable pace. Forces working against the flow have been matched by forces working in favour. The recession years in the Western World in 1992-93 worked in favour of increased capital inflow into India and other developing countries. the fall in the interest rate differential in India and U.S. led to a decreased flow of speculative capital.

Over the years, the number of investment approvals have been on the increase. The amounts involved increased nearly fifty-fold over a six year period after reforms. The increase in inflows is nearly ten-fold.

A large share of investment approvals and inflows went into telecom, power generation and services. But an in-depth probe does not give a very rosy picture.

The number of approvals indicates that there has been a phenomenal spurt in the technological co-operation between India and other countries. Technology transfer agreements have been signed with a large number of countries and these agreements have encompassed almost the entire Indian industrial spectrum. When we look at the concomitant inflow of investment, we find that often most of these agreement have remained on paper with little follow up to ensure that the agreements fructify and give the much needed fillip to the industrial productivity qualitatively and quantitatively. There is reason to believe that a large number of companies have entered into investment and technology transfer agreements and simultaneously diverted their productive resources.

FOREX RESERVES

Opinions oscillate between an extreme estimate of uncomfortably high levels of forex reserves which could lead to money supply management problem and the other extreme of inadequate reserves in the light of asymptomatic liabilities and a further liberalisation of capital account transaction.

The tendency to worry incessantly and evade decision making with an inferiority complex result in waste of time and resources. China has many times more than the forex reserves that India has but does not believe that managing reserves of that magnitude is an insurmountable obstacle.

India had better start appreciating and taking cognisance of what is happening in a developing country like China and learn a lesson or two in discipline and firmness. In fact India should stop her almost total dependence on the opinions and dictations of developed countries and think in terms of her long term interests. Of course, there is much to learn from the experience of other developing countries.

The influx of foreign capital through various routes can be a boon only when the deployment of the accumulated forex resources is done profitably and judiciously. The present scenario is symptomatic of anything but the reverse.

EXPORTS

Export promotion directly and indirectly through industries having high export propensity of the right type is needed. The use of capital has to be productive and should be conducive to exports. Capital can be most usefully employed in building infrastructure and in sustaining industries that require large investments having a long gestation period and make use of advanced technology here.

There is an increasing trend in short term external commercial borrowings which if continued unabated can have dangerous portents because the economy can take the Mexican route. The FDI and NRI funds cannot be relied on for stability. Profitability may not be a criterion in this respect but profligacy need not be. If the reserves are deployed at an abysmal rate of return, simultaneously allowing short-term liabilities to mount, that too at relatively higher rates of interest, it is bad economics, to say the least.

The strategy of fiscal reforms should significantly reduce the fiscal deficit and finance the remaining deficit with a minimal recourse to the inflation tax. In this context, a large fiscal deficit even when financed by bond issuances may not be compatible with an open capital account if it undermines the credibility in servicing debt. It is also mentioned that the central fiscal deficit could be used as a summary measure for assessing fiscal performance. It is equally applicable to the federal framework of the Indian economy since a significant part of financing of states' fiscal deficits occurs through central assistance. Against this background, the post-pay Commission scenario should be stunning to the dispassionate observers. Without political will to withstand the sustainable pressure from any group, whether it be trade unions or exporters or any other vested interests, no perspective policy making is possible in India. (Vike Tarapore CAC Report).

There was supposed to be national consensus on the reform agenda and as such even with a change in the Government at the Centre, India's creditworthiness was not adversely affected. In fact, India was marketed as a profitable business opportunity with immense potential. But this myth was exploded when the Tata-Singapore Airlines joint venture episode badly dented the credibility of the protagonists of the slogan of liberalisation/

globalisation. It also prove that political expediency will over-ride the economic common sense. The Enron chapter also was a pointer in this direction.

The present day scenario makes one pause and ponder. There is distinct possibility of a reverse flow of capital or capital flight in the days to come and the comfortable BOP position may only be a passing phase. The fiscal profligacy of the central government, closely followed by the state government will undermine the macro-economic fundamentals which eventually will lead to a setback in the reform process. Conspicuous consumption is a vice not just for the individual; it is very much so even for the State.

CHAPTER

19

Women's Participation and Unorganised Sector : A Study of Pre-and Post-Reforms Period

PRAHLAD KUMAR AND RENU JAIN

I feel greatly honoured to contribute an article in a felicitation volume in honour of Professor Baidyanath Misra who had been an alumni of my *alma mater*, the University of Allahabad. Prof. Misra was a brilliant student who stood first class first both in M.A. (Economics), and faculty of Arts in the University. My revered teacher and guide, (Late) Prof. Mahesh Chand had high admiration for Prof. Misra and often talked about his qualities as a man and a scholar. This inspired me to contribute an article in his honour on a topic, so dear to his ideas on development—the role of women and women force in the process of development, particularly the working women in the unorganised sector of the Indian economy.

The vital role of women in the Indian labour force and their contribution to the national economy has been established beyond doubt. Women have to take dual responsibility at home and at work, and are expected to do both duties simultaneously. However, they have accepted the challenge. Women spend on an average 7-10 hours a day on domestic chores besides collection of fuel, water and child care. A large amount of time and energy expended on these domestic chores, however, remain invisible as no productive economic value is attached to these tasks. The process of development could not be accelerated in the third world because nearly half the proportion of the population consisting of women had no access to process of development and their problems were not taken care of.[1] The unpaid economic activities of women and their contribution through work in the domestic sector remain unreported. The value of unpaid household work constitutes 25.39 per cent of the gross national product in developing countries.[2]

With the increase of population, the pressure on organised sector employment also increases but since employment opportunities in organised sector are limited and also with the era of liberalisation flowing in the economy- its scope has further narrowed down, especially in the public organised sector for females. Naturally the pressure has increased to create new employment avenues in the unorganised or informal sector. Informal sector not only generates employment and capital but also is 'eco-friendly' as against the formal sector that destroys the ecological balance by exploiting the natural resources heavily.[3] Employment in the unorganised sector for women has wide variety.

In rural areas, such work includes care of cattle, sowing, transplanting and harvesting, working on handlooms, producing handicrafts etc. and are lowly paid. In the urban informal sector, women work as petty traders, producing and selling vegetables and many other things. In both the areas, women work as domestic workers. Moreover, the socio-economic condition of unorganised sector women is not satisfactory. Banerjee[4] reported that about 70 per cent of the women working in the informal sector occupations were below the poverty line. Even when they are employed by larger formal sector firms, they are generally hired as casual labour and therefore, remain in the informal sector.

The present paper is divided into three sections. Section I examines the work participation rates for male and female as well as rural-urban differentials. It also presents the sectoral employment growth and trend of un-organised sector female employment. Section II discusses the constraints that account for low socio-economic status of informal sector working women. The last Section III gives suggestions and recommendations for improving the socio-economic status of unorganised sector working women.

I

Table 19.1 below gives the percentage of workers in rural and urban areas separately and jointly, as per 1991 census. It shows that the work participation of female category is very low, both in absolute terms and percentage terms. Female participation rate is less than half that of the males among total population.

Similar trend can be seen both in rural and urban areas. The work participation is higher both in male as well as female categories in the rural areas as compared to urban areas. This difference is more pronounced in the female category. Thus, where the rural-urban difference of work participation in the male category is by nearly 4 percentage points, in the female category this difference is by nearly 18 percentage points. It is to be

TABLE 19.1
Total Workers in India, 1991

Population/Workers	*Persons*	*Males*	*Females*
1	2	3	4
		Total	
Population	836,605,522	433,791,705	402,813,817
Workers	314,903,642	223,506,135	91,397,489
% of workers	37.64	51.52	22.69
		Rural	
Population	621,267,297	320,062,940	301,204,357
Workers	249,330,072	167,822,985	81,507,087
% of workers	40.13	52.43	27.06
		Urban	
Population	215,338,225	113,728,765	101,609,460
Workers	65,573,570	55,683,168	9,890,402
% of workers	30.45	48.96	9.73

Source : Census of India, 1991, p. 3.

noted that female work participation in rural areas is three times that of urban areas (9.73 per cent).

Table 19.2 below gives sex-ratio, male and female work participation rates and number of female workers per 1000 male workers.

TABLE 19.2
Work Participation Rate of Female in India (1901-2001)

Year	*Sex Ratio*	*Female workers as % of female population*	*Male workers as % of male population*	*Female workers in 1000 male workers*
1	2	3	4	5
1901	972	31.70	61.11	504
1911	964	33.73	61.90	525
1921	955	32.67	60.52	516
1931	950	27.63	58.27	450
1941	945	—	—	—
1951	946	23.31	54.04	408
1961	941	27.93	57.12	460
1971	930	14.22	52.75	215
1981	936	20.85	53.19	367
1991	927	22.69	51.52	408
2001	933	25.60	—	—

Source : Women and Society in India by Neera Desai and Krishna Rai, p. 66. Various Census Reports.

The column 2 of the Table shows the continuous fall in sex ratio till 1971. Though the year 1981 showed 6 point increase but again in 1991, it fell by 9 points. The latest Census, 2001 has again shown improvement in the sex ratio by 6 points which is a positive sign.

The female workers as a percentage of the female population shows declining trend till 1951. It improved by 4 percentage points in 1961 but in 1971, it declined sharply and became almost half of 1961. Since then it is showing gradual improvement, partly because of definitional change. Though WPR also declined during this period for male population, it was not as drastic as for female workers. This trend may further be observed by column 5 that shows number of female workers per 1000 male workers. In 1991, it reached to 1951 level but is still far below the 1901 figure.

Table 19.3 shows that sex-wise WPR had been fluctuating both in rural and urban areas. In the rural areas, the WPR among males and females fell by 5 percentage points and 15 percentage points respectively during 1961-71. Among females, it fell from 30 per cent to about 16 per cent i.e., it nearly halved. It improved slightly for males and appreciably among females in rural areas during the next decade (1971-81) though improvement was also visible in urban areas. This improvement was maintained for the period 1981-91 in both the categories. But for males, it was still below the 1961 level in rural as well as urban areas.

TABLE 19.3

Rural-Urban Differences in Work Participation by Sex (%)

Year	*Rural*		*Urban*	
	Male	*Female*	*Male*	*Female*
1961	58.00	30.00	52.00	11.00
1971	53.70	15.92	48.88	7.18
1981	53.77	23.06	49.06	8.37
1991	52.50	27.00	48.95	9.74

Source : Census of India, 1991, p. 11.

In the urban areas, WPR differences among male and female is very pronounced. Where it was 52% for males in 1961, it was only 11% for females in the same period. This had further fallen from 11% to 7% in the next decade but improved slightly in the following decades. This improvement could not equalize the fall during the period 1961-71. Due to definitional changes, census data cannot be completely relied upon for comparisons but it is true that it has a declining trend. Mukhopadhyay and Ghosh have analysed the census data for 1961-81 by making adjustment for definitional changes and concluded that the displacement of the female worker by the male worker was the most dominant factor for the falling female work participation rate. If we look for reasons for the reduction in the female work participation rate, the following points attract our attention :

> New industrial structure were urban based. These created difficulty for the women to combine child care and domestic work along with paid work outside : firstly, urban activities required some level of education, and secondly, unlike in the rural areas, women had no kith and kin or neighbour's support.

Though work organisation changed in form and content yet women's role did not change for they still carried the sole responsibility for child care and domestic work.

The disappearance of older household industries created problems for women workers because they faced more immobilities in seeking work than men. On the demand side, the secondary sector rejected women, the service sector did not expend sufficiently and the primary sector overcrowded itself. The impact of fall in labour demand fell most harshly on women because of the difficulty of their gaining new skills and altering their social role in the system. As a result unorganised sector activity increased speedily.

According to degree of 'organisation', the workers were classified into two broad categories—organised and unorganised sectors. The difference between these two is not as between agriculture, industry and services. The real difference between them is the organisation of productive relations, regulations and recognition by data collecting agencies and scientific investigators.

The exact data for the work participation in unorganised sector is not available. The scanty data available on the unprotected worker is mainly drawn from the Census, the National Sample Survey Organisation, central and state Government departments and micro level studies conducted by scholars but it is frequently incomplete and lacking in details. Table 19.4 presents the distribution of main workers according to various sectors in the economy. It is clear that majority of women are working in the primary sector which is lowly paid and of casual nature of work. Out of total main workers, 81.57% of female workers are engaged in the primary sector. In both the years 1981 and 1991, the share of primary sector in providing employment is maximum. But the share has fallen by 2 percentage points during the decade. Similar fall (by one percentage point) was also registered for the secondary sector. The tertiary sector showed an increase of 3 percentage points in its share. The total main workers increased by 63.42 million in 1991 i.e., an increase of 28.50 per cent.

Comparing the male-female ratios, it is seen that a higher proportion i.e., 80 per cent of the females are engaged in primary sector (mainly in agriculture) as compared to males (68 per cent). The share of females in secondary has marginally declined during the period (by 1.08 percentage) whereas for males also, it has declined but by 0.85 percentage. Though the

TABLE 19.4
Distribution of Main Workers in Different Sectors in India

(in percentage)

Sectors	*1981*			*1991*		
	Persons	*Males*	*Females*	*Persons*	*Males*	*Females*
Primary	69.35	66.26	81.57	67.53	63.57	81.20
Secondary	12.98	13.97	09.06	11.97	13.12	07.98
Tertiary	17.67	19.77	09.37	20.50	23.31	10.82
Total	100.00	100.00	100.00	100.00	100.00	100.00
Total Main Workers (in millions)	222.51	177.54	44.97	285.93	221.66	64.27

Source : Census of India, 1991.

share of males as well as females has improved in the tertiary sector by 3 percentage points and 1 percentage point respectively but the disparity between these two still remains marked and has even aggravated in 1991.

According to the various rounds of NSS, employment and its annual growth is presented in Table 19.5, sector-wise and sub-sector wise. It is clear that the share of agriculture has increased in absolute terms but in terms of proportion, it has fallen from 63 per cent in 1983 to less than 57 per cent in 1999-2000. The proportion of population engaged in the industrial sector has increased during the period 1993-94 to 1999-2000 by 2 percentage point. This increase has been fluctuating in the industrial sector, but in the service sector there has been a gradual increase during these years. Following points emerge-out from the Table :

(i) During the pre-reform period (1983 to 1993-94), employment growth in the agriculture sector was 2.23 per cent per annum whereas it was almost nil (0.02 per cent per annum) in post-reform period (1993-94 to 1999-2000).

(ii) In the industry sector, the proportion of workers initially increased during 1983 to 1987-88 but declined in the next period (1987-88 to 1993-94). In the post-reform period, it again rose to 1987-88 level (i.e. 17.56 per cent). This increase in the employment in post-reform period in the industry-sector was due to the increase in employment in 'manufacturing' and 'construction' sub-sectors. In fact, mining and quarrying; electricity, gas and water supply registered high level of negative annual growth.

(iii) The employment in the service sector in absolute terms as a proportion of total employment has registered positive growth. Annual growth rate in employment in the post-reform period was found to be more than pre-reform period except in the 'community' social and personal services' sub-sector which registered a negative

TABLE 19.5
Sectoral Employment Growth (CDS basis)

Sector	*Employment (in million)*							
	1983	*1987-88*	*1993-94*	*1999-2000*	*1983 to 1987-88*	*1987-88 to 1993-94*	*1983 to 1993-94*	*1993-94 to 1999-2000*
Agriculture :	151.35 (63.17)	163.82 (60.14)	190.72 (60.38)	190.94 (56.70)	1.77	2.57	2.23	0.02
Industry :	37.43 (15.62)	47.85 (17.57)	49.99 (15.82)	59.15 (17.56)				
Mining & Quarrying	1.74	2.40	2.54	2.26	7.35	1.00	3.68	-1.91
Manufacturing	27.69	32.53	35.00	40.79	3.64	1.23	2.26	2.58
Electricity, Gas & Water supply	0.83	0.94	1.43	1.15	2.87	7.19	5.31	-3.55
Construction	7.17	11.98	11.02	14.95	12.08	-1.38	4.18	5.21
Services :	50.78 (21.20)	60.72 (22.20)	75.11 (23.78)	86.65 (25.73)				
Trade, Hotels and Restaurant	18.17	22.53	26.88	37.54	4.89	2.99	3.80	5.72
Transport, Storage and Communication	6.99	8.05	9.88	13.65	3.21	3.46	3.35	5.53
Financial, Insurance, Real Estate and Business Services	2.10	2.59	3.37	4.62	4.72	4.50	4.60	5.40
Community, Social and Personal Services	23.52	27.55	34.98	30.84	3.57	4.06	3.85	-2.08
All Sectors	239.57 (100.00)	272.39 (100.00)	315.84 (100.00)	336.75 (100.00)	2.89	2.50	2.67	1.07

Source : Economic Survey (2002-03).
Note : Figures in Parentheses show the percentages to the total.

growth. In other sub-sectors, the growth rate was between 5.40 – 5.72 per cent per annum.

(iv) Inspite of the above remarkable facts, it is noteworthy to observe that the over-all employment growth in the post-reform period (1993-94 to 1999-2000) was found to be sufficiently low (1.07 per cent per annum) than the pre-reform period (1983 to 1993-94) growth rate (2.67 per cent per annum). Should it be concluded that economic reforms have worsened the employment situation in the country ?

Again, if we look at the employment figures in the organised and unorganised sectors, it is observed that the share of casual labour in total employment has gone up.[5] Only a small percentage (8 to 9 per cent) of the total workforce of the country is employed in the organised sector (refer to Table 19.6). While employment growth in the private organised sector significantly improved in the 1990s, the growth of employment in the public sector was negligible. Since the public sector accounts for more than two thirds of the total organised sector employment, there was slow down of the overall growth in organised sector employment. Employment in the organised sector has been hardly 8.34%, of which public sector accounts for 5.77% and private sector only 2.58% in the total employment generated. (Economic Survey, 2002-03).

Table 19.6
Trend of Unorganised Sector Work Participation

Year	*Employment in (Millions)*			*Share of unorganised sector employment in terms of percentage*
	Organised	*Unorganised*	*Total*	
1971	20.20	206.70	226.90	91.10
1981	20.90	214.00	236.90	90.33
1991	26.70	259.38	286.08	90.66
2001	27.80	—	—	—

Sources : 1. Draft Five Year Plan—1978-83.
2. Economic Survey, 1994-95.
3. Sarvekshna, Vol. III, No. 1, July 1979.

The main employment generating activities, according to Economic Survey are; (a) Agriculture and allied activities, (b) Trade, restaurant and hotels including tourism, (c) Some of the social sectors like education and health, (d) The small and medium enterprises, mainly in the rural non-farm sector, (e) Transport and construction.

Table 19.6 reveals that out of total workers, more than 90 per cent are engaged in unorganised sector activity. The accounting of female workers in unorganised sector in the Census and NSSO suffers from serious enumeration and reporting drawbacks. According to Mitra,[6] the under reporting of female workforce participation rates in the Census varies from 30 to 40 per cent. He estimates that the participation of females in the urban informal sector is as high as 49 per cent as against 15 per cent to 17 per cent in the case of males.

Jain and Chand find that the measurement of female labour force participation and analysis suffers from serious problem—"There are poor conceptualisations of female work styles, mistaken perception of female economic roles, by respondents and interviewers. The statistical information is generally collected through male interviewers who do not correctly report the economic activities of women.

Report on Status of Women in India[7] (1974) estimated that in 1971 out of total women workers, 94 per cent were found in the unorganised sector, leaving only 6 per cent in the organised sector, out of this 2.7 per cent being in industry and 3.3 per cent in service and professions. In the organised sector, the concentration of women in professions of teaching and medicine and recognition of certain low prestigious jobs in the clerical services were particularly suited to women.

The employment figures in the organised sector show that though the share of women in total employment is low yet it has gone up from 12% to 14% during a decade. On the other hand the share of women in the unorganised sector in total employment has also climbed by 10 percentage points.

The disparity of male female employment in the organised sector is more than that in the unorganised sector but this disparity has lessened in 1991. The share of employment in both organised and unorganised sectors among females has increased but this increase is more pronounced in the

TABLE 19.7

Employment of Male and Female in Organised and Unorganised Sectors 1981 and 1991

(in Lacs)

Year	*Organised Sector*			*Unorganised Sector*			*Total (Organised + Unorganised)*		
	M	*F*	*T*	*M*	*F*	*T*	*M*	*F*	*T*
1981	200.86	27.93	228.79	1625.75	427.59	2053.34	1826.61	455.52	2282.13
	(87.79)	(12.21)	(100.0)	(79.17)	(20.83)	(100.0)	(80.04)	(19.96)	(100.0)
1991	229.53	37.81	267.34	2014.11	859.86	2873.87	2243.64	897.67	897.67
	(85.85)	(14.15)	(100.0)	(70.08)	(29.92)	(100.0)	(71.42)	(28.58)	(100.0)

Notes : 1. Figures in parentheses are percentages.
2. M denotes Males; F denotes Females and T denotes Total.

Sources: 1. SAARC Guide Book on Women in Development, p. 245.
2. DGE and T, Ministry of Labour, Govt. of India, New Delhi.
3. Status of Women in India—A Report of the National Committee, New Delhi.

unorganised sector where the share of females increased by 9.09 percentage points as compared to 1.94 percentage points increase in the organised sector.

National Sample Survey (1987) stated that on overwhelming proportion of women 93 per cent or more are engaged in the unorganised sector mainly as self employed wage-earners and casual workers. The incidence of casual wage-earners in agriculture and construction work amongst females ranges from 75 per cent to 96 per cent of the total female wage earners. The wage offered to them for the same work is generally one half or less than that of males.

A World Bank study also reported the work participation of women in the unorganised sector of India. As seen in Table 19.8, work participation of women in the rural areas is more dominant, predictably due to the importance of agriculture.

Table 19.8
Women in the Unorganised Sector 1981

	Urban	*Rural*	*All India*
Main and marginal workers	6,137,000	57,388,000	63,525,000
Organised	2,899,500	2,899,500	2,899,500
Unorganised marginal workers	3,237,500	54,488,500	60,625,500
Unorganised as % of main and marginal workers	53%	95%	95%

Source: A World Bank Country Study, Gender and Poverty in India, 1991, p. 337.

The vast majority (95%) of rural women work in the informal sector. Among urban working women, this proportion is substantially lower (53%) which generally captures a large number of working women, the proportion of informal sector workers among economically active urban women rises to 75 per cent and overall work participation of women in unorganised sector is approximately 85 per cent.

Women employment in the unorganised sector consist of self-employed, trader, wage-earners, salary paid, agricultural workers and other agriculture related activities.

II

This section presents the details of the constraints which are faced by working women in the unorganised sector in particular, and that also account for their low socio-economic status.

Labour market leads to two major type of discrimination against women. The most glaring discrimination against women is in wage inequality, not only unequal pay for equal work but unequal pay for work of comparable worth. Second discrimination in terms of concentration of women in particular primary sector and in certain types of jobs. Sethi[8] in her field survey found that not only all occupations in which females are engaged carry a lower wage rate is always higher than the female wage rate. Farm owners say that they prefer female because they are 'cheap' and 'hard working'. Wage inequalities persist not only in the unorganised sector but also in the organised sector. Among highly qualified science and technology personnel, while women's wages are 90 per cent of men at entry point, stagnation in career produces a wage gap of 60 per cent by the time.

In the unorganised sector, women are concentrated in occupations which are usually at the lowest rung of the ladder. In most occupations they are engaged in the more arduous and less skilled areas of work. For example in construction industry, men do brick laying while women carry bricks and mortar.

In the unorganised sector most of the poor working women are in agriculture if they are unpaid family worker, or if they work in household industry, their contribution is unrecognised and under-valued and if they work outside, they work as labourers and their family is mainly dependant on her earnings.

Poverty and female-headed households go together as established by both Visaria[9] and Parthasarathy.[10] In Visaria's analysis the household expenditure of female headed households was half that of male headed households. According to Parthasarathy among the poor households of every agricultural class, the proportion below poverty line for females was consistently higher.

It is also well established that children's nutritional status mainly depends on the wage of mother rather than the employment of the father or his wages. Various studies among the poorer households with gross deficiency and malnutrition, the deficiency among women was found 25 per cent more than for men.

Women also have unequal control and access to cash. Wages for agricultural work even when paid to women are taken over by men. In some regions where husband wife teams or family labour is employed the cash is handed over to the male. Seasonal fluctuations in employment affect women much more than men. The status of family workers with no direct control over earnings is low where patriarchal control is most closely exercised.

Technological advancement has eliminated the traditional employment activity and adversely affected women. Mazumdar[11] stated that "rural women who constitute the largest group have not only been bypassed by the development process but those traditional roles and status in society have been adversely affected by the nature of development process itself. Technological modernisation eliminating traditional activities are well known. Powerlooms have put handloom weavers women out of work. Modern herbicides and rice mills displaced women and eliminated their traditional incomes from weeding and milling. There are a number of other mechanisms through which technological progress has adversely affected females' income and opportunities.

The lack of organisation and unionisation hampers the bargaining position of women especially in the unorganised sector. Unorganised women have no political power and no bargaining strength. The unorganised sector presents a number of difficulties in implementing protective labour laws and relating to wages, conditions of work, insurance, provident fund, maternity leave etc. in unorganised sector most of the women are working on casual basis. The growing use of casual labourers reflects a common strategy used by formal sector firms to avoid legal and collective bargaining. Even a large registered firm can employ casual workers who remain in the informal sector, for the unorganised sector working women hours of work are long, wages are poor, conditions are hazardous, benefits are not existent, and wages are below survival needs. Channelling inputs such as literacy, health, family welfare etc. is also difficult in this sector. As a result, there are marked disparities between women in the organised and unorganised sector. Investment policies too continue to award low priority to the unorganised sector.

One of the major drawbacks to the development of employment opportunities for women is the lack of adequate training. While the women and child development department has a number of schemes such as short stay homes, working hostels, women's development corporations, but it has no national programme for women's training. It is evident that the mixed programmes such as the TRYSEM have not reached women as effectively as visualised. Currently there are atleast 45 schemes in the 17 departments of the Government of India catering to training for women but they do not present a systematic integrated approach to women's training.

The vast majority of women are engaged in the unorganised sector, forming nearly 90 per cent of the total female labour force. Therefore, we should provide training to improve their productivity as well as to explore new avenues of employment to facilitate occupational shifts wherever possible.

After independence, the Govt. of India through constitutional changes and legal reforms, provided equal opportunity for women as men. Reviewing the position of the women under the Indian Constitution, Upender Baxi pointed out the basic weaknesses of laws and argued that even after the independence, efforts to combat the patriarchial ideology of the law, have not led to even blunting of the edge of male domination. Enforcement of legal provisions has been very ineffective. These provisions did not apply to unorganised sector and so most of the women workers were not covered by any legislation safeguards.

III

We recommended below some of the suggestions that can help in improving the socio-economic condition of unorganised sector working women in India.

(1) There is a need to develop positive attitude towards unorganised sector. It should not be treated as inefficient or less important sector as the term perhaps itself suggests. It bears a negative dimension.

(2) Allocation of resources for women should be enhanced in basic areas like education, training and welfare programmes.

(3) Activities of voluntary organisations should be increased. At present, there are two types of voluntary groups working in the field of women. One is only espousing the cause of women and, the other mobilising them into organised groups to work for their welfare and empowering them through economic activities—such as SEVA and LIZZAT Papad organisations. For the women's welfare, both types of organisations should be strengthened.

(4) Hostel facilities at a lower cost should be provided especially to unorganised sector working women in urban areas. The experience of some countries has shown that it is possible to accelerate women's employment in new areas of work by finding broad solutions to their problems of family life and child care by public policy. The establishment of day care centres, crèches and balwadis should be promoted on a large scale in rural, semi-rural and urban areas to help working mothers. Hostel facilities for working women of the lower income groups should also be expanded.

(5) Other facilities related to their working environment such as lighting, ventilation, drinking water, toilets and crèches need to be provided. In shopping and office complexes facilities for schooling including non-formal education and health care be provided.

(6) Workers organisation should be started for 'women workers' to enhance their bargaining power and level of skill. Lack of organisation of women workers is the root cause of exploitation of women labour. At present the process of organisation of women workers is very limited and fragmented. Individually women are not is a position to fight against law, discriminatory wages and exploitative working conditions and it is necessary to promote organisations of women and for women on a large scale.

(7) There is often a wide gap between the legislative intent and the use of laws and legal processes in reality. It is necessary that legal reforms such as minimum wages act, fixation of working hours act etc. should be implemented effectively. Inspite of illiteracy and problem of inadequate communication, legal literacy and free legal aid programmes for women have become popular and widespread.

(8) It is necessary to increase the level of education and rate of literacy among women. The spread of education among women is generally described as a key element for ameliorating their position in the society. In order to raise the educational level of females especially in those areas which have problems of low literacy and low income, cost free educational facilities, full of incentives should be provided.

(9) Self employment opportunities should be increased. The rapid increase of unemployment and underemployment has further underscored the need to promote self employment opportunities for women. The current programmes tend to display an urban bias and cannot meet the employment needs of the masses of women in villages and small towns. Training and finance facilities should be provided for enhancement of productivity of self employed women.

(10) Another important problem faced by the self employed women is related to marketing of their products. This is faced by the large section of women doing their own work or family occupations. Their major marketing channels are in haats and weekly markets which are now being flushed by mass produced goods. Non-availability of a network of marketing facilities is one of the important obstacles to their advancement. To deal with this problem several alternatives may have to be worked out. Setting up of co-operative societies which can collect and sell products is one of them. This will enhance the bargaining power of members and they will have reliable information about the current trend of the market.

(11) Separate economic planning for women within the overall planning system should be evolved. Emphasis should be laid on non-economic factors like human dignity and social justice which might be effective to end discrimination against women.

(12) It is imperative that appropriate and reliable techniques are developed to quantify the economic contribution of women, particularly their non-monetary contribution.

(13) It is necessary to initiate more micro level studies area-wise and sector-wise to study the condition of working women especially of unorganised sector. Proper data bank be developed and planning for the future should be based on these works.

(14) It is suggested that Census Survey of the unorganised sector working women be carried out in order to get detailed and complete information about heir condition.

(15) The unsatisfactory and inadequate data base on the role of women should be improved to get a clearer and more accurate picture and o make the data comparable over time.

It can be concluded that there is need to adopt an integrated and holistic approach towards upliftment and empowering of women. While educated and trained women will find increasingly more avenues or employment as teachers, nurses, doctors, engineers, administrators, executives, clerks, etc., the real problem is of illiterate and unskilled women workers who seek whole-time jobs. We are convinced that together with the various programmes for increasing employment of women., it is necessary to raise the economic and social status of women so that they may be brought into the mainstream of national development. This requires a systematic human resource development strategy towards women, with special focus on the unorganised sector. However, the emancipation of women would ultimately depend on the change in the social value system, attitudes and social structure prevailing in the country. This would require coordinated and concerted efforts on the part of political leaders, social reformers and other members of social strata, including women themselves.

(The authors acknowledge the assistance given by Ms. Tinku Paul in providing some latest data and sharpening the arguments. However, for any errors or omissions, the authors are solely responsible).

Notes and References

1. Banerjee, N.K., (1985), 'Women Workers in the Unorganised Sector', Sanyan Book, Hyderabad.
2. Govt. of India (1974), Report on Status of Women in India Towards Equality, New Delhi.
3. Govt. of India (2002-03), Economic Survey, New Delhi.
4. Mazumdar, Vina (1978), Role of Rural Women in Development, Allied Publication, New Delhi.
5. Mitra, Ashok (1981), Participation of Women in Socio-Economic Development, Women and Development, UNESCO.
6. Parthasarathy, G. (1982), Rural Poverty and Female Heads of Household, Technical Seminar on Women, Work and Employment, ISST, New Delhi.
7. P.S. Baidyanath (1989), Effective Utilisation of Women Power Resources in India—A Study of Trial Women Working Force, *Economic Affairs*, Vol. : 34, July-Sept. issue.
8. Sethi Raj Mohini (1981), A Study of Agricultural Labour in Punjab, Department of Sociology (Unpublished Ph.D. dissertation), Chandigarh.
9. Sue Ellen & M. Chariton, (1984) Women in the Third World Development, West View Press, London.
10. Tripathy, B.B. (1998), Problems and Prospects if Informal Sector, Paper presented in the National Seminar Organised by Bhartiya Arthik Shodh Sansthan, Allahabad.
11. Visaria Praveen and Leela Visaria, Indian Household with Female Heads in Devaki Jain and Nirmala Banerjee (Ed.) Women and Poverty in India.

CHAPTER

20

Commercial Banks as a Pacesetter of Rural Development : The case of Orissa in the Post-Reform Period

S.N. MISRA

INTRODUCTION

Commercial banks, as catalytic agents of economic development, have the mandate to involve themselves in rural development on the following grounds. First, before public ownership of commercial banks, the rural areas were devoid of any branches of these banks, except for the presence of a few co-operative societies. Hence after nationalisation, the banks were called upon to open bank branches in the rural centres to promote banking habit of the people in the countryside (Dagli : 1976). Secondly, the rural economy was mostly dominated by non-institutional credit agencies, such as the usurious money lenders. After nationalisation it was considered necessary to win away rural clientele from these usurious money lenders and to place them under the fold of organised commercial banking (Rangarajan : 1998). Thirdly, the rural income, though small it is, was left untapped by any organised financial institution. Accordingly it was considered necessary to tap those untapped income in the form of deposits for purpose of utilisation in productive activities of the rural economy. The banks are considered as more deserving institutions to fulfil this goal (Subrahmanya : 1982). Finally there is growing incidence of poverty and unemployment in rural areas. The government considered commercial banks as the suitable vehicle for the implementation of anti-poverty programmes for the benefit of the rural people. It is against this background that in this paper an attempt is made to study the role of commercial banks in the promotion of rural development. We shall, in particular, look at the relative level of credit deployment and credit absorption in rural Orissa. The importance of this can be hardly overemphasised, given significant investment gaps in several productive sectors of the rural economy notably agriculture.

RURAL ECONOMY OF ORISSA

'Orissa lives in villages', a statement that seems to be more appropriate when considered from the analysis of available statistics. As per 1991 census, 86.6 per cent of the total population of the state live in rural areas. On the country, percentage share of population living in urban areas is 13.6. Furthermore, 64.0 per cent of the work force again depend upon agriculture for their livelihood and occupation. In agriculture again, the number of both marginal and small operational holdings stood at 79.9 per cent out of the total operational holdings, which covered 46.7 per cent of the total area under different operational holdings. On the other hand, the number of medium and large operational holdings constituted about 19.1 per cent of total operational holdings but they covered 53.3 per cent of the total area under different operational holdings (GOI : 2001). There is, thus, a skewed distribution of land holdings in the agricultural sector. Marginal and small farmers though constituted a sizeable segment of farming class yet they owned and operated a smaller percentage share of cultivated area. On the contrary, the medium and large farmers, though constituted a small proportion yet they owned and operated a larger proportion of the cultivated area. consequently, it is those big farmers who have greater access to all the available inputs compared to marginal and small farmers. The rural population again are steeped in poverty. Percentage share of population living below the poverty line as per 1993-94 prices was about 48 as against the all-India average of 26. This indicates that quite a sizeable chunk of rural population in the state live with a minimum per capita expenditure of less than Rs.1000 per month. Furthermore, there is growing incidence of unemployment in the state. The backlog of unemployment at the beginning of 1999-2000 was of the order of 8.27 lakhs. Bulk of this unemployment in the true sense has taken place in the countryside where there is already the phenomenon of disguised unemployment (Misra : 1982). Besides, the rural areas are devoid of several 'opportunities' in the forms of roads, transport & communication, irrigation, electricity, education and health services. The rate of infant mortality is quite high in the state. Bulk of the infant mortality is again visible in rural areas than in urban areas.

The bleak picture outlined above, therefore, calls for a massive dose of investment by institutional financing agencies, the important being the commercial banks, outside the investment made by government through budgetary sources. It is in this context, that the role of commercial banks in the promotion of rural development in Orissa appears to be more significant. The study is confined to the post-economic reform period covering the years 1991-1999. However, comparison will be made with pre-economic reform period (1981-1990) in order to find out the relative performance between the two periods.

The study is pursued with the following aims: (a) to study the performance of commercial banks with respect to branch expansion, deposit mobilisation and deployment of credit in rural areas, (b) to examine as to what extent commercial banks have utilised credit in rural areas out of the deposits mobilised from these areas, (c) to analyse the problems confronted by commercial banks while working in rural areas and to suggest measures to overcome these problems.

PERFORMANCE OF COMMERCIAL BANKS DURING PRE-REFORM PERIOD

- During pre-reform period, the rural bank offices of commercial banks increased from 670 offices in 1981 to 1560 offices in 1990, an increase of 2.3 times over the period (Table 20.1). As a result of this average annual growth rate of rural offices stood at 8.2 per cent (Table 20.3).

TABLE 20.1

Population Group-wise Distribution of Offices, Deposits, Advances and Credit- Deposit Ratio by Commercial Banks in Orissa : 1981-1999

(Rupees in Lakhs)

Year	*Pre-Reform Period*							
	RURAL				*SEMI-URBAN*			
	Offices	*Deposits*	*Advances*	*C/D Ratio (in%)*	*Offices*	*Deposits*	*Advances*	*C/D Ratio (in%)*
1981	670	9827	9879	100.53	183	14917	8742	58.60
1982	902	12291	13235	107.68	211	15385	10348	67.26
1983	968	15766	18101	114.81	220	19927	12330	61.88
1984	1120	19454	23966	123.19	187	18117	12661	69.88
1985	1239	20071	26666	132.86	247	25263	18581	73.55
1986	1283	25101	32467	129.35	257	30807	22377	72.64
1987	1311	31268	38721	123.84	259	39684	26226	66.09
1988	1347	42022	48547	115.53	217	29384	19456	66.21
1989	1422	49344	75632	153.27	259	56672	38714	68.31
1990	1560	60884	75300	123.68	260	66671	48955	73.43

Year	Post-Reform Period							
	RURAL				SEMI-URBAN			
	Offices	Deposits	Advances	C/D Ratio (in%)	Offices	Deposits	Advances	C/D Ratio (in%)
1991	1611	76071	62736	82.47	263	73364	44193	60.24
1992	1623	88677	74208	83.68	264	89758	50489	56.25
1993	1635	107452	83995	78.17	265	98200	54366	55.36
1994	1638	127955	92014	71.91	270	109640	56391	51.43
1995	1616	155028	100468	64.81	295	140659	65907	46.86
1996	1617	189279	113516	59.97	297	169337	80274	47.40
1997	1610	231835	124351	53.64	297	200280	83023	41.45
1998	1610	277345	149088	53.76	303	233082	98120	42.10
1999	1614	335306	164765	49.14	312	272194	110943	40.76

Source : R.B.I., Banking Statistics (1981-1999), relevant issues, Mumbai.

- The rural deposits of commercial banks stood at Rs. 98.3 crores in 1981, which increased to Rs. 609.0 crores in 1990, an increase of 6.2 times over the period. As a result of this, average annual growth rate of rural deposits stood at 26.0 per cent as against the state average of 18.6 per cent.
- The loans and advances of commercial banks in rural areas stood at Rs.98.8 crores in 1981. Which increased to Rs.753.0 crores in 1990, an increase of 7.6 times over the period. The average annual growth rate of advances was 22.1 per cent during the pre-reform period.

WEAKNESSES OF THE SYSTEM

In spite of the impressive quantitative performance of commercial banks in rural areas during the pre-reform period, several weaknesses were detected on account of systemic failures.

- There were large number of bank offices in rural areas no doubt but the business of most of the branches was at a low level. There was low-income generation and growing inefficiency in those rural branches (GOI : 1992).
- There was lack of competitiveness among rural branches. Area demarcation that forced commercial banks to operate only in rural centres having less than 10 thousand population could not prompt much of efficiency and productivity in rural bank offices.
- Loans and advances of banks in rural areas mostly reached into the hands of beneficiaries who failed to testify the sound canons of viability and profitability. In a majority of cases beneficiaries were improperly identified and this caused the woe of the banks. They

failed to repay the loans or repeatedly asked the banks to rescheduled the loans. This seriously affected the business of banking in rural areas.

- Loans sanctioned to honour the commitment of the government towards alleviating poverty of the poor through several programmes failed to generate assets and could not sustain the poor in the activities of their adoption on long term basis on account of the poor quality of the assets (Misra & Behera : 2000).
- There was also the problem of decision making. Most of the branches were manned by a few staff. Branches having surplus staff, in certain localities, experienced dearth of business activities due to low level of development in those areas. The branch managers enjoyed very little decision making power and always looked upward for guidance and flow of decision. The reluctance of bank staff to serve in rural centres also affected banking business in rural centres (Misra : 1994)

BANKING SECTOR REFORMS

For strengthening commercial banks in general and the rural banks in particular, the financial sector reforms were adopted. Some of the basic features of the reform are the following :

- the organisational structure of commercial bank was revamped. There was proposal for four types of banks; (a) International banking, (b) National banking, (c) Regional and local banks, and (d) Rural banks. The committee put utmost confidence on the continuance of rural banks. For viability it suggested that weak and dormant rural banks be amalgamated with strong ones. For branches of commercial banks doing good business the committee preferred to put them in a separate category called the Rural Subsidiary Banks, free from onerous regulations and controls from the apex bank (GOI : 1992).
- Recovery of loans by commercial banks was made compulsory. For this, banks were required to take the help of State Recovery Tribunals. In course of time, more of such Tribunals would be established in rural areas to take care of unrecovered loans. Particularly this would reduce growing NPAs in rural branches of commercial banks which presently account for more than 25 per cent.
- More emphasis was given for decentralised decision making. As a result, a rural bank manager now enjoys the benefit of taking decision at the rural branch level upto Rs. 25 Lakhs.
- For writing-off bad and doubtful loans. Asset Reconstruction Fund was created. The Fund would particularly take care of those loans which have outlived its longevity.

- In order to strengthen the staff position in rural banks, the commercial banks were asked to pursue their own recruitment policy for the selection of suitable persons for rural branches. Persons to be selected for rural branches must be committed to serve in rural centres and must have thorough knowledge about the geography, social and cultural conditions prevailing in rural areas.
- There was also the proposal for all banks including the rural banks maintaining capital adequacy norm of 8 per cent to risk weighted assets for running banking business in a sound manner.
  There was further the proposal for scaling down priority sector advance in rural areas which is about 45 per cent of the total bank credit. The committee was of the view that this be brought down to the level of 10 per cent in a phased manner to release more funds in favour of key and strategic sectors of the economy.
- The committee also pleaded for reducing administered rates of interest now given to poor persons in rural areas. Even there is the suggestion for reducing subsidies, which is given in various proportions to different class of borrowers in rural areas, as it has put serious financial burden on the exchequer. Instead, borrowers are advised to manage with market related rate of interest which is mainly determined by demand for and supply of loans. This would increase the competitive strength of the borrowers and at the same time improve income generating capacity of the banks in the rural centres.

COMMERCIAL BANKING IN THE AFTERMATH OF ECONOMIC REFORMS

The progress of commercial banks in the aftermath of financial sector reforms revealed several peculiar signposts.

- Branches of commercial banks in the rural areas stood at 1611 in the year 1991, which increased to 1614 in the year 1999. Percentage variation over the period was only 0.2. It is further worth observing that average annual growth rate of bank offices in the post-reform period was negative at –0.10 per cent. This was partly the result of merger and amalgamation of weak banks with strong banks which prevented further decline of income generation by the banks in rural areas. The negative decline was also partly due to 'over consciousness' of rural bank offices to handle rural accounts on account of frustrating experience of banking business in rural centres in the past.
- Deposits mobilised from rural centres was Rs.760.7 crores in 1991, which increased to Rs. 3350.0 crores in 1999 i.e. an increase of 4.4 times over the period (Table 20.1). There is increase in the quantity

of deposits in the absolute sense no doubt but when considered from qualitative angle it is noticed that average annual growth rate of deposit in rural areas was 20.7 per cent as against the state average of 18.3 per cent (Table 20.2). The performance with regard to deposit mobilisation even appears to be lower compared to pre-reform period (21.2 per cent).

TABLE 20.2
Population Group-wise Distribution of Offices, Deposits, Advances and Credit-Deposit Ratio by Commercial Banks in Orissa : 1981-1999

(Rupees in Lakhs)

Year	*Pre-Reform Period*							
	Urban				*Total*			
	Offices	*Deposits*	*Advances*	*C/D Ratio (in%)*	*Offices*	*Deposits*	*Advances*	*C/D Ratio (in%)*
1981	122	22134	13691	61.86	975	46878	32312	68.93
1982	142	24584	16157	65.72	1255	52260	39740	76.04
1983	154	29329	21460	73.17	1342	65022	51881	79.79
1984	172	35841	31048	86.63	1479	73452	67675	92.13
1985	192	42849	36616	85.45	1678	88183	81862	92.83
1986	194	51307	44310	86.36	1734	107214	99154	92.48
1987	196	59766	50001	83.66	1766	130718	114948	87.94
1988	166	39887	38472	96.45	1730	111293	106475	95.67
1989	223	81582	85309	104.57	1904	187599	199654	106.43
1990	226	108955	87880	80.66	2046	236511	212135	89.69
Year	*Post-Reform Period*							
	Urban				*Total*			
	Offices	*Deposits*	*Advances*	*C/D Ratio (in%)*	*Offices*	*Deposits*	*Advances*	*C/D Ratio (in%)*
1991	229	127557	84734	66.43	2103	276992	191663	69.19
1992	240	137694	93282	67.75	2127	316130	217980	68.95
1993	258	155192	103377	66.61	2158	360844	241738	66.99
1994	266	176846	1000576	56.87	2174	414441	248981	60.08
1995	268	231836	121198	52.28	2179	527523	287573	54.51
1996	273	247025	144943	58.68	2187	605641	338733	55.93
1997	276	297495	127666	42.91	2183	729610	335040	45.92
1998	296	360480	167145	46.37	2209	8709907	414353	47.58
1999	312	428436	172942	40.37	2238	1035936	448651	43.31

Source : R.B.I., Banking Statistics (1981-1999), relevant issues, Mumbai.

- Loans and advances of commercial banks in rural centres was Rs. 627.4 crores in 1991, which increased to Rs. 1647.7 crores in 1999 i.e., an increase of 2.4 times over the period. During the period, average annual growth rate of advance was 12.3 per cent in rural areas as against 11.0 per cent at the state level (Table 20.2). In this sphere also commercial banks faired not so well compared to pre-reform period (Table 20.3).
- The credit-deposit ratio, which indicates utilisation of fund by commercial banks out of the deposits mobilised from rural areas, has also decelerated in post-reform period. The average annual credit-deposit ratio in the pre-reform period was 122.5 per cent in rural areas as against the state average of 88.2 per cent between 1981 and 1990. On the other hand, in the post-reform period the average annual rural credit-deposit ratio was 56.3 per cent as against the state average of 66.9 per cent during 1991 to 1999.

The sharp decline in the credit-deposit ratio in rural areas during post economic reform period was due to following factors.

(a) After financial sector reform there has taken place a shift of emphasis from financing traditional sectors like agriculture, small scale and village industries etc. to more in favour of modern sector like infrastructure, construction of building and durable assets such as automobiles, electronic appliances, etc. Since such activities are not widespread in rural areas, the financing pattern of banks have therefore, more tilted towards semi-urban and urban centres.

(b) There is the growing volume of Non-Performing Assets (NPAs) in banks. A sizeable chunk of these NPAs in banks is due to poor recovery of loans from rural areas. Owing to poor income generation, the banks have deliberately reduce the quantum credit to rural sectors.

(c) Absence of diversification of rural economy having viable entrepreneurs is another cause of poor credit-deposit ratio in rural centres. Agriculture in Orissa is the only occupation of the majority of population in the state. It is not diversified. Food crops alone account for about 70 per cent of total production. Commercialisation of agriculture has not taken place in a large scale. As a result of this banks have expressed reluctance to supply credit only to food crop growers who are more affected by natural factors.

(d) The experience derived from state sponsored poverty alleviation programmes where in sizeable amount of bank credit was locked in due to poor generation of income by the beneficiaries and non-repayment of loans by them, grossly affected the lending activities of the commercial banks.

(e) The poor performance of co-operative banks and the Regional

TABLE 20.3
Distribution of Annual Growth Rates of Offices, Deposits, Advances in Different Population Group-wise Centres by Commercial Banks in Orissa : 1981-1999

(in percentage)

Year	Pre-Reform Period											
	Annual Growth Rate (in %)											
	Rural			Semi-Urban			Urban			Total		
	Offices	Deposits	Advances	Offices	Deposits	Advances	Offices	Deposits	Advances	Offices	Deposits	Advances
1981	—	—	—	—	—	—	—	—	—	—	—	—
1982	34.63	25.07	33.97	15.30	3.14	18.37	16.39	11.07	18.01	28.72	11.48	22.99
1983	7.32	28.27	36.77	4.27	29.52	19.15	8.45	19.30	32.82	6.93	24.42	30.55
1984	15.70	23.39	32.40	-15.00	-9.08	2.68	11.69	22.20	44.68	10.21	12.96	30.44
1985	10.63	3.17	11.27	32.09	39.44	46.76	11.63	19.55	17.93	13.46	20.06	20.96
1986	3.55	25.06	21.75	4.05	21.95	20.43	1.04	19.74	21.01	3.34	21.58	21.12
1987	2.18	24.57	19.26	0.78	28.81	17.20	1.03	16.49	12.84	1.85	21.92	15.93
1988	2.75	34.39	25.38	-16.22	-25.96	-25.81	-15.31	-33.26	-23.06	-2.04	-14.86	-7.37
1989	5.57	17.42	55.79	19.35	92.87	98.98	34.34	104.53	121.74	10.06	68.56	87.51
1990	9.70	23.39	-0.44	0.39	17.64	26.45	1.35	33.55	3.01	7.46	26.07	6.25

TABLE 20.3 (Contd.)

Year	Post-Reform Period											
	Annual Growth Rate (in %)											
	Rural			Semi-Urban			Urban			Total		
	Offices	Deposits	Advances	Offices	Deposits	Advances	Offices	Deposits	Advances	Offices	Deposits	Advances
1991	—	—	—	—	—	—	—	—	—	—	—	—
1992	0.74	16.57	18.29	0.38	22.35	14.25	4.80	7.95	10.09	1.14	14.13	13.73
1993	0.74	21.17	13.19	0.38	9.41	7.68	7.50	12.71	10.82	1.46	14.14	10.90
1994	0.18	19.08	9.55	1.89	11.65	3.72	3.10	13.95	-2.71	0.74	14.85	3.00
1995	-1.34	21.16	9.19	9.26	28.29	16.88	0.75	31.09	20.50	0.23	27.29	15.50
1996	0.06	22.09	12.99	0.68	20.39	21.80	1.87	6.55	19.59	0.37	14.81	17.79
1997	-0.43	22.48	9.54	0.00	18.27	3.42	1.10	20.43	-11.92	-0.18	20.47	-1.09
1998	0.00	19.63	19.89	2.02	16.38	18.18	7.25	21.17	30.92	1.19	19.37	23.67
1999	0.25	20.90	10.52	2.97	16.78	13.07	5.41	18.85	3.47	1.31	18.95	8.28
Average Annual Growth Rate:												
1981-90	8.17	21.19	25.17	3.42	17.85	19.49	5.92	17.06	22.08	7.17	18.58	22.59
1991-99	0.10	20.69	12.28	2.39	18.07	12.14	3.44	16.90	9.40	0.65	18.34	11.05

Source : R.B.I., Banking Statistics (1981-1999), relevant issues, Mumbai.

Banks in rural areas are to a large extent restricted the lending behaviour of rural branches of commercial banks who preferred to avoid further risks in rural lending by concentrating more in semi-urban and urban centres.

FINANCIAL SECTOR REFORMS : WHAT HAS GONE WRONG IN RURAL AREAS?

Inspite of the laudable propagation of the merits of financial sector reforms, the commercial banks seem to have come across with certain difficulties in rural centres in the aftermath of financial sector reforms.

1. In the post-reform period, the commercial banks are more engaged in the consolidation of their activities which in the past reached to several directions most of which were not strictly in accordance with banking norms and guidelines. The 'internal house keeping' is more directed towards putting banks in sound footing particularly in rural centres which in the past exhibited signs of distortion (Misra : 1996)
2. Priority sector finance still continued to claim nearly 60 per cent of gross bank credit. This happened in Orissa due to preponderance of large mass of poverty stricken people leaving below the poverty line. On account of this, commercial banks failed to supply credit to economically deserving and viable sectors which offer large scope for income earning. Improvement of the living conditions of the poor thus calls for a determined and deliberate effort by the government, in order to reduce the 'pressure' on the commercial banks.
3. On account of the growing Non-Performing Assets in rural banks, the banks themselves adopted go-slow methods in financing the rural centres. The poor recovery of loans still persists although its magnitude has declined to some extent. This is corroborated by the fact that most of the loans sanctioned under poverty-alleviation programme were turned out to be bad loans affecting the income earning capacity of the banks (Misra & Meher : 1997).
4. The organisational structure which is mooted under financial sector reforms has not been given any practical shape to promote the development of rural centres. In the rural areas almost all nationalised banks have their rural branches competing with each other for the same class of rural customers who live with scarce means. Even there is severe competition between rural branches of commercial banks and the offices of Regional Rural banks in undertaking banking business with the same class of customers (RBI : 1982).
5. It is further seen that whatever rural banking has been done by commercial banks they are mostly confined to developed coastal

areas of the state. The most backward and hinterland areas have not been very well served by commercial banks. There was thus a sizeable gap in the development of rural centres between developed coastal areas and backward tribal areas.

In order to promote rural development in real terms the following measures be considered.

- Rural development needs to receive topmost priority in any scheme of economic development. This is particularly important with reference to the construction of roads, bridges and embankments i.e all types of rural capital formation essential for economic development. Besides, more attention be paid for the spread of education, expansion of health services, sanitation and environmental protection in the rural areas.
- Agriculture which is the key sector in rural economy needs to receive further attention by undertaking measures like irrigation, soil conservation, land reforms, distribution of inputs and agricultural marketing etc. Rural upliftment may not be possible only by agricultural growth. There need to be a linkage between agriculture and industry, particularly agro-industries for improving income and well being of the farming class. The raw materials generated from agriculture will find larger opportunity of exploitation by agro-industries which would not only improve the productivity of agriculture but also lead to value addition. (Misra : 1999).
- There is need for further consolidation of rural bank branches. The low income yielding branches be merged with high income earning branches in order to have a minimum number of viable rural branches (Sen, K. and Vaidya, R.R. : 1997). It is suggested that the commercial banks to gradually withdraw its rural branches for an effective fairplay by Regional Rural Banks.
- Once the rural branches of commercial banks are withdrawn, the RRBs need to improve their operational efficiency by reducing losses and earning higher profits. In this context two suggestions seem to be relevant. First, the RRBs be totally detached from the sponsored banks to stand on their own leg. Secondly, as independent units they be affiliated to an apex corporation like Rural Banking Development Corporation to be created for the purpose who would undertake all promotional and regulatory activities in favour of rural banks. This would help to improve the efficiency of such banks (RBI : 2000).
- The rural banks need not be exclusively confined to rural areas alone. While having a rural thrust, they can go in search for profitable investment of their funds in semi-urban and urban areas. Even they need not be attached to rural customers only. They may

be permitted to deal with all types of customers for all types of loans (Misra : 2000).

CONCLUSION

Rural development is a complex phenomenon. The people and their activities are so heterogeneous in character that they require systematic treatment by any institutional organisation. Commercial banks, more specifically rural banks, are to be motivated to approach rationally the complex situation prevalent in the rural centres. They cannot, however, remain as a passive onlooker. Most of the developmental thrust can only be translated into practical aspect of providing economic and social infrastructure which can attract private investment that, in turn, will increase credit absorptive capacity of rural producers. The observed sharp decline in credit-deposit ratio in the post-reform period is thus of concern insofar as it is a reflection of declining investment demand.

REFERENCES

Dagli, V. (1976), Financial Institutions of India (Edited), Vora, Bombay.

Govt. of India (1992), Report on Financial Sector Reforms, New Delhi.

Govt. of Orissa (1992), *Op. cit.*

Govt. of India (2001), Economic Survey, D.E. & S., Bhubaneswar.

Misra, S.N. (1982), Commercial Banking and Rural Development in Orissa, Utkal Economic Papers, Vol. 1, No. 1, Bhubaneswar.

Misra, S.N. (1984), Growth of Commercial Banking in Orissa, Anu Books, Meerut.

Misra, S.N. & Meher, S. (1997), Freedom from Hunger—A Study of Begunia Block of Puri District, Nabakrushna Choudhury Centre for Development Studies, Bhubaneswar.

Misra, S.N. (1999), Can Agro-Industries be an effective tool for promoting rural development in Orissa, Journal of Rural Development—A Quarterly of NIRD. Vol. 18, No. 2, April-June issue, Hydrabad.

Misra, S.N. (1999), Commercial Banks and Agricultural Development, Anmol Publications, New Delhi.

Misra, S.N. & Behera, M. (2000), An Evaluation of Anti-poverty programmes in Mayurbhanja District, Nabakrushna Choudhury Centre for Development Studies, Bhubaneswar.

Misra, S.N. (2000), Development of Commercial Banking in the Post Banking and Financial Sector Reform periods in India in Banerjee, Amlesh and Singh, S.K. (edited), Banking and Financial Sector Reforms in India, Deep and Deep Publications, New Delhi.

Rangarajan, C. (1998), Indian Economy—Essays on Money and Finance, UBS Publishers' & Distributors, New Delhi.

R.B.I. (1982), Working of the Regional and Rural Banks (Chairman : D.R. Gadgil), Mumbai.

R.B.I. (2000), Report of the Working Groups on Agricultural Finance (Gupta Committee), Mumbai.

Sen, K. and Vaidya, R.R. (1997), The Process of Financial Liberalisation in India, Oxford University Press, Calcutta.

Subrahmanya, K.N. (1982), Modern Banking in India, Deep and Deep Publications, New Delhi.

SECTION III

Strategy of Development and its Sustainability

CHAPTER

21

Ecological Sustainability and Economic Development in Low Income Economies : A Case Study of Wet Land and Mangrove Ecosystem in Sundarban

RAJ KUMAR SEN AND SOMNATH HAJRA

With the increasing awareness of the importance of any ecosystem and its sustainability on the quality of life specially in low income economies with high population density like India, the current pattern of economic development can be more effective to achieve its goals of uplifting human welfare, if it adequately accommodates the above concern. This paper tries to elucidate the ecological sustainability and economic development of Sundarban mangrove ecosystem.

This paper is divided into the following sections. Concept of sustainability occurs in section I. Section II describes the concept of ecological sustainability and its relations with economic development. Characteristics of wet land and mangrove ecosystem of Sundarban in the context of ecological sustainability are described in section III. Section IV develops the relation between the wetland and mangrove ecosystem of Sundarban and economic development in the context of ecological sustainability and describes the present situation of Sundarban mangrove forest. The last section is for conclusion and policy prescription.

I

In the last decade sustainable development has become an important objective for many governments and other decision-making bodies across the world. Sustainable development and environment are closely related. But what do we mean by the world sustainable development? Sustainable development refers to creating a style of economic development which is sustainable within the context of planet's ecosystem and human society. The concept is a synthesis of economic and ecological ideas. World is currently exploring the concept of sustainable development—it is an approach that will permit continuing improvements in the present quality of life at a lower density of resource use thereby living behind the future generation undiminished or even enhanced stock of natural resources and other assets.

The dictionary meaning of sustainable development is an economic development that takes full account of environmental consequences of economic activity and is based on the use of resources that can be replaced or renewed and therefore are not depleted. In the context of sustainable development the definition of Burntland Commission (1987) is most appropriate—sustainable development is a development which meets the needs of the current generation without jeopardizing the needs of the future generations.

II

The ecological view of the sustainable development focuses on the stability of the biological and physical systems. Once ecological sustainability is considered, the notion of a fixed quantum and composition of environmental resources as well as commitment to traditional pattern of land use can affect potential economic growth. Ecological sustainability could be achieved by "locking up" resources but there is an overwhelming case for economic growth and development, to provide goods and services and to create employment opportunities for increasing populations. Ecological sustainability is not necessarily a goal in its own right, unless degradation of ecosystems leads to reduction of welfare of mankind. Particular importance is the viability of subsystems that are critical to the global stability of the overall ecosystem. Protection of biological diversity is a key aspect. Loss of diversity in an ecosystem can cause environmental changes. Loss of one species may cause a chain reaction, resulting in a change to the ecosystem itself. Every organism has its suitable position in the environment. Once it is gone it may not be able to be replaced by any other organism. The functioning of the biosphere is dependent on the combination of all existing ecosystems. Furthermore, natural system may be interpreted to include all aspects of the biosphere including man made environments. Biodiversity conservation does not require the preservation of all species or the maintenance of current environment conditions. An evolutionary system requires that a level of biodiversity be maintained that will guarantee the resilience of the ecosystem on which human consumption and production and therefore human welfare depend.

Now the question arises that how sustainable development was neglected and even degraded in developing economies. For sustainable development of a developing economy it is useful to distinguish between necessary and sufficient conditions for it. For development to be sustainable it is necessary to enhance the capital stock on which the development depends, capital stock includes human made capital and natural capital. In developing economy the amount of human made capital is not sufficient for development but the natural capital occupies a very strong position. Poverty is the main reason for degradation of sustainable development in developing countries like India. Poor people of the developing countries are fully dependent on natural resources and primary production because of the lack of resources and economic opportunities in other sectors of the economy and insufficient man made capital formation. Institutional and policy failures in poor economies are important determinants of their inability to innovate sufficiently to achieve higher long term growth rates. Controlling environmental degradation in developing economies is difficult because of the poverty-environment trap. If the poverty and environmental degradation exist at a high level then it can be said that the environmental degradation is the main cause of poverty. Poverty and environmental degradation are positively related.

Out of the 12 mega diversity zones India is one. India has abundant natural resources and insufficient man made capital. Protection of natural capital is important in India because over 50% or more the export earnings come from this natural capital and also it helps mankind to live in. India is trying to develop during the past 50 years since independence in both agricultural and industrial sectors. For sustainable development, without jeopardizing the environmental asset proper development of the above two sectors is needed.

III

We choose Sundarban for our study because due to its remoteness and underdeveloped nature of transport system and many other factors, most of the people here are living below poverty level. The population of this area increases at a very high rate. It also exposes the forest system to continuous degradation. Sundarban is the largest mangrove forest of the world, it provides protection to the inland habitations against the fury of cyclones. The mangrove forest is a great protector of coastal natural calamity. It directly or indirectly helps the welfare of the people in this locality.

Sundarban is the largest deltaic region of the world and is situated at the southern part of West Bengal in India and spreading over to Bangladesh. Almost 62% of the Sundarban is situated in Bangladesh while the remaining western portion i.e, 38% of the region lies within India. The Southern area of South 24 Parganas district is known to us as Sundarban. Sundarban of West Bengal consists of 9630 sq. Km. of mangrove swamps. There are 102 islands among which 54 have human settlements. Population is nearly 3.5

million. The Sundarban is the gift of the river Brambhaputra and Ganges. The land area is very low and full of forest. The Indian Sundarban lies at the apex of the Bay of Bengal and includes the area bordering the Hooghly, Muriganga, Saptamukhi, Thakuran, Gosaba, Vidya, Matla and Harinbhanga estuaries, known as Hooghly Matla estuarine complex (*Roy Choudhury,*

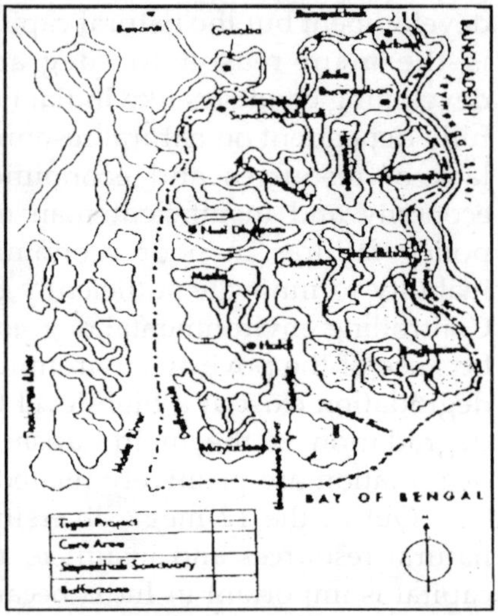

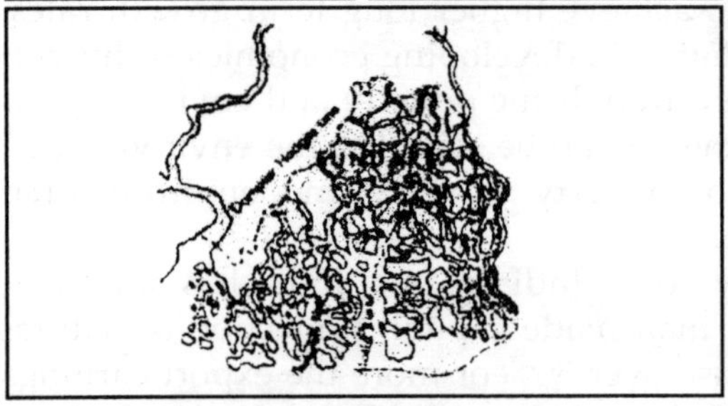

Datail Map of Sunderban

Tiger Project Area

Mangrove species of Sunderban

Fishing in Sunderban

B. 2003). In a broader sense the rivers Saptamukhi, Thakuran, Ajmalmari, Dhulibhasani and Matla (part) with all connecting the channels comprising about 1500 sq. Km. come under the area of wetlands. This area has a vast fish and floral and faunal resources including birds, tigers, crocodiles etc. Some ecologists consider wetlands as transitional ecosystem of a landscape that occupy a status intermediate between terrestrial aquatic ecosystems. These are most productive sites which have a wide range of natural functions. The wetlands play a significant role of global cycling and geochemical balance of carbon, nitrogen and sulphur. Sundarban wetlands have an enormous ecological, economic, commercial and socio-economic importance. Such lands contents have very rich components of bio-diversity. Sundarban is the only mangrove area where tiger survives. Total number of tigers, popularly known as Royal Bengal tigers according to latest census are 253. Since 1973 "Project Tiger" was initiated with an area of rich bio-diversity. People of Sundarban are mainly fisherman. They depend on the forest for fishing, wood and honey collection.

IV

Coastal ecosystems are important natural resource base of India. In spite of ecological and economical significance, current resource use pattern of coastal areas has resulted in degradation and putting stress on the coastal ecosystem. The Sundarban ecosystem has a particular significance on coastal areas from ecological as well as economic point of view. The ecological significance of mangroves is important as they serve as a storehouse of bio-diversity and also as a natural defence against coastal erosion. The economic significance of mangrove is equally important because it provides direct benefits in the form of timber, fuel wood, animal feed, manure as well as indirect benefits in terms of profitable fisheries. In spite of all these significances the mangrove ecosystem is under a serious threat due to the overuse caused by the population pressure and land diversion caused by expansion of agricultural land and urbanization. While wetlands have been conserved and managed with great care for their economic values in developed countries of the temperate regions, their importance has not yet been understood in India. At present wetlands are used in different societies for different needs depending on their demands. Sundarban wetland is a highly productive area with a rich and varied flora and fauna. It is a habitat for spawning and a nursery ground for several species of fish and shellfish and seasonal home for birds and rich feeding ground for duck. These wetlands are cultivated for the production of edible plants, and rich sources of protein food for the people e.g. mussels, oysters, shrimps, prawns, crabs and fish. They also play a role in the recycling of wastewater and function as a natural filtering system.

Now we describe how wetlands and mangrove ecosystem of Sundarban have been affected under developmental planning in India.

To maintain a steady density of the mangrove forest in the Sundarban region it is highly essential to increase the breeding power of the mangrove forest and side by side there should be huge supply of sweet water from rivers along with the sea water. In the early ages due to huge availability of sweet water from the Hooghly river and the Bhagirathi river, there was no problem. But in recent years the availability of sweet water became scarce to the agricultural areas due to the establishment of some new dams. This shortage of supply of sweet water from river is the main cause for decreasing the breeding power of the mangrove forest.

Diagram 21.1
Functions of Wet Lands

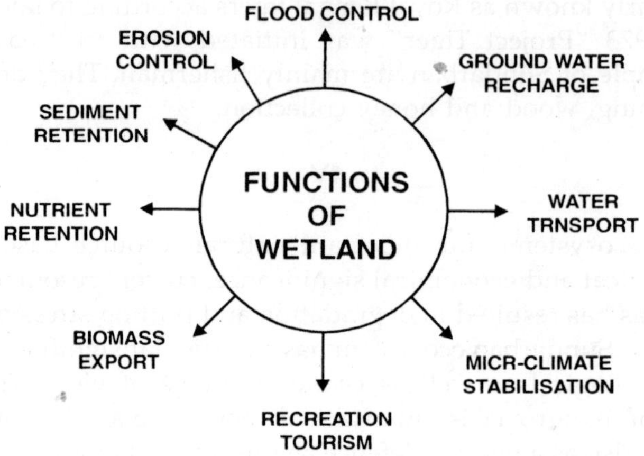

The second most important reason is the huge population pressure. Due to high birth rate and low death rate in this region and side by side migrating people from our neighbouring country Bangladesh there is increase in population pressure in Sundarban region. These people are very much dependent on these mangrove forest directly or indirectly and by over use they endanger these precious species.

Diagram 21.2

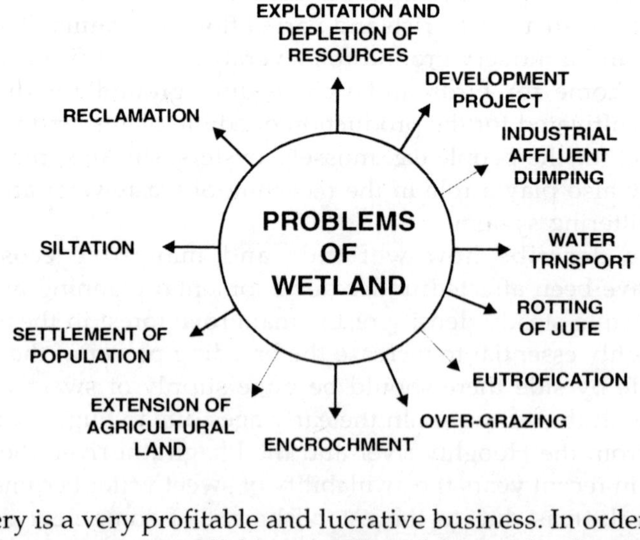

Fishery is a very profitable and lucrative business. In order to earn high profits fishermen are establishing small and big embankments by cutting down the trees. The fishing in river, damages the small fish and other water

DIAGRAM 21.3

bodies which creates an ecological disorder and affects the ecosystem and bio-diversity of Sundarban.

In the recent past there has been an increase in the number of brickfield. Because of this, the size of the agricultural area has come down. But agriculture is another occupation among the population in this region. So they have to increase the agricultural areas and they are doing this by cutting down the trees.

The very recent problem of Sundarban is pollution. Everyday the chemicals and oils from the speedboats, motorboats, wastes from the industrial areas and town areas are mixing with river water and creating pollution and damaging the healthy environment of Sundarban. Wetlands are also vanishing rapidly. The rich population of fish, fauna, amphibians, reptiles, are also declining as the wetlands are vanishing. Ruthless persecution of Setal birds and eggs by some people have caused substantial decline in the number of such birds. Wetlands are being reduced to provide farming and building settlements. The use of massive quantities of artificial fertilizers to boost agricultural production and pesticides, in particular insecticides to protect the crops from pests disturbs the Sundarban wetlands and ecosystem.

Mustafa K. Tolaba, Secretary General of UNEP started in 1991 in *Environment and Development* that government needs to review budget priorities to ensure subsidies, project finance, energy transformation, fiscal and other policies to work towards environmental protection as well as economic expansion. New revenue generating mechanisms like green taxes and charges on so called free goods like air, water, user fees pricing adjustments, concessionary loans, rebates and fiscal incentives need to be introduced at the national level (*Naidu, K.2000*). A new measure GPI

(Genuine Progress Indicator) is being suggested which takes into account the environmental besides the social and economic well-being for assessing the quality of life of the community. NGOs are providing medical aids to the villagers. Awareness camps have been set up. More NGOs should come forward and join with forest department to tackle man-animal conflict which is now the real crisis of the Sundarbans.

V

Ecological sustainability of mangrove ecosystem is more important and it can be achieved through grass roots level plans and programmes. A national policy is needed for protection of Sundarban mangrove ecosystem and wetlands. Environment degrading issues were responsible for depletion of several species of flora and fauna. No one was serious about conservation of natural habitat and genetic resources of Sundarban during the phase of green revolution in India. The only objective of the Government was to produce more and more food and increase urbanization by any means. These types of development activities are planned on a sustainable basis with long term objectives rather than with short term objectives and immediate benefits. Protection of mangrove ecosystem can be made through minimizing the current use pattern of mangrove and encouraging indirect and non-exploitative uses of the mangrove forest on a sustainable basis. To provide for a sustainable livelihood security of the population it is not enough to stop only at the ecological sustainability of the mangrove ecosystem. It is also essential to provide the population, especially the lower strata, with alternative sources of fuelwood and building materials. A green tax can be imposed on all depleting users of mangroves and wetlands of Sundarban to cover the social cost of the reduced biodiversity or ecological damage. Such a tax can be used to ecological fund to be used for restoration or other preservatory efforts and also to improve GDP. There is need to take concrete steps to ensure the sustainable management of the coastal ecosystem. Given the economic and ecological significance of coastal ecosystem, the need for a careful study is necessary to identify the issues involved in ecological sustainability of mangrove forest and wetlands of Sundarban. From a system's point of view the sustainable development will be one that improves the quality of life while living within the carrying capacity of supporting ecosystem.

References

Agrawal, Anil (1997), The Challenge of the Balance—Environmental Economics in India Proceedings of National Environment and Economic Meeting, pp. 1-56, population 101-110 pp. 207-260, Centre for Science and Environment, New Delhi.

Agrawal, Anil (1992), The Price of Forests, Proceedings of a seminar on the Economics of the sustainable use of Forest Resources, pp. 1-62, Center For Science and Environment, New Delhi.

Allaby, Michel (ed. 1998), Dictionary of Ecology, Oxford University Press, New York.

Balakrishnan, M. (1993), Environmental Problems and Prospects in India, pp. 1-93, Oxford and IBH Publishing Co. Ltd. New Delhi.

Banbithi (2002), Environment and Aranya Saptaha Issue, Forest Department Government of West Bengal.

Banbithi (2001), Forest and Environment Issue, Forest Department, Government of West Bengal.

Bergh, Jeroen C.J.M. Vanden (1999), Handbook of Environmental and Resource Economics Edward Elger Publishing Limited, Cheltanham.

Biswas, K.R. (1998), Sundarbans—A Statistical Account of Bengal—W.M. Hunter. West Bengal District.

Gazetteers, Department of Higher Education, Government of West Bengal, Calcutta.

Bhattacharya, Rabindra N. (2001), Environmental Economics—An Indian Perspective, Oxford University Press, New Delhi.

Chaudhuri, A.B. (1998), Wetland Ecology—Resources, Research and Conservation—An Indian Scenario. MEPS Publishers, Kalyani, West Bengal.

Moore, Ron and Ryan Jan (1995), Sustainable Development Policy and Practice. pp. 2-38, 76-96 New Age International (P) Ltd., New Delhi.

Naidu M.K., (2000), Impact of Economic Reforms our Environment Protection, Environment and People, (August), Society for Environment and Education, Hyderabad.

Naskar, Kumudranjan (2002), Sundarban Bipannya Prakriti, pp. 9-17, Yojona, March, 8, Esplanade East, Kolkata.

Rao, N.S. (2001), Sustainable Forest Management, pp. 28-32, Kurukshetra, March, Ministry of Rural Development, Government of India.

Roy Choudhury, B. (2003), Sundarbans : An Overview. pp. 46-48, Environ.Vol. 8, No. 4. Vision Publications Pvt. Ltd. Kolkata-67.

Roy, Biswanath (1993), West Bengal Today———A Fresh Look, pp. 107-123, Mittal Publications, New Delhi

Shekar, C. (2001), Externally of CPR Degradation, Indian Journal of Agricultural Economics, Vol. 56, No. 3.

Sengupta, Ramprasad (2001), Economics, Oxford. University Press, New Delhi.

State Forest Report (1999), Forest Survey of India, Dehradun.

State Forest Report (2001), Government of West Bengal, Department of Forest.

Tisdel, Clem (1993), Environmental Economics, pp. 69-128, 140-169, 239-249, Edward Elgar Publishing Limited, England.

CHAPTER

22

Institutional Aspects of Sustainable Aquaculture Development and Abatement of Conflicts in Resource Sharing

N. RAJALAKSHMI

INTRODUCTION

"A major portion of the conflicts arising from the expansion of shrimp farming are the result of environmental and social degradation that is not included in the costs of shrimp production, where the industry assumes no responsibility for damages to other groups arising from its activities, economists call them "externalities". For example, abandoned ponds are usually virtually unusable for other purposes for indefinite periods without costly rehabilitation which is seldom undertaken. Mangrove destruction, flooding of crops, salinization or pollution of land and water associated with the expansion of shrimp farming all affect the local people depending on these resources", the UN report on conflicts and externalities due to aquaculture has presented the problems associated with aquaculture in the above paragraph. (Supreme Court's Judgement, 1996).

Rana and Immink (2000) in Home Page FAO High Lights site, have given details about Trends in Global Aquaculture Production during 1984-96. They also say that as we move into next millennium, finfish and other aquatic products will be in greater short supply as domestic and international demand for both high and low valued species increases due to rising populations, living standards and disposable incomes. This page also tells that the potential of aquaculture to meet the challenges of food security and to generate employment and foreign exchange is clearly demonstrated by the rapid expansion of this sector, which has grown at an average annual rate of almost 10 percent since 1984, compared with 3 per cent for livestock meat and 1.6 per cent for capture fisheries production.

One implication of environmental change or resources scarcity is the increasing likelihood of conflict among people or nations. Human activity can contribute to environmental degradation or resource scarcity in 3 ways. First, human activities can result in a decrease in the quality and or quantity of resources if they are used or harvested at a rate faster than they can be renewed. A second source of degradation or scarcity is population growth, a set amount of land or water, must increasingly be shared among more people resulting in a steadily reduced amount available per person. Third, unequal access to resources or the environment may cause problem. Unequal access is usually the result of laws of property rights which lead to or encourage the concentration of supply in the hands of relatively small number of people leaving others subject to scarcity.

Conflict is a clash of interests, values, action or directions and has been a part of life since time began. Thus, conflicts are inescapable but they can be positive as well as negative. Conflict or no conflict, man has to subsist. Hence it is attempted to study the conflicts of coastal resources over the sustainable development of aquaculture.

Objectives

- To assess the socio-economic benefits of aquaculture farms in Tamil Nadu.
- To examine economic and environmental impacts of aquaculture farms in Tamil Nadu at Bay of Bengal region.
- To analyse the extent of conflicts of common property resources for multiple uses.
- To arrive at institutional solutions for sustainable aquaculture production.

Based on the above objectives the following hypotheses have been formed.

Hypotheses

1. There is no linear relationship between profit and cost, turnover and land size.
2. There is no linear relationship between initial work time on aquaculture farms and initial investment, pond size and land size.
3. There is no linear relationship between public opinion on the future of farms and the benefits they receive, educational level and pollution problems.

Study Area

The data to be collected for the successful testing of hypothesis and for achieving of the objectives have been called out from 3 different levels.

1. *Schedule—A* : The owners or chief executives of the selected farms who were made to respond to the questions in schedule A.
2. *Schedule—B* : The labour or the work force in the selected farms numbering 60, responded to the questions in Schedule B.
3. *Schedule*—C : The general public drawn at random from the surrounding areas of the selected farm, numbering 180, responded to questions in Schedule.

Public or the workforce who were illiterates, the researcher read out and sometimes translated the questions in order to elicit a valid and reliable answer. Necessary data have been collected from 10 shrimp farms spread over the above mentioned 4 villages for the present study.

The enclosed map shows the location of Nagapattinam district and the location of Sirkali taluk.

Table 22.1 shows the number of farms in each selected village.

TABLE 22.1
Number of Aqua-farms in the Selected Villages

Name of village	*Number of Existing Farms*	*Number of Farms selected*
1. Vanagiri	10	2
2. Perunthottam	7	2
3. Thennampattinam	21	3
4. Thirunagari	15	3
Total	53	10

Table 22.1 shows a total of 10 farms which is 20 per cent of the existing farms and a judicious selection of 2 or 3 per village has been effected for a homogeneous random sampling. An initial survey conducted through discussion with Village Administrative Officers and others shows that the owners of the shrimp farms are mostly male members in the age group 45 and above. Most of the people in the villages (60 per cent to 65 per cent) are literates. Those engaged in the agricultural farming constitute about 60 per cent of the population. Generally, the size of the family is small i.e., less than 5 on an average.

MULTIPLE REGRESSION

Regression models are used to analyse the dependence of one set of variables over another set of independent variables. If y is a dependent variable and x's are independent variables then the regression model is

$$Y = a1x1 + a2x2 + \ldots \ldots \ldots + anxn.$$

a's are constants. After fitting the regression equation, the validity of the model will be tested using F-Statistics as shown below.

TABLE 22.2
Correlation between Profit and Other Variables

	Profit	*P-Value*
Work Time	0.6979	>0.05
Land Size	0.5883	>0.05
Ponds	0.7171	>0.05
Cost	0.9209	<0.001
Turnover	0.9661	<0.001
Investment	0.9654	<0.001

Correlation between dependent variable profit and other important variables are given in the Table 2. Since there is high correlation between profit and cost, turnover and land size, the linear relationship between these variables has been analysed with the help of multiple regression.

Dependent Variable: Profit
Independent Variable: 1. Cost 2. Turn over in Rupees
3. Land size

Model Summary

Multiple R = 1.000
R. Square = 1.000
Adjusted R. Square = 1.000
Standard Error = 1.285673 E-08

TABLE 22.3
Analysis of Variance

	Sum of squares	*DF*	*Mean Square*	*F-Value*	*p-Value*
Regression	0.59554	3	0.19851	1.19E+15	<0.00001
Residual	0	6	0		
Total	0.59554	9	0.19851		

TABLE 22.4

Coefficients of the Variables in the Regression Equation

Variable	*B*	*SE of B*	*Beta*	*t-Value*	*p-Value*
TURN_OVER	1.00E+00	4.72E-08	2.8073	2119880	<0.00001
LAND_SIZE	-4.15E-17	2.65E-10	-4.39E-10	0	1
COST	-1	7.65E-08	-1.8592	-1307107	<0.00001
(Constant)	6.79E-16	6.28E-09		0	1

Inference

The analysis of variance is given as an overall summary of the multiple regression analysis. The total sum of square represents the total variability in the dependent variable 'Profit'. The error (as residual) sum of square here is equal to 'Zero', that is the complete measure of variance explained by the independent variables (Turn over, Land size, Cost) in the regression equation.

The general null hypothesis,

H1: all the 3 independent variables considered together do not explain a significant amount of variation in 'Profit'.

The F value – 1.1918301E+15 with (3,6) degrees of freedom and p-value (<0.00001) of the model under study suggests that the hypothesis Ho is rejected. It is concluded that there exists a significant relationship between 'Profit' and other variables namely Turnover, Land size and Cost.

The linear relationship between dependent variable profit and independent variables land size, initial investment and number of ponds is also analysed using multiple regression tool, since the correlation between profit and the above variables is significant.

Dependent Variable: Profit

Independent Variables:
1. Land size
2. Investment
3. No of Ponds

Model Summary

Multiple R = 0.99805
R. Square = 0.99611
Adjusted R. Square = 0.99417
Standard Error = 0.01965

Inference

The analysis of variance table is given an overall summary of the multiple regression analysis. The total sum of squares represents the total

TABLE 22.5
Analysis of Variance

	Sum of squares	*DF*	*Mean Square*	*F-Value*	*p-Value*
Regression	0.59322	3	0.19774	5.12E+02	<0.00001
Residual	0.00232	6	0.00039		
Total	0.59554	9	0.19813		

TABLE 22.6
Coefficients of the Variables in the Regression Equation

Variable	*B*	*SE of B*	*Beta*	*t-Value*	*p-Value*
Investment	0.350544	0.013491	0.995808	25.984	<0.00001
LAND_SIZE	-0.00649	6.52E-04	-0.685746	-9.946	0.0001
No. of Ponds	0.021761	0.0026	0.611079	8.371	0.0002
(Constant)	-0.018654	0.010993		-1.697	0.1406

variability in the dependent variable "Profit". The error (on residual) sum of square represents the amount of variation in 'Profit' that is not explained by the independent variables (Land size, Investment and No. of Ponds) included in the regression equation. And (Total SS-Residual SS) is called the model sum of squares and is a measure of the variance explained by the independent variables in the regression equation.

H1: All the independent variables consideral together do not explain a significant amount of variation in 'profit'. With the calculated F-value=512.30653 with (3, 6) degrees of freedom and the corresponding p-value (<0.00001) it is concluded that there exists linear relationship between dependent variable Profit and independent variables, Land Size, Investment and No. of Ponds and hence the hypothesis is rejected. The second hypothesis formulated for the present study is that there is no linear relationship between initial work time (dependent variable) and initial investment, pond size and land size (independent variables). Initial work time is the time taken by the farm to do all preparatory work and start functioning. Generally, the initial work time will be more or less dependent

TABLE 22.7
Correlation between Work time and Other Variables

	Work time	*p-Value*
Ponds	0.9564	<0.001
Investment	0.7550	>0.05
Land size	0.9297	<0.001

on a variety of factors. The quantum of the initial investment, land size and number of ponds is to be considered as independent variables and initial work time as dependent variable in order to arrive at the result of dependency or otherwise. The linear relationship between these sets of variables have been analysed using the multiple regression tool.

Correlation between dependent variable work time and other variables are given in Table 4.4.1a. This shows high correlation between work time and pond size, investment and land size.

Dependent Variable: Initial Work Time
Independent Variables: 1. Initial Investment
2. Land Size
3. Ponds

Model Summary

Multiple R = 0.964a
R. Square = 0.930
Adjusted R. Square = 0.895
Standard Error = 1.33

TABLE 22.8
Analysis of Variance

	Sum of squares	*DF*	*Mean Square*	*F-Value*	*Sig.*
Regression	141.466	3	47.155	26.605	0.001[a]
Residual	10.634	6	1.772		
Total	152.100	9			

TABLE 22.9
Coefficients of the Variables in the Regression Equation

Variable	B	*SE B*	*Beta*	T	*Sig. T*
INI.INVEST	4.65E-03	0.009	0.083	0.509	0.629
LAND_SIZE	4.40E-02	0.044	0.291	0.996	0.358
PONDS	.355	0.176	0.624	2.017	0.090
(Constant)	1.798	0.745		2.414	0.052

a Dependent variables: WTIME.

Since F table value for (3,6), d.t. at 5% as well as 1% is higher than the calculated value of F in the Annova Table, the regression model is not a good fit. Therefore, the second hypothesis – no linear relationship between initial work time and pond size, initial investment and land size is accepted.

Hypothesis 5 is that there is no linear relationship between public opinion on the future of farms and benefits they receive, the educational level and pollution problems.

MULTIPLE REGRESSION

Dependent Variable	:	Future
Independent Variables	:	1. Disadvantage
		2. Education
		3. Benefit

Model Summary

Multiple R	0.805
R Square	0.648
Adjusted R Square	0.609
Standard Error	0.61

TABLE 22.10
Analysis of Variance

	Sum of squares	*DF*	*Mean Square*	*F-Value*	*Sig.*
Regression	110.196	18	6.122	1.65E+01	0
Residual	59.865	161	0.372		
Total	170.061	179	6.494		

Inference

From the ANOVA Table 22.11 it is concluded that there exists no linear relationships between future of aqua-farms and the education level, benefits they receive and pollution/disadvantages they face, since the significant F value is zero. Therefore the hypothesis 5 is accepted. In order to analyse the most prominent factor among benefits on the one hand and disadvantages on the other, the factor analysis tool has been used. Factors such as education; benefits pollution and future of aqua-farms have been analysed.

TABLE 22.11
Coefficients of the Variables in the Regression Equation

Variable	*B*	*SE of B*	*Beta*	*t-Value*	*Sig.*
Constant	1.943	0.183		10.598	0.000
EDUC	2.02E-02	0.035	0.028	0.570	0.569
BENE1	0.804	0.154	0.403	5.211	0.000
BENE2	0.513	0.264	0.247	1.940	0.054

(Contd.)

TABLE 22.11 (Contd.)

Variable	*B*	*SE of B*	*Beta*	*t-Value*	*Sig.*
BENE3	-0.803	0.373	-0.198	-2.151	0.033
BENE4	0.554	0.488	0.110	1.135	0.258
BENE5	-0.399	0.260	-0.190	-1.535	0.127
BENE6	-1.6E-02	0.240	-0.077	-0.067	0.947
BENE7	0.354	0.492	0.054	0.720	0.473
DISAD1	0.230	0.120	0.177	1.919	0.057
DISAD2	-0.152	0.142	-0.077	-1.066	0.288
DISAD3	-0.151	0.224	-0.036	-0.673	0.502
DISAD4	-0.984	0.266	-0.473	-3.697	0.000
DISAD5	0.164	0.287	0.079	0.573	0.567
DISAD6	-0.322	0.112	-0.162	-2.866	0.005
DISAD7	-0.137	0.258	-0.065	-0.530	0.597
DISAD8	0.354	0.167	0.169	2.115	0.036
DISAD9	-0.157	0.498	-0.017	-3.14	0.754
DISAD10	0.265	0.345	0.040	0.769	0.443

Factor Analysis

Communalities	*Initial*	*Extraction*
Education	1.000	0.188
Benefit	1.0000	0.898
Pollution	1.000	0.842
Future	1.0000	7.005E-02

Total Variance Explained

Component				*Ex*		
	Total	*% of Variance*	*Cumulative % %*	*Total*	*% of Variance*	*Cumulative %*
1	1.998	49.947	49.947	1.998	49.947	49.947
2	0.966	24.157	74.104	—	—	—
2	0.966	24.157	74.104	—	—	—
3	0.907	22.665	96.769	—	—	—
3	0.907	22.665	96.769	—	—	—
4	0.129	3.231	100.000	—	—	—
4	0.129	3.231	100.000	—	—	—

Since, benefit has the highest value of 0.948, Benefit is the most important factor and pollution has the least value of –0.917. Therefore pollution is not given importance in deciding about the future of the farms. Having accepted hypothesis 5, the researcher moves on to other areas of analysis such as demographic details and public opinion on the working and maintenance of aqua-farms. Age is an important factor in detaining both utility and experience the agewise distribution of employees in aqua-farms studied shown in Table.

Education wise Distribution of Employees

Sl. No.	*Educ. Level*	*No. of Persons*	*Percentage*
1.	Upto 8th Standard	26	43.3
2.	8th Standard to High Secondary Level	20	33.3
3.	Graduate	1	1.7
4.	Illiterates	13	21.7
	Total	60	100.00

Income wise Distribution of the Employees

Sl. No.	*Income Level*	*No. of Persons*	*Percentage*
1.	Less than Rs.1000	9	15.0
2.	Rs. 1000-1500	31	52.0
3.	Rs. 1501-2000	15	25.0
4.	Rs. 2001 & Above	05	09.0
	Total	60	100

As per the above table, out of the 60 employees contacted about their monthly income, 15 per cent of them, get a sum upto Rs. 1000. A majority (52%) get income ranging between Rs. 1000 and Rs. 1500. There are 25 per cent of the employees getting an income ranging between Rs. 1501 and Rs. 2000/- per month and 8 per cent of them get income above Rs. 2001/. The average income of an employee works out to be Rs. 1550 per month.

Items of Expenditure after increase in Income

Sl. No.	*Items of Expenditure*	*No. of Persons*
1.	On Voluntary Saving	37
2.	On Education	12
3.	On Festival	4
4.	On Jewels	1
5.	On Others	18

The above table shows the items of expenditure of the employees after the increase in their incomes due to the impact of shrimp farms it is seen that 37 employees are voluntarily saving since their entry in to aqua farms and because of the increase in the incomes. This saving will ultimately help in capital formation. Another 12 employees spend their increased amounts on education due to their employment in shrimp farms.

There are a few (4,1) who also spend on festivals and jewels because of the increase in their income level.

Distribution of Benefits

Sl.No.	Benefits	No. of Persons
1.	Increase in Wages	50
2.	Transport Facilities	28
3.	Shrimps at Low Price	6
4.	Electricity/Water Supply	25

The above table gives about the benefits received by the employees working in the shrimp farms. A vast majority of employees (83.3%) feel higher wages to be the most important benefit, while 28 persons (46.6%) have expressed transport, facility to be beneficial. Those who feel electricity/water facility as beneficial are 25 persons (ie 41.6%).

INCOME GENERATION

Shrimps are highly valued species, especially in the external markets. As a result, not only the owners of the farms get more profits, but also the workers of the farms get better wages. This has been revealed by many respondents of the questionnaire in Sirkali region. The following tables shows the district wise production of prawns in the State.

District wise Production of Prawns in Tamil Nadu

(in Tonnes)

Sl. No.	Districts	1994-95	1995-96	1996-97	1997-98
1.	Chennai	1187	876	844	858
2.	Thiruvallur & Kanchipuram	464	534	973	570
3.	Villupuram	17	4	140	12
4.	Cuddalore	704	717	631	622
5.	Nagai & Thiruvarur	4199	4440	3744	4092
6.	Thanjavur	977	1248	902	1107
7.	Pudukottai	2197	2452	3966	3604
8.	Ramanadapuram	9445	6961	7539	6279
9.	Tuticorin	3369	2205	2925	622
10.	Thirunelveli	429	73	158	24
11.	Kanniyakumari	337	767	180	210
	Total	23325	20275	22002	18000

Source : Statistical wing, Directorate of Fisheries, Govt. of Tamil Nadu.

The above table shows that the trend in the production of prawns in the coastal districts of Tamil Nadu for a period of 4 years from 1994-95 to 1997-98. It is clear that the district, Ramanathapuram tops in the production, but with lot of fluctuations. In 1994-95 the production stood at 9445 tonnes, but it has declined to 6961 tonnes in the very next year, again a slight increase in 1996-97 but slipped to 6279 tonnes in 1997-98.

The next important region, Nagai and Tiruvarur districts have produced above 4,000 tonnes every year except in 1996-97. The third important district, Pudukottai has increased the production of prawns steadily from 2197 tonnes in 1994-95 to 3966 in 1996-97 and slipped to 3604 tonnes in 1997-98. Likewise, Thanjavur district has also produced around 1,000 tonnes every year. The production is negligible in the district of Villupuram. The production of prawns in the district of Tuticorin has drastically declined from 3369 tonnes to 622 tonnes.

Shrimp culture in Sirkali taluk and in the entire district was actually introduced with full support from the Government as viable alternative for paddy cultivation and also for utilizing the barren and uncultivable, alkaline lands profitably. This culture has helped the area directly and indirectly with more business and economic activities in the region. The unexpected protests due to various reasons gave a dead blow to the growth as well as to the future of the industry. But, in spite of the country's apex court's rulings, the industry is still surviving and considerably contributing to the State economy.

Most of the aqua-farmers in Sirkali taluk have taken up the Shrimp culture mainly for export purposes. Actually good quality shrimps are not made available to the local people, but they are sold to the agencies who are handling the exports. As it has already been stated, aquaculture is financially lucrative venture from individual entrepreneur point of view. This has been revealed by the information collected from individual aqua-farmers. Profits have ranged from 20 to 50 per cent per annum which cannot be thought of in any other activity. This increased profits and better wages are also responsible for the overall improved economic activities and better standard of living of the people in the region. In the case of shrimp farming drinking water is polluted and the society is forced to spend money for getting drinking water. This cost incurred by the people are the external costs. The external costs are not included in the costs of production of shrimps. As per NEERI's estimate value of environmental costs are more than the value of shrimps produced and exported. For Andhra Pradesh, the report estimated the annual earnings at Rs. 1,500 crores, but the annual value of the damage caused by aquaculture at Rs. 6,300 crores. Thus for each rupee of gain, there would be four rupees of damage. For Tamil Nadu the estimated annual earnings of Rs.280 crores are outweighed by damage costed at Rs. 430 crore.

EMPLOYMENT

The importance of fisheries as a source of employment is even more significant. It has been seen that fisheries are more productive than comparable agricultural activities and that income and profits generated from aquaculture are generally higher than those derived from other age activities. Fisheries provide employment directly to about 2.52 lakh people out of a total of 5.5 lakh fishermen in Tamil Nadu whose livelihoods depend upon marine and inland waters (Rajalakshmi, 1999). About an equivalent number of people take up fishing as part time job. Nearly 2 lakhs persons earn their livelihood from associated vocations such as fish transportation, basket-making, ice and salt manufacturing, etc. It is a way of life for the whole fishermen population. In Sirkali taluk about 2800 fishermen and 200 women are directly employed in aqua farms and depend on aquaculture for their living.

Besides providing direct employment, the industry is also an important income generator as it supports canneries, and processing establishments, gear and equipment manufacturers; boat yards; refrigeration and ice-making plants, and transport services in addition to those working in state fisheries department, fisheries corporation and other government fishery based institutions.

COMMON PROPERTY RESOURCES AND RIGHTS

Munro and Scott (1985) distinguished between 2 types of common property problems. The first which they call a class I common property problem, is the result of complete non regulation of a fishery; unlimited members of fishermen are allowed to complete for an uncentered number of fish. The second type of common property problem identified by Munro and Scott (1985) is called a class II problem. In class I situations, fisheries effort is not regulated but the total catch is limited. This includes setting total allowable catches as well as "Escapement targets" which are targets with respect to the number of fish allowed to escape the fishermen and be free to spawn. Another approach is to restrict the number of fishermen as well as the total catch. All of these methods establish differing types of property rights.

Howe (1979) developed a set of six principles for responsible natural resources policy. They encompassed both exhaustible and renewable resources, but two are particularly useful for developing resources policies.

1. The avoidance of irreversibilities in all renewable resources system: Howe advocates using a safe minimum standard (SMS) approach which he says must be defined specifically for each renewable resource system. A SMS for a unique natural system, Yellow stone park, for eg., might be defined as a contiguor area needed to permit natural perpetuation of the system.

2. A clear determination of the role of free markets and prices; when Howe wrote his principles in 1979, he said that "current practices consists of a bad mixture of attempts at public control and partial reliance on private markets". Almost two decades later, current practice remains glaringly similar. Market prices should be allowed to define actual condition of scarcity. Subsidies that encourage destructive practices should be eliminated. Regulations should provide market signals wherever possible to encourage efficient behaviour.

Walters and Hilborn (1978) classify into 3 categories from least difficult to address to most difficult:

1. Random effects whose future occurrence can be determined from past experience.
2. Parameter uncertainty that can be reduced by additional research and information gathering.
3. Ignorance about the appropriate variables to consider and appropriate model forms.

The resources which are not owned by a single person, yet used by many, are known as Common Property Resources. Generally nobody is willing or able to control the use of such resources. Common Property Resources may be divided into local and regional common property resources and global common (Berkes, 1989). Examples of the former include many of the world's grazing lands, fisheries, deep ocean mineral deposits and the Antartic. Examples of global commons include the world's atmosphere or ozone layer and geo-synchronous orbits. Biogeochemical and Biogeophysical cycles are crucial for the maintenance of a number of global commons and are at risk from or are already disrupted by human activity.

Common Property Resources are also divided into open access, community owned and state owned.

1. Open access resources belong to no one and have no restriction as who makes use of them. These can be very difficult to manage.
2. Community owned resources mean that the co-ownership can exclude outsiders.
3. State owned resources might be better managed, although that is not always true.

Creeks and coast lines have been used to set up shrimp farms along the East coast as they are Common Property Resources. The same as well as the sea have been used by the local fishermen community for their living from time immemorial, due to open access. These interests have come to conflicts and clashes resulting in protests and threats to destroy the shrimp farms in the State of Tamil Nadu.

TYPE OF CONFLICTS

Conflicts between Fishermen and Aqua Farm

The shrimp farms do not provide access to the beach for traditional fishermen who have to reach the sea from their villages. As Aqua farms are located on the sea front and entry is restricted, the fishermen have to take a longer route to sea for their operations. The traditional, local fishermen, doing fishing for years are subjected to such hardships because of the newly emerging aqua farms.

Social Conflicts

Social conflicts arise between the nearby people and aqua farms due to salinisation of drinking water, salinisation of land and fear of floods during the rainy season. It is reported that salinisation of land is spreading further and the wells yielded only salinised water. The Agricultural farms adjoining the shrimp farms are reported to be affected. Aqua farms are constructed right on the banks of the creeks without leaving any space for draining of flood water. Due to physical obstruction caused by the dykes, the natural drain is blocked and flood water gets accumulated in these lands. Therefore protests have been voiced by the affected people.

Conflicts in the Land Use Pattern

Indiscriminate conversion of fertile agricultural lands into aqua farms leads to many problems. This practice aggravates landlessness among the farmers. Absentee landlords sell away their lands to aqua enterprises, getting high price. Those who were doing jobs or cultivation under tenancy farming lose their livelihood occupations and agricultural production of crops is also affected.

In the earlier years, vast areas of mangroves were destroyed for agriculture. Though mangroves are protected by law, in the recent years they have been destroyed for constructing aqua farms.

Conflicts between Aquaculture and Agriculture

Water and land are finite resources, and their use for fish production is highly competitive with other economic uses. Competition can be expected to increase with population growth, demand for food, energy and employment. The growth of aquaculture will depend on its ability to compete successfully for these resources (FAO).

As a matter of fact, economists typically recommend stringent controls to protect common property resources from over exploitation due to population pressure. Yet it cannot be denied that the recommendations, here as elsewhere in the resource and environmental areas, tend to draw attention of those who make policy in these areas. Managing common property resources, for example, will carry more weight when we are able to identify more precisely maximum incentives faced by those who will use, or misuse, our environmental resources which will affect their choice of technology. Pollution can even be considered a "negative resource" rather than an externality. Climate and the processes regulating it may become regarded a fundamental, vital resources managed under this paradigm. (Rajalakshmi, 1999).

Conflicts between Profits and Survival

It is the market mechanism and the invisible hand which drive it that underlines the choice of new fishing technologies and the harvesting patterns which they involve. Conflicts at sea today are essentially conflicts between the few, spurred by the motive of profits, and the many whose objective is survival. The former are largely catering to ever increasing demand for sea food of the over fed metropolitan consumer in the developed countries and the latter to the basic protein needs of the rural masses of the region.

Scitorsky's distinction (1954) between "Pecuniary and technological" externalities dates from his period as does the distinction made by Meade (1952) and Bator (1958) between "unpaid factor" and "public good" technological externalities. But the examples used to illustrate these concepts were mostly examples of external economies in production, occasionally of external diseconomies in production. They largely ignored the direct interaction between one or many producers, on the one hand, and large numbers of stake holders on the other, that characterizes the forms of environmental disruption today.

When water resources are abundant in relation to the demand for them, there will not be any difficulty, but the reality at present is entirely different. As the population grows, economies develop and megacities expand, freshwater will be in even greater demand. Unlike a resource like oil, for which coal, wind or nuclear power can be an alternative, water has no substitute (Gorbachev and Peres, 2000).

The indiscriminate exploitation of basic natural resources for development has begun to flicker the warning signal about the limited potential left over for future. Development, in its recent appearances, has been an ecological issue because the Contemporary development has caused the humanity to grapple to find man's place in his environment (Taylor and Humpstone, 1973).

ENVIRONMENTAL KUZENTS CURVE

In a series of papers [Boulding (1966), Cumberland (1966), Ayres and Kneese (1969), Victor (1972) and Maler (1974)] the environmental significance of the economic growth was explored. IN 1972, Meadows and others drew the startling conclusion that continued growth was not sustainable due to exhaustability of resources.

To quote from the paper by Panyotou (1993) and Beckermann (1992)- "At low levels of development, both the quantity of environmental degradation is limited to the impacts of subsistence economic activity on the resource base and to limited quantities of bio-degradable wastes. As economic development accelerates with the intensification of agriculture and other resource extraction and the take off of industrialization, the rates of resource regeneration and waste generation increase in quantity and toxicity. At higher levels of development, structural change towards information—intensive industries and services, coupled with increased environmental awareness, enforcement of environmental regulations, better technology and higher environmental expenditures, result in levelling off and gradual decline of environmental degradation. There is clear evidence that, although economic growth usually leads to environmental degradation in the early stages of the process, in the end stages of the process, in the end the best-and probably the only way to attain a decent environment in most countries is to become rich".

The EKC debate is important as the environmental quality through wealth creation is the solution to environment damage which is economic growth itself. This immediately suggests reassuring aquaculture growth and generating income in coastal society that will lead to pollution control in the long run and retain sustainable aquaculture production.

The relation between aquaculture income and environmental pressure can be sketched in a number of different ways. On a first level, one can distinguish between monotonic and non-monotonic curves representing this relationships. Monotonic curves show either increasing pollution with rising income or decreasing pollution with rising income. In reality, non-monotonic patterns may be more likely. More complex patterns are possible especially when longer time horizons are taken into account. In fact, it has been found that an inverted U-curve is possible in aquaculture production where environment quality can be maintained due to increase in income which can be diverted into investment as pollution abatement cost (PAC). It has been found that the conflicts in resource arise in coastal zone with regard to aquaculture production mainly because of the fact that the knowledge on pollution abatement and waste disposal is not available but rather it has been treated with less seriousness. The amount of pressure is lesser than industrial toxic effluents.

The hypothesis is based on the notion that more has been spent on the environmental quality as income rises. Environmental concerns were down played as a transitional phenomenon which increases in income that will resolve in due course leading to sustainable aquaculture. This is the crux of application of environment Kuznets curve to aquaculture production.

SUSTAINABLE PRODUCTION

The origin of modern fisheries economics is the seminal article by Gordon (1954). Gordon developed a static (due independent) model of a fishery. His fishery model is best thought of as showing a long run equilibrium between fishing effort and fish stocks. Clarke (1988) developed a simple dynamic model assuming that there existed one species each of predator and prey. The vadratic or logistic function discussed originally by Lotka (1956) was introduced into the economics of fisheries by Shaefer (1954), Beverton and Holt, 1957.

The level of sustainable production is often estimated using the Fox model. This model shows that the production level decreases as the conflicts of aquaculture increases, with all the other factors remaining constant. The following equation was used (Accounting and valuation of Environment. Vol. II.).

$$Y = E \exp(a + bE)$$

Where

Y = production or yield from the resource
E = Conflicts effort per unit time
a = constant
b = regression coefficient

The regression coefficient was derived by establishing the relationship between the time series data on the aquaculture production and the conflicts with an R-square of 0.7960.

Unlike the models we have discussed so far, most fisheries are to a no. of species. The Georges Bank, for eg, which lies east of cape god is one of the most productive fisheries in the entire world partly because of the variety of species that can be caught there. (Pontecorvo, 1986).

Ryther (1969) in an oft cited article has suggested that the maximum yield from the world's ocean fisheries is about 100 million tonnes. Strictly speaking the figure of 100 million tonnes does not refer to MSY but, rather to maximum potential harvest, since a good fraction of the fisheries production too has to be left unharvested on ecological grounds. Thus, Ryther (1969) estimates that the world's potential total fish production is about 240 million tonnes annually.

Depletion

Aquaculture products (fish and shrimp) are renewable biological resources that will eventually die if not harvested. When the harvest of fish exceeds natural growth, depletion occurs. Depletion is computed in the following way:

Depletion = Actual production less sustainable production

In monetary terms, the value of depletion, expressed as net rent was using the Net price method,

Net rent = Net price per unit x Depletion

The ASE of the NSO provided the basis for arriving at the net rent. To arrive at the net rent, costs of intermediate inputs (fuel, compensation to employees, indirect taxes, depreciation and a 15.0% opportunity cost based on experts opinion—for holding assets) were subtracted from the gross output valued at producers price (gross revenue). Based on the above computations, the ratio of net rent to gross output was derived.

CONCLUSION

A developing country like India needs more foreign exchange for importing basic raw materials, advanced technology etc. Export of marine products is also encouraged in order to earn foreign exchange. Shrimps continued to be the largest item realising the highest foreign exchange earning among the marine products. As we have already seen, shrimp culture has been undertaken in many parts of the country, mainly due its lucrative export earnings. Since capture fisheries are unable to supply sufficient volume of shrimps to meet the increasing demand and as a result of the new techniques of producing shrimp seeds in hatcheries, shrimp culture has become an attractive enterprise in many countries including India. But this shrimp culture is creating some side effects also, as already seen.

- There exists a linear relationship between profits and cost, turnover and land size.
- There is linear relationship between profits and factors such as land size, investment and number of ponds.
- There is no linear relationship between dependent variable, viz. initial work time and independent variables viz., initial investment, land size and number of ponds.
- The public opinion about the closure of existing aqua farms and the pollution problems are interdependent. Moreover opinion of the people regarding the closure of the aquafarm is divided. A section of the public has said that these farms must be closed. Another section has said that aquaculture is the panacea for all the ills there and aquaculture has to be encouraged for promoting the economic welfare in the region.
- There is no linear relationship between public opinion on the future of farms and the benefits the public receive, their education level and the pollution problems.
- Analysis of various factors involved indicates that the benefits the people receive from aqua farms are the most important factor.
- It is found that more than 35 percent of the employees working in the aquafarms are educated.
- It is found that 75 percent of the employees in the aquafarms are getting a salary of Rs. 1000/- and above each, per month.

- Many employees working in the aquafarms are able to save because of their higher incomes since they are employed in shrimp farms.
- Many of the employees (83 percent) have felt that they have got increased wages in aquafarms.
- Facilities like roads, electricity and water supply have improved according to 28 and 25 employees respectively.
- More than 60 percent of the general public feel that they get better value for their lands.
- About 30% of the general public feel that they have got better road facilities due to the development of shrimp industry.
- Among the disadvantages experienced by the general public, the reduction of job opportunities in agriculture is given importance by most of the respondents (60 percent). Likewise about 42 percent of them have revealed their concern about the conversion of agricultural lands into aquafarms.
- It is understood that the number of respondents who are happy about the creation of job opportunities in aquafarms is less than the number of respondents who have stated the reduction of jobs in agricultural farms.
- Groundwater pollution and foul smell have also been reported a important disadvantages by the respondents.
- Many of the respondents have stated that the aquafarms should be allowed to continue, but at the same time measures should be taken to check pollution.
- Foreign exchange earnings from the export of marine products in general and from the export of shrimps in particular have increased over the years.
- The share of shrimps in the export value of marine products from the country is more than 70 percent. Therefore, the shrimp culture will be bringing in more of foreign exchange to the country.
- Shrimp aquaculture and environmental preservation must be achieved as a unified motto for sustainable development.

Based on the above findings the following conclusions are drawn.

If agricultural landless labourers and the local fishermen community are directly involved in shrimp culture, the entire benefits will be enjoyed by these grass root people. Some fishermen in the area have taken up shrimp farming and derived better benefits. Since profit rate is high, if the capitalists are allowed to capitalise the situation, inequalities in income and wealth will get accentuated. The start of shrimp farming and earning huge profit have resulted in clashes between the locals and the shrimp industrialists. Therefore the Government must protect the interests of the weaker sections with necessary legislations and also by implementing them effectively. Though shrimp farming is highly profitable, its pollutive effects should not be undermined.

RECOMMENDATIONS

Any development may have some ill effects also, that too in the initial stages. After understanding the nature of the problem, it is possible to solve it. This is the case in the shrimp industry also. Development activities, in general, are associated with some degree of depletion of resources. When the supply of resources is plenty in relation to the demand for it, problems are not acute. With the increase in population, the awareness of the people to live better lives and with the technological revolution, resources are fast depleting. Some of these resources are non-renewable and so they may not be available for the generations yet to come. The renewable resources also need careful management, since they are not sufficient in relation to demand for it. Groundwater is renewable if properly managed. On the other hand, groundwater is drawn for use at present, without knowing whether it gets recharged or not. It takes many years for rain water or stream water to enter into the deep layers of earth and stay there.

Proper land lease policy will be very helpful in making the landless labourers aqua farmers, which in turn will help the aqua farmer. Setting up of aqua farms based on co-operative principles will be helpful to the small farmers, as well as, to the industry. It will improve socio-economic conditions of the people in the region.

If shrimp industry is to thrive, the conflicts between aquaculture and agriculture and also the conflicts between aquaculture and other uses of coastline should be minimised. If the fishermen and landless agricultural labourers are encouraged to practice shrimp culture, unwanted clashes and conflicts would be avoided without any loss of foreign exchange. Though shrimp aquaculture is polluting the surroundings, if proper measures are introduced the level of pollution will become tolerable and the loss or damage will become manageable. This is not the only industry which is polluting the water or land. Industries like dyeing, leather processing also do the same. When these industries, are allowed to function with necessary checks, the aquaculture industry may also be permitted with certain provision to minimize the pollution problem.

Efforts should be made to ensure that the local people are motivated to accept the steps taken to protect the environment. Without the co-operation of the local people, any solution will not be a lasting one.

The 'precautionary' principle as well as 'Pollutor pays' principle should be used wherever necessary. This suggestion has originated from the verdict of Supreme Court of India. EIA, (Environment Impact Assessment) must be made compulsory wherever necessary notably in aquaculture.

Considering the benefits received, disadvantages experienced and the favour shown by the general public as a group for the analysis, the results show an independent behaviour. Whereas, any one among the above group is considered individually, the results of the analysis show a dependent nature. Hence, the above results of this analysis from primary data lead to an elaborate analysis of each individual variable. The possibilities of analysis along these lines may be explored in future.

Various government authorities and research institutes, as also private sector and coastal management projects could organise and exchange information periodically and regularly. A specific system may be evolved to help improve cross – sectoral co-ordination and co-operation in the development and management of coastal areas.

References

Bater, F. (1958), 'The Anatomy of market failure' *Quarterly Journal of Economics*, 72: 351-79.

Bell, f.w. (1978), Food from the sea; the Economics and Politics of Ocean Fisheries, West View Press, Boulder, Colorado.

FAO Rana and Immink. (2000), Downloaded Homepage from internet.

Gordan, H. (1954), 'The Economic Theory of a Common Property Resource: The Fishery' *Journal of Political Economy* 62(2): 124-142.

Howe, C. (1979), Natural Resource Economics, New York, Wiley.

Lotka (1956), Elements of Mathematical Biology, Dover, New York.

Meade, J.E. (1952), "External Economics of Diseconomics in Competitive Situation". *Economic Journal* 62:54-67.

Mikhail Gorbachav and Simon Peres (2000), *The Hindu*, 28th May.

Munro, G. and A. Scott (1985),The Economics of Fisheries Management in the "Hand Book of Natural Resources and Energy Economics", Vol.2, ed:A. Kneese and J. Sweeney, New York.

Pontecorvo, G. (1986), "Supply, Demand and Common Property: The Historical Dynamics of the fisheries of the Georges Bank – some Preliminary Observations". In 'Natural Resources Econbmics and Policy Applications": Essays in honour of James A. Crutchfield, ed: E. Miles, R. Pealy and R. Stokes: Seattle, University of Washington Press.

Rajalakshmi, N.(1999), Environmental and Economic Development, Manak Publications Pvt., Ltd.

Rajalakshmi, N. (1999), Tamil Nadu Economy. Business Link Corporation, Mumbai.

Ryther, J.H. (1969), Photosynthesis and fish production in the sea. Sciences, 166, 72-76.

Scitorsky, T. (1954), "Two Concepts of external Economics'. *Journal of Political Economy* 62:143-151, 1954.

Shaefer, M.B. (1978), Some Aspects of the dynamics of population important to the management of commercial marine fisheries, inter-american tropical Tuna, *Bulletin*, 27-56.

Supreme Court of India, (1996), Judgement in the case relating shrimp farms.

Walters, C. and R. Hilburn. 1978), "Ecological Optimization and adaptive management" Annual Review of Ecological System 9: 157-188.

CHAPTER

23

An Analytical Review of Issues Concerning Agrarian Structure, Poverty and Rural Development

R. ARUNACHALAM

An agriculturally predominant Indian economy is striving hard for decades together to alleviate poverty to make rural development a successful one to ultimately sustain higher level of growth and development. It should be noted that no rural development programme can be meaningful and effective without making a major break through in rural poverty alleviation. Analogously, overall high growth rate of the economy is well nigh impossible in the absence of successful rural development measures.

Backtracking economic history of India one can recapitulate that high growth has been a crucial objective of our five year plans with a fervent hope that the 'Trickle down' will operate and the gains of development would automatically percolate down. The problem of poverty and its impact on growth rate was realized at the beginning of Fifth plan. Since then, concerted efforts are made to reduce poverty coupled with greater level of rural development.

It is in this context, this paper attempts to analytically review the progress made on these lines and the issues confronted in achieving the desired objectives. The present work is organized into 3 sections. Section I reviews the issues concerning rural development and rural poor as they were ably discussed by leading economist, at the time of Introduction of New Agricultural Strategy.

Section II deals with the social dimensions of poverty and rural development and in section III, an attempt is made to evaluate the recent policy measures connected to rural poverty and rural development.

I

The differentiation of rural economy into a dynamic subsystem represented by large scale agricultural producer and a backward subsystem characterized by small peasant producer and a floating mass of landless population. The dynamic sub sector is represented by capitalistic sector. The nature of interaction between these subsystems in the long run context is a vital aspect of rural development.

There is a view that these subsystems are complementary to each other and equally opposite view was also held in certain quarters. The development process chosen in India seems to be more favourable to the large land holding households rather than the small peasant farmers and the landless labour. For example, the adoption of High Yielding Varieties (HYV) and the Green Revolution. It is reported in several studies that the Green Revolution and the HYV are crop and area or region friendly implying that these are not widely followed in all states and also not applicable to all crops. As a result, the poor farmers and the landless are not major beneficiaries. Another aspect of the development process is the advent of new technology. In a dynamic economy, the relative incomes of different groups, according to Mellor, do change. At the same time, the new technology is reported to be providing increasing job opportunities.

The wonder seeds technology is not conducive for widespread adoption of dry farming as the crops cultivated under this category require copious supply of water. More particularly, the small and marginal farmers along with sharecroppers resort to cultivation of paddy and other wet crops, which require huge quantity of water. Therefore, neither the new technology nor HYV are very poor farmers friendly. Another issue concerning land utilization pattern is constrained by irrigation water. As a result, sizeable percentage of even operational holdings are left fallow during the 1st and 2nd crop seasons. Tables 23.1 and 23.2 present a clear view of the extent of land utilization at the national level.

TABLE 23.1
Magnitude of Fallow Land in India

(in million ha.)

Year	*Current Fallow*	*Other Fallow*
1950	10.7	17.4
1960	11.6	11.2
1970	11.1	8.8
1980	14.8	10.0
1985	9.5	7.0
1991	13.9	9.6
2000	8.0	5.0

Source : GISTNIC, Dept. of Economics and Statistics, Chennai-6.

TABLE 23.2
Magnitude of Fallow Land as % of Total Cropped Area (State-wise)

State	*1970-71*	*1980-81*	*1992-93*
Andhra Pradesh	9.7	14.3	15.9
Arunachal Pradesh	3.0	2.3	1.3
Assam	3.7	2.3	2.2
Bihar	14.1	15.3	18.8
Goa	—	—	0
Gujarat	4.0	4.6	4.2
Haryana	3.4	4.0	5.9
Himachal Pradesh	2.1	1.8	2.1
Jammu & Kashmir	2.8	2.2	2.4
Karnataka	10.6	9.7	7.3
Kerala	1.2	1.8	1.8
Madhya Pradesh	3.6	4.6	3.8
Manipur	—	—	—
Meghalaya	—	13.9	10.1
Mizoram	—	21.1	21
Nagaland	—	—	—
Orissa	—	21.1	21.0
Punjab	7.9	4.1	2.5
Rajasthan	11.0	12.2	9.9
Sikkim	11.0	12.2	9.9
Tamil Nadu	11.8	19.8	15.5
Tripura	0.5	0.4	1.9
Uttar Pradesh	4.7	6.3	6.7
West Bengal	4.1	1.6	5.0
UT	1.8	3.6	2.0
Maharastra	5.3	5.4	6.3

Source : Same as in Table 23.1.

In Table 23.1 the magnitude of both current fallow land and other fallow land is given. The range is between 8 and 15 million hectares in the case of current fallow and between 5 and 17 million hectares in the case of other follows. Table 23.2 shows the situation at the national level. An important feature of Table 23.2 is that in relatively well developed states like Andhra, Karnataka, Tamil Nadu, Punjab and Maharastra, the magnitude of fallow land is fairly high. No wonder, in the case of Orissa, Rajasthan, Sikkim, Meghalaya and Mizoram, it is still high. All these only indicate the magnitude of under utilization of landed asset and the consequent lack of agricultural employment and income generation.

Another development in this connection is the conflict between landlords and peasants as pointed out by Mellor[2]. This view is referred to by Dantwala stating that the rigid and stable division between the privileged and the disadvantaged would be more characteristic of static, rather than under dynamic agriculture.[3] Besides he points out the new forces of technological change instead of contributing to the emergence of dualism have in fact made a great contribution towards softening of dualism. This view of Dantwala is based on three premises.

1. The new technology is not depending on large size. It has reduced the threshold of non-viability to something like three irrigated acres.
2. Equal distribution in favour of small peasants has assumed greater significance in a dynamic context than in a static one.
3. Institutional reforms without technical progress are neither feasible nor capable of leading to any appreciable and sustained improvement in the conditions of the vulnerable class of socially and economically disadvantaged persons. It is also stated that technical progress in agriculture treats the possibility of achieving growth with justice by two methods: (i) Economics of institutional reforms and (ii) by development of non-agricultural sector's growth within the rural sector to expand employment opportunities. But the critics maintain their stand that Dantwala speaks of only potential rather than realistic situation of our economy.

Turning to the observations of Dandekar and Rath we find that new technology has made owner cultivation in sizeable farms a distinctly profitable proposition.[4] They finally conclude stating that the landless labour cannot be accommodated effectively in agriculture. It is futile to resolve the problem of rural poverty in an over populated country by redistribution of land which is in short supply and therefore, they advocated the need for jobs outside agriculture. While Minhas urges in favour of consolidation of holdings like Ambedkar and complementary policies, Khusro advocates land reforms and redistribution of lands.[5]

Hunter is more apprehensive in saying that the growth of dynamic sector destroys the economic security which the vast majority of the poor enjoyed in the traditional economy. He is of the view that in the context of technical change vast majority of small landholders are "much more likely to be driven off their land or to sell it to pay debt".[6]

Raj contends that the size of distributional holdings is often not markedly different from that of ownership holdings.[7] Besides Raj observes that the distribution of credit is skewed with the result that the gains of new technology tend to be concentrated in large holdings. He concludes that the gap between the rates of growth in large farm sector on the one hand and the small farm sector become wider in the dynamic context of technical change than in the static context.

Amit Bhaduri refers to the existence of feudalism[8]. The structure of production relations is the dependence of small peasants on land-lords for credit. Whereas Minhas refers to an interesting association between performance of agricultural sector and people below poverty line.

II

SOCIAL DIMENSIONS OF RURAL DEVELOPMENT

Whether it is rural poverty or rural development, they are obviously determined by socio-economic, technical and political factors. In the Indian context, social dimensions of the issues on hand have not been tackled to the extent techno-economic issues are attempted so far.

Both Adam Smith and Ricardo strongly believed that capital accumulation and technology promoted growth, but the capitalistic system was not successful in distributing the gains of development to weaker sections of society. In fact, in a class based society, the dominant class/region appears to have usurped the benefits of development and the percolation of benefits hardly takes place. In addition, in a class dominated situation, government actually functions in such a manner as to hinder the process of percolation and facilitate the process of concentration of economic and social power both across individuals and regions.

Mahatma Gandhi was of the view that economics is untrue which ignores and disregards moral values. He spoke of democratic decentralization and rural development. He pleaded for reconstruction of villages on a self governing basis, self sufficient, egalitarian and spiritual basis. Rurality is the epitome of socio-economic, political and cultural life of India, but the saddest story of its being in the grip of centuries old poverty. Though many efforts have been made to improve the conditions of poor, yet the sky remains overcast with only a few patches of development. Rural poverty keeps increasing both in terms of households below poverty line and in terms of the intensity of poverty. Saini et. al. observed that several economic factors which neglected socio-economic aspects are limited resources, failure to exploit local resources, sectarian approach in planning, incompetent implementing agencies and urban bias in development.

Indian villages most often suffer from discontent, violence against persons and property, hunger and disease, illiteracy, ignorance, free fights for land, water scarcity, caste rivalry, competition and so on. In recent times, the caste hierarchy along with class and illiteracy have become intense. These two act and react on each other and also overlap and ultimately lead to many factions which are motivated by self-interest. (Dubey : 1975).

The factions which exist in India are divided into hierarchical groups of different castes which are close to each other and shut all doors to social mobility (Baljit Singh 1996). The caste hierarchy is followed by economic class hierarchy, following almost in the same order as generally higher classes are economically better off than the lower castes and the landless ones comprising two major classes in the society.

These castes and classes being on the same track make the village society self contained in social affairs but interdependent in economic affairs and preparing the ground for another divisive force, that is, the faction. Factions are social alignments as the basis of self-interest and interest through class and caste groups. These are an old ingrained pattern in village life and be considered as a structural aspect of traditional village organization along with caste, totals, pannar, gotras, and other groupings[9].

Rostogi views that village factions develop vested interests and are generally related to land, social status and power ego, satisfaction and ideological differences. Rostogi also contends that village factions not only divide the entire village leading to fighting and litigations and permeating such of these feuds to other villages. The abolition of Zamindari system and introduction of Panchayati Raj all have brought out greater antagonisms among different factions.

Two features of rural society mentioned earlier namely factions and hierarchical organizations make the village society even more complicated than urban society. The exogenous factors which affect the factional society make progress extremely difficult, they react sharply to any change with a more suspicion that the change may place their opponents, in a more favourable situation. Such a factional society hinders all progress and explains why village people in general are so indifferent to the plans and the development programmes and even making legislation's ineffective in such a context.

III

POVERTY SCENARIO

Definition, measurement and magnitude of poverty in India continue to be a matter of controversy and debate. More so, in the context of the on going economic reform measures. A jointly sponsored workshop on "Poverty, Measurement and Evaluation held in New Delhi on January 11-12, 2002 came up with a host of interesting research papers on the theme. The workshop was sponsored by Planning Commission, Government of India and the World Bank.

The Planning Commission's estimates suggest that India recorded one of the developing world's fastest reductions during the 1990's.[10] As per the official estimates poverty fell from 36 percent of the population in 1993-94 to nearly 26 percent at the end of the decade 1999-2000. The paper by Angus Deaton explains a method that can be used to adjust the NSS 55th Round Poverty estimates so as to make them comparable with earlier estimates.[11] Another paper of Sundaram et. al. debates over Indian Poverty trends in the 1990s. Raising questions about the comparability of the Quinquennial 50th and 55th rounds of the Consumer Expenditure Survey (CES) carried out by the NSS in 1993-94 and 1999-2000, the paper focuses how the rate of reduction in poverty in the last six years of 1990's is greater than the period between 1982 and 1993.[12] Yet another paper by Gaurav et al deals with an econometric model of poverty assessment in India and its reduction in 1990s.[13] In its assessment, this paper provides for state fixed effects, state specific time trends and state specific elasticities of poverty to non-farm output growth, while also allowing poverty measure to depend on yield per hectare, per capita development spending and inflation rate in the state. Another paper by Kozel and Parker adopts a diagnostic approach to poverty in Uttar Pradesh and throws light on the challenges in reducing poverty in its various economic and non-economic dimensions and improving security and well being for all citizens.[14]

Not withstanding copious literature and empirical works on poverty both at the micro and macro level; regional, national and international level and at the level of Government agencies and individual researchers, the basic definition of rural poverty is still unclear. Several studies have come out with the findings that in the rural areas the incidence of poverty is concentrated among small and marginal farmers, landless agricultural labour, share croppers and tenants. The empirical work of this author in Tamil Nadu relating to poverty and agrarian structure brings out that poverty is associated with 'land status' of households[15]. But the land status in turn depends on possession of land holdings acquired by means of inheritances as well as by households own efforts over the years.

The point of contention in this context is that there is no guarantee that households belonging to different classes such as larger farmers, medium, small and petty or marginal farmers are able to maintain their position intertemporally. Based on genealogical survey, this author could ascertain that there are several factors which account for the upward and downward movements (meaning economic progress as well as impoverishment). For instance, in the study of the village of the author, out of 382 households 15 percent of them had upward mobility; around 37 per cent had downward mobility; nearly 48 per cent remained stagnant during the period 1920-84. The ratio of upward to downward mobility was 1 : 2.6. Field investigations clearly revealed that upward mobility was caused by good agricultural performance, money lending, power structure, trading in agricultural products and capital from Urban areas, through descendants settled down and employed in organized sector. Down ward mobility or impoverishment was caused by partition of land holdings, major illness and the resultant huge medical expenses, death of cattle assets, demographic factors and debts incurred for agriculture and consumption purposes.

This study reveals that rural poverty is basically associated with land size and its use in income generation, and its distribution. Recent empirical works in several villages of Uttar Pradesh also came out with the finding how certain categories of households are vulnerable to be trapped in poverty for various reasons, though presently they may not qualify to be poor.

EVALUATION OF VARIOUS RURAL DEVELOPMENT PROGRAMMES

Various programmes being implemented by the Governments ever since their commencement have a dual objective of reducing poverty on the one hand and promoting rural development on the other. For instance, Jawahar Rozgar Yojana and Employment Assurance Schemes came under rural employment. It is found over the years, (Table 23.3) the total allocation for rural employment schemes ranges between 41.5 per cent to 70 per cent of the total plan outlay. Between JRY and EAS, the former enjoys greater allocation than the latter. There are other schemes such as Rural housing, Million Wells Schemes, Integrated Rural Development Scheme, TRYSEM, Development of Rural Women and Children, DPAP, water supply and rural sanitation schemes. The Table reveals that for water supply, the outlay ranges between 11 per cent in 1994-95 to 21 percent in 1991-92. The outlay for other schemes barring wells scheme and IRS, happens to be less than one percent. A glaring features of plan outlay allocation is that, in general, it seems to decline over the years. It will not be out of place to state that the reduction of outlay for various schemes in recent times may be due to Government Policy of prudent expenditure and fiscal management as part of reform measures. However, total outlay for rural development and social sectors as a percentage of GDP, increased from 1.77 in 1991-92 to 2.23 percent in 1998-99. In absolute terms it recorded 3 fold increase. But a discouraging feature is that the actual utilization of expenditure ranges from 37 percent to 78 percent as on 1997-98. JRY records highest utilization along with EAS. IRDP accounts for nearly 79 percent utilization. The DPAP accounts for only 48 percent utilization. The average utilization in the case of nearly 11 programmes is only 64 percent. The under utilization to the tune of around 35 percent of the sanctioned expenditure speaks for the efficacy of these measures.

Table 23.4 gives an idea of distribution of plan outlay which is the sum of allocation by Centre, State and Union territories. It also shows the allocation of agriculture, irrigation and flood control. It is noticed that the allocation to rural development, though keeps on increasing from 5.5 percent of total plan outlay to 7.5 percent between 1980-85 and 1995-99, the allocation to both agriculture and irrigation and flood control programmes has been reduced during the same time period. It is mentioned earlier, these programmes are complimentary to each other and so the overall rural development may not fructify in the absence of agricultural development. Many of the employment generating programmes such as DPAP, CSRE and TRYSEM and such others lack co-ordination and integration at various levels. In fact, Minhas argued for the starting of some sort of co-operative technology to improve the lot of small framers and marginal farmers.[16] How

TABLE 23.3

Distribution of Outlay for different Programmes under Rural Development

Programme	*1998-99*	*1997-98*	*1996-97*	*1995-96*	*1994-95*	*1993-94*	*1992-93*	*1991-92*
Rural Development Total (Rs)	9844	8319	7797	8268	7337	5620	3613	3021
1. Rural Employment	41.50	46.37	44.82	57.70	63.72	69.50	70.47	60.41
(a) Jawhahar Rozgar Yojana	51.29	50.62	47.35	61.94	75.61	84.64	100.0	100.0
(b) EAS	48.71	49.38	52.65	38.06	24.39	15.36	—	—
2. Rural Housing	100.0	100.0	100.0	100.0	100.0	100.0	100.0	100.0
3. Million Wells Scheme	4.60	4.48	4.98	2.55	—	—	—	—
4. Integrated Rural Development	7.52	6.20	7.57	7.74	8.52	10.98	10.40	11.78
5. TRYSEM	0.61	0.55	0.12	0.17	0.12	0.14	0.22	0.13
6. Development of Rural Women and Children	1.02	0.75	0.83	0.79	0.42	0.37	0.36	0.40
7. Drought Prone Areas	0.97	1.21	1.41	1.51	1.16	1.37	1.41	1.69
8. Water Supply	16.54	15.67	14.06	13.44	11.05	13.15	12.76	21.15
9. Rural Sanitation	—	1.01	1.20	0.77	0.73	0.57	0.55	0.13

Source : Economic and Political Weekly, July 18, 1998

Notes : 1 (a) and (b) are percentage of 1, which add upto 100%

The remaining rows are % of total Rural Development outlay.

TABLE 23.4
Distribution of Plan outlay for Rural Development, Agriculture, Irrigation and Flood Control (Central, State & Union Territories)

(% of Total outlay)

Particulars	1980-81-1984-85	1985-86-1989-90	1990-91-194-95	1995-96-1998-99
Rural Development	5.5	4.9	7.48	7.45
Agriculture	5.8	5.8	5.56	4.45
Irrigation & Flood control	10.24	9.3	6.42	5.32

Source : Economic Survey, Govt. of India (various years).

can we complete a scientific consolidation of holdings and attempt to bring together lands of small land holders? To what extent non-farm employment opportunities can be generated to gainfully employ the landless?

Besides lack of co-ordination, there is the problem of effective delivery system. The Ninth Plan Approach Paper (1997) identifies that the delivery system with its existing resources is not in a position to undertake all the needed actions within the time available to implement qualitatively and to ensure the Sustainability of the Programme[17]. The World Bank in its recent paper on rural development referring to an appropriate strategy mentions that rural entrepreneurship, off farm employment and natural resources should be integrated with human capital, infrastructure and social development. Participation of rural beneficiaries and Panchyati Raj Institutions is another issue. The lack of effective participation of local people and institutions coupled with lack of local level expertise were stumbling blocks in the part of accelerating development. In these days of growing computerization and information technology, village records need to be updated for appropriate development strategy and implementation.

THE POST REFORM CONCERNS

Long back Harriss referred to the development of capitalistic tendencies in Indian agriculture. The new economic policy initiatives in the name of liberalization, globalization and marketization along with WTO compulsions seem to pose new threats to rural development and employment generation in the rural sector. For example, Swaminathan, the agricultural scientist refers to the various challenges to be encountered due to WTO regime. The paper by Chadha et al brings out the post-reform set backs in rural employment. Analysing the preliminary 1999-2000 NSS estimates many studies bring out that rural employment had suffered tremendously during the decade of economic reform measures. The works of Chadha and others point out that at the national level, employment friendly claims of 1991-92 reform measures are nowhere in sight. The state level evidence according to this study shows that the rate of growth of rural non-farm employment witnessed slowdown during the post, compared with the pre-reform period. The pace of investment in agriculture and allied sectors, particularly irrigation slackened during the post-reform period.

In the light of the above developments, a sort of permanent cleavage between the large landholding category of households on the one hand and the smaller households and landless seems to be existing. This is rather characteristic of the Indian agrarian structure which is nurtured by not only the development process adopted at various times but also by the social system hidden with class, caste and factions. Legal steps to eliminate the social conflicts have not been successful.

Empowerment of the weaker sections including women may be effective as a solution to all these in the long run. At the same time, in the short and medium term certain appropriate techno-economic and administrative steps to be taken to bring about sustained growth with social justice. They include; (a) Extension of appropriate technology including full utilization of available operational holdings (b) Meaningful education of weaker sections including women, (c) Timely supply of credit and other inputs to the needy through the institutions concerned, (d) special attention to be paid to safeguard the interests of poor farmers in the rural areas in the light of fast changing economic conditions and the implementation of economic reform measures.

Notes and References

1. Arunchalam, R. (2002): Intertemporal Dynamics of Peasant Households and Poverty, Deep and Deep Publications, New Delhi.
2. Bhaduri, A. (1973) : 'Study in Agricultural Backwardness under Semi Feudalism', Economic Journal, Vol. 83, No. 329, March.
3. Dandekar, V. M. and N. Rath (1971): Poverty in India, Gokhale Institute of Politics and Economics, Pune.
4. Dantwala, M.L. (1970): From Stagnation to Growth: Relative Roles of Technology, Economic Policy and Agrarian Institutions, Presidential Address, Indian Economic Association, 53rd Conference, Guhati.
5. Datt, Gaurav, V. Kozal and M. Ravallion (2003) : 'A Model Based Assessment of India's Progress in Reducing Poverty in the 1990's, EPW, Vol. XXXVIII No. 4, Jan. 25-31.
6. Deaton, Angus (2003): 'Adjusted Indian Poverty Estimates for 1999-2000', EPW, Vol. XXXVIII, No. 4, Jan. 25-31.
7. Economic and Political Weekly (2003): 'Poverty Measurement, Monitoring and Evaluation in India—An Overview', EPW, Vol XXXVIII, No. 4, Jan. 25-31.
8. Govt. of India, Planning Commission (1997), VIII Plan approach paper, New Delhi.
9. Hunter, G. (1969): Modernizing Peasant Societies: A Comparative Study in Asia and Africa, Oxford University Press, London.
10. Joshi, P.C. (1974): ' Some Problems of India's Economic Policy', Social Change, Vol. iv, September-December.
11. Khusro, A.M. (1972): The Economics of Land Reform and Farm Size in India, Mac Millan, New Delhi.
12. Kozel, V. and Barbara Parkar (2003) : 'A Profile and Diagonistic of Poverty in Uttar Pradesh', EPW, Vol. XXXVIII No. 4, Jan. 25-31.

13. Lewis, O. (1953) : Peasant Culture in India and Mexico in Village India (ed), Mackin Marriot.

14. Mellor, J.W. (1968) : Developing Rural India: Plan and Practice, New York, Cornell University.

15. Minhas, B.S. (1977) : Rural Development for weaker Sections—Experience and Lessons in Some Problems of India's Economic Policy (ed) C.D. Wadhava, Tata Mac-Graw-Hill Publication Co. Ltd.

16. Raj, K.N. (1969): Ownership and Distribution of Land, Centre for Advanced Studies, Delhi School of Economics.

17. Sundaram, K. and S. Tendulkar (2003): 'Poverty had Declined in the 1990's, EPW, Vol. XXXVIII No. 4, Jan. 25-31.

CHAPTER

24

Changing Role of Rural Credit Institutions and Support Services in Kolahapur District

V.B. JUGALE

INTRODUCTION

The significance of Primary Agricultural Co-operative Credit Societies (PACS) in the Indian rural credit market, actuates the policy makers to restructure the PACS rather than trying for the welfare of the rural masses within the framework of Financial Sector Reforms (FSRs). PACS, have endured a series of reorganisation since decades prior to their inception. The present co-operative credit system in India is a mere credit delivery system, which is in fact blocked up in an orthodoxy of traditional functioning. Creditworthiness is the basis of loan transactions of almost all financial agencies. That is, one who proves, how loan borrowing is not required, he is granted the credit. During the decades the pattern and practice of rural economy in general and the agricultural economy in particular have undergone a sea-change with a diversification entrusted from production fronts to that of business fronts. The horizontal linkages of the agri-business have been widened and deepened with multi-facet forward and backward linkages. This tends to restructure the co-operative credit system into the Co-operative village Banking (Jugale, 1998) which is in fact an opportunity as well as a challenge to the existing co-operative structure. The PACS as visualised initially, are in fact the village banks, which are expected to create a habit of thrift and savings among the ruralites. Unfortunately they failed to enhance in this front.

The existing PACS are pitiably admired as grass without root agencies and totally condemned. They are accomplishing little as the agents of District Central Co-operative Banks (DCCBs) mainly engaged in disbursement and recovery of the loans granted by the DCCBs. As a result rise of Self-Help Groups (SHGs) and Poverty Lending Working Groups in India are due to disregard of the co-operative agencies towards the poor people.

PARADIGM

Money, since decades could not be revolved within the Indian village markets. Consequently the funds for lending began to flow from urban to rural areas. This is the outcome of the policies so far adopted by the Government since decades. Agricultural savings have been attracted by the urban institutions. As a result capital is formed in urban areas and import of capital to rural area becomes inevitable, correspondingly, causing less employment generation-low demand-low standard of living of the rural people. Hence dependency increased, ultimately causing the bottlenecks in the process of development of rural area. This false paradigm of development, is required to be revised, refined and revitalised.

The Gandhian policy reiterated the need to mobilise the agricultural savings within the rural area, which would help to accumulate capital in the rural economy. This tends to increase the agricultural income—investment—employment opportunities in the rural area. As a result of this the rural economy would have experience of self-reliance. The choice and preferences for industrial products in rural area would have motivated the ruralites to adopt the non-farm industrial technology. Which in turn would have generated investment, employment and income in the rural economy. A positive flow of development with a cycle of self-reliance would have continued with a wider path of expansion of the rural economy. But this has not been adopted so far since a few decades. The cumulative effects of backwardness consequently created many bottlenecks in the process of rural development. However, greater the backwardness, greater are the opportunities of development. Let the opportunities be identified and harnessed.

A.I.R.C. Committee has rightly pointed out that the viability of rural financial institutions depends upon the viability of the economy and the activities pursued by the borrowers. The agro-industrial co-operative commonwealth in Western Maharashtra State (India) has supported this ideology.

RESTRUCTURING THE PACS AS CO-OPERATIVE VILLAGE BANKS

Restructuring the rural financial system has now become inevitable. Particularly restructuring of PACS is empathised to augment the functioning of the agricultural credit system and assumed to fulfil the credit needs of the rural India. The ACRC has rightly pointed out that "the essence of basic feature of co-operative banking system must be a larger reliance on resource mobilised locally and lesser dependence on higher credit institutions. Heavy dependence on outside funds has, on the one hand, made the members less vigilant, not treating these funds as their own, and on the other hand led to greater outside interference and control. Overall this has made the co-operative a mediocre, inefficient and static system."

The present PACS should be restructured as Co-operative Village Banks, which will initiate in mobilising the potential savings from the rural economy. Shivaram Committee was confident enough in this endeavour of the PACS. The Committee felt that, "the PACS should immediately take steps for greater mobilisation of deposits. They should have to adopt an approach and a system that will bring confidence to the rural saver irrespective of whether he becomes the potential depositor of the PACS."

Even the historical perspectives at the beginning of the co-operative movement in India have proved the required thrust of the village banking. The term village banks was first used by Nicholson in his report of 1896. Two such banks were established in the erstwhile Madras Province as indicated by him. The idea of establishing Agricultural Banks had been a much discussed subject ever since the Deccan Riots. Sir Wedderburn and Justice Ranade were the first proponents of agricultural banks, which was recommended after conducting an exhaustive survey of Purander Taluka (Pune District). H. Dupenex, after his intensive study of United Province (U. P), recommended the People's Bank. In 1937, Ambegaonkar and Nanavati in the RBI Bulletin, published a theme of "Co-operative Village Banks" which was found out as the best solution for betterment of the rural people. Same title has been reiterated by the author, as a restructured version of the PACS. CVB as suggested by the author, is not for solving the problem of indebtedness, but to mobilise the savings and integrate village activities. The bank which fulfils, at once, the requirement of thrift and credit, while promoting in a high degree those qualities which are essential to high national character are the CVBs. They are not formed by the capitalists seeking investments for their funds with the hope of earning dividends thereon..."CVBs are, of the villages, for the villages, run by the villages and banking with the villages. Hence it is advocated in a restructured form.

The specific features of CVBs (Jugale, 1997) are as under:

1. The cannons of good credit viz. Adequacy, proximity, reasonable rate of interest, timely supervision of self management can be served through CVBs.

2. A special feature of CVBs will be to ensure mobilisation of rural saving for accelerating the economic growth in rural area. Thakurdas Committee (1950) has rightly pointed out the significance of the rural savings by stating that, "In case of similar people in rural areas, the extension of banking facilities should aim at mobilising small savings and also a part of the income likely to be generated as a result of public investment in various projects".
3. Lending at low rate of interest can be made possible through CVBs due to the minimum spread (Margin) of 2 to 2.50 percent, if CVBs are mobilising their own deposits and disbursing the loans to their members. This is accessible again due to low cost of intermediation.
4. An integration of ST, MT and LT credit delivery can be made feasible through CVBs. If the long term deposits have been attracted by the CVBs, it is worth to disburse the long term loans to its members. Normally rural people save for a medium and long period. The Regional Seminar for Asia on Agricultural Credit for Small Farmers, Bangkok (Thailand) (Oct. 1974) has given stress on all credit needs (ST, MT and LT) to be met at one place, which has been accepted as criteria for suitability and viability of credit system. Besides the credit facilities must be as near the door step as possible when needed. By integrating the ST, MT and LT loans an adjustment in the type of loans can be made at the level of CVBs for strengthening the repaying capacity.
5. Direct refinance from the upper agencies like NABARD to CVBs can be made practicable. The middle agencies are swallowing, the margin of about 4 to 4.5 percent and creating burden on the borrowers.
6. The CVBs will thus lead to meet all financial needs of farm and non-farm communities in the rural area.
7. The repaying capacity of the borrowers can be strengthened through CVBs by increasing the equity, removing the imbalance in resource availability, adjusting the time period of loan requirements, resource planning, enhancing micro-enterprises and by creating proper market links.
8. Kisan Credit Cards may be issued by assessing the borrowing capacities of the farmers for consecutive three agricultural seasons.
9. Co-operative commonwealth can be attained by establishing vertical and horizontal links in the institutional framework.

Fredrick Nicholson, who principal supporter of the village banks had enumerated some advantages, which may be taken up as the supportive feature of the CVBs. (i) CVBs as the absolute proximity to borrower can issue loans as and when need arises. (ii) They create local confidence and local capital. (iii) The CVBs know the borrowers and their capabilities. (iv) Supervision on loan utilisation. (v) Cheap credit can be assured through direct refinance. (vi) Profit remains within the villages. (vii) Can work as agent of the members' other activities. (viii) Unity and integrity can be maintained.

However, some conditions have to be fulfilled for successful operations of the CVBs. For example : (i) Credit availability, (ii) Adjustments of credit terms, (iii) Reduction in the cost of credit, (iv) Assistance for hi-tech agriculture, (v) Whole village within the ambit of CVBs, (vi) Include every one in the village, (vii) Adherence to co-operative principle, (viii) Sense of belongingness etc.

If the Indian rural co-operatives are not restructured as CVBs, the concept of village banking as it has entered worldwide will substitute the present PACS in India. Hence a model of PACS is required to be designed as CVBs for the development of rural co-operative credit system in India (Jugale, 2000). PACS are entrusted with only loans to land owners and not to the productive poors.

VILLAGE BANKING WORLDWIDE

The initial trust of the co-operative banking was much oriented towards agricultural banking. The system so designed also covers the provision of credit help to weaker section. But the condition of creditworthiness in loan business to weaker section, altogether spoiled the common men's will to develop themselves. This mechanism gave a way to spring up the SHGs. Poverty lending village banking was thought essential in the mid 1980s with participant base and reliance on a group mechanism for loan processing. The informal credit system does not signify the creditworthiness of the borrowers. The institutional lending stresses on the norm of creditworthiness of the borrowers. Creditworthiness can be generated by regulating the productive capabilities hidden in the non-creditworthy people. This has been properly identified by the system of village banking. The poor helps the poors is the principle of the village banking so far development in the world.

The model of village banking was based on the assumption that the village communities would make the best managers of their own banking system. Hatch designed a method to organise informal banks, which could use a line of credit form, a financial intermediary to provide non-collateralized loans to members, a place to invest savings and promote social solidarity (UNDFW, 1996).

The rural credit system did not keep the agriculture sector outside its purview. Even the earlier village banks in Bolivia offered one year agricultural loans primarily to male farmers. Financial help both to creditworthy and non-creditworthy is urged for their upliftment. Historically this process focussed on offering services to the self-employed, who did not qualify for commercial credit, but who did have established business and some assets.

In Bangladesh, the Grameen Bank pioneered "Peer Lending", which is now reached to more than 2 million women and spurred a movement known as poverty lending village banking, developed in Latin American is another approach that is strengthening the poverty lending movement through the creation of community institutions and networks striving to meet the enormous demand for credit for those most in need and most ignored (UNDFS, 1996). The term village banking is used commonly in USA. Other terms like community banking, credit association, group guaranteed saving and lending agencies etc. are used worldwide.

The village banks though created for the use of the productive poors, can be applied to even small and marginal farmers. The methodology of VBs highlighted the usefulness to the farm committees. The modified version of VBs in the system of Regional Private Banks may possibly be introduced by the Private Sector banking. The rural sector has large amount of saving potentials which remained unharnessed since a few decades. The bank deposits in the non-metropolitan urban areas have grown at a faster pace than the national average since last four or five years. (E.T. 12th Jan. 2001). The rural savings are still flowing towards moffusil urban areas. The number of savers is rising in these areas. But the other saving instruments beyond banking are not fully available there (Semi-urban & rural) as yet. All India average of growth of rural deposits in banks between September 1996 to September 2000 remained at 17.3 percent, and that of Semi-urban at 17.3 percent, urban area experiences the growth at 18.6 percent and that of metropolitan deposits remained at 16.7 percent during the period. Co-operatives have well built network, through which, if they entertained, can harness the rural savings further. The CVBs are qualified for such type of mobilisation of saving potentials in rural area. The Kolhapur DCCB in Maharastra through the viable PACS, whose nomenclature has been changed as Mini Kisan Banks, is experiencing good result in mobilising the savings.

AN EXERCISE OF RESTRUCTURING : A CASE IF MINI KISAN BANKS IN KOLHAPUR DISTRICT

The Kolhapur DCCB (Maharashtra States, India) has come up with a scheme of Mini Kisan Banks earmarked under the existing structure of co-operative credit system in mid 1980s. It is justified as an innovative banking ideology of the practitioners, within the existing structure of co-operative credit system in Maharashtra. The history of MKBs goes back to the early 1980s, when the Easy Crop Loan Scheme (ECLS) was introduced as an outcome of operational experiences in the crop loan policy. Easy loan indicates the process of way out from the strict adherence to the scheme of crop loan, which had been softened in terms of length of time, process of sanction etc. for the benefit of the farmers. ECLS was applied to selected PACS (Those who have obtained the audit class of A and B) with 100 per cent recovery for corresponding 3 years and those having linking facility of credit to marketing. The scheme of ECLS was revised in 1987-88. The Board of Directors of Kolhapur DCCB decided to offer the viable PACS to work on the banking lines. Six viable PACS were selected for implementing the scheme of MKB. Out of these only two have adopted the scheme initially. On 2nd January 1996, the scheme of MKB has been revised. At present there are 43 MKBs working in the Kolhapur District (Maharashtra).

The main features of the MKBs are as under :

1. The scheme of MKBs is applied to only viable PACS. Whose audit class remained at 'A' with 100% recovery for more than 3 years.
2. The MKBs are permitted to collect deposits and are allowed to intermediate between savers and borrowers (investors).
3. The scheme of loan disbursement other than the DCCB crop loan scheme can be designed by the MKB, but should get sanctioned from the DCCB.
4. The MKBs have to keep 30 per cent deposit liabilities with the DCCB for which the DCCB charges the rate of interest at 14.5 per cent. Remaining 70 per cent of deposits are used by the MKBs for loan disbursement to their members.
5. The rate of interest on deposits and loans is fixed by the MKBs in consultation with the DCCB.
6. The MKBs are eligible to borrow (cash credit) from the DCCB within their limit after utilization of 70 per cent deposits. Saving account is also opened up for depositing the 30 per cent deposits collected by MKBs.
7. Tallying of asset and liabilities are exercised daily.
8. MKBs are allowed to lend for other than farm activities, the essential provisions prior to this should be made in the by-laws with a scheme of loans disbursement.
9. 30 per cent of deposits are allowed to be used for M.T. loans and another 40 per cent for short term loans like crop loans.
10. Each MKB has to prepare a schedule of maximum credit limit every year like that of all PACS, for prior approval of the Central Office (DCCB) and individual credit disbursement to its members after approval.
11. Operational guidelines are issued to each MKB for smooth functioning of the scheme.

The idea behind the scheme is to facilitate the farmers by quick services and to facilitate the MKBs to harness the deposits in rural area, so as to provide access of the financial support for making loan business with their members.

The MKB is empowered to constitute a five member committee to deal with the urgent matters and to disburse the loans in time. Every member is given a pass book for his observations and record. In the case of higher loan demands the MKB can borrow the DCCB. Exhaustive guidelines have been issued to each MKB for smooth functioning of the system. All types of bill payment e.g. sugarcane bills are routed through MKBs. Cash credit facility upto the limit of 30 per cent of the deposits mobilised by the MKB is granted by the DCCB.

The PACS are normally borrowing the Cash Credit at the rate of 9 per cent from the DCCB within their limits and disbursing the crop loans to its members at the rate of 12 per cent with an addition of 3 per cent as their margin. The MKBs are intermediating the deposits and loans other than above mentioned cash credit. For deposits, on an average, they are paying 10 per cent rate of interest, while that on loans they are charging, on an average, 16 to 18 per cent. As a result, the margin of 6 to 8 per cent is retained with the MKBs. Earlier the PACS were getting only 3 per cent margin.

To carryout the whole work of MKBs, the Secretaries are being paid extra allowances, along with some assistants helping on the transactions, whose payment are made out of the interest margin. The cost of intermediation of the MKBs has remained less. As a result most of the MKBs are in profit.

The composition of the business consists of crop loans, hire purchase loans (consumer durables) and M.T. and L.T. loans for agricultural implements etc. crop loan shares 40 per cent of loans and another 30 per cent business is covered by hire purchase (M.T.) and L.T. loans for agricultural implements and remaining amount of deposits are kept with the DCCB as working capital. Crop loan is the major attraction of the members. The L.T. loan borrower has used his loan amount for purchasing tractor, while hire purchase and M.T. loan are used for purchasing TV, scooter, cycle, minor agricultural implements and for irrigation installations, etc.

Continuation of the MKB scheme basically depends on the recovery of the loans. It is expected that, the MKB should attain at least 90 per cent of loan recovery. Timely grant of loans is possible through CVBs. On the contrary the PACS system takes much time for grant of crop loans. The quality of lending is quite good. The supervision on loan utilisation is being made by the Board members, because the MKBs are using the local deposits not the DCCB funds.

Table 24.1 indicates the performance of the deposit mobilisation by MKBs (28) since their nomenclature as MKBs of which 13 MKBs are operating for more than last 5 years. Remaining 15 MKBs have their recent origin, but are performing well. Short term and long term deposits have been mobilised by the MKBs. The annual growth rate of deposit mobilisation is positive with increasing trend therein. Only seven MKBs have not initiated in collecting L.T deposits. Performance of a few MKBs is noteworthy. Growing L.T. deposits qualifies the MKB to make L.T. investment in rural activities. Moreover, this indicates the credibility of the MKBs. The scheme of MKBs is successful in mobilising rural resources.

The PACS are very much known for their borrowing from DCCBs. The scheme of MKBs has reduced the borrowings from DCCB. As a result the MKBs are using 6 to 8 per cent margin for their development. Micro finances by the MKBs for Micro enterprises have been developed in the respective

Table 24.1
Annual Average Growth Rate of Deposits and Loan Borrowing from KDCCB

(In per cent)

Sl.No.	Name of MKB	Year	Deposits	Cash Credit from KDCCB
1.	Nagav MKB	1989-1999	24.60	8.06
2.	Yashwant (Rashiwade)	1995-1999	184.89	-2.24
3.	Amarapur (Aurwad)	1995-1999	62.02	6.09
4.	Laxmi (Gadhinglaj)	1997-1999	35.93	62.74
5.	Dinabandhu (Shedshal)	1994-1999	50.48	22.75
6.	Bharat (Gualwad)	1995-1999	57.85	-9.24
7.	Shriram (Waghapur)	1997-1999	351.38	100.65
8.	Kedarling (Chuye)	1997-1998	11.24	29.47
9.	Abdullat MKB	1995-1999	38.43	21.42
10.	Jaybharat (Kanwad)	1996-1999	15.15	2.62
11.	Laxmi (Basarge)	1994-1999	51.77	13.96
12.	Udgaon MKB	1993-1999	22.37	25.89
13.	Janaseva (P. Khurd)	1995-1999	73.99	25.15
14.	Shahu Chh. (Sabalewadi)	1991-1999	8.88	1.26
15.	Alas MKB	1994-1999	85.59	28.12
16.	Balbhim (Khupire)	1997-1999	108.52	-16.06
17.	Mahalaxmi (K. Sangav)	1995-1999	114.38	26.85
18.	Amroli MKB	1995-1999	81.64	9.23
19.	Naganwadi MKB	1995-1999	19.97	0.05
20.	Balbhim (K.Nul)	1996-1999	8.36	0.16
21.	Datta (Khupire)	1995-1999	0.36	-0.81
22.	Janaseva (Danoli)	1995-1999	0.68	0.83
23.	Mahavir (Chokak)	1995-1999	0.42	0.15
24.	Hirwade Khalasa	1995-1999	0.77	-0.05
25.	Ramling Hebbal (K. Nul)	1996-1999	6.75	-0.10
26.	Sarvodaya (Hasur)	1998-1999	3.09	0.10
27.	Kothali MKB	1993-1999	0.38	0.20
28.	Krishi Sadhana (Kurundwad)	1993-1997	6.85	48.03

Notes : (1) The names in brackets are the names of the village.
(2) The information of 7 MKB was not available.

Source : Towards the village Banking, V.B. Jugale, 2000.

rural areas. MKBs are making four types of loan business, (a) Crop loan, (b) Cash Credit (Hire Purchase), (c) M.T. loans and (d) L.T. loans. Crop loan is a regular PACS' activity governed by the DCCB. Cash Credit is given under the direction of DCCB for purchase of household consumer durables like TVs and motorcycles etc. L.T. loans are also given to the villagers (as a special case) for purchase of tractors and other agricultural equipments. The MKBs are free to make their bye-laws regarding the loan disbursement to agricultural activities in their respective village areas duly approved by the DCCB.

It is further observed that, the annual growth rate of borrowing from DCCB in most cases is negative. Crop loan shares major portion of loan disbursement. The trend of borrowing for M.T. and L.T. loans has also declined. This is what the CVBs are expected to do.

It is very difficult to operate the banking activities in the given system of co-operatives. The DCCB is dominating and regulating the funds in almost all MKB's transaction.

The rate of interest on S.T. loans (out of deposits) except crop loans handly varies among the MKBs. The borrowers are happy with the MKBs.

The MKBs have to carryout lot of paper work as guided by the DCCBs and for the benefit of DCCB. The entries have to be made at 13 places in various register books. The secretaries are burdened by extra work, consequently they are reluctant to have such credit system.

The MKBs and PACS are the kingpin of the co-operative credit system, they should be emphasized in the overall rural money market. An experiment of the MKBs is a landmark effort of freedom and innovation by the Kolhapur DCCB. Such type of innovations are essential for succeeding the financial sector reforms. Restructuring of rural finance is essential rather than reorganising the co-operative credit system. Otherwise the alternative agencies will occupy the space provided by the existing co-operative credit system. MKBs is a lesson to the policy makers. Supply of credit, to carry out all agricultural activities is a pre-requisite, as the complexities are also observed in the rural credit system. Therefore, the enterpreneurship in farm activities is different from that of industrial enterpreneurship. The risk and uncertainties in agricultural sector have direct implications on the risk and uncertainty management of the financial institutions who are issuing the credit to the agricultural sector. The lenders are more safer than the borrowers. The farmers neither have a guarantee of agricultural production due to vagaries of the monsoon, nor they predict favourable agricultural returns in the form of money income.

The mismanagement of the agricultural credit is normally seen among the farmers, which disturbs the family budget of the farmers. Credit is a bad master if it is mismanaged. It is like, "credit supports the farmers as the hangman's rope support the hanged". However, if it is used properly, "it can serve as a elevator." Economically, socially and technologically we can improve the positions of the farm and farm families by way of supplying the credit timely, cheaply and adequately. Thus the role of agricultural finance is immense in improving the economic conditions of the farm families.

Co-operatives provide good credit to the farmers, because co-operatives can mobilize rural savings and promote national thrift. Prudence of self control arouses new ideas among the masses including self help and mutual help and removes the isolation, suspicious exclusiveness of the farmers and suggests new departures in the conservative methods of cultivation.

An attempt to raise a logical and rational structure of co-operative credit must involve conceptual, organisational and financially well designed ideology. The continuing need for financial resources of rural co-operatives in India is the result of three elements-prevention of exploitation, investment of fresh resources and steady and integrated growth system. The co-operative structure in India fulfils the principles of better credit. Hence the co-operative structure should be advocated. However the co-operative structure should not carryout the credit disbursement mechanism only. D.G. Karve (1960) has rightly remarked, "Only lending money to the farmers under co-operative regulation cannot be defined as an activity, contributing to economic development". In this respect, to make co-operative credit more effective, a well developed model of Co-operative Village Bank be supported with adequate institutional support, which suits within the framework of financial sector reforms. If not, the concept of village banking for the poors and the concept of local private banks will occupy the empty space in the rural credit system. The MKBs is a right step towards the viable village banking within a framework of co-operative structure. At present the scheme of MKB is running on the line of suggested CVB model. To revitalise the model, it is required to enact the co-operative law and some regulations and permission from Reserve Bank of India are also essential so as to work at par with the banking units. The MKB scheme is a replica of CVB Model. Restructuring the PACS into CVBs is an opportunity rendered under the FSRs. Co-operation as an alternative to privatization and nationlization suits in the framework of the mixed economy. However, proper mindset is strictly required for restructuring the rural credit system. The strength and ability of the co-operative system lies in, how the sector converts challenges into opportunities.

References

Berry, Peter J. & Robinson Liden J. (1987): Port Folio Theory & Financial Structure : An Application of Analysis, Agricultural & Financing Review, Vol. 47.

Choubey, B.N. (1968): Principle and Practices of Agricultural Finance, Asia Publishing House.

Fiedler, Edgar R. and assisted by Peck Maude R. : Measures of Credit Risk and Experience, National Bureau of Economic Research, New York, General Series, 95.

Johi, S.S. and Moore C.V. (1970) : Essentials of Farm Management, Today & Tomorrow Printers and Publishers, New Delhi.

Jugale, V.B. (1991) : Theories of Agricultural Finance, Atlantic Publishers & Distributors, New Delhi.

Jugale, V.B. (1993) : Co-operative Credit in India Agriculture : It's Socio Economic & Technological impact, Mittal Pub., New Delhi.

Jugale, V.B. (1996) : A Model of PACS, Symposium, Dept. of Economics, Shivaji University, Kolhapur December.

Jugale, V.B. (1996): Restructuring the Rural Credit System, NABARD Chair Unit, VAMINICOM, Pune.

Jugale, V.B. (2000): Towards Village Banking: Working of Mini Kisan Banks in Kolhapur, Monograph-10, UGC-SAP-DRS, Department of Economics, Shivaji University, Kolhapur, March.

Karve, D.G. (1960): Failure and Success in Indian Co-operative Movement, Third International Congress on Co-operation.

Nelson, A.G. and Murray W.C. (1967) : Agricultural Finance, IOWA State University, Press, Ames LOWA, USA, 5th Edition.

Penson, Johan B. Jr. (1987) : Evaluating Financial Trend, Agricultural and Financing Review, Vol. 47.

RBI (1998) : Report of the High Level Committee on Agricultural Credit Through Commercial Banks, (Gupta Committee).

Report on Risk and Uncertainty in Agriculture, Chicago.

Singh, B.K. & Nantiya J.C. (1986): An Empirical Estimation of Risk in the Application of Chemical Fertilizers in HYV of Wheat & Paddy in Different Regions of U.P.I.J.A.B., Vol. 4, No. 2, April-June.

UNDFW (1996): Village Banking.

CHAPTER

25

Contribution of Tobacco Sector to National and Local Economy—Should it be Banned?

GYANA CHANDRA KAR

Christopher Columbus discovered the use of tobacco as a narcotic in Sansalvador Island in 1492. One of the crew members accompanying Columbus found the natives of the island smoking tobacco leaves through pipes which are locally known as "Tobacco". He also noticed snuff taking habits among the natives. The Spaniads in the year 1502 discovered the use of tobacco for chewing purposes in South Africa. Tobacco plant was brought to Europe in 1560. The entry of tobacco to Europe through France has a very interesting historical background. In the mid sixteenth century, the the-then emperor of France, Francois II was having severe and constant headache which existing medicines could not cure. A courtier named Jean Nicote sent some tobacco powder to the King's mother (Catherine). It is said that Francois II, after consuming the tobacco powder, got relieved from the headache. The gratified emperor named the product after the name of the courtier and tobacco in France was named as "Nicotina Tobaccum". In no time, thereafter, the use of tobacco for smoking, chewing and inhaling spread rapidly throughout the globe. Lo behold ! the French named the product as 'Nicotina tobaccum', and praised its virtue. Today they call it "Wicked Plant" because in France alone nearly 30,000 people die every year due to smoking-related diseases. (Lungs/Throat Cancer etc.)

Tobacco came to India in the 17th century. It was found to be cultivated in Bijapur State. As a cash crop it achieved its commercial status in 1829 when the Britishers made experiments to commercially grow tobacco. By the year 1888-89 it was recorded that nearly eight lakh hectares were under tobacco cultivation. 'Mr. O' Conor (1873) in his report on "Tobacco in India" has given many details of area under tobacco in different parts of British India. The major districts in India growing Tobacco from the beginning have been east and west Godavari, Krishna and Nellore in Andhra Pradesh; Coimbatore in Tamil Nadu; Rangpur and Tiruhut in West Bengal and Gujarat. Orissa, certainly is not, a major tobacco growing state. Tobacco was a major item of export in mid nineteenth century and in 1866-87 India exported tobacco worth 5.62 lakhs of rupees to Aden, Mauritious, U.K., France, U.S., etc. In next 10 years its export went upto 8.914 lakhs.

The area under tobacco in Orissa has been gradually declining (Table 25.1) since 1972-73. It was 15.3 thousand hectares, whereas, in 1999-2000, it became 7 thousand hectares.

TABLE 25.1

Area, Production and Yield Rate of Tobacco in Orissa and India during 1972-73 to 2000 -01

Area in -'000 ha.
Production in '000 tns.
Yield Rate in 'kg/ha.

Year	Orissa			India		
	Area	Production	Yield Rate	Area	Production	Yield Rate
(1)	(2)	(3)	(4)	(5)	(6)	(7)
1972-73	15.3	13.2	863	444.9	372.2	837
1973-74	15.4	12.4	8.5	461.5	462.1	1001
1974-75	15.4	11.1	721	380.6	363.1	954
1975-76	16.7	11.0	659	368.2	349.8	950
1976-77	14.8	6.9	466	432.4	418.8	968
1977-78	16.6	7.1	428	504.4	493.6	979
1978-79	19.6	9.6	490	409.3	453.8	1109
1979-80	18.1	8.6	475	425.4	438.5	1031
1980-81	21.2	11.3	533	428.2	481.0	1123
1981-82	16.6	7.8	470	444.0	520.0	1171
1982-83	15.9	7.2	453	503.0	582.0	1157
1983-84	18.6	10.2	548	440.0	493.0	1120
1984-85	17.8	9.4	528	436.6	485.9	1113
1985-86	18.2	9.6	528	397.0	441.2	1111
1986-87	16.2	9.7	599	389.0	462.0	1188
1987-88	14.4	5.0	347	318.0	367.4	1155
1988-89	14.0	6.3	450	377.0	493.0	1308

(Contd.)

TABLE 25.1 (*Contd.*)

(1)	(2)	(3)	(4)	(5)	(6)	(7)
1989-90	15.2	9.1	599	413.0	552.0	1337
1990-91	15.0	8.1	540	411.0	556.0	1353
1991-92	14.9	10.8	725	427.0	584.4	1369
1992-93	12.9	9.9	767	418.5	596.5	1425
1993-94	10.0	6.1	610	384.8	562.9	1463
1994-95	10.3	6.0	582	381.7	566.7	1485
1995-96	9.1	6.7	736	394.6	535.2	1356
1996-97	9.3	5.5	591	428.0	617.9	1444
1997-98	8.0	5.0	625	463.5	646.0	1394
1998-99	8.6	4.4	512	508.1	736.2	1449
1999-2000	7.0	4.0	571	433.4	609.0	1405
2000-01	NA	NA	NA	290.0	490.0	1690

r = -2.76 r = -2.76 r = 3.16 r = -0.305 r = 1.623 r = 1.935

NA - Not Available

Source : Agriculture, CMIE, December 2002.

Similarly, the total production of tobacco has also declined in Orissa. It was 13.2 thousand tonnes in 1972-73, and these declined to 4 thousand tonnes in 1999-2000. At all-India level, the area under tobacco in 1972-73 was 444.9 thousand hectares, and in 2000-01, it decreased to 290 thousand hectares. With regard to yield rate of tobacco, no systematic trend is found. Again, the percentage share of area under tobacco to total cropped area in Orissa during 1972-75 was 0.2 per cent which declined to 0.1 per cent in 1998-01. Similarly, at all- India level, it was 0.3 per cent in 1972-75 as against 0.2 per cent in 1998-01 (Graph-I).

GRAPH 25.1

Percentage Share of Area under Tobacco to Total Cropped Area in Orissa and India

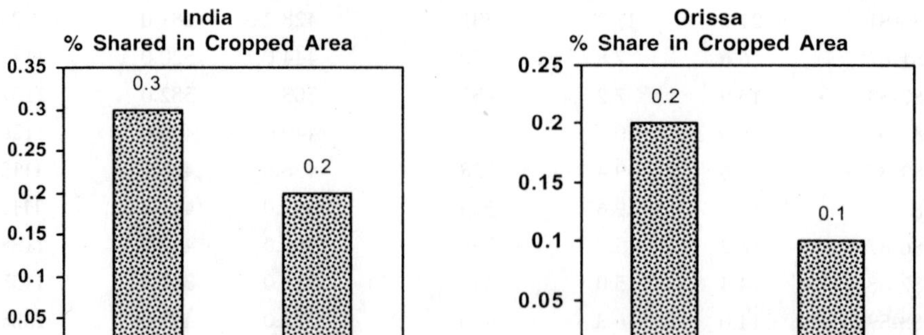

Orissa		India	
1972-75	0.2	1972-75	0.3
1998-01	0.1	1998-01	0.2

Source : Agriculture, CMIE, December 2002.

The above analysis shows that, day-by day, people are switching off the cultivation of tobacco both in Orissa and all India level, which is a very good sign considering the major harmful end use of the product. Nevertheless, if tobacco cultivation is banned, large number of people would be temporarily unemployed. But it is hoped that they subsequently could switch over to other cash crops.

On the face of declining area under tobacco and total output, surprisingly we find an increasing expenditure on tobacco by household. The average monthly per capita expenditure on tobacco is found to be increasing between 51st Round NSS and 56th Round NSS both in Orissa as well as at all-India level, which can be seen from Table 25.2. As expenditure on tobacco is harmful as well as wasteful expenditure, the increasing expenditure of the people on consumption of tobacco should be of great concern.

TABLE 25.2
Average Monthly Per Capita Expenditure on Tobacco in Rural and Urban Areas of Orissa and at All-India Level

NSS Round		Orissa: Amount (in Rs.)	Orissa: % to expenditure on non-food items	Orissa: % to total expenditure	India: Amount (in Rs.)	India: % to expenditure on non-food items	India: % to total expenditure
July 1994 to June 1995	Rural	2.60	3.29	1.07	5.14	4.26	1.66
(51st Round NSS)	Urban	2.99	1.55	0.68	5.18	2.19	1.02
January 1997 to Dec. 1997	Rural	2.53	2.39	0.85	6.53	4.00	1.65
(53rd Round NSS)	Urban	3.49	1.36	0.62	6.25	1.92	0.97
January 1998 to June 1998	Rural	2.03	1.91	0.68	6.31	4.22	1.65
(54th Round NSS)	Urban	3.61	1.26	0.56	6.62	1.92	0.97
July 1999 to June 2000	Rural	3.38	2.52	0.90	7.57	3.84	1.56
(55th Round NSS)	Urban	3.20	1.2	0.52	8.10	1.82	0.95
July 2000 to June 2001	Rural	3.11	2.13	0.79	8.36	3.87	1.69
(56th Round NSS)	Urban	3.99	1.00	0.52	8.70	1.69	0.95

Source : Economic Surveys of different years, Directorate of Economics and Statistics, planning and Co-ordination Department, Govt. of Orissa.

TOBACCO—THE BANE—(THE WICKED PLANT)

The health risk factors associated with tobacco consumption in its various forms (smoking, chewing, tooth paste and inhaling) are very high. One of the 10 major causes of cancer is tobacco related-emerging in forms of lungs, throat, mouth or stomach cancer.

As per WHO study (1995) every year 5.75 lakh new cases of cancer are detected and an overwhelmingly majority cases are tobacco related cancer cases and nearly 2.20 lakh deaths are reported world wide every year. In India 50 to 70 per cent of all cancer patients are in the category of tobacco related cancer cases. A study in Mumbai (reported by WHO 1995) that the incidence of cancer is 16.4 per lakh of population in case of males and 8.8 per lakh in case of females.

It may be pointed out here that cases reported at hospitals are much less than actual cases of occurrence due to poor access to hospital facilities in India as also poverty of the people. That is why the number of tobacco related cancer cases are far too lower in comparison to advanced countries like UK and US. It is only 2-3 per cent of such cases of cancer of UK and USA.

In oral cancer lower lip cancer is quite common due to consumption of chewing tobacco and smoking of Bidi.

Let us take the case of Orissa. As usual getting data on anything is difficult and that too, tobacco related diseases, are either not maintained or no one has tried to categorise such cases. But it may be presumed that what is true of Mumbai study, may be true of Orissa, and the incidence of tobacco related cancer could be around 15.7 to 16.4 for males per one lakh population and 3.5 to 8.8 females per one lakh population.

Bidi smoking may be more injurious due to two reasons-one in the smoke of tobacco inhaled and the other is the 'heat' which the lips (particularly the lower lip) bears while smoking Bidi. Hence, apart from holding chewable tobacco between the inside lower lips and teeth becoming a cause of cancer, smoking bidi could also be another major cause of mouth cancer.

STATUS OF BIDI IN ORISSA

In Orissa (Office of the Labour Commissioner, Orissa) as many as 6365 no. of workers work in licensed premises for Bidi manufacturing and 1,75,323 Bidi rollers work as home workers (2002). Together, they make a total of 1,81,688 workers working in the Bidi industry directly. There are a large number of people who are engaged in Bidi trading, whose number could not be known.

Associated with Bidi manufacturing there is Kendu leaves plucking, drying, bundling and sizing that provide huge employment to a large number of people in Orissa. These people are mostly poor and belong to the scheduled caste and scheduled tribe. It is found that nearly 18 lakh people, mostly women, receive 10 to 40% of their annual income from Kendu leaf related activities. In lean season, when other agricultural activities are absent, about 2 lakh people are engaged in the processing, binding, and bagging Kendu leaves deriving an estimated income of Rs.42 crores. There are at present 18 thousand binders.

Kendu Leaf (KL) in Orissa

- About 18 lakh poor people—mostly women depend on KL and derive 10% to 40% of their annual income from it.
- Orissa Government gets good revenue (Rs.69.0 crores in 2001-02) as royalty.
- Revenue from Kendu Leaves has doubled (214% in 1999-00 over 1973 at current prices).
- More than two lakh people are engaged in processing, binding and bagging and earn Rs.42 crores during lean season from Kendu Leaves.

There is apprehension that if Bidi manufacturing is banned it would lead to a serious livelihood problem involving not only the 1.82 lakh Bidi workers but also inflict severe deprivation and threat to livelihood of nearly more than 18 lakh people, (of which women constitute a sizeable proportion) engaged in Kendu leaf business. The state would also lose considerable revenue derived from this leaf. Orissa Govt. receives about 70 crores of rupees as royalty from Kendu leaf operation.

These, however, do not include the expenses made for Kendu Leaf Corporation (indirect income there) and the profit of the Corporation. So far no alternative use of Kendu leaf has been found, and thus, a ban on Bidi making would affect substantial number of people belonging to backward classes and the government in terms of huge revenue losses. This would pose a great problem to the state administration, which is currently passing through one of the greatest financial crisises. Deprived of the revenue from Kendu leaf source, handling such a social problem of rehabilitation would have great political consequence.

THE BOON OF TOBACCO—GROWING TOBACCO FOR ALTERNATIVE USES

Tobacco has a wide spectrum of several chemical compounds in abundance which can broadly be classified as alkaloids, nitrogenous constituents, acids, phenolics, lipids and inorganic substances. Nicotine could be converted to various value added products. It could be the source for botanical pesticide. Some of the recent scientific evidences suggest that nicotine and nicotine—like compounds may slow the progress of or ameliorate the symptoms of certain diseases such as Tourettes' Syndrome,

TABLE 25.3
Status of Kendu Leaves from 1980-81 onwards in Orissa

Year	*Revenue from Kendu Leaves (In Crore Rs.)*	*Quantity Production (In Lakh Quintals)*
(1)	(2)	(3)
1980-81	8.88	3.08
1981-82	9.00	3.02
1982-83	14.00	2.95
1983-84	18.50	3.42
1984-85	17.00	3.94
1985-86	13.00	3.79
1986-87	15.69	3.84
1987-88	27.48	4.28
1988-89	23.64	3.9
1989-90	82.44	4.55
1990-91	76.85	3.97
1991-92	51.57	4.97
1992-93	78.26	5.09
1993-94	75.35	4.98
1994-95	84.16	4.91
1995-96	43.58	3.86
1996-97	24.10	5.11
1997-98	40.60	4.96
1998-99	63.50	3.9
1999-00	74.50	4.69
2000-01	55.00	5.04
2001-02	69.00	3.97

Source : Office of the PCCF, Government of Orissa.

Alzheimers', Parkinsons disease. Solanesol is the starting material for many high value biochemicals like vitamin-K analogues, vitamin-E and coenzyme Q-9. In pure form, Malic acid and citric acid find use in food and pharmaceutical industries. Apart from these phyto-chemicals, there are other possibilities such as edible protein recovery from green tobacco leaf, oil from the seed, rutin from the cured leaf and furfural from the stalk.

All parts of tobacco plant, from seed to stalk, can be a great source value-added chemical. Fraction-I is the most abundant protein in tobacco and accounts for 50 per cent soluble protein. It is composed of amino acids including essential ones. In tobacco seed, oil content is about 35 per cent which can be used in paint industry. Refined tobacco oil has properties similar to edible oil which is used for edible purposes in Turkey and Tunisia. The residue can be converted to the de-oiled cakes which can be used for making organic manure.

In 1994-95, 600 tonnes of nicotine sulphates worth Rs. 12.4 crore were exported to Japan, UK, Switzerland and other countries. There is a steady increase in the international values of nicotine sulphate. Nicotine sulphate is being successfully used as a pesticide, the spray of which generally does not leave any residue on the crop. The alkaloid, being biodegradable, leaves no hazardous residues on vegetables and fruits bound for the market. The US Food and Drug Administration permits a nicotine residue of 2 ppm on foods. Most crops spread with nicotine sulphate exhibit residue levels far below 2 ppm- thus making the chemical a safe pesticide. The total export of tobacco and tobacco-based products are on in the increase in value terms. In 1998-99 India's total exports were US 181 million dollars (Rs. 868 crores). In 1999-2000 the export has gone upto US $ 191 million (Rs. 960 crores). Tobacco constitutes 3.2 per cent of India's total agri-export. But it constitutes about 1 per cent of total world export of tobacco.

Tobacco cultivation gives rise to large employment in agricultural sector. Cost of cultivation of tobacco in Andhra Pradesh shows the requirement of 1700 to 1800 man hours per hectare (Andhra Pradesh estimates), converted to mandays at 8 hours per day works out to nearly 211 to 240 mandays of labour employment for different types of tobacco under different soil texture. Thus, tobacco provides very large employment opportunities in the agricultural sector. A ban of tobacco cultivation in India will lead to about 974 lakhs of mandays withdrawal from tobacco cultivation and their immediate engagement in some other form of agricultural activities may pose a great problem for the planners. In Orissa a ban on tobacco cultivation would cause 16 lakh mandays of labour withdrawal requiring alternative engagement in the agricultural sector.

As growing tobacco for phyto-chemicals is very relevant, tobacco can be cultivated for its alternative use in all potential areas of the country and state. Its use must be made selective. A plant which is now knick named as 'wicked plant' can be converted to a 'money spinning plant' if its uses are in the right direction.

CHAPTER

26

Political System of Corruption : A Villain for Civilised Societal Development

A. Ranga Reddy

The analysis of paper is divided into six parts, part one deals about the nature of corruption, levels of corruption, place and position, cognizable crimes, ecology and development and remedial measures.

I

Corruption is defined as the abuse of office for private gain. Corruption is a big crime, in extent, in scale and in impact because it can derail any process, be it political, electoral, social, cultural, administrative, any development, or even war. It is a menace to the moral well-being of the community.

Corruption has different *avatars*. It is bribe, commission, greasing palm, kickbacks, lubricant, pay off, seed money, rent seeking, winding charges, underhand dealings and scams. The most corrupting influence on politics is exerted by business and industry. Politics is the fountain head of corruption not only in India but also in the world over. Corruption develops with development. It is submitted that lack of integrity in the holders of offices is the real and vital cause of corruption. Infact, higher the office, lower is the integrity. Greater the wealth, greater is dishonesty.

Moguls and British ruled India by bribing Indian rulers. It is the legacy and heritage of India. Because of increased government expenditure now as an instrument of fiscal policy, it is a most convenient channel for official corruption. Now it is more or less a global phenomena. A new dimension is the infiltration of mafia money into the political and socio-economic fabric of many nations. One sad result of this is that substantial amounts of wealth have been taken away from poor countries by the mafias and deposited in rich countries. An Argentinean delegation complained that 200 millions had been legally transferred from his country to foreign shores, and all attempts to freeze those assets had met with failure. The Nigerian delegate reported that over the past 20 years, $ 55 to $ 100 billions had been looted from his country by corrupt officials, locking them up in financial institutions in 20 different places. The 95 member expert group of the UN (2001) identified that this type of corruption has now become a common feature. Accordingly, it recommended that international cooperation should be strengthened to fight illicit fund transfers and their laundering. Corruption money should be defined as proceeds of crime and an act of corruption may be established as a predicate offence in relation to money laundering.

Prevention will be the key feature of the new convention and that could mean integrity, transparency in governance, effective and impartial civil service, transparent public procurement rules, independent supervisory bodies, development of code of conduct, effective systems of financing political parties, regulation of financial systems, free and transparent media, an independent judiciary and implementation of the rule of law. Nevertheless, an anti-corruption culture is not that easy, to develop especially in countries with poor resources.

ORGANISED CRIMES : WANT OF MORAL CRUSADERS

Crime is a global phenomena. In legal terms crime is an act of human behaviour which is banned by criminal law. Actually not all acts that are penalised under the law are really criminal. When we consider crime from development point of view the white collar crimes/organised crimes emerge as the main limiting factor of development. The organised crimes are a large scale racket run by extensively organised crime syndicates carried on over long period of time and relying in political corruption for protection from the law. The growing power and influence of organised crime syndicates, involved in the corruption of gross 1.5 trillion a year are a global concern. Crime syndicates have emerged as a major economic power rivalling Multinational Corporations.

Central Bureau of Investigation (CBI) has reported that all over India crime syndicates have become a law into themselves. Even in the smaller towns and rural areas, musclemen have become the order of the day. Hired assassins have become a part of these organisations. The nexus between the criminal gangs, police, bureaucracy and politicians has come out clearly in various parts of the country. The existing criminal justice system, which was essentially designed to deal with individual offences crimes is unable to deal with the activities of the Mafia. The provisions of law in regard to economic offenses are weak; they are insurmountable legal difficulties in attaching confiscation of the property acquired through Mafia activities. Vicious circle of crime is the main obstacle in the way of economic development. It limits the functioning of the market. The overall scenario is much beyond the imagination of *Soft State* of Gunnar Myrdal. It is time to awaken mass consciousness against the crime syndicates. A crusade for moral generation for change is the need of the hour.

LIFT STYLE OF INDIA'S MESSIAH POLITICIANS

Nonetheless, the details of Chief Minister of Uttar Pradesh, Mayawati's birth day party make compelling reading: over one lakh Ladoos, 60 quintals of flowers, a birth day cake, a size of a mini-bus. The U.P. Government's Finance Department was apparently forced to grant permission for withdrawal of Rs. 1.35 crore from State's contingency funds. When Chief Minister of Bihar, Rabri Devi's and Lallu Prasad Yadav's second daughter got married, their henchmen decided they needed certain goods, they just helped themselves. The inventory went like this: 45 brand new cars forcibly taken from Patna Showrooms, over 100 sofa sets and other furniture taken from a dozen shops, suits and shirts worth Rs. 7 lakhs 'borrowed' from Raymond's outlets, 50 kg dry fruits, confectionery worth thousands, etc. No one dared complain, when one of the car dealers (the upright Tatas), lodged FIR with the police, they took the precaution of keeping all their premises locked out and moved to Kolkata. No wonder, one of Laloo's close relatives Subhas Yadav said of the allegation. Mayawati and Yadavs not only head the two poorest states in India, they are self-styled "Messiahs of the Poor".

LOOT AND SHARE SYSTEM: LOK PAL—A PIPE DREAM

Kleptocracy can be broadly described as a system of non-governance characterised by rampant greed and corruption. Politicians and bureaucrats have lorded over this country for over five decades keeping up and in fact adding to the oppressive and draconian laws that were imposed upon us by colonial masters. Politicians are the largest beneficiaries of state kleptocracy, bureaucrats are their main perpetrators either by complicity or through compliance. In Kleptocracy merit is the first causality. The super-bureaucrats who willingly formed part of the 'loot and share system' have spearheaded this betrayal. Unfortunately parliamentarians are blocking the passage of the Lok Pal Bill to escape the definition of 'Public Servants' while feasting themselves on high pay and perks.

The fruits of corruption are enjoyed by a fraction of the population while its disastrous consequences are borne by the whole population. The clients of the state supply inferior quality of goods and the authorities meekly approve of sub-standard works. Broken bridges are no longer the news in India. Corruption breeds poverty. Violence, by definition, signals the loss, lapse and negation of a spiritual way of being. We live in a time when no definition can be taken for granted. All these *adharmic* actions and philosophies have sought and received religious sanction.

II

LEVELS OF CORRUPTION AND ETHICS

Corruption may be presented as following in a formula

$$C = M + D - A$$

Corruption (C) equals monopoly (M) plus Discretion (D) minus Accountability (A). Generally corruption undermines democracy and destroys the credibility of government. Corruption is stealing from the poor.

CORRUPTION IS CLASSIFIED IN FOUR CATEGORIES

(a) Kleptocracy State

Few recipients are concentrated at upper levels of Government. It is either extortionery state or a weak state or bilateral monopoly state. Bribers are found among very few.

(b) Bilateral Monopoly

A corrupt ruler faces a single major briber. Multiple recipients at lower level of government. It may be mafia dominated state. Eg: Asia.

(c) Freelance Bribery States

It is weak and dis-organised with many officials engaged in freelance bribery. Private group dominates the state, buying the low level officials.

(d) Competitive Bribery State

Many corrupt officials deal with large number of ordinary citizens and firms. The situation is the political for an upward spiral of corruption. The corruption of some officials can encourage others to accept bribes until all but the un-reconstructed moralists are corrupt. Eg.India, of course, most developing countries fall somewhere between these two extremes.

The truth is that in some parts of the country a person can get away with murder if he has enough money to pay the police and if he has close contacts with the local heavy weights. On the other hand, false cases can also be registered against innocent people and can be pursued with the convenience of the police to harass or extract money. In many localities, policemen are suspected of being in league with thieves and decoits. Apart from it a substantial portion of political class has thus become highly corrupted. Democratic institutions have become polluted. Corrupt India of today is their legacy.

Do not blame the politicians solely for all the ills of the country today. The bureaucrats are equally responsible for defiling India's administration. If 5,067 I.A.S. officers decide to use enormous powers to fight corruption in an un-yielding manner and to run governmental administration honestly, efficiently and transparently, they will achieve amazing success. An honest index at nation, state and district level is to be developed.

The bulk of corruption in India originates in the realm of business and industry. Over the years important business houses have made arrangements through their contacts men posted in New Delhi and state capitals for the discreet disbursement of cash funds. The confederation of Indian Industries (CII) published in April 1998 a document entitled "Desirable Corporate governance—A Code". In fact, the word ethics does not appear at all in any of the CII recommendations.

III

PLACE AND POSITION OF CORRUPTION IN INDIAN SOCIETY

Impact of Corruption on Society

Corruption undercuts the macro economic efficiency, equity, and institutional functions of government. It is helpful to distinguish these four types of costs imposed by corruption. They are macro-fiscal, reduction in productive investment and growth, costs to the public and to the poor in particular and loss of confidence in public institution.

Size of Corruption in India

India had a dubious distinction of a high rate of corruption, high incidence of AIDs, widespread poverty, having a large number of disabled persons etc. Thousands of crore are being exchanged as bribe in the country.

State Intervention

Andhra Pradesh Advisory Commission on Peoples' Empowerment (COPE)

It is headed by the former Central Vigilance Commissioner N. Vittal. He said that he could look into the issue of pending corruption cases against 56 IAS and IPS officers in Andhra Pradesh. It was the commitment of William Gladstone and Lee Kuan Yew that helped to check corruption in Britain and Singapore respectively. Each member of COPE, eight would meet once a month and submit reports to the Government. Each member would be assigned two departments and asked to visit two districts in two months.

EMPIRICAL WORK ON CORRUPTION

N. Vittal the former Chief Vigilance Commissioner, in the "Vigilance Awareness Week" of Oct. 31-Nov. 4, 2000 organised a exit poll in five cities—New Delhi, Lucknow, Chennai, Hyderabad and Pune and six departments, power, telephone, civil supplies, city government, driving license and local urban department office, where a large number of people usually go. Out of 2,576 sample visitors from each city not less than 500 visitors were covered as sample. The structural questionnaire was canvassed by local premier institutions like IIM, Lucknow, Symbiosis. The findings are as follows: (a) 50 per cent of visitors who availed of the services had experience of giving bribe at one time or other, (b) 2/3 of people think corruption is real, (c) in Lucknow and Hyderabad 60 per cent had given bribe against only 38 per cent in Chennai and 42 per cent in Pune, (d) In Chennai more than 60 per cent had named politicians as responsible for corruption. Middlemen menace seems to be far more in Hyderabad and Lucknow, (e) Road Transport Authority and civil supplies were viewed as most corrupt in all the five cities, (f) Relatively more among businessmen and self employed agreed giving bribe in all cities, (g) Interestingly, even among government employees more than 40 percent agreed giving bribe at one time or other in all cities covered, (h) A little over 40 per cent of people think that judiciary in the country is not able to tackle corruption cases. Recently, a former Prime Minister, a few former Chief Minister and a few politicians were adjudged in indulging corrupt practices but nobody was punished. Former Chief Justice S.P. Bharucha reported that 20 per cent of judicial officials were corrupt and expressed concern at the absence of an effective mechanism to deal with the allegations of corruption in respect of High Court and Supreme Court judges.

IV

COGNIZABLE CRIMES IN INDIA

In this country, the value of life is based on your socio-economic status. For richer class making crime is like killing an innocent lamb. Law is at richer side due to corruption among police and lawyers. Murders are taking place due to poverty, unemployment, vengeance and jealousy. The murders committed are given below:

TABLE 26.1
Incidence of Congnizable Crime

Year	*Murder*
1991	39174
1994	38577
1995	37464
1996	37671
1997	37543
1998	38584
1999	37170

Source : GOI, Statistical Abstract India, 2000-01, p. 385.

TABLE 26.2
Incidence of Cognizable Crime

State	*Murder*	
	1998	*1999*
U.P.	8303	7854
Bihar	5311	5116
M.P.	3266	3225
Maharashtra	3003	3024
A.P.	2972	2711
W. Bengal	2122	1902
Tamil Nadu	1974	1726
Karnataka	1693	1651
Rajasthan	1514	1520
Assam	1665	1517
Gujarat	1407	1353
Orissa	936	1019
Haryana	826	839
J & K	664	765
Punjab	756	746
Kerala	443	484

Source : Same as Table 26.1.

TABLE 26.3
Incidence of Cognizable Crime

Cities	*Murder*	
	1998	*1999*
Delhi	514	523523
Mumbai	340	365
Kanpur	208	239
Patna	226	243
Bangalore	203	206
Hyderabad	115	115
Ahmedabad	105	104
Lucknow	129	118
Nagpur	135	114
Surat	106	108

Source : Same as Table 26.1.

Table 26.1 has shown that crime of murder is very high and constant in 1990s. At state level, in Table 26.2, proves that poverty leading murder is common in U.P., Bihar, M.P. At metropolitan level, Table 26.3, reveals that Delhi is the highest place in murder. Southern states are less prone to this degree of violence.

CONCLUSION

The following remedial measures may be adopted to control corruption.

(1) More of privatisation provided there is transparency in operation of private business.
(2) Encourage to honest officials and punishment to the dishonest.
(3) Independent and effective judiciary system.
(4) State has to function as a facilitator to help different agencies to operate their assignments effectively.
(5) Vigilance authorities must have more teeth to effectively control corruption without government interference.
(6) State funding of elections to avoid misuse of political power to indulge in corrupt practices of collecting money from businessmen and favouring them when they come to power.
(7) Vigilant civil society & independent media.

A strong political will, quality education, people's participation, good governance, transparent and accountable administration may go a long to control corruption.

References

Aekarman, Susanrose (1997), Corruption and Development, Annual World Bank Conference on Development Economics.

Chakko, George (2001), UN Clears way to fight Global Corruption, *The Hindu* (Aug, 20).

Dharkar, Anil (2003), Official Birthdays, *The Hindu* (Feb, 9).

Doraiswamy (2002), Ministers and Officers—Who's Corrupting Whom, *The Hindu* (April, 16).

Dubhasi, P.R. (2002), Criminalisation of Politics—Beyond Vohra Committee Report, *The Indian Journal of Public Administration*, July-September Issue.

Mani, Lata (2003), Confronting Violence: Bridging the Sacred—Secular Divide, *The Hindu*, (Feb. 9).

Mensah, S. Nil-Aheleh (2000), Official Corruption and Underdeveloped Markets: Africa's Economic Policy Dilemma, Indian Journal of Public Administration (April—June issue).

Singh, N.P. (2002), Set back to fight against Corruption, the Hindu (March, 22).

Sinha, Ajit Kumar (1999), Organised Crime and Economic Development in India, Forum of Free Enterprise, Mumbai.

Vittal, N. (2001), Human Capital to meet the emerging trends and Strategies, University News (Sept. 10-16 issue).

CHAPTER

27

Development of Small Scale Industries in Orissa—A Spectrum in Emerging Global Perspective

SUKANTA KUMAR SAHOO

INTRODUCTION

The Small Scale Industries have acquired pre-eminent position in the economic structure of the country. It acts as a vibrant and dynamic segment of Indian economy. The contribution of the sector both towards the economic advancement/development and removal of economic disparities among cross section of the society has been tremendous. With 3.6 million small units in the country, the sector produces over 7500 items of different product ranges varying from traditional items such as pickles to modern sophisticated items of components for plane and space crafts. The structural transaction of Indian Economy through Information Technology, Bio-technology, Food Processing, Drugs and Pharmaceuticals, Electronics etc. is prominently manifested through the SSI sector of the Indian Economy. The sector currently contributes 40% of industrial production, 35% of direct exports and provides employment to 19.3 million persons which is second only to agriculture. The significant contribution in terms of national exports not only links this sector globally, but also speaks volumes about the quality and competitiveness of its products. During tenth plan a target of 12% growth per annum has been fixed for the SSI sector with creating 44 lakh additional jobs. The sector gives emphasis on the impact of globalization, credit, marketing, technology, infrastructure, cluster development and access to information.

DRAMATIC CHANGE

Change is the only constant mantra in the present world. All economic activities including small scale industrial (SSI) sector in India have undergone a sea change in the past 50 years. The SSIs that we see today are not the same which existed 50 years ago and will not be the same after another 50 years. The process of change has been catalysed in recent years due to macro economic transformation taking place both domestically and globally. In the present era of borderless and market oriented economy, the two big global economic forces which are competing for world attention are (a) the emergence of a 'new economy', underpinned by information and communication technologies and (b) growing instability and un-certainty linked to globalization. With the WTO coming into existence, a new trade environment has been emerging. With the removal of Quantitative Restrictions (QRs) on import of 715 items with effect from 1st April, 2001 and those done earlier, a large number of items are now under Open General License (OGL). There has also been reduction in import duties in recent years. These have emerged as challenges before the SSI sector since these warrant that the SSI sector must be more competitive and efficient. There are changes in the type of products demanded in the quality of products and change in fashion and tastes. There has also been changes in the mode of production and technology. To cope up with these changes, the SSI sector will have to undergo many internal and external transformations. Will it be able to do so? Since it has changed in the past, it is assumed that it will change in future as well as it has the advantages of flexibility and innovativeness.

The SSI sector might witness changes in the following areas :

(a) Concept of SSI
(b) Role of Government
(c) Concept of Market
(d) Nature of Credit flow to SSIs
(e) Changes in Technology Use
(f) Changes in Entrepreneurship
(g) Changes in the Regulatory Environment including labour laws and
(h) Changes arising out of WTO Conditionalities.

INDUSTRIAL PROFILE OF ORISSA

Orissa is one of the industrially backward states in the country as well as in eastern region. The state is experiencing highest incidence of poverty in the amidst of plenty, serious unemployment problem, devastating super cyclone, hazardous drought, havoc of flood etc. At present, there are only a few large and medium scale industries existing in the state and providing gainful employment to a certain category of people. As day-by-day the employment position is squeezing in the economy there is no alternative to solve the problems of employment except setting up of small scale industries which is the only ray of hope.

The state is known for its traditional craftsmanship and handicraft industries. The excellence of the skill of the craftsmen can be made useful to resurge this sector in an impressive manner by improving the productivity and also diversifying the products in different ranges. In addition, there is an urgency to uplift the socio-economic status of the manpower involved in this sector by providing requisite assistance both from Government and industrial sectors. The overall performance of small sector is not very much impressive compared to other states, but also not discouraging. Till today small scale industries, agro industries, handicrafts industries are playing a vital role in solving the socio-economic problems of the state and are involved in manufacturing of different types of products like food, chemical, pharmaceuticals, textiles, plastics etc.

Taking into consideration the geographical situation, there is tremendous scope to develop agro, plastic and engineering industries in the state. Plastic industry is a new concept to the entrepreneurs in the state and it has got a phenomenal growth in the last decade compared to other sectors. But the textile industry shows a declining trend, though there is a lot of scope to develop this sector in a big way, as this sector contributes 20% of industrial production and more than 30% export of our country. Similarly, handicraft industry in the state does not show any encouraging feature in export, though there is a big demand for handicraft items in international market. In the recent years, marine products have got an impetus in export, despite some controversies have arisen in this sector.

INDUSTRIAL DEVELOPMENT

Small Scale Sector plays a crucial role in the process of economic development in general and industrial development in particular by value addition, employment generation, removing regional disparities and contribution to export etc. Prior to independence, industrial activities in the state were virtually non-existent, excepting that of exploitation of iron ore and coal to cater to the needs of industries in other states and railways. The so-called manufacturing activities were confined to traditional caste-based, village and tiny industries servicing local needs.

However, after independence some medium and large scale industries were set up in the state to produce cement, ceramics, textiles and engineering goods. The foundation for industrial development of the state was laid with the establishment of a steel plant at Rourkela, an aluminium factory at Hirakud, ferro-manganese plant at Joda, Keonjhar and expansion of the existing engineering, cement and paper industries during the second five year plan. During the subsequent plans, a few more large and medium industries were set up to produce cement, chemicals, cast iron, spun pipes, steel furniture, sugar etc.

In recent years, small scale industries of Orissa are mainly engaged in the manufacture of various products like food and allied, chemical and allied, electrical, electronics, engineering, paper products, rubber products, textiles etc. It is observed that industries are mostly established in Cuttack, Balasore, Ganjam, Sambalpur, Rourkela, Bhubaneswar, some parts of Paradeep etc. By the end of 1980-81 the state had 11.123 SSI units with an investment of Rs. 81.87 crores and employment opportunities for 89,962 persons. Because of some aggressive and target oriented policies adopted by both state and central government from time to time, the number of SSI units by the end of Seventh Plan stood at 35,867 and total investment and employment in these units was 437.26 crores and 2,65,332 persons respectively. With the addition of new units in the subsequent years, the no. of units increase to 59,057 nos. with investment of 1231.38 crores and employment of 3,98,873 persons in this sector of the state by the end of March, 1999. By the end of March, 2002, the no. increased to 70,125 with investment of 1712.72 crores and employment of 4,52,180 persons.

Growth of SSI units with investment and employment set up during 1985-86 to 2001-2002 is presented in the table below :

TABLE 27.1
Growth of SSI Units in Orissa

Sl. No.	*Year*	*During the Year*			*By the end of the year*		
		No	*Investment (Rs. In lakh)*	*Employment*	*Nos.*	*Growth rate*	*Share to all India (%)*
1.	1985-86	2513	4640.10	23424	25950	—	1.90
2.	1986-87	3482	4506.81	16977	29432	13.4	2.00
3.	1987-88	2292	4266.79	14828	31724	7.8	2.00
4.	1988-89	2096	4909.28	13917	33820	6.6	2.00
5.	1989-90	2025	4986.27	14049	35845	6.0	2.00
6.	1990-91	2249	6099.87	15657	38094	6.3	2.00
7.	1991-92	2233	5203.38	15545	40327	5.9	1.90
8.	1992-93	2117	5499.96	13344	42444	5.2	1.90
9.	1993-94	2311	5620.64	13807	44755	5.4	1.90
10.	1994-95	2327	6808.15	13096	47082	5.2	1.80
11.	1995-96	2507	7481.90	13019	49589	5.3	1.80
12.	1996-97	3098	10452.52	15629	52687	6.2	1.80
13.	1997-98	3186	13408.70	16716	55873	6.0	1.90
14.	1998-99	3184	19006.26	16776	59057	5.7	1.90
15.	1999-2000	3473	16293.82	18608	62530	5.9	1.90
16.	2000-2001	3676	15317.70	18115	66206	5.9	2.00
17.	2001-2002	3919	16522.32	16582	70125	5.9	2.00

Source : Directorate of Industries, Government of Orissa.

From the above table it is observed that the share of Orissa in the national index is very meagre and not able to bring much attention despite of availability of resources. Adequate emphasis is given by the Government for rapid progress of small sector in the state. Importance has also been given to gear up rural development programmes through diversification of the rural economy by promoting village and small industries in the rural areas.

The growth of investment and employment per SSI unit, over the time is presented in the table below :

TABLE 27.2
Investment and Employment per SSI Unit in Orissa

(*Rs. in lakh*)

Sl. No.	*Year*	*Employment (Nos.) per small scale industries unit*	*Investment per SSI Unit*	*Investment per unit of employment*
1.	1980-81	8.08	0.73	0.09
2.	1990-91	7.37	1.30	0.17
3.	1994-95	7.14	1.54	0.21
4.	1997-98	4.97	2.88	0.58
5.	1998-99	4.97	3.84	0.77
6.	1999-2000	5.06	4.03	0.80
7.	2000-2001	4.92	4.17	0.85
8.	2001-2002	4.23	4.22	1.00

Source : Compiled by collected data from Directorate of Industries, Govt. of Orissa.

It may be observed from the table that per unit employment has declined but per unit investment has kept an increasing over the years. As a consequence of which investment per unit of employment has kept on increasing proportionately. It shows small scale industries have become more capital intensive over the period.

RESOURCES AVAILABILITY

The state of Orissa has caught the attention of the major investors of the country and abroad due to the availability of vast resources. The state is richly endowed with agricultural, horticultural, livestock, forest, marine and mineral resources. Agriculture occupies a predominant position in the economy of the state due to its agrarian nature. It has contributed 28.13% of the net state domestic product during 2001-2002. Different types of cereals, pulses, oil seeds, fibre and other cash crops are grown in the state and the surplus production is being utilised in the industrial purposes. The state has vast potential for development of horticulture. Different agro climatic zones are operating in the state and producing a wide range of fruits, vegetables and spices. Congenial situation is also prevailing for production of commercial fruits, use of hybrid vegetables seeds, propagation of off season vegetable cultivation etc. Animal resources are considered as important resources of Orissa through cattle development and production of milk, egg and meat. The role of forest in the economy of the state hardly needs any elaboration. Despite widespread deforestation causing shrinkage in forest coverage the forest area of the state in 2001-02 was 58,135.47 sq. kms which is 37% of its geographical area. The forest in Orissa is not only the source of major products like timber and fire wood but also the source of valuable minor products like Bamboo, Kendu Leaf, Sal seeds, Lac, Gum, Cane etc. Orissa is generously endowed with mineral resources. The mineral resources of the state encompasses a wide range of products. Apart from concentration of many minerals deposits, the state possess about 1/4th of the total resources of Iron Ore, Manganese Ore and Coal 92% of Chromite, 60% of Bauxite, 35% of Graphite, 95% of nickel reserves of the country. The resources of Lime stone, Dolomite, Fire Clay, Chine Clay, Quartzite, Mineral bearing sands are vast and extensive. The other important possessions include Ores of Vanadium, Copper, Lead, Tin & Columbium and Lent alum, Precious and semi precious stones, Kyanite, soap stone, mica, limonite, selimanite asbestos and pyrophyllite. Recently, resources like gold, diamond, platinum and gemstone have also been identified in the state making it the most enviable region of the country. Orissa has a coastal line of 480 kms and the lake of Chilika with its vast expanse of brackish water covers a significant part of the coastal length and thus also contributes to the source of marine potential in Orissa. The important species of marine fish catch are prawn, sciaenids, pomfret, hilsa, plynemids, clupeids, catfish, elasmobrancus and other varieties. The state has also rich water resources with a large number of rivers flowing its mountains to the Bay of Bengal.

INFRASTRUCTURAL DEVELOPMENT

Development of infrastructure, often called social and economic overhead is a sine-qua-non of economic development. These facilities consist of energy, transport, communication, financial institutions, health, education etc. Orissa continues to lag behind many states in the country as regards to provision of infrastructural facilities for industrial development. Realising the above facts, the state government through IDCO have taken bold steps to accelerate the pace of development of infrastructure in core areas. The persistent efforts of state government have got a tremendous response from investors in and outside the country, as a result of which a number of proposals could be attracted to the state under industrialization programme. Although the state Government has set up the Orissa Industrial Infrastructure Development Corporation in 1981, the infrastructural sector has remained neglected and failed miserably in accelerating the pace of development. The state has very poor power supply having a total installed capacity of 4621 MW, which is only 4.33% of the country's power generation. Although per-capita consumption of power has increased in the overall sector, the industrial per capita consumption is very low and very unfavourable for continuous progress of the industrialization in the state. The development of the Railways in Orissa has not received adequate attention. With a railway network of 2390 kms only, the railway route length per 1000 sq. km. works to be 15.3 kms. against all India average of 19.80 kms. The share of rail route in Orissa is only 3.5% of the total railway network of the country. Roads, ' the major means of transport in Orissa are quite inadequate. The total road length and surfaced road per 1000 sq. kms. of area is 333 kms as compared to the all India average of 363 kilometres. Modern communication systems, such as, telephone, e-mail, website, faxes, etc. are yet to make a dent in the state despite rapid expansion in recent years. Despite rapid strides made by the banking system throughout the country, many areas in the state remain unbanked. There are thirty three commercial banks and nine Regional Rural Banks operating in the state with 2225 branch offices unevenly distributed in the state. Co-operative structure in the state is very weak as elsewhere in the country. Expenditure on social overheads like health and family welfare, education, sports art and culture etc. are quite discouraging. In a nutshell, the infrastructural facilities in the state are poor and inadequate.

INDUSTRIAL CULTURE

During 1980's the massive industrialisation slogan was given by the Government. On this basis both experienced and inexperienced entrepreneurs entered into this field with b\vested interest. At that time there was no industrial culture in the state. Promotional agencies, financial institutions like banks were also not well experienced to match the demand and to tackle the situation. As such in course of times, several units became sick and investment became Non-Performing Assets (NPA) in financial institution and banks. Due to various reasons the Orissa State Financial Corporation which is only premier financing Institution of the state to industries becoming the 2nd highest loss making corporation of the state. Though Government could not spell out the realistic sickness figure but every body will agree that the industries are not running well and vanishing day by day.

INDUSTRIAL SICKNESS

Sickness and non development of industries are due to various reasons such as faulty industrial policy which could not be implemented due to bureaucratic hassles, non clearance and delay of various matters by Government, non-availability of finance in time from financial institutions and banks, wrong selection of product and location of the unit, non-cooperation on purchases by Government and some public sector undertakings. Non-payment of dues from government in time, Taxation complication, High Power Tariff, Management failure and lack of understanding between entrepreneurs and industry promoting agencies and above all susceptible attitude towards entrepreneurs from all sections. Leaving apart now under WTO agreement, globalisation process very much affected the industries specially consumer goods producing units.

INITIATIVE TAKEN BY THE STATE GOVERNMENT

Realising the poor industrial scenario the State Government has set up various specialized organizations to promote industries in the Private, Joint, and State Sectors. For this purpose, the Industrial development Corporation Ltd. (IDCOL) was set up in 1962, followed by Industrial Promotion and Investment Corporation Ltd. (IPICOL) in 1973. To develop ad provide infrastructural facilities like industrial sites and sheds etc., to the small scale industries in the state, the Orissa Industrial Infrastructure Development Corporation was set up in 1981. Small Scale industries were adequately emphasized by the government only from 1980 and there after till today 6 Industrial Policies formulated and implemented by the State Government. As a result considerable progress has been made in the small scale sector of the state. Rural Development Programmes have also been geared to diversifying the rural economy by promoting village and small industries in the rural areas.

STRUCTURAL CHANGES

There has been no structural change in the small scale sector of the state during the last two decades. The agro based industries accounted for the largest percentage of SSI units in terms of number, investment and employment. The relative position of other categories of small scale industries has not changed significantly.

STRENGTH

The state started its industrialization process in early 80's and could not come in the industrial map of the country till today. The time is opportune to take advantage of the opportunities emerging out. Chandikhol—Duburi area is coming up in steel sector. Berhampur is potential in port based steel plants. Tatas and L & T have started implementing steel plant. Paradeep port for industrial park and petro-chemical complex will open up avenues for globally competitive industries. Koraput having rich in Bauxite has been nurturing largest Alumina complex and their expansion is, on the anvil. Western part of Orissa, such as Sambalpur, Sundargarh etc. will have their potential dominance for rich and abundant coal reserves. River systems will provide hydroelectricity and irrigation, thus achieving the twin objectives of Agricultural production and power.

The vast mineral resources, ample of sweet water in the river networks, potentially unexploited coastline, marine resources, fertile agricultural land awaiting the treatment of modern scientific inventions and more importantly, the peaceful industrial climate has been thought to be investors' paradise.

Global investors have been evincing interest in technological development besides investment. Infosys, the computer magnate of international repute has already negotiated with government for production, training etc. inside the state, with internet facilities available through computer system. The state is connected globally for information sourcing. All these potentialities would call upon further development of infrastructure such as Roads, Railway lines, Air Ports, Housing etc.

Youth force is on the increase fortified with synergy and vitality. What required of the society is to infuse experience and skill so as to bring them to the mainstream of state's development. Institutions like SICI, CIPET, CTTC, IED besides many NGOs are available to impart necessary training and prepare them with requisite skill. Industries Associations are available to provide bridge between the society and the institutions available for this.

WEAKNESSES

The development of small scale industries have failed to correct regional imbalances within the state as these industries continue to remain concentrated in the non-backward districts. Various incentives and subsidies given to industrial units in the backward districts could not attract investment on a large scale primarily because of lack of infrastructural facilities, entrepreneurship, Government support etc.

Suzuki registered maximum profit from their Indian operations (MARUTI) as compared to any other countries in the world. NALCO has achieved the best export award of the country being located in Orissa. Then what are the problems leading Orissa as a poor industrial state. Some of the burning examples are cited below:

(1) Power

Large scale industries can install captive power plants but small industries have to live with power interruptions which create wastage, quality problems, damage to machineries and productivity loss. If the interruptions are as many as 4 to 10 times as day there can not be any industry in the present scenario which can still be viable.

(2) Stores and Purchase

Presently most items are being purchased through tender being supplied by contractors from mostly outside the state. If the earlier system of purchase from small scale industry will resume with regular payment atleast 40% of the small and medium enterprises will again revive. This will generate huge employment and the Government can also fetch a good amount of taxes by which the system of defaulted payment to the financial institutions can be regularised and make profits specially OSFC can be revived.

(3) Telecommunication

Today all contacts are established through phone, e-mail or faxes. Telecom is considered a fixed installation in all developed countries. In case we wish to achieve this we must first ensure that at all times e-mail, telephone and faxes are in operation. This is never the case and we are existing with "sometimes working" telecommunication system with huge loss of business.

(4) Sales Tax Loan, Soft Loan and Purchase Loan

Waiving out the interest on above loans and principal will be paid with mutual understanding of entrepreneurs and concerned financial institutions, otherwise such industries will yield no result and sickness will result in closure.

(5) Waiving out Collateral Securities upto 25 Lakhs

After the reform and privatisation in power distribution system the industries suffered a lot. Though, Government of India announced for SSI units waiving collateral securities upto 25 lakhs loan, now banks and financial institutions are demanding 200% of collateral security including the cash security, which will definitely have negative impact fir the growth of industries.

(6) High Interest Rate

OSFC and IPICOL extending financial help but the interest rate is as high as 24% per annum, if defaulted. In this case the rate of interest to be rationalised and for small scale industries the interest rate to be charged at the Prime Landing Rate (PLR). The interest benefit must be provided to small scale industries in comparison to large scale industries as the former affects adversely.

(7) Access to Finance

The Biggest challenge for small enterprises today is to find availability of adequate funds for running of their plants specially low cost fund. The banks in general are conservative to small enterprises and the application of Naik Committee report of financing maximum 20% of their turnover as working capital is ridiculously wrong and can never be generalised.

(8) Cluster Approach

The state suffers due to lack of cluster approach development of SSIs. Many problems of infrastructure, support services, marketing etc. persist due to this draw back in location of industries.

Today market has become a global village and our competitor could be any industry located anywhere in the world. In the changed scenario of economic reforms, globalisation and liberalisation after WTO agreements, there are many challenges SSI sector is facing. Any product manufactured or services provided, it should be at a very competitive price with desired quality. In this scenario, to make the SSI sector more vibrant and competitive there is a need of reorientation and repositioning as well as concentrating in the area of core competency and products with comparative advantages from resources and other angles.

SUGGESTIVE MEASURES

(1) There is a need of a single window clearance system to solve the problems of entrepreneurs with a stipulated time.

(2) Bank should provide adequate financial assistance at a reasonable rate of interest, within the time frame and guide the industrial unit for its successful operation.

(3) Agro based, marine, minerals and other resources based industries to be promoted in rural area to provide employment and advance rural economy.

(4) Need of revival of sick units within a time limit. If the sick units cannot be revived they should be closed through one time settlement (OTS) scheme and the entrepreneurs should be free from all liabilities.

(5) Stress should be given to promote micro-projects, self help groups based activities on agricultural produce, handicrafts, handloom, tourism etc.

(6) Rehabilitation of OSFC and flexibility of labour laws need of the hour on urgent basis.

(7) Awareness programme like symposia, workshop, campaigns, negotiation with mother plants, information from the existing large scale industries, massive entrepreneurship programmes and project identifications etc. will be of vital necessity. The financing agencies may have to re-engineer their strategies to provide single window timely service and state industrial development agencies have also to bring out action plan to make the facilities available to the promotions in time.

(8) Any industry that will set up should be equipped with all pollution control measures and ensure strict adherence to pollution control norms. Besides, they should have adequate plantation inside the premises for ecology.

(9) Informal and format arrangements may be made with large industries to pass on required technological up-gradation inputs to small enterprises to enable them to cope with the time to produce quality goods and become globally competitive for their mutual benefit.

CONCLUSION

To conclude, it may be said that despite rich potentials in Orissa resources, various packages of assistance were given by both the state and Central Government to boost industrial activity but the small scale sector has not got the adequate momentum in this state. The existing provisions through financial, technical and other institutions have not effectively worked to ameliorate the problems. The state still remains backward in the sphere of export. Small scale sector also does not show any significant contribution in different areas. So it is evident that there is urgency to take concerted effort jointly by industries and State Government including Government of India to boost the industrial activities of the state which will in turn bring an opportunity to the industrialists to get an access in international arena and generate employment in the state which will bring prosperity in the state. Above all the entrepreneurs should understand the situation and realise the output of hard work, building up team spirit and fight for the common cause of industrialisation of the state.

References

Bryce, Murray, D., "Industrial Development", International Student Edition, Tosho Printing Co. Ltd., Tokyo, Japan.

Chadha, G.K., "WTO and the Indian Economy", Deep & Deep Publications Pvt. Ltd., New Delhi -110027.

Dhar, P.N. & Lydall, H.F., "The Role of Small Enterprises in Indian Economic Development", Asia Publishing House.

Kalam, A.P.J. Abdul & Ranjan Y.S., "India 2020—A Vision for the New Millennium", Penguin Books India (P) Ltd., New Delhi-1998.

Laghu Udyog Samachar (Various Issues)—A Journal of Small Scale Industries published by O/o the Development Commissioner, Small Scale Industries, Government of India, Ministry of SSI, New Delhi.

Mandelbaum, K., "The Industrialisation of Backward Areas" Basil Blackwell, Oxford.

Mishra, Ramachandra, "Orissa Economy", Home Printers, Puri—2000.

Roy, Prithwish, "Economic Geography—A Study of Resources", New Central Book Agency (P) Ltd., Calcutta-700 009.

Sinha, B.N., "Geography of Orissa", National Book Trust, India—1999.

Small Industries in India—An Engine of Growth : A Publication of O/o the Development Commissioner, Small Scale Industries, Government of India, Ministry of SSI, New Delhi.

SSI in India—The Growth Sector for the Millennium: A Publication of O/o the Development Commissioner, Small Scale Industries, Government of India, Ministry of Textiles, New Delhi-110 011.

CHAPTER 28

A Reflection on Budget Priorities in Orissa

BHAGABATA PATRO

INTRODUCTION

Orissa happens to be one of the most backward states in the country with no sign of improving its position in the next few years. The state attributes to be rich in physical and natural resources with a very long coastline, fertile coastal plains and rich mineral base. All these endowments put the state in a position of comparative advantage vis-à-vis the other states, which should have been exploited for quick and adequate economic growth.

In the recent years, the state has adopted a carefully designed reform program under the guidance, supervision and monitoring of the DFID and World Bank. The central government has also insisted on fiscal discipline and linked its assistance programmes to satisfactory implementation of reform agenda. The Government of Orissa has signed a memorandum of understanding (MOU) with the centre on 15th April 1999, and the MOU promised to achieve reduction in non-plan expenditure in the revenue account, to take measures for more resource mobilization, to impose user charges on social and economic services, to proceed quickly on disinvestments programme and finally to involve the community in implementing development programme. (GOO White Paper, 2001).

With this background, the purpose of this paper is to identify the priority heads in different components of the state budget. The components examined in the paper relate to revenue account, capital account, non-plan account and plan account. The methodology followed for the purpose is to collect data from secondary sources and to analyse these by using statistical tools. The Finance Account, of the State classifies the budget expenditure into 21 major heads under four groups of services. The share of expenditure for each major head over a 10-year period from 1990-91 to 1999-2000 is calculated. Then the coefficient of variation for each major head is calculated to know the variation in emphasis given to a particular sector.

PATTERN OF ECONOMIC GROWTH IN ORISSA

An assessment of performance of the state economy since independence indicates that it has got trapped in a low level equilibrium. Table 28.1 narrates the growth of total income and per capita income of the state economy and compares it with that of the national economy.

TABLE 28.1

Annual Growth Rate of Income of Orissa and India Since Independence

Sl. No.	*Period*	*Total Income*		*Per Capita Income*	
		Orissa	*India*	*Orissa*	*India*
1.	1951-52 to 69-70 (in 70-71 Prices)	2.71	3.62	0.62	1.51
2.	1970-71 to 79-80 (in 70-71 Prices)	0.73	2.86	-1.20	0.56
3.	1980-81 to 89-90 (in 80-81 Prices)	4.76	5.38	2.90	3.16
4.	1990-91 to 96-97 (in 80-81 Prices)	2.85	5.59	1.01	3.69
5.	1993-94 to 97-98 (in 93-94 Prices)	4.45	3.10	2.93	4.08

Source : White Paper on State Finances, Government of Orissa, BBSR, 2001, p. 6.

Comparison of total income growth for Orissa and India reveals very poor performance of the state economy in seventies. For fifties, sixties and eighties, the growth rate for Orissa is closer to the national figure. The state income growth has exceeded the national income growth for the period of 1993-94 to 1997-98 (at 93-94 prices). However, the performance for the period from 1990-91 to 96-97 at 80-81 prices is not that encouraging. The per capita income growth for Orissa is always lower than that of India for the entire fifty-year period. Negative growth of per capita is noticed for the decennial period of seventies. Satisfactory growth rate is noticed for eighties and nineties for the state as well as for the nation.

In spite of all these adversaries, it is hoped that the state will emerge successful in the battle of economic growth due to three reasons. (DFID, 1999). These are,

1. Orissa is growing, though slow, but not in a downward trend like Bihar and U.P.
2. The Government of Orissa has taken several positive fiscal policy measures since 1994-95 and
3. In reform programme, it went ahead of many other states in key sectors.

The success of all these initiatives primarily depends on the optimizing financial performance and achieving productivity of investment to the highest extent.

EXPENDITURE MANAGEMENT STRATEGY

Sectoral distribution of scarce resources is a very complicated and complex procedure. One of the very difficult proposition for the government is to achieve reconciliation of short-term and long-term economic goals. While the government is compelled to arrest starvation death in some parts of the state on humanitarian consideration, it is not possible and desirable to continue such aid in a continuous basis. The government has to find a long-term solution to the problem by creating independent employment and food security on a sustainable basis.

Choosing an appropriate investment-mix in a developing economy is subject to fulfilling the aspiration of a number of pressure groups. Strikes, protests have been organized continuously in the state capital to make administration aware of the problems faced by the common man through pressure groups, maximising voters' favour to a political party is also an important dimension in a democratic set up. In such a framework, deciding the share of each of the governmental function requires sound judgement and needs to be evaluated periodically. Ideally, a regional government is supposed to construct an interdependence table for the whole economy and to spend more on those with high forward and backward linkage. But in Orissa no such exercise is carried out and the priority attached to public expenditure is more based on the practice and pressure of the different lobbying units of the economy. It is noticed that at times the judiciary intervenes to regulate the flow of resource to a particular state function on the basis of public interest.

In the recent years, the Government of Orissa has taken a number of steps to downsize the bureaucracy and eliminate unproductive expenditure. The DFID suggested the government to introduce medium term expenditure framework, linking expenditure to outcomes, increasing accountability and strengthening performance budgeting. In the last 3-4 years, the government has successfully stalled many expenditure programmes on the plea of economic reform under the guidance of World Bank and DFID. The immediate impact of such reform measure is on the growth rate of the GSDP and the level of employment in the state economy. It is noticed that the government's feeling that there is too much spending on maintenance of capital assets is perhaps not based on sound logic. Maintenance expenditure is necessary for the purpose of ensuring longer life for the capital asset created out of government money. The traditional idea of going for new investment (plan) always to satisfy the voters has its repercussion on reduce productive capacity due to negligence of maintenance expenditure of the economy. Lack of co-ordination among different government departments also results in delay in using capital assets for years after installation.

REVENUE BUDGET PRIORITY

The receipt side of the revenue budget consists of tax revenue from own sources and from shared taxes, non-tax revenue and grants-in-aid from the centre for different purpose. Latest figures suggest that the state government is mobilizing around Rs. 7000 crores annually to meet its revenue requirements. Another two thousand crores are borrowed from different sources to put the total revenue expenditure at Rs. 9000 crores. Borrowed funds normally mean payment of interest and thus invite careful planning in the spending programme. Items of expenditure creating socio-economic infrastructure has to be given priority to boost the productive activity in the state. Table 28.2 presents the revenue account allocation to 21 major heads of the state government. The 22nd item ralates to the contribution of the state government to different local government units. Out of the 21 major heads 5 relate to general services, 8 to social services and the rest 8 to economic services.

Revenue account allocation indicates about one-fifth of the total goes towards interest payments. Similarly, more than one-fifth also goes towards promotion of education, sports and culture. Expenditure on administrative services and pension claims around 8 per cent of the total revenue expenditure. Expenditure on administrative services reflects a stable behaviour whereas pension liability of the government is steadily increasing over the period. In 1990-91, it was around 4 per cent of the total but rapidly shoot up to 8 per cent by the end of the century. The third group of major head is agriculture and rural development. Each one of these two heads is responsible for consuming around 6 to 7 per cent of the total expenditure. A falling share is noticed for agriculture and rural development. Social welfare and nutrition head have gained importance and got a steady share of 5 to 6 per cent throughout. In 1999-00, the share of social welfare and nutrition has increased all of a sudden to the extent of two times of the trend value for the entire period. This is due to unprecedented cyclone in October 1999. Other major heads like health accounts for 5 per cent, water supply and urban development with 4 per cent, and welfare of SC/ST with 3 per cent and irrigation with about 2 per cent. Expenditure under energy was visible till 1995-96 and negligible thereafter. This is due to adoption of power sector reform in the state. Reduced burden for power sector resulted in rise

Table 28.2
Revenue Account Allocation to Different Major Heads in Orissa

(Rs. in Crores)

Items	*1990-91*	*1991-92*	*1992-93*	*1993-94*	*1994-95*	*1995-96*	*1996-97*	*1997-98*	*1998-99*	*1999-2000*
Organs of State	17	32	24	24	79	41	77	65	67	116
	(0.8)	(1.2)	(0.8)	(0.7)	(2.0)	(0.9)	(1.5)	(1.2)	(1.0)	(1.4)
Fiscal Services	57	66	73	78	95	99	114	122	170	170
	(2.6)	(2.5)	(2.4)	(2.2)	(2.1)	(2.1)	(2.2)	(2.2)	(2.5)	(2.0)
I.P. & S.D.	365	481	542	683	787	929	1079	1292	1485	1238
	(16.6)	(18.3)	(17.5)	(19.6)	(19.5)	(19.8)	(21.0)	(23.3)	(21.8)	(14.8)
Adm. Services	168	207	250	245	288	339	43	445	558	675
	(7.7)	(7.9)	(8.2)	(7.0)	(7.2)	(7.2)	(8.4)	(8.0)	(8.2)	(8.1)
Pension	75	95	122	148	165	195	253	675	476	476
	(3.4)	(3.6)	(4.0)	(4.3)	(4.1)	(4.2)	(4.9)	(5.7)	(7.0)	(8.3)
Education	452	621	687	816	942	476	1066	1208	1480	193
	(20.6)	(20.8)	(20.4)	(20.0)	(20.3)	(20.0)	(20.8)	(21.8)	(21.7)	(23.1)
Health	136	157	172	188	216	255	274	30	401	426
	(6.2)	(6.0)	(5.6)	(5.4)	(5.4)	(5.4)	(5.4)	(5.5)	(5.9)	(5.1)
W.S. & Urban Dev.	65	96	120	105	128	152	160	197	285	312
	(3.0)	(3.6)	(3.9)	(3.0)	(3.2)	(3.2)	(3.1)	(3.6)	(4.2)	(3.7)
I & B	4	5	5	5	6	7	7	8	11	10
	(neg)	(neg)	(neg)	(neg)	(neg)	(neg)	(neg)	(neg)	(neg)	(neg)
Welfare of SC/ST	76	86	103	116	134	163	162	166	226	230
	(3.5)	(3.3)	(3.4)	(3.3)	(3.3)	(3.5)	(3.2)	(3.1)	(3.3)	(2.8)
Labour	10	11	12	14	16	14	19	16	24	22
	(neg)	(neg)	(neg)	(neg)	(neg)	(neg)	(neg)	(neg)	(neg)	(neg)
S.W. & Nutrition	94	129	156	200	165	289	313	305	270	1046
	(4.3)	(4.9)	(5.1)	(5.8)	(4.1)	(6.2)	(6.1)	(5.5)	(4.0)	(12.5)
Other S.S.	7	7	8	9	10	12	13	13	16	25
	(neg)	(neg)	(neg)	(neg)	(neg)	(neg)	(neg)	(neg)	(neg)	(neg)
Agr. & Allied	273	249	290	259	278	426	443	431	505	540
	(12.4)	(9.5)	(9.5)	(7.5)	(6.9)	(9.1)	(8.7)	(7.9)	(7.4)	(6.5)
R.D.	195	187	218	337	254	195	259	233	342	511
	(8.9)	(7.1)	(7.2)	(9.7)	(6.3)	(4.2)	(5.1)	(4.2)	(5.0)	(6.1)
Irrigation	62	79	98	107	112	131	180	147	147	147
	(2.8)	(3.0)	(3.2)	(3.1)	(2.8)	(2.8)	(3.5)	(2.7)	(2.5)	(2.1)
Energy	7	34	46	79	255	273	273	8	14	5
	(neg)	(1.3)	(1.5)	(2.2)	(6.3)	(5.8)	(neg)	(neg)	(neg)	(neg)
Industry	34	50	60	60	66	66	67	65	89	75
	(1.6)	(1.9)	(2.0)	(1.3)	(1.6)	(1.4)	(1.3)	(1.2)	(1.3)	(0.9)
Transport	51	71	85	85	107	116	122	122	107	107
	(2.3)	(2.7)	(2.8)	(2.6)	(2.7)	(2.5)	(2.4)	(2.0)	(1.6)	(1.7)
S & T	2	3	4	8	5	6	9	13	24	13
	(neg)	(neg)	(neg)	(neg)	(neg)	(neg)	(neg)	(neg)	(neg)	(neg)
General E.S.	25	25	26	29	40	35	43	48	65	
	(1.1)	(1.0)	(0.9)	(0.8)	(1.0)	(0.7)	(0.8)	(0.9)	(1.0)	
G-I-A	18	15	13	20	5	13	17	27	24	20
	(0.8)	(0.6)	(0.4)	(0.6)	(neg)	(neg)	(neg)	(0.5)	(0.4)	(neg)
Grand Total	2193	2634	3048	3478	4027	4697	5188	5543	6809	8341

Source : Finance Accounts, Government of Orissa, Bhubaneswar.

TABLE 28.3
Statistical Parameters of Revenue Allocation

Item	Standard Deviation	Mean	Coefficient of Variation
Organs of State	31.81474	54.2	58.6988
Fiscal Services	40.1807	104.4	38.4873
Interest Payment	378.8003	888.1	42.6529
Adm. Services	189.3772	321.8	58.8494
Pension	194.3252	253.5	76.6569
Education	382.5912	801.4	47.7404
Health	119.9558	225.5	53.1955
W.S. & Urban Dev.	80.89225	162	49.9335
I & B	2.299758	6.8	33.82
Welfare of SC/ST	53.53462	146.2	36.6174
Labour	4.638007	15.8	29.3545
S.W. & Nutrition	274.5218	296.7	92.5251
Other S.S.	5.436502	12	45.3042
Agr. & Allied	110.8264	369.4	30.0017
R. Development	100.1371	273.1	36.6668
Irrigation	40.93301	125.8	32.5382
Energy	103.2471	73.2	141.0479
Industry	15.43481	61.7	25.0159
Transport	26.61432	100.1	26.5877
S & Technology	6.600505	8.7	75.8679
General E.S.	13.35103	33.6	39.7352
G-I-A	6.214678	17.2	36.1318

Source : Compiled.

in the share of interest payment, education, rural development and irrigation. A fall in the allocation for health, industry and transport continuously reveal lesser priority for these heads in the revenue budget.

The statistical parameters like standard deviation, mean and coefficient of variation are calculated for the entire period to know the extent of variation. The average value is the highest for the interest payment head followed by education. Information and broadcasting head got the lowest average allocation. With regard to standard deviation, it is highest for education head and quite low for industry, transport, science and technology, labour, information and broadcasting. Moderate standard deviation is noticed for water supply and urban development, irrigation, welfare of SC/ST, fiscal services and expenditure on organs of state. Coefficient of variation is the highest for energy sector followed by social welfare and nutrition. It is the lowest for industry head followed by transport. Among other heads coefficient of variation is on the higher side for pension, science and technology, organs of state, administrative services and health.

PRIORITY IN THE CAPITAL BUDGET

Capital account of the state budget is titled heavily towards economic services. Around 60 per cent of the allocation goes to irrigation and energy. Transport and industry come next. The share of industry became negligible perhaps due to the impact of economic reform. Other heads finding allocation in capital budget are agriculture, water supply and urban development, administrative services, education and health. Negligible allocation is made for welfare of SC/ST, information and broadcasting, labour, science and technology and other social and economic services. All these are presented in Table 28.4.

The average capital expenditure is the highest on irrigation followed by transport and energy. The standard deviation is also the highest for irrigation followed by energy and transport. Very low value of average and standard deviation is noticed for administrative services, education, health, and welfare of SC/ST, agriculture and general economic services. The coefficient of variation is highest for transport followed by industry. Table 28.5 presents the statistical parameters with regard to capital account.

PRIORITY IN NON-PLAN EXPENDITURE

Tables 28.6 and 28.8 analyse the priority in the budget from the point of view of non-plan and plan category. This distinction, which was not originally embodied in the constitution, arose due to the emergence of the Planning Commission in 1950 as a separate autonomous body. The present practice is to charge all new programmes of expenditure in the plan expenditure category. This means priority in the non-plan side of the budget is mostly dictated by the past expenditure under a particular head. However, this logic is not applicable in case of interest payments and pension as these are related to the debt burden and employee burden of the state arising due to expenditure on all the sectors. The non-plan expenditure allocation is given in Table 28.6.

Around 25 to 30 per cent of the total non-plan expenditure of the state goes to payment of interest on the growing debt liability of the state government. Expenditure on administrative services and pension claims another approximate 10 per cent each. In this way 50 per cent of the total non-plan goes to only general services whose basic purpose is to keep the government machinery operational. In the social sector; education owes around 20 per cent of the total non-plan expenditure of the govt. The health sector follows with 4 to 5 per cent. The shares of other sectors are agriculture allied sector around 6 per cent, social welfare and nutrition around 5 per cent, transport around 3 per cent and water supply and urban development,

TABLE 28.4
Capital Account allocation to Different Major Heads in Orissa

(Rs. in Corres)

Items	*1990-91*	*1991-92*	*1992-93*	*1993-94*	*1994-95*	*1995-96*	*1996-97*	*1997-98*	*1998-99*	*1999-2000*
Organs of State										
Fiscal Services										
Interest Payments	9	11	10	9	12	13	10	11	18	15
Adm. Services	(1.6)	(1..6)	(1.7)	(1.6)	(1.7)	(2.9)	(1.4)	(1.3)	(2.0)	(1.9)
Pension										
Education	10	5	11	7	13	3	13	3	4	8
	(1.8)	(0.8)	(1.9)	(1.2)	(1.8)	(0.5)	(1.8)		(0.4)	(1.0)
Health	5	16	4	5	29	11	10	11	6	6
	(1.0)	(2.3)		(1.0)	(3.6)	(2.5)	(1.4)	(1.3)	(0.7)	(0.8)
W.S. & Urban Dev.	24	28	24	38	44	37	52	54	48	35
	(4.4)	(4.0)	(4.1)	(6.5)	(6.1)	(8.4)	(7.1)	(6.3)	(5.2)	(9.4)
I & B										
SC/ST	3	3	4	4	5	3	3	3	3	3
Labour										
S.W. & Nutrition		52	1		91	1				
		(7.4)	(neg)		(12.7	(neg)				
Other S.S.										
Agr. & Allied	15	17	21	29	13	28	32	28	25	57
	(2.7)	(2.4)	(3.6)	(5.0)	(1.8)	(6.3)	(4.4)	(3.2)	(2.7)	(7.1)
R.D.										
Irrigation	207	239	224	195	195	241	393	590	610	534
	(37.8)	(32.0)	(38.4)	(33.7)	(26.0)	(54.4)	(53.8)	(69.3)	(67.0)	(66.8)
Energy	151	180	163	160	84	-44	198		64	11
	(27.6)	(25.6)	(27.9)	(27.6)	(11.7)	(-9.9)	(27.1)		(7.0)	(1.4)
Industry	41	52	15	11	83	1		1	5	-1
	(7.5)	(7.4)	(2.6)	(1.9)	(11.5)				(0.5)	
Transport	82	100	106	120	156	150	18	150	132	132
	(15.0)	(14.2)	(18.2)	(20.8)	(21.8)	(33.9)	(2.5)	(17.6)	(14.4)	(16.5)
S & T										
General E.S.										
G-I-A	547	703	583	578	716	443	730	851	915	800

Source : Finance Account, Government of Orissa, Bhubaneswar.

rural development, irrigation, SC/ST around 2% each. It is important here to mention that in the social sector, some heads like education, health and social welfare had no major capital investment in the earlier years but have high non-plan liability due to the predominance of salary components.

TABLE 28.5
Statistical Parameters of Capital Account Allocation

Item	*Standard Deviation*	*Mean*	*Coefficient of Variation*
Organs of State			
Fiscal Services			
Interest Payment			
Adm. Services	2.859681	11.8	24.23459
Pension			
Education	3.917199	7.7	50.87271
Health			
W.S. & Urban Dev.	7.572611	10.3	73.5205
I & B	10.99697	38.4	28.63794
Welfare of SC/ST			
Labour	0.699206	3.4	20.56488
S.W. & Nutrition			
Other S.S.	43.70641	36.25	120.5694
Agr. & Allied	12.51	26.5	47.20753
R. Development			
Irrigation			
Energy	173.7485	341.9	50.81852
Industry	83.57947	96.7	86.43172
Transport	29.24228	20.8	140.5879
S & Technology	41.54837	114.6	36.25512
General E.S.	1.309307	4.0	32.73268
G-I-A			

Source : Compiled.

Calculation of the standard deviation for the major heads of expenditure indicates highest value for interest payments followed by education and social welfare. Pension and administrative services also reflect high standard deviation. The average expenditure is also highest for interest payment followed by education and administrative services. standard deviation is on the lower side for science & technology and information and broadcasting heads. The coefficient of variation is the highest for industry followed by social welfare and butrition. Rural development and pension also characterises with high value of coefficient of variation. Low coefficient of variation is associated with transport, industry, information and broadcasting, fiscal services, irrigation and labour.

PRIORITY IN PLAN EXPENDITURE

Pattern of plan-expenditure in the state reveals that a prominent place is given to irrigation followed by education. Agriculture and rural

TABLE 28.6

Budgetary Allocation of Non-Plan Expenditure in Orissa

Items	*1990-91*	*1991-92*	*1992-93*	*1993-94*	*1994-95*	*1995-96*	*1996-97*	*1997-98*	*1998-99*	*1999-2000*
Organs of State	17 (1.1)	32 (1.6)	24 (1.0)	24 (0.9)	79 (2.5)	41 (1.2)	77 (2.0)	66 (1.6)	67 (1.3)	116 (1.8)
Fiscal Services	54 (3.8)	63 (3.2)	69 (3.4)	74 (2.9)	87 (2.8)	94 (2.6)	106 (2.8)	114 (2.7)	136 (2.6)	164 (2.5)
Interest Payments	365 (25.4)	481 (24.5)	542 (23.6)	683 (26.5)	787 (25.3)	929 (26.2)	1079 (28.7)	1292 (30.9)	1485 (28.8)	1238 (18.7)
Adm. Services	161 (4.2)	205 (10.4)	248 (10.8)	241 (10.5)	290 (9.3)	334 (9.4)	423 (11.2)	423 (10.4)	549 (10.7)	669 (10.1)
Pension	75 (5.2)	95 (4.8)	122 (5.3)	148 (6.4)	165 (5.3)	195 (5.5)	253 (6.7)	317 (7.6)	476 (9.2)	689 (10.4)
Education	333 (23.1)	464 (23.5)	542 (23.6)	594 (23.1)	667 (21.5)	764 (21.5)	724 (19.7)	813 (19.4)	975 (18.9)	1298 (19.6)
Health	70 (4.9)	98 (5.0)	108 (4.7)	118 (4.0)	134 (4.3)	151 (4.3)	176 (4.7)	189 (4.5)	246 (4.8)	277 (4.2)
W.S. & Urban Dev.	26 (1.8)	58 (2.9)	69 (3.0)	51 (2.0)	60 (1.9)	64 (1.8)	71 (1.9)	83 (2.0)	152 (3.0)	179 (2.7)
I & B	2	3	3	3	4	4	4	5	6	5
SC/ST	22 (1.5)	28 (2.4)	33 (1.4)	34 (2.3)	39 (1.3)	46 (1.3)	48 (1.3)	52 (1.2)	76 (1.5)	77 (1.2)
Labour	6 (0.4)	8 (0.4)	9 (0.4)	10 (0.4)	11 (0.4)	12 (0.3)	13 (0.3)	14 (0.3)	20 (0.4)	19 (0.3)
S.W. & Nutrition	69 (4.8)	94 (4.8)	113 (4.1)	148 (5.7)	112 (3.6)	156 (4.4)	159 (4.2)	179 (4.3)	138 (2.7)	927 (14.0)
Other S.S.	6 (0.4)	7 (0.3)	7 (0.3)	8 (0.3)	9 (0.3)	11 (0.3)	12 (0.3)	12 (0.3)	23 (0.4)	24 (0.4)
Agr. & Allied	87 (6.0)	127 (6.4)	150 (6.5)	163 (6.3)	159 (5.11)	252 (7.1)	288 (7.7)	296 (7.1)	359 (7.0)	417 (6.3)
R.D.	20 (1.4)	27 (1.4)	28 (1.2)	30 (1.1)	37 (1.2)	38 (1.1)	43 (1.1)	46 (1.1)	130 (2.5)	196 (3.0)
Irrigation	34 (2.4)	45 (2.3)	58 (2.5)	58 (2.2)	62 (2.0)	71 (2.0)	91 (2.4)	91 (2.1)	101 (2.0)	121 (1.8)
Energy	1 (neg)	27 (1.4)	29 (1.7)	73 (2.8)	241 (7.8)	216 (6.1)	2 (neg)	(neg)	2 (neg)	2 (neg)
Industry	11 (0.8)	27 (1.4)	38 (1.7)	18 (0.7)	28 (0.8)	22 (0.6)	28 (0.7)	26 (0.6)	41 (0.8)	34 (0.5)
Transport	46 (3.2)	63 (2.2)	77 (3.4)	88 (3.4)	104 (3.4)	114 (3.2)	123 (3.3)	113 (2.7)	107 (2.1)	145 (2.2)
S & T			1	1		1	1	1	1	1
General E.S.	11 (0.8)	15 (0.7)	16 (0.7)	19 (0.7)	20 (0.6)	22 (0.6)	27 (0.7)	28 (0.7)	42 (0.7)	(0.8)
G-I-A	18 (1.3)	13 (0.4)	11 (0.4)	13 (0.5)	13 (0.4)	13 (0.4)	14 (0.4)	14 (0.3)	18 (0.3)	16 (0.2)

Source : Finance Account, Government of Orissa, Bhubaneswar.

TABLE 28.7
Statistical Parameters of Non-Plan Expenditure in Orissa

Item	*Standard Deviation*	*Mean*	*Coefficient of Variation*
Organs of State	31.81474	54.2	58.69879
Fiscal Services	34.63925	96.1	36.04501
Interest Payment	378.8003	888.1	42.65289
Adm. Services	194.3252	355.6	54.64713
Pension	194.3252	253.5	46.65688
Education	273.9255	717.4	38.18309
Health	66.03206	156.7	42.13916
W.S. & Urban Dev.	47.23005	81.3	58.09354
I & B	1.197219	3.9	30.69792
Welfare of SC/ST	18.73944	45.5	41.18559
Labour	4.516636	12.2	37.02161
S.W. & Nutrition	254.2839	209.5	121.3765
Other S.S.	6.471304	11.9	54.38071
Agr. & Allied	108.935	229.8	47.40428
R. Development	57.25625	59.5	96.22899
Irrigation	26.97324	73	36.94964
Energy	94.82088	67	141.5237
Industry	9.006788	27.3	32.9919
Transport	29.63106	98	30.23578
S & Technology	0	1	0
General E.S.	9.216531	22.22222	41.47439
G-I-A	1560.493	3468.8	44.98652

Source : Compiled.

development are the two other major heads claiming around 10 per cent share each. In the social sector four heads like health, water supply & urban development, welfare of SC/ST and social welfare are found to have almost equal importance with around 5 per cent allocation to each of them. The transport head is also favoured with around 5 per cent share. Industry, S & T, labour, information & broadcasting have very negligible share of the total plan expenditure. The energy head had got very good amount till 1996-97 and then got reduced share thereafter.

Average plan expenditure (Table 28.9) is the highest for irrigation department followed by education. The standard deviation of plan expenditure is the highest for agriculture followed by education. The co-efficient of variation is in the higher range for agriculture, education, science and technology, fiscal services and energy. The coefficient of variation is associated with administrative services, rural development, health and welfare of SC/ST.

TABLE 28.8

Allocation of Plan Expenditure among Different Heads in Orissa

Items	*1990-91*	*1991-92*	*1992-93*	*1993-94*	*1994-95*	*1995-96*	*1996-97*	*1997-98*	*1998-99*	*1999-2000*
Organs of State	0	0	0	0	0	0	0	0	0	0
Fiscal Services	0 (neg)	3 (neg)	4 (neg)	4 (neg)	8 (neg)	5 (neg)	8 (neg)	8 (neg)	24 (neg)	7 (neg)
Interest Payments	0	0	0	0	0	0	0	0	0	0
Adm. Services	16 (4.2	13 (1.0)	14 (1.0)	13 (0.9)	10 (0.6)	17 (1.1)	16 (0.8)	17 (0.8)	25 (1.0)	21 (0.8)
Pension	0	0	0	0	0	0	0	0	0	0
Education	129 (10.0)	90 (6.7)	90 (6.6)	100 (6.8)	160 (10.2)	181 (11.3)	355 (17.3)	400 (18.2)	509 (19.9)	569 (21.6)
Health	71 (5.5)	75 (5.6)	68 (5.0)	75 (5.1)	86 (5.5)	115 (7.2)	107 (5.2)	118 (5.4)	161 (6.3)	155 (5.9)
W.S. & Urban Dev.	63 (4.9)	66 (4.9)	75 (5.5)	92 (6.3)	106 (6.8)	126 (7.5)	135 (6.6)	168 (7.7)	181 (7.1)	137 (5.2)
I & B	2	2	2	2	3	3	3	3	5	5
Welfare of SC/ST	57 (4.4)	61 (4.6)	74 (5.4)	86 (5.9)	97 (6.2)	120 (7.5)	117 (5.7)	118 (5.4)	153 (6.0)	156 (5.9)
Labour	4	3	3	4	5	2	6	2	3	3
S.W. & Nutrition	25 (1.9)	87	44 (3.2)	52 (3.6)	109 (7.0)	133 (8.3)	155 (7.6)	126 (5.7)	130 (5.1)	118 (4.5)
Other S.S.	1	0	1	1	1	1	1	1	1	1
Agr. & Allied	201 (15.6)	139 (6.5)	162 (11.9)	125 (8.5)	130 (8.3)	201 (12.6)	184 (9.0)	163 (7.4)	172 (6.7)	359 (13.6)
R.D.	193 (15.0)	160 (11.9)	190 (13.9)	307 (21.0)	217 (15.9)	217 (9.8)	216 (10.5)	187 (8.5)	187 (8.3)	315 (11.9)
Irrigation	235 (18.2)	273 (20.4)	264 (19.4)	244 (16.7)	227 (14.5)	301 (18.8)	459 (22.4)	648 (29.5)	679 (26.6)	585 (22.2)
Energy	157 (12.2)	187 (14.0)	170 (12.5)	166 (11.4)	98 (6.3)	-18 (-1.1)	207 (10.1)	8 (neg)	76 (3.0)	14 (0.5)
Industry	64 (5.0)	75 (5.6)	43 (3.2)	39 (2.7)	121 (7.8)	83 (5.2)	83 (1.9)	40 (1.8)	43 (1.7)	41 (1.6)
Transport	87 (6.7)	108 (8.1)	114 (8.4)	121 (8.3)	159 (10.2)	152 (9.5)	152 (0.8)	149 (2.2)	133 (5.2)	131 (5.0)
S & T	2 (neg)	3 (neg)	3 (neg)	7 (neg)	5 (neg)	5 (neg)	8 (neg)	12 (0.5)	23 (0.9)	15 (0.6)
General E.S	14 (1.1)	14 (1.0)	14 (1.0)	17 (1.2)	23 (1.5)	15 (0.9)	19 (0.9)	23 (1.0)	22 (0.9)	0
G-I-A		2	2	7	-8	0	3	13	6	4
Total	1290	1340	1363	1462	1561	1599	2048	2196	2552	2640

Source : Finance Accounts, Government of Orissa, Bhubaneswar.

TABLE 28.9

Statistical Parameters of Plan Expenditure in Orissa

Item	*Standard Deviation*	*Mean*	*Coefficient of Variation*
Organs of State			
Fiscal Services	6.488451	7.1	91.38664
Interest Payment			
Adm. Services	4.289522	16.2	26.47853
Pension			
Education	312.4484	258.3	120.9633
Health	34.25217	103.1	33.22228
W.S. & Urban Dev.	41.47945	114.9	36.10048
I & B	1.154701	3	38.49002
Welfare of SC/ST	35.0506	103.9	33.73494
Labour	1.269296	3.5	36.26559
S.W. & Nutrition	43.82402	97.9	44.76406
Other S.S.	0.316228	0.9	35.13642
Agr. & Allied	426.2411	183.6	232.1574
R. Development	54.52665	215.4	25.31414
Irrigation	183.2559	391.5	46.80866
Energy	82.64012	106.5	77.59635
Industry	27.27962	58.8	46.39392
Transport	41.72929	117	35.66606
S & Technology	6.617317	8.3	79.72672
General E.S.	6.773314	16.1	42.07027
G-I-A			

Source : Compiled.

CONCLUSIONS AND POLICY OPTIONS

The statistical analysis carried out for 21 major heads of the state budget generates many interesting features worth noting and designing appropriate policies.

1. In the revenue budget, the rising expenditure requirement on account of pension and interest payment is likely to create a very difficult situation in the coming years if not slowed down. As pension is related to the age of superannuating of the workforce, the govt. has very limited option to control it. What the govt. can do now is to create a separate pension fund and mobilize resources for it separately. On interest payments, it is necessary to convert the high interest bearing loans into low interest bearing ones and to reduce the interest burden. In the social sector, the revenue budget

indicates too much emphasis on education only and neglecting other core areas like health, housing and water supply. More revenue expenditure on economic services like agricultural and rural development may not result much benefit to the economy. It is desirable to keep revenue expenditure on important economic services at the minimum. High coefficient of variation for science and technology indicates volatile allocation to this head, which requires examining and stabilizing.

2. Capital account allocation clearly indicates concentration of expenditure in two, three departments. These are agriculture, irrigation and transport. Surprisingly, the end-result of these investments indicates no significant change in agricultural production, area under irrigation and better transport services in the state. This means a sizable part of the capital expenditure on these items is leaking away through different agencies and has no impact on the state economy. Capital expenditure on social sector consists of less than 10 per cent of the total. out of this, around 5 per cent goes to water supply and urban development sector. Capital expenditure is normally met from borrowed funds and is supposed to ignite other production activity in an economy. It is also required to generate minimum rate of return to cover the interest burden. Both these aspects are not working properly in the state economy. In the coming years any capital investment programme must be taken up after properly assessing the benefits that are likely to be gained by the economy through direct and indirect means.
3. Non-plan expenditure incurred in the state is assumed to be of committed type and cannot be reduced easily. The growth of non-plan expenditure from Rs.1436 crores in 1990-91 to Rs.6614 crores in 1999-00 reflects fast rising committed expenditure of the state and calls for immediate control. Except normal price-rise of 3 to 4 per cent, anything more than this is required to be disallowed. Non-plan liability arising out of interest payment is the fastest growing item. Reduction of this liability requires co-operation of the Central Government and can only be built up through strong political pressure. Other non-plan items have to be curtailed very carefully so that minimum maintenance cost of the assets can be allowed.
4. Plan expenditure in the state is being carried out without following any established growth model. Even though the state is agriculture-oriented yet it is not always true that investment in agricultural sector will yield higher return over others due to soil and climatic conditions. The suitable head of investment can be identified only through estimating a detailed input-output matrix and estimating the linkage and multiplier impact of each sector. At a preliminary level such an exercise was carried out in a study for Orissa (Patro,

2002) and requires to be further refined. The plan investment resembles the situation associated with capital expenditure and requires solution as suggested there.

References

Govt. of Orissa, (2001) White Paper on Orissa State Finances, Finance Dept. Bhubaneswar.

Govt. of Orissa, (2003) Orissa Budget (2003-04) at a Glance, Finance Dept. Bhubaneswar.

Jena, P.K. (2003) Expenditure Pattern and Revenue Generation in Orissa. State Misplaced Priorities. The Indian Journal of Economics, Allahabad.

Patro, Aditya Kumar: "Regional Dimension of I-O Model for Orissa—A Study for Orissa": Unpublished Ph.D. dissertation to Berhampur University.

Premchand, A. and Chattopadhya, Saumen, (2002). Fiscal Adjustment and Expenditure Management; Discussion Paper, NIPF, New Delhi.

Reserve Bank of India (2003). State Finances; A Study of Budgets of 2002-03, Mumbai.

Sen, T.K. Orissa Finance in Eighties; National Institute of Public Finance and Policy, New Delhi.

Sharma, Partha Sarathi, Sen T.K., Gopal Krishanan, S., (1996) Public Expenditure Policy and Management in India: A Consideration of Issues: Working paper, NIPF New Delhi.

CHAPTER

29

Economic Development and the Tribals : An Experience from Orissa

JAGANNATH LENKA

INTRODUCTION

Orissa occupies a unique position in the map of India as far as the tribal problem is concerned. Next to Madhya Pradesh, Orissa has the second largest tribal population (70,32,214) in the country. As per the 1991 census the tribals constitute 22.43 per cent of the total population of the state. Six two ethnic tribes including 12 primitive groups are found in Orissa out of 400 in the country. In terms of variety of tribes, the ethnic difference and the bewildering complexity of customs and social practices, Orissa is far more heterogeneous and exciting a place than any other state in the country. There are not only physical differences among these groups, their economic occupations, social practice, customs, beliefs etc. are very different from one another. This makes it difficult to evolve any standard pattern for the study of these groups or any set of strategies for the solution of their problems. A modest attempt is made through this paper to explore the impact of alternate development strategies on tribals of Orissa.

ECONOMY OF THE TRIBALS

Tribal communities in Orissa are very backward and very vulnerable. These people inhabit in jungles and hilly areas. Their food is deficient in quantity and quality. The huts, they dwell in are 'Kachha' houses. What they wear nothing but rags. They are easily exposed and fall prey to epidemic diseases. Their social life is narrow but full of festivities. They are exploited by different sections of the society. This description of the picture of subhuman existence stands substantially unaltered even after 50 years of independence and adoption of planning as an instrument of economic development since 1951.

Agriculture constitutes an important source of livelihood for the bulk of the tribal population. According to 1991 Census, about 80 per cent of the tribals depend on this sector. But the agricultural practices adopted by the tribals are more crude and primitive than that of other inhabitants in the state. Average tribal families depend mostly on the collection of forest produce such as turmeric, tamarind etc. and to some extent on shifting cultivation on the hill slopes and raising a few dry crops which do not provide enough to last round the year. This is sometimes supplemented by causal employment in PWD or other works or in the operation of timber coups by contractors. In other words, cultivation and exploitation of forest produce constitute the main sources of their livelihood.

Some of the tribals are particularly backward and lead a subhuman existence by subsisting on wild fruits and tubers drawing their main source of nutrition from Mahua and a type of palm juice locally called 'salap'. In fact, the Bondas in Koraput district are the best examples of this category. The Lanjia Souras of Parlakhemedi, the Juangs of Keonjhar are also not very different from Bondas in terms of relative backwardness.

As a first step towards evolving realistic and special programmes for the development of these particularly backward tribes, it was considered necessary to classify them keeping in view the degree of their economic backwardness, illiteracy and the extend of acculturisation. Thus the tribals have been classified into A, B and C by the government, the categories being determined by the degree of assimilation and acculturisation of a particular tribe. The 'A' category tribes are economically the most backward and this list includes the Bondas, Koyas and Kandhas of Koraput and Phulbani, the Lanjia souras of Parlakhemedi, the Juangs and hill Bhuyans of Keonjhar, Paudi Bhuyans of Bonai of Sundargarh districts. The total population of the 'A' category tribes would be about 12 lakhs. In spite of the special schemes formulated for their economic development, it appears that we have not made much headway in the desired direction.

CONSTITUTIONAL PROVISION AND DEVELOPMENTAL STRATEGIES

Till independence development of tribal areas did not receive any special attention. It is only after the Constitution came into force that some attempt was made to accelerate the pace of development of the scheduled tribes. Article 46 of the Indian Constitution requires the State Government and the Union Government to promote their educational and economic interests and to protect them from social injustice and exploitation.

Moreover, the Constitution recognizes the special nature of this tribal problem in some states including Orissa and therefore lays down that in these states there shall be special Department of Tribal and Rural Welfare under a minister (Article 164). Accordingly the state government is committed to implementing the constitutional mandate and ensuring speedy development of these communities.

For better administration and effective implementation of development programmes. Scheduled Areas have been demarcated taking into consideration the concentration of tribal population in different parts of the state. Around 44.7 per cent of the geographical area of Orissa has been identified and declared as Scheduled Areas covering all tribal groups. At present the whole districts of Mayurbhanja, Sundargarh, Koraput, Raygada, Nawarangapur, Malkangiri, Nilgiri Block of Balasore, Keonjhar and Champua Tahasil of Keonjhar, Kuchinda Tahasil of Sambalpur, R. Udayagiri of Gajapati, Sorada Tahasil of Ganjam, Lanjigarh block of Kalahandi, Kandhamala and Baliguda Tahasil of Phulbani belong to Scheduled Areas. In these areas, developmental programmes are being implemented through 21 Integrated Tribal Development Agencies and 17 micro projects.

Apart from the aforesaid projects, Modified Area Development Approach (MADA), Cluster Approach, Orissa Tribal Development Project (OTDP) Dispersed Tribal Development Programme (OTDP) etc. are some the developmental programmes to look after the health of the tribal economy. Moreover, Tribal Development Co-operative Corporation of Orissa ltd. (TDCCOL), Orissa Scheduled Caste and Scheduled Tribe Development Finance Co-operative Corporation (OSFDC) etc. are expected to provide the financial needs of the tribals in the state. Finally, poverty alleviation programmes like TRYSEM, JRY, IAY, EAS, MWS, SFPP, DPAP etc. are extended to cover 50 per cent of the SC and ST families.

Tribals being the minority who are mostly in the weaker sections of the society, the Constitution of India makes provisions to safeguard their interests. Various protective regulations have been promulgated and measures taken in the Scheduled Areas in a continuous manner. Noted among them are the Orissa (Scheduled Area) Transfer of Immovable Property (by Scheduled Tribes) Regulation, 1956; Money Lenders Regulation, 1967; Orissa Land Reforms Act, 1960; the protection of Civil Rights Act, 1956; Bonded Lab(urers (Abolition) Act, 1976; the Orissa Reservation of vacancies (in posts and services) Act, 1975, Scheduled Castes and Scheduled Tribes (prevention of atrocities) Act. 1989.

REVIEW OF THE ACHIEVEMENTS

After five decades of planning and spending of huge amount for the tribal people we cannot assert that the standard of living of these people has really zoomed. Improvement is only marginal. Still more than 70 per cent of the tribals live is jungles. The literacy achieved by them is only 22.3 per cent as against 49.9 per cent among the total population. The corresponding figure for women is 10.21 per cent and 34.7 per cent respectively (1991-Census). About 80 per cent of them are marginal farmers and agricultural labourers. Many villages are yet to be supplied with the drinking water facilities. The jobs reserved for them are never filled in due to unavailability of qualified candidates. More than 64.9 per cent live below poverty line. Infant morality rate is highest among the tribals. They are still exploited by the village money lenders, sahukars and other middlemen and it is observed that intra-tribe exploitation is more now-a-days.

Jharkhanda problem of North and the Naxalite problem of the South are the manifestation of their dissatisfaction and anger. The qualities of life they live remain lusterless. Large-scale conversion into Christianity reveals the fact that inspite of all our development programmes we have failed to make much headway in bringing them to the main stream of social and economic development.

DEVELOPMENT DUALISM

In the dazzles of economic development of the tribals, what our planners and administrators have done is nothing but a paradigm of development dualism. On the one hand, it is proposed to bring about progressive material advancement in such a way that they can be eventually integrated with the rest of the Indian People. On the other hand, it is emphasized to preserve, protect and foster all that is good and beautiful in their culture and to do least violence to the essential harmony of their lives. Tribal economy and culture is by and large static. It does not encourage dynamism and change. A major change with the tradition is a precondition to economic development which is bound to necessitate drastic changes in the totality of social, culture and religious institutions and habits and thus in their psychological attitude, their philosophy and way of life. Certain habits of the tribals are inimical to progress such as overemphasis on enjoyment and merry making, rituals and festivals that last for days together and their attitude of self-complacency and non-challenge towards future. These need drastic revision to effect development. How best and smoothly their culture shall be tailored and to what extend persuasion and direction shall be used depend upon how best we understand and guide tribal people. What is to be emphasized is that the policy should have singular aim of economic development.

ALTERNATIVE STRATEGIES AND THEIR IMPACTS

It is needless to say that with our existing constitutional commitments no model of economic development will be sustainable unless it ensure social justice. In Orissa where a majority of population is deprived of basic human needs, social justice is not just a value but has to be an objective and obligation of the planners. It is therefore imperative to examine alternative strategies of economic development to ensure social justice.

(i) Accelerating Production

Conceding the fact that the existing consumption level of majority population and that of tribals in particular is very low and the rate of population growth is relatively high, even a marginal increase in the desired standard of living will require a large increase in the production. Increase in production and productivity is bound to put more pressure on the natural capital stock and result in higher environmental fallout.

The path of enhanced production also puts more burden both economically and ecologically on the deprived sections (tribals of the society those who depend on forests). The percolation of the benefits is slow while the cost of living increases at a faster rate resulting in a decrease in real wages. On the ecological side, the tribals living in marginal areas and pursuing marginal economy have to bear the brunt of a large share of the negative consequences of environmental degradation. Thus in the path of rapid economic growth, the tribals are benefited only marginally on the income side while they have to sacrifice more with reference to negative impact of eco-degradation.

Therefore, the linkage with the macro production system at the national level and the path of rapid economic progress are inherently exploitative in nature and cannot have any in-built mechanism of distributive transfer to the tribals who are in the lower strata of the society, and lowest bracket of economic opportunities.

The experience of the under developed nations vindicates the fact that the capitalistic path of development is exploitative in nature and has widened the economic disparity. The whole system has a strong centripetal force by which resources are mobilized towards the core, while the trickledown benefits towards the periphery are extremely low. The core thus develops at the cost of periphery and the poor are expected to become poorer in the system.

(ii) Social Obligation

The most publicised and politically very attractive strategy is the one which starts with the priority of tribals who carry the voting rights. The model emphasizes on equality of opportunities, mobilization of core groups and capture of political power. The poor and particularly the tribals are given utmost priority. But in reality it is observed that it does not lead to social justice. It has been experienced that the policy of reservations has not helped the downtroddens, but instead has spawned a 'Dalit Elites' that has cornered all the benefits. The group in power, aiming at maintaining the power and personal gains override the social justice. The end result is therefore centralization of power and money with a few privileged persons. What is distributed is poverty.

Areas where the above process is in operation are not able to attract capital due to inherent danger of inefficiency and system collapse. Therefore, spatial disparity and imbalance also increase.

(iii) Market and Liberalization

With the collapse of Marxist model of socialization of capital, there is no other alternative than to accept the market and economic liberalization. If the market economy and on going economic reforms are treated as God, the presumption would be that all players are equally endowed with skills and there is no hindrance to access. But in reality there is serious market imperfections. The state has a highly skewed income distribution and asset ownership together with a massive work force of varying skills and characters. The market that believes in capital-intensive methods of large-scale production will throw out surplus labour. Since lower caste workers are not able to achieve excellence because of socio-economic environment, it can only result in ruthless elimination of inferior caste workers. Face to face with this economic reality there is also political compulsion of the power groups to look pro-poor who form vote banks. This paradoxical situation has resulted in a patchwork or window dressing approach. The rationale of this approach lies in pursuing patch work here and there by welfare measures tó club dissatisfaction of the tribals. At the same time social and economic orders are designed in the interest of socially and economically dominant groups. Thus the problem is not solved rather it is postponed without taking into account its future dimensions.

CONCLUSION

Under the circumstances, unless committed and strong controls are exercised from outside the system, a justified share cannot accrue to the tribals. The state therefore has to see that the weaker and vulnerable sections in the society are not only protected from the predators of the market, but that they are enable to participate in it and derive benefits of the expanding economy. Liberalization does not mean, not even in the most liberalized economies of the world that government cease to rule and surrender the fate of the Country's poor and deprived to market forces. For the market to really become an equalizing force, the state has to perform more astutely its role of maintaining level-playing fields. The state cannot escape this responsibility. If it does, not just economic reforms but our very existence as a democracy will be imperiled. Therefore, it is suggested that the state will have to exercise its regulatory roles with reference to :

(a) Developing a mechanism of direct and forced transfer of resources from the privileged section to the tribals.
(b) Discontinuing all public expenditure on the sectors which are not directly relevant to the poor in general and tribals in particular.

(c) Encouraging non-governmental organizations working for the development of the tribals and,

(d) To create a congenial atmosphere where the tribals will have the natural inducement to develop socially as well s economically. The sooner the better.

REFERENCES

Economic Survey, 1998-99, Government of Orissa.
Fifth Five Year Plan of Orissa, 1973.
Joshi, Y.G. and Verma D.K. (ed), 1998-"Social Environment for Sustainable Development".
Lewis, W.A. (1974); "Theory of Economic Growth".
Palit, S.K.—1969, "Some Aspects of Tribal Economy in Orissa" OEJ 1973.
Planning Commission, 1969—Report of the Study Team on Tribal Development Programmes Committee on Plan Projects.

Index